Origins of Possession

Human possession psychology originates from deeply rooted experiential capacities shared with other animals. However, unlike other animals, we are a uniquely self-conscious species concerned with reputation, and possessions affect our perception of how we exist in the eyes of others. This book discusses the psychology surrounding the ways in which humans experience possession, claim ownership, and share, from both a developmental and a cross-cultural perspective. Philippe Rochat explores the origins of human possession and its symbolic development across cultures. He proposes that human possession psychology is particularly revealing of human nature, and also the source of our elusive moral sense.

PHILIPPE ROCHAT is Professor of Psychology at Emory University in Atlanta and the head of the Emory Infant and Child Laboratory. His research focuses on the developmental origins of human self-awareness and social cognition in infants and children growing up in different social and cultural circumstances. His work includes *Others in Mind* (Cambridge University Press, 2009), *The Infant's World* (2001), *Early Social Cognition* (1999), and *The Self in Infancy* (1995).

Origins of Possession

Owning and Sharing in Development

Philippe Rochat

CAMBRIDGE
UNIVERSITY PRESS

CAMBRIDGE
UNIVERSITY PRESS

Shaftesbury Road, Cambridge CB2 8EA, United Kingdom

One Liberty Plaza, 20th Floor, New York, NY 10006, USA

477 Williamstown Road, Port Melbourne, VIC 3207, Australia

314–321, 3rd Floor, Plot 3, Splendor Forum, Jasola District Centre, New Delhi – 110025, India

103 Penang Road, #05–06/07, Visioncrest Commercial, Singapore 238467

Cambridge University Press is part of Cambridge University Press & Assessment, a department of the University of Cambridge.

We share the University's mission to contribute to society through the pursuit of education, learning and research at the highest international levels of excellence.

www.cambridge.org
Information on this title: www.cambridge.org/9781107032125

First published 2014
First paperback edition 2015

A catalogue record for this publication is available from the British Library

Library of Congress Cataloging-in-Publication data
Rochat, Philippe, 1950–
Origins of possession : owning and sharing in development / Philippe Rochat.
pages cm
ISBN 978-1-107-03212-5 (hardback)
1. Property – Social aspects. 2. Property – Psychological aspects. 3. Possessiveness. I. Title.
HM856.R63 2014
306.3′2–dc23

2014006986

ISBN 978-1-107-03212-5 Hardback
ISBN 978-1-316-50281-5 Paperback

Contents

Foreword

It is a privilege, though a somewhat daunting one, to introduce the reader to this striking book. For though the subject of possession is an ancient one, it is a forever difficult and controversial one. While "possessing" something is a crucial feature of what we call ownership, it is by no means the only aspect of that conventionalized phenomenon. Indeed, as Rochat puts it, the "transition from possession to property" is the main issue of this challenging book.

It is argued that this "possession-to-property transition" is governed by three distinctively human characteristics: human self-consciousness, human symbolic capacity, and characteristically prolonged human immaturity, and this volume sets forth a rich and detailed account of each of these.

What is particularly striking about Rochat's account of this transition is the breadth and depth of his inquiry. This is a scholarly book in the deepest sense. It scans a vast body of literature and treats it with genuine respect – whether it is in a close look at Aristotelian essays, particularly well explored, or in considering the most recent literature on the behavior of young infants carried out in the last decade or two. Indeed, the discussion of changing conceptions of mind in the early and late nineteenth century as well as in our own times is masterly – not to mention his rethinking of the years leading to the French Revolution at the close of the eighteenth century.

It is no exaggeration to classify this book as an excursion into the cultural history of our conceptions of human development, and yet we must recognize its vivid contemporaneity as an exercise in classic intellectual history. I, for example, am currently much concerned with the evolution of legal systems (as in my recent *Making Stories: Law, Literature, Life* (2002)). I wish there had been the opportunity of reading Rochat's book before I'd written mine!

One last point. I have long felt that the human sciences risk superficiality by moving further and further from the classic epistemic concerns of philosophy – concerns about the nature of "knowing." I see this book as a sign that things are changing. For surely it is concerned as much with epistemology as with psychology. And so it should be!

Jerome S. Bruner

Preface

This book was on my mind for some years, particularly while doing cross-cultural research with children in the South Pacific, Brazil, and other regions of the world. As far as I can remember, possession always struck me as a crucial aspect of psychology, rarely considered in full by intellectuals and other researchers in the behavioral and developmental sciences. It always seemed to me that most conflicts and concerns in the animal mind pertain to protection of what one controls and feels entitled to. Everything always appeared to me as deriving from issues revolving around possession or ownership. I became obsessed with the idea and started to look at the world in terms of possession as others tend to reduce psychic life to sex or violence.

After a few aborted attempts, I started writing the book while visiting and teaching at PUC University in Rio de Janeiro in August 2012, a first fresh breath of great freedom surrounded by welcoming friends and colleagues: my friend Pedro Salem, my generous host Carolina Lampreia, and Octavio Domont de Serpa and his wife Fernanda who offered me a quiet, bright, and comfortable place to stay and write. I enjoyed every minute, thank you. I finally got down to it and wrote the book in one intense period in the spring of 2013 while on sabbatical leave in Paris, enjoying a total absence of constraints to drift and explore the topic *ad libitum*. I want to express my appreciation to my employer institution, the College of Arts and Sciences of Emory University in Atlanta, for allowing the absolute freedom and open horizon required for such an enterprise.

Warm appreciation to my faithful friend François Bertrand, who followed my progress every step of the way and with whom I shared ideas almost twice weekly, taking long walks, roaming the streets, and having lunches, each time at a new, memorable place with memorable people in a city he knows, inhabits, and loves like nobody else. He gave me constant encouragement and undivided attention, always ready to share his vast experience and knowledge, at time even with bibliographic references ... Thank you Francesco, I'm lucky to have you as a friend.

While writing this book, I met people on the streets of Paris, at random talks, cafés, and old bookstores, particularly the one on my street, the Librairie des Alpes, on rue de Seine, in the shadow of the Institute and the French Academy cupola building, as well as the adjacent Bibliothèque Mazarine where I wrote almost daily. I had conversations with the bookstore manager and now friend, Pierre Masson, an erudite, curious, and irreverent storyteller. We talked over cups of bitter coffee at this soulful bookshop, surrounded by old mountain climbing books and pictures of victorious mountaineers bending pine shelves. Conversations with Pierre and all the bookworms, history bum derelicts constantly roaming the shop, oriented some of the book's content and certainly influenced its spirit.

My appreciation also to Barbara Carnevalli, whom I met by luck at a crisp talk on "glory and the struggle for reputation in Thomas Hobbes" she gave in Paris early in my stay. I enjoyed her brilliance and benefited from her intellectual passion and philosophical guidance.

Michael Heller, my childhood friend, has been instrumental, as always, in cleaning up my ideas, playing devil's advocate, and giving me renewed intellectual impetus in my research and soul searching. There is nothing I value more than his wit at detecting wrong intellectual paths and weak arguments, his ability to zero in to what's important. Since adolescence, I have benefited from his encyclopedic culture and provocative thoughts. I continue to do so. His friendship is invaluable. Likewise, my gratitude to another, more recent friend Gustavo Faigenbaum, whom I finally located in the Argentinian town of Gualeguaychú, of all places, after reading his 2005 precious book on children's economic experience. We eventually taught together at FLACSO in Buenos Aires. Riding buses and driving across the pampas toward other teaching gigs (Parana and Gualeguaychú), with Gustavo lecturing me on Hegel and Greek tragedies, and hanging out with his lovely family, we had long conversations that changed and shaped my views on possession but also my views on psychology in general that I always tend to construe too much in individualistic terms, isolated from institutions – to a fault – probably because of my Piagetian background. He keeps reminding me of the collective and it has been a real education, even though he thinks this book is still lacking much of the institutional view he tries to instill in me. What can I say? I confess that I am primarily attached to the temporality of embodied experience. I cannot take as seriously as I should all the things that will survive us.

A warm thanks to my faithful former doctoral student Erin Robbins, for letting me keep rambling on and bouncing ideas for the past six years, for her friendship and support, and for all her diligent help in making sense of the mountain of data we collected together in the USA but also in remote places of the South Pacific and Central America. Her good work, kindness, humor, understanding, and intelligence made a huge difference.

Finally, thanks to the French taxpayers for maintaining and allowing public access to wonderful historical and very aristocratic study places like the seventeenth-century Bibliothèque Mazarine, the oldest public library in France. That is where most of this book was written, under the gaze of old dignitaries' busts lining the vast reading room with its high ceiling, three-story-high book shelving, tall ladders, and parquet floor crackling under each step of the roaming librarians desperately trying to be quiet. Descartes and the French illustrious intellectual past haunted the room. It was very solemn and reverential.

While writing, I had the spirit of these long-gone ancestors hovering over my shoulders, keeping me in check. They comforted me. My hope is that I did not betray the tradition of excellence they are supposed to stand for. I dedicate this book to all of these illustrious ghosts and the French taxpayers allowing them to remain alive.

Introduction
Making sense of human possession

Death is the issue. Knowing that one day we shall be dispossessed shapes our lives in unique ways. In the broadest and deepest sense, this is what this book is about, as dispossession is the necessary counterpart and defining element of possession. Without the knowledge of losing, we would not have any reasons to control and hold on to things the way we do. It gives us reasons to hope and discover faith, but also to despair and suffer existential angst like no other animal can. This knowledge comes with a sense of awe and absolute puzzlement. It has inspired millions of books, and shaped rituals and artistic expressions since the dawn of humanity. All can be said to revolve around the knowing of our pending dispossession of embodied self-experience.

The bottom line is that human psychology, unlike any other animal psychology, is in essence self-conscious: a psychology whereby subjects constantly reflect and elaborate upon their own value and place in the world, particularly the social world. Arguably, this is unmatched in the animal kingdom. As a case in point, humans are the only species having "fashion instinct," putting makeup on, wearing clothes, decorating themselves with accessories manifesting insatiable care for their own reputation and what they project to the public eyes. We are the only species self-objectifying through the evaluative eyes of others.

Self-consciousness and possession

This book is about how being the self-conscious creatures we are changes the way we relate to things, how we possess and experience having exclusive control over things, an inclination we share with all other living creatures. It is about how being self-conscious transforms the way we relate both affectively and cognitively to things: the way we get attached to them, how we cherish and fetishize what we own, fighting for it, but also how we are capable of relinquishing exclusive control over things by giving, sharing, or simply being forcefully dispossessed of them.

The question of interest here is what underlies the human experience of possession. Likewise, and as a necessary counterpart, what underlies the human experience of *dispossession*? Indeed, in order to share one first needs to own. So, what is the interplay between possession and dispossession in the context of human self-conscious psychology?

In an earlier book with the same publisher,[1] I wrote about the social underpinnings of self-consciousness, which I view as a unique human adaptation. Unlike any other, human psychology is both symbolic and self-conscious. These two cardinal characteristics of human psychology are in fact inseparable, supporting each other: in order to be self-conscious one needs to have some capacity to be symbolic, and vice versa. By symbolic I mean the basic ability to be referential in thoughts, capable of holding and manipulating multiple representations about things, the capacity of fathoming that something might stand for something else. Symbolic means the mental ability of going beyond the literality of experience, capable of becoming "meta" and not just *literal* about the world. As part of this symbolic and self-conscious psychology, the goal now is to capture how humans develop their ways of expressing and dealing with possession.

I try to show that we develop specific ways of possessing and organizing our social lives around possessions. There is a necessary counterpart to the human ways of possessing expressed in irrational fears of being dispossessed and losing control over what we own and feel entitled to. As part of the same package, humans also develop devastating envies, insatiable needs for more ownership and control, more power over the environment, be it physical or social. These ways can be pathological and devastating, but also the source of great cultural and legal codifications meant to buffer deleterious effects on group harmony.

Onion metaphor

As a general model, what is proposed here is to look at the phenomenon from a multilayered awareness perspective, what I call the *onion metaphor* of mind states. The idea is simple: in the course of development, as well as in evolution, various levels of awareness emerge or have emerged, piling up on top of each other, like the layers of an onion. Our awareness of the world is made of these various layers through

[1] Rochat, *Others in Mind.*

which we constantly navigate, through being non-conscious, unconscious, aware, co-aware, conscious, or co-conscious. Attached to these layers of awareness are a variety of possible mind states. Mind states are part of the experience of sentient creatures that are not just sensing the world but *feeling it.* I am referring here to creatures that, unlike machines, even minimally experience pain or fear for example – in other words and bluntly put, creatures that have affective life in them. It is within this simple schema that we want to approach the complexity of human possession psychology, particularly from a developmental perspective.

Facts and ideas about possession

Important works exist on the psychology of possession. They come from a broad array of perspectives including interdisciplinary,[2] marketing/consumerism,[3] organizational/management,[4] or social psychology (social identity and social constructionist views on identity).[5] However, only a few major developmental works exist, primarily from the 1970s and 1980s.[6] Recently a timely resurgence of interest on the topic has occurred from the point of view of infant and child development. New experimental and theoretical takes are proposed.[7] For sure, books and articles abound on topics like attachment, money, property, territoriality, copyrights, etc., but there are few on the psychology of possession with a particular focus on the "origins" question from both an ontogenetic and a phylogenetic point of view, particularly from a more phenomenological and developmental perspective.

The book compiles a large body of selected empirical and "falsifiable" facts relevant to the question of what the human experience of possession is made of at its origins and in development. What can be critically seen as less falsifiable is the meaning making of such facts and conceptual ideas that the book primarily intends to provide. The reader should know that this is not a survey textbook providing an exhaustive inventory of findings spanning the "possession field" as a whole. The book instead proposes a fresh look at the topic with the intention of providing

[2] Rudmin, "To own is to be perceived to own."
[3] Belk, "The ineluctable mysteries of possessions."
[4] Pierce and Jussila, *Psychological Ownership and the Organizational Context.*
[5] Dittmar, *The Social Psychology of Material Possessions.*
[6] Furby, "Possession in humans."
[7] See Ross and Friedman, "Origins of ownership of property."

novel ideas and integration of ideas by digging abundantly and opportunistically into philosophy, biology, sociology, anthropology, and developmental psychology, my own specialty. The goal is *meaning making*, not cataloguing or dressing a laundry list of existing research. It is to make sense of human possession psychology by providing new ontological parsing and a new framing of three main questions: *what makes human possession psychology unique compared to other animals? Where does it come from? What determines it?*

Possession and morality

Probably the boldest, most provocative idea running through the book is that the human sense of what is right and what is wrong (i.e., shared and explicit morality) could arise from conflicts over possession. Think of it: six of the Ten Commandments are directly linked to issues surrounding possession and exclusive control over things: "Thou shalt not covet, steal, kill, commit adultery, bear false witness, or have other gods." This is the Old Testament's vindication that possession, particularly the risk of social disharmony via possession conflicts, is not estranged from the genealogy of morality. This is arguably true from both an evolutionary and a developmental perspective.

In the midst of competition over limited resources, moral principles are necessary requirements for group survival, be they implicit as in the reluctance to kill or engage in incest, or explicit as in the codified systems of retributive justice that exist across human societies. At a very basic level, human moral principles arise from the necessary selective pressure of avoiding conflicts and maintaining social harmony. Once again, these principles can be explicit as in written laws, or implicit as in the normative ways one ought to behave in relation to others. This would be the bottom-line warranty of group preservation and growth of the species, but also the preservation of individuals in relation to their social group.

If we accept that such a broad statement holds some truth, then we can gauge how relevant it is to engage in trying to make sense of the human psychology of possession, and its origins in both evolution and development. Group harmony and harmony of the individual within the group demand some solutions as to *who owns what and why*. It requires some shared principles on how to distribute justice when resources are scarce. Individuals are required to abide by these principles in order to survive and avoid being ostracized as freeriders or bullies. There is indeed an instinctive, innate need to affiliate with others and a universal fear of being socially rejected, the driving idea of my earlier book *Others in Mind*.

The prevalence of conflicts over possession is an emotional minefield, both in human history and in the life of the developing child. For children and from the outset of their development, these conflicts are rich soil for the early learning of shared values and social norms. Possession conflicts provide the young child with the opportunity to experience and observe most conspicuously normative ways of handling social stress, the active attempts by adults and other peers at restoring group harmony, the enforcement and assertion of shared social practices, etiquettes, and ultimately shared moral principles.

Possession, as we shall see, is unquestionably an important part of social learning, because of what it reveals when conflicts occur, but also because it is in the context of possession that children can learn, in the most conspicuous fashion, normative ways of sharing with others, and hence can learn shared, acceptable (normative) ways of relinquishing and transferring ownership. It is also in this context that children explore, often with playful delight, how to transgress the norms, and the limits of these transgressions within their social group. Last but not least, it is also fertile soil for the development of self-conscious emotions like shame, guilt, or pride.

As already mentioned, in order to share, one needs first to possess. The ways we possess and experience possession, and relinquish it to others via gift, sharing, or any sorts of bartering exchange, is another central theme of the book that can be summarized as *the human psychology of owning and sharing informed by research in child development.*

Book summary

There are three main parts to the book comprising a total of nine chapters. In Part I, basic aspects and principles of human possession psychology are laid out. In a second part, these aspects and principles are reconsidered, but this time specifically from the perspective of child development. Finally, in Part III, possession psychology is considered in relation to culture and context from both an adult and a child perspective. Below is a summary of the book as a whole, chapter by chapter. It is meant to provide an overview of the main ideas. To help the reader, two simple tables are included, providing a synopsis of the main ontological distinctions made in Part I (Psychology) and the developmental "roadmap" discussed in Part II (Development).

Part I Psychology: principles of human possession

BASIC ONTOLOGICAL DISTINCTIONS

KINDS OF POSSESSION TRANSFER	KINDS OF OWNERSHIP PRINCIPLES	KINDS OF POSSESSION PATHOLOGY
Violent (theft and usurpation)	Strongest ("lion's share" and physical strength)	Expulsive (centrifugal dynamics), e.g., gambling
Generous (giving and obliging)	First possession (precedence of control)	Retentive (centripetal dynamics), e.g., hoarding
Agreed (exchanging and reciprocation)	Labor (effort and energy investment)	
	Creation (invention and originality)	
	Familiarity (history and ancestry)	
	Blood (biological relatedness and inheritance)	
	Luck (haphazard and chance windfall)	

Chapter 1 ("Experiencing possession") discusses possession from a phenomenological (experiential) point of view. The goal is to emphasize the centrality of possession as experienced in our lives, as well as in the mental life of any other animals that live in groups. Etymologically, possession means to throw one's weight over. At a generic level, possession is thus linked to the forceful experience of gaining control and agency over things. A strong case is made for the basic claim that, in order to possess, one must feel and have emotions. Machines cannot possess because they can only sense but cannot feel. They have no affective lives, nor any mental states. Feeling is indeed different from sensing. Feeling, including the feeling experience of possession, refers ontologically to mental states, and our task as psychologists is to document such states. All social animals qualify and meet criteria for having feeling experience. It does not require higher cortical involvement. The chapter goes on to show that we need to distinguish between implicit (non-conscious, self-contained, or private) and explicit levels of possession experience. These are ontologically different. At the explicit level, the experience of possession is shared and publicly articulated, but not at the implicit. In general, I suggest that the human capacity for feeling experience emerges very early on, with first signs already in the womb, by the middle of gestation. A crucial aspect of possession as feeling experience is *self-evidence*: the immediate embodied evidence of possessing oneself, the "mine-ness" of experience. Schizophrenia but also drug- and other trance-induced psychosis demonstrate the foundational role of the immediate embodied experience of being the sole possessor of one's own experience. In healthy feeling creatures like us, there is immediate experiential self-evidence. The chapter goes on to discuss the psychological mechanisms underlying possession as an experience. The mechanisms are construed as combining differentiation, projection, and identification processes. These mechanisms, in general, tend to blur the distinction between the Me and the Mine. The Me–Mine blurring is directly related to experiential phenomena like envy or jealousy, two specific emotions that are directly related to the experience of possession. The chapter then comes back to the basic fact that, from the outset, most conflicts are related to possession (envy and jealousy). It is therefore a fertile soil for the emergence of morality. I propose that possession experience is at the origin of our normative ways of being and sharing with others.

Chapter 2 ("Claiming ownership") deals with the process by which the experience of possession is objectified in the claim of ownership. The claim of ownership is an active assertion of power and control over things ("That's mine!"), made public by the mere fact that it is *enacted*, whether this enactment is instinctual or deliberate. At the most basic level, animals enact their feeling of possession in defense and attack postures. The neurobiological control of such enactment evolved from automatic and instinctual responses like freezing, and fight or flight responses, to more complex and inter-subjective regulations in social exchanges and communication. An analogous evolution is observed in child development. In general, animals need to carve secure space, evolving sophisticated ways to build nests and shelters. The instinct to mark and defend territory, as well as progeny and sexual partners, is the most basic and pervasive enactment of possession across species. Against this evolutionary and basic adaptive background, property emerges as a human invention that elevates the claiming of ownership to a formally recognized concept, legislated by implicit (etiquettes) or explicit rules (laws) that are normative and mutually binding to all group members. We are the only species that has created ownership codes. These codes specify in formal terms *who should own what and why*. Such codes, like the original Roman Law, are symbolic tools providing objective rationales for the ruling and arbitration of possession conflicts. From a less formal and motivational point of view, the case is also made that taking ownership is driven by an intensely rewarding and self-aggrandizing experience. It is an intrinsic part of possession psychology, and de facto what amounts to the engine of all economies. Dismissing such pleasures is only ascetic, religious, or ideological wishful thinking. In general, in the footsteps of Thomas Hobbes and Adam Smith, I argue that greed is the trademark of social (group) psychology. Social harmony and avoidance of the tragedy of the commons can only rest on some formal ruling. It appears that the invention of private property is probably one of the necessary by-products of the pressure for formal ruling. The chapter then tries to show that delineating exclusive (private) as opposed to public ownership (the commons) is fuzzy at best, particularly in the current era of economic globalization and looming ecological threats. At this global scale, ruling on possession hits deadlock because threatened commodities like air or water cannot be fenced in. This second chapter concludes with an articulation of the idea that, from a general psychological and anthropological point of view, "belongings" are only tools to gain social control and for individuals to measure the extent to which they "belong" to the group. Possession and ownership are part of our affiliation capital.

Chapter 3 ("Possession and ownership transfer") focuses on the psychology revolving around the transfer of possession. Dispossession is the counterpart of possession. Both are co-defined like two sides of the same coin. Possession does entail the possibility of its loss or transfer in exchange. Yet different ontological kinds of possession and ownership need to be distinguished from the point of view of transfer. *Proud possessions* define personal as opposed to interpersonal values of possession. Personal possessions echo who we feel we are, what defines us: ideas, creations, personal and family roots, traditions, past actions, moral rectitude, and principles we abide by as the foundation of our moral (idealized) identity. Some possessions are *inalienable*, like body parts, family members, or gifts that cannot be transferred outside of the social bonds they create. Across cultures, languages and traditions mark the ontological distinction between inalienable versus alienable possessions. Alienable possessions are those that allow transfer of possession and ownership. The chapter goes on to distinguish at least *seven principles* from which ownership of alienable possessions can be determined. These principles form deeply rooted intuitive and rational biases when trying to answer the question of who should own what and why: (1) *the principle of the strongest*; (2) *first possession*; (3) *labor*; (4) *creation/invention*; (5) *familiarity*; (6) *blood*; and (7) *luck*. Furthermore, at a more general level and on the whole, possession transfer appears to be of three basic kinds with radically different psychological experiences and consequences linked to each. In psychological and sociological terms, these basic kinds of transfer are distinguished and discussed as respectively: (1) *violent transfer* via theft and usurpation; (2) *generous transfer* via giving and obliging; and (3) *agreed transfer* via exchanging and reciprocating. It is argued that the agreed kind of possession transfer entails a particular form of reciprocity that is of much greater psychological complexity compared to all other forms. A case is made for the distinction of various levels of reciprocity. These levels are, from low to high complexity: (1) symmetrical and reverberated reciprocity (*direct reciprocity*); (2) reputable reciprocity (*indirect reciprocity*); and (3) moral reciprocity (*strong reciprocity*). Each of these levels is thought of as entailing radically different cognitive and social capacities. The psychology surrounding negotiation (the agreed kind of possession transfer) requires complex mindreading, an exercise in which humans particularly excel. What is peculiar in the *Homo negotiatus* we are is the constant need to agree on things, to create inter-subjective values about alienable possessions. We always try to find agreements regarding the worth of our possessions in the *eyes of others*, hence in reference to our self-conscious capacity.

Chapter 4 ("Symbolic spinoffs of possession") concludes the first part of the book. The main argument is that human possession psychology is particular and vastly complex because it is for the most part symbolic. It tends to be re-described into phantasms, sublimated phenomena, and compulsive obsessions, or what we call *symbolic spinoffs*. At the origins of the symbolic spinoffs of possession there is the unique human propensity to *project* feelings and mental states into things. We tend to impute forces and intentions where there are none, creating uncanny attractors to things. Human symbolic endowment changes the nature of the phenomenal experience of being in the world. From direct and literal, this experience becomes also referential and non-literal (i.e., *symbolic*), changing fundamentally our relation to things, hence their possession. In general, objects participate in peculiar ways in the lives of symbolic individuals. They become part of individual and group identity. They start to stand for personal and interpersonal ideas and beliefs projected into the past and into the future. The idea that possessions are part of the symbolic capital of individuals and groups is central to human possession psychology. Beyond exchange or commercial values, objects of possession stand also for the reputation and prestige of possessors, the marks of social distinction and stature in relation to others. Symbolic dimensions of human possession make their transfer connoted with higher meanings. This is evident when considering that human possession transfers tend to be highly ritualized across cultures, from the most primitive to the most technologically advanced. Across cultures and social strata, the tendency to breathe life into things (i.e., animism) is pervasive, the source of superstition and magical thinking in relation to possessions. In humans in particular, objects of possession can become objects of affective fixation and cult. *Fetishism* is a concept that captures the three pillars of human possession psychology: symbolic creation, compulsion, and animism. I try to show that fetishism is pervasive in humans. Another important point made in the chapter is that human possession psychology can become pathological, and its symbolic spin the mark of many extravagances. In general, a case is made that this happens when the circle of reciprocal exchanges is broken, spinning out of control. All pathologies of possession have compulsive and obsessive components. In general, they are of either retentive or expulsive kinds, characterized by centripetal or centrifugal dynamics that break normal give and take circles of reciprocal exchange. The chapter ends by showing that decoration (aesthetics and intentional beautifying) is an intrinsic aspect of human possessions, particularly one's own body. Cultivated as a mark of distinction, aesthetics is part of the symbolic capital of individuals and groups. Even money, the most fungible of all possessions, carries ornamentation.

Part II Development: human ontogeny of possession

DEVELOPMENTAL ROADMAP OF UNFOLDING LEVELS

AGE (approx.)	MIND STATE	OWNERSHIP	SHARING	RECIPROCITY
Around birth	Aware and feeling	Biological (innate latching)	Innate (biological) co-regulation	Direct (reverberated)
2 months	Co-aware	Controlled (self-agency)	Inter-subjective	Direct (tit-for-tat turn taking)
7–9 months	Co-aware	Shared (jointly attended)	Referential	Direct (tit-for-tat + initiated)
18 months	Conscious	Inalienable ("Mine!")	Intentional	Direct tit-for-tat + initiated + Indirect (projected)
3 years	Co-conscious	Alienable (exchangeable and reciprocal)	Mutual	Direct + indirect (reputable)
5 years and up	"Conscientious"	Ethical property (normative and codified)	Negotiated	Direct + Indirect (reputable) + strong (moral)

Chapter 5 ("First possession"), is the first of three chapters dealing specifically with possession in the perspective of development. What is tentatively discussed here is the nature of infants' subjectivity in general, which I term primordial subjectivity: what newborns feel and live as sentient creatures, the early experiential context from which first feelings of possession would arise. The aim of the chapter is to lay down what might constitute the origins and development of possession as a *feeling experience*. The prenatal dawn of feeling experience is considered. Research shows that the various perceptual systems are already at work in the womb: skin and bodily (somatic) movements, taste and smell, sounds and voices, rudimentary vision in light versus dark contrasts and movement. Based on such evidence, the first manifestation of putative mental states in fetuses is discussed. We elaborate on the fact that newborns are best described as active explorers and actors in their environment, rather than just reflex machines. Behavior from birth is indeed organized around functionally oriented action systems and there is evidence that we are born with minimal self-awareness and not in a state of confusion with the environment (the "blooming buzzing confusion" proposed by William James). From birth, objects are discriminated and can be acted upon, potentially controlled, and hence minimally "possessed." Action is first organized primarily around the mouth as main attractor. There is a dual, opponent dynamics of centrifugal and centripetal attractor forces taking their reference point in the body, the mouth in particular. From birth, children produce feeling experiences of object injection and dejection, in and out of the oral cavity. It is fundamentally in the interplay between centrifugal and centripetal forces in relation to the body that infants, from the outset, would develop first feelings of control over things, what constitutes and is meant by possession feelings: the perception of having exclusive self-control over things. This primordial feeling experience of possession quickly generalizes from oral to manual capture, and eventually to the control of others' attention via dyadic exchanges and joint attention by the second half of the first year. Interestingly, this appears to coincide with first signs of social attachment and the particularly exacerbated fear of separation of infants around this age, a fear that is not without link to the human uniquely prolonged immaturity following their biological birth. The early inclination to control things is associated with powerful endogenous reward or built-in pleasure systems. The origins of our untamed propensities toward envy and jealousy, our insatiable thirst for power and self-assertion, are to be found in the addictive pleasure experience of newborns. Drawing on the animal literature, the chapter goes on to show that there may be a built-in primordial grammar of feeling values translating into approach and avoidant motives for action. This grammar, expressed from birth in humans and in which possession feelings would find their developmental roots, has deep evolutionary origins. We share such grammar in terms of approach and avoidant motives with most ancestral animal species. Even fish show analogous avoidant responses and feeling experience of pain, as revealed in precise neurophysiological indices.

Chapter 6 ("Ownership in development") tackles how ownership, hence the public expression of possession feelings, develops in the child. As for all domains of child psychology, this development unfolds from being first implicit and non-conceptual, to becoming explicit and conceptual or symbolic. The question is how ownership development unfolds and what leads children to eventually reason about ownership in relation to values that are collectively shared and recognized, as in the highly conceptual notion of property with all the abstract rights putatively attached to it. In other words, we discuss what leads children from the implicit feeling of possession to the highly abstract and explicit sense of property. I first try to put these questions in the context of children's developing mind states, using the proposed *onion metaphor* to capture various constitutive layers of general awareness.

In order to deal with these crucial questions, we need to place them in the larger context of general awareness and its development, in particular what might constitute our awareness of things and how such awareness develops to become conscious, ultimately co-conscious, and collectively shared with others like the notion of legal property. To do so, I use a simple *onion metaphor* to capture what would amount to various constitutive layers of mental awareness in general. These wakeful mind states are respectively and in the proposed order of their emergence in development: (1) non-conscious, (2) unconscious, (3) aware, (4) co-aware, (5) conscious, and last but not least (6) co-conscious. Each is described with the idea that these layers of awareness, once constituted in development, form the various aggregated levels of awareness individuals navigate through as they experience and make sense of events and things in the environment. The development of ownership is discussed in this context, to which would correspond distinct psychological kinds of ownership developing from birth. The developmental unfolding of ownership kinds is described, from the first inalienable ownership kind expressed in newborns, to the first inalienable ownership of agency and effects by 2 months, followed by the first signs of a differentiation of inalienable and alienable ownership from approximately 9 months, the first explicit concept of inalienable ownership from the end of the second year, the emergence of a reputable concept of alienable ownership, and finally the normative and ethical kind of ownership children begin to express from approximately 5 years of age. Each would represent a psychological landmark in the development of ownership, the natural history of the public expression of possession feelings as they unfold in human ontogeny. Based on this natural history, and in order to understand further the unfolding of ownership kinds, three developmental matrices are proposed. One is the development leading the child from a preconceptual (implicit) to a conceptual (explicit) sense of possession. Another is the development leading children toward the objectification of their feelings of possession. Finally, another matrix is the development toward the explicit differentiation of alienable as opposed to inalienable possessions. Each represents various lines of developmental progress witnessed in children from birth. Within the context of the onion metaphor, we try to extract distinct levels of meaning and value of ownership as they emerge in child development: from biological and pre-adapted value of ownership at birth, to the value of deliberate control over things from about 2 months, the shared value of ownership expressed in joint attention from 7 to 9 months, the exclusive value of inalienability by 18 months, and finally the exchange and reciprocal (normative) values of ownership that are evident from about 4 years of age and beyond.

Chapter 7 ("Sharing in development") considers how the relinquishing or trade of control over things, hence the ability to relinquish possession more or less voluntarily, comes to children. We ask: where does sharing come from and how does it evolve in the life of children? Again, we inscribe such inquiry in the general onion metaphor schema, whereby children in development accumulate layers of meaning forming strata around a basic biological core. This core in relation to sharing would be the interplay of tension between gaining and losing control, first for self, then for somebody else. This tension forms a universal affective core, the source of basic pleasures we share with all other animals that play, and therefore that engage in not strictly utilitarian games of losing and gaining possession over things like a ball, prey, or in the case of humans a hand of cards or an idea. Compared to other social animals, humans add much complex symbolic veneer to sharing games and the question addressed in the chapter is how this veneer comes about and accumulates in development. We first discuss the ontological difference between utilitarian and playful activities, particularly sharing games. Play and sharing games give children privileged access to their own limits and possibilities as agents in their environment. It is primarily in affective, face-to-face playful exchanges (sharing games) of gazes and smiles that infants first gauge their social situation: the impact they have on others, the quality of social attention they are able to generate and receive from others. From a psychological, hence subjective and inter-subjective perspective, there are different kinds of sharing, each paralleling the chronological unfolding of the six mind states discussed in the chapter on ownership in development (i.e., non-conscious, unconscious, aware, co-aware, conscious, and co-conscious). We distinguish and discuss six corresponding kinds of sharing that would map onto these mind states in the order of their emergence in development: (1) biological sharing at birth, (2) intersubjective sharing by 2 months, (3) referential sharing by 7–8 months, (4) intentional sharing by 12 months, (5) co-conscious sharing by 21 months, and finally (6) negotiated and ethical sharing from 3 years of age. Once again, in the context of the onion metaphor, each kind would form a new, exponentially more powerful and encompassing stratum adding novel ways of sharing possession, while not cancelling the possibility of sharing in any of the other, more archaic ways. In a last section, we consider the development of sharing in relation to morality and the perennial idealistic view that sharing in child development would represent the natural history of social progress: the progressive emergence of enhanced solidarity and fair reciprocity. But from a psychological perspective and considering the human capacity to hold multiple moral standards, this idealistic view is seriously put into question. Instead, what appears to emerge in development is greater complexity in ways of sharing. Psychologically, this growing complexity can only be understood in the context of self-consciousness and the care for reputation, trademark of our species.

Part III Culture: human possession in context

Chapter 8 ("Culture and possession") discusses and tries to circumscribe the elusive concept of culture, in reference to how it has been historically construed in philosophy and the social sciences, but also in relation to possession and group views on property. In the broadest sense, culture is the sedimentation of collective ways and group norms of co-existence and sharing of resources. It is also what children learn and assimilate to integrate with their group and region, as they adapt to the circumstances they inherit by birth. These circumstances are sociocultural and economic. They are also geographical, hence climatic (i.e., atmospheric) and physical, thought from antiquity to be the source of reliable differences in cultural institutions (laws and political regimes) as well as in the psychological profile of people within a culture. The idea of culture is something that is everywhere in the human environment. At a primordial phenomenological (sensory) level, what emanates from group living is a distinct *atmosphere* that we feel and smell. This is all-important when considering what distinguishes places and people around the world. We do not simply adjust to culture, we breath it; it is in the air, the temperature, the smell, the noise, and the light. There is indeed an atmospheric, phenomenal dimension to culture that contributes to its conceptual elusiveness. However, collective ways, social norms, group traditions, cultural practices, and behavioral manners corresponding to sedimentation of group habits and practices are learned and internalized by each individual child, transmitted from one generation to the next, spreading at the group level, sometimes over very long but also very short periods of time. The recent fad of "love padlocks" adorning many public landmarks around the world is a good example of a recent emerging cultural tradition. In this new global ritual inspired by an Italian novel, lovers write their names on a padlock, locking it to the monument, then throwing the key away in a symbolic gesture that seals their relationship. Aside from new global fads, there are ancestral cultures of possession that can vary in deep ways, corresponding in particular to radically different views on property. We review some striking exemplary contrasts drawing from various ethnographies, including the aboriginal tribes of Sri Lanka and the traditions that are still very much alive in small island villages of Melanesia and Polynesia. In all cultures, there are differences in the personality profile of each individual, particularly in relation to possession (e.g., various levels of stinginess, generosity, propensity to be jealous or attached, etc.). However, it appears that inter-individual variations are different across cultures, each culture favoring and fostering particular individual profiles. We propose that culture plays a role as a buffering or "limiting" factor of such variability. We then discuss the extent to which material scarcity within a culture might shape the way people experience possession, own, and eventually share. We debunk the idea that poor people tend to be more generous, showing that possession and possession conflicts exist even in the most egalitarian societies like some hunter-gatherer tribes from southeast Africa. Although there may be tamer expressions of possessiveness in more egalitarian cultures, the experience of possession remains the psychological cornerstone of both human evolution and child development.

The final chapter ("Possession in children across cultures") emphasizes first the fact of the great material poverty of most children around the world. Eighty percent of all people on this planet live on a family income of less than $6,000 a year. The question is whether great variations in children's developmental niche impact on the way they might experience possession, and ultimately the way they own and share with others in their group. Aside from relative material scarcity, there are many other levels of cultural variation that may have an impact on the development of owning and sharing. We review some of these levels described in the anthropological and social personality literature, all trying to capture various ways of being together and sharing values as a group. These ways are reflected in child care (e.g., maternal versus distributed child care), family living arrangement (e.g., joint versus individual space and activities), or the forms of early education (e.g., rote learning versus instruction). Various attempts exist at circumscribing culture as a factor in child development, each proposing more or less systemic and encompassing conceptualizations of cultural influences. We review some of these theoretical attempts. At the level of the immediate family and intimate relations within the family circle, early cultural dressage of the body takes place systematically, leading to the early dispositional habitus of children: the "engraving" of social ways into the body of the child. Dispositional habitus depends, in general, on parenting practices that can greatly vary across cultures. We review some of these variations, such as the relative flexibility and diffusion of parenting responsibility within the community, above and beyond the nuclear family of the child. Cultural variations in parenting practices are shown to have an impact on children's early attachment to people, but also to physical, so-called transitional objects. Early possession of and attachment to transitional objects vary across cultures and are predicted, in part, by sleeping arrangement practices surrounding the young child. We review existing research showing cultural variations in the way young children spontaneously share desirable objects with others and distribute justice. There are differences in the way young children (3–5 years) tend to share and reason about ownership depending on demographics (village versus urban living) and the more egalitarian or less egalitarian environment of the child. Depending on such factors, the rate of development toward more equitable sharing and justice distribution (a universal tendency) varies. In general, it appears to be more accelerated in rural and more traditional group living environments. These environments also appear to determine how children perceive what is fair, and the extent to which they are willing to correct unequal sharing via retributive justice or even costly punishment. Multiple cross-cultural studies show that if there are universal trends in children's reasoning about ownership, these trends are mixed with marked cultural differences in the way children deal with inequity. Five-year-olds from all over the world recognize, for example, that someone who has created something should own it (labor principle). However, depending on culture, they diverge on whether the poorer of two protagonists has precedence in owning something they fight over (equity principle). There are signs of comparable aversion to inequity in land ownership among children growing up in extremely different circumstances, such as Palestinian children living in a dilapidated refugee camp in Beirut compared with upper-middle-class suburban children in the United States. However, the highly charged political context in which Palestinian children grow up probably explains their greater tendency toward parochialism or in-group favoritism. Stress and poverty surrounding children do have an impact on their reasoning about possession and how justice should be distributed.

In the Conclusion, the transition from possession to property is discussed, and identified as the main issue running through the book. Reasons for this transition, identified as a "Great Transformation," are tentatively provided, emphasizing in particular three distinct factors: (1) human self-consciousness, (2) human symbolic capacity, and (3) human prolonged immaturity following biological birth. A developmental "just so" story is proposed to account for what may have constrained and contributed to the uniquely human transition from experiencing possession to reasoning about possession in terms of property as a shared notion. The story is built around the universal conundrum of separation and proximity maintenance that all human infants face over a period of incomparably protracted social dependence.

Part I

Psychology

Principles of human possession

1 Experiencing possession

All psychologically endowed creatures feel possession at some implicit and basic level. Humans share these roots. This is particularly evident with the territoriality instinct that cuts across species, from vertebrates to invertebrates. However, humans also feel possession at some highly symbolic, often irrational and devastating level. Unlike other animals, in order to contain their – often uncanny – symbolic propensities to possess, humans had also to evolve cultural artifacts like tribunals, books of law, or religions as explicit moral systems promoting (often tenuous but still successful) stability and social harmony.

The goal of this chapter is to bring forth what is foundational in the feeling experience of possession: a feeling construed as central to our own as well as most other living creatures' awareness of being alive in this world. My goal is to convey the idea that the feeling experience of possession is no less than the cornerstone of our conscious lives, possibly also the source of our morality, the origin of the *conscientiousness* that links us to others in some ethical way. But first, what is the bottom-line prerequisite for feeling possession? What characterizes and who qualifies as having feeling experience in general and possession experience in particular?

Under my thumb

In English, as well as most early modern Indo-European languages (i.e., the Romance, West Germanic, and Russian languages that spread into the colonized world from the sixteenth century on), possession as a word derives from the Latin verb *possidere*, which means literally "to sit or to put one's weight or foot over."

The bottom-line, dictionary meaning of possession is thus the act of grabbing things or forceful control and physical binding over them. Literally speaking, it refers to an act of control, more specifically an "in-corporation" of things that exist outside of the body and are assimilated, one way or another, to the body and its action, be it intentional or not, conscious, non-conscious, or even unconscious.

The etymology of possession refers to a forceful experience, an act of power over things. Inversely, and as a case in point, a person is qualified as being "possessed" when forcefully controlled and dominated via the incarnation of an occult power (under someone's thumb). So possession is literally, following its etymological root, linked to a psychological experience that, in essence, is imbued with force and the drive to control. The question is, of course, what kind of force and what sort of control?

Beyond a physical act of power and control over things, possession also carries a meaning that is "hot." The forcefulness of possession in its etymological meaning also means that the psychology behind possession is imbued with passion. It conveys the meaning of something that is irrevocable, something that is compulsive in nature, like jealousy or envy, the possession of the possessed. It refers to something we have little to no control over. It also refers to something that potentially can be the source of defensive acts, a source of personal and interpersonal confusion.

Possession as experience

How to circumscribe feeling experience? How to capture subjectivity and other "what it is like" experiences of possession that presumably we share with other animals? What is the affectivity and emotional life that cuts across species at some basic implicit levels?

A machine does not experience possession. It does not possess. It might be programmed to say "mine!" when detecting something in the environment but that does not qualify it as experiencing possession. We might consider "Siri," the virtual interlocutor of my smartphone, to be an actual person. But that is just a figment of our imagination, our irresistible tendency to project mental attributes into inanimate things and other simulacrums. When talking to Siri and listening to "her" answers, we are interacting with a host of Apple Inc. engineers who came up with this smart feature mimicking reality. Siri is a programmed avatar, not a person. Our proclivity to project mental attributes into physical things and artifacts should not be simply derided as in the common spoofing of our inclinations toward superstitions and other "pseudo-" and "pre-"scientific claims. Those are indeed revealing of who we are psychologically and probably what makes us unique in the animal kingdom: imaginative and fantasy prone creatures inclined to impute intentions and complex mental states to physical, inanimate things. I will have more opportunities to come back to the particularly unique human propensity toward animism and the projection of intelligent life into material things (i.e., see Chapter 4).[1] This propensity is central to the psychology of possession, the necessary ingredient for most of our irresistible attachment to things.

Machines sense but don't feel. We, like other animals, do feel the world around us; we do not just sense it as a thermostat would. Most animals, including us, are much more than thermostats. A thermostat *senses* temperature changes, serving the specific function of controlling and regulating the ambient air of a contained environment. Thermostats, as "autonomous" feedback loop systems, do control the atmosphere but they do not *feel* it in the way we feel warm or cold. Self-regulation happens at a very different level, a subjective level that defines psychology as a distinct field, in contrast to the deterministic fields of physics and engineering in particular. This explains why there is a world of engineers and a world of psychologists, two professions that should not be confounded. Both professions have their own specific, ontologically different objects. Some grey areas exist of course (e.g., machine–user interaction) but machines are not people, because they do not feel and have no emotions. They do not have feelings, but are just astute detectors that sense with no meanings attached to it.

Feeling experience entails mental states, sensing does not. For example, we do not "sense" pain, but *we feel it*. Pain is an experience referring to a particular mental state that we recognize and eventually can describe to ourselves or someone else, or simply refer to via specific emotional expressions. The expression of pain makes its corresponding mental state public, hence readable and shareable with other "feeling" creatures who can relate, resonate, sympathize, maybe even empathize with it.

Fundamentally, most animals are feeling creatures, communicating with each other in reference to mental states: happiness, contentment, arousal, pain, sadness, disgust, eagerness. The world of feeling creatures is colored by affective values that pull and push. It is a "hot" and emotionally colorful world that is much more than the cold world of machines, however complex those machines might be, and however closely they might

[1] This is particularly evident in Albert Michotte's classic demonstrations of perceived causality in dynamic events involving inanimate protagonists that we irrepressibly perceive as "agents and patients" of intentional actions (Michotte, *The Perception of Causality*). The same is evident in Heider and Simmel's pioneer demonstration of the obligatory inference of intentions that we tend to engage in automatically, trying to make sense of dynamic displays that involve the relative motion of geometric figures like squares and triangles that are compulsively described by viewers as "chasing each other and escaping one another," an unmistakable sign of higher-order projection (Heider and Simmel, "An experimental study of apparent behaviour").

simulate the colorful world of feeling experience. They are just approximations of the real thing.[2]

The point I am trying to drive home here is that possession is primarily a feeling experience, like pain. It refers to complex mental states that are the foundation of the psychology of possession. Like pain, joy, or sadness, possession is felt and not merely sensed by those creatures endowed with feeling experience and the accompanying "what it is like" phenomenal or P-awareness. The question, however, is how feeling experience and its accompanying awareness compares across ages and species, as well as across levels of psychological complexity and depth. One way to address this question is to consider first what might be the criteria for endowing a creature with "feeling" as opposed to just machine-like sensing experiences.

Criteria for minimal feeling experience (as opposed to mere sensing)

It is common to link feeling experience to higher-order cognitive processes associated with late-developing cortical structures. From this perspective, one should not attribute any kind of feeling awareness but rather just sensing, machine-like awareness to creatures that are not, or not yet, endowed with higher cortical structures, namely a *mammalian forebrain*. But this view is challenged by empirical evidence of goal-directed, purposive behaviors in decorticated animals and anencephalic children (children born without cortex).[3] In general, it appears that feeling experience does not have to be explicit and mediated by higher symbolic processes like language. Infants as well as most animals could be endowed with the potential for feeling awareness, depending on what criteria are used.

In his argument in support of a consciousness without cortex, Merker proposes that in "the most basic and general sense" what qualifies for consciousness (here by extension the putative awareness and the feeling experience of possession) is "the state or condition presupposed by any experience whatsoever" (p. 63). This would mean that only "experiencing" creatures could possess as construed here: those who are capable of having subjective "what it is like" experiences. This proposal, however, begs the question of what qualifies as having "any feeling experience

[2] See John Searle's famous Chinese room thought experiment for a thorough discussion of the limits of machine simulation, and the extent to which machines can equate human intelligence, in particular higher-level competence like language. The conclusion is that comparable performance does not necessarily entail comparable competence. A machine can only perform in comparable ways, it cannot speak as such.

[3] For a cogent review, see Merker, "Consciousness without a cerebral cortex."

whatsoever." In particular, what is having feeling experience and awareness versus not having any of it or just machine-like sensing experience?

I propose that to have feeling experience is to have an affective life that is made of perceived values (or qualities) such as pain, pleasure, or cravings. Having experience, hence having an affective life, should transcend the mere recording of raw sensations as "signals" by an organism functioning like a thermostat. Inversely, not having experience is to sense the world by simply recording raw sensory signals that trigger automatic, predictable responses as in the output behavior of computers or thermostats. Again, these automata sense but do not feel. One entails minimal subjective experience (feelings), not the other, even though output behavior might be homologous for third party observers (e.g., fleeing of a cockroach versus the fleeing of a foot soldier under attack).

Feelings as opposed to raw sensory signals are expressed in emotions via particular bodily movements (e.g., facial expression, or a particular dynamic of motion or signaling as in screaming). As already mentioned, it is the affective life revealed in expressive emotions that distinguishes sentient creatures from mere machines and automata. The former feel and are potentially conscious, the latter are not. Feeling experience adds values to an organism's encounter with the world. More importantly, in relation to possession, it gives *purpose* and *orientation* to actions performed by that organism (e.g., defending, protecting, acquiring, controlling).

This is the constitutive element of any form of what we refer to as consciousness (the state or condition presupposed by feeling experience), and by extension the necessary prerequisite of a minimal possession awareness that can be imputed to most animals and very young infants.

In short, affectivity and emotions guide actions and elevate behaviors above the register of mere automatic and mechanistic responses. Automata respond; they do not act proper. Contrary to sentient (feeling) organisms, they respond like thermostats do in relation to temperature fluctuations within a pre-set, calibrated range. Thermostats do not act to avoid hot or cold, nor are they oriented toward a gain of comfort (pleasure or the maintenance of good feelings). Machines do have, however, the superior power to find and apply algorithms to resolve complex problems with reliable success (see the chess match between the IBM Deep Blue machine and Garry Kasparov). Machines can, in some cold sense, think and resolve problems, but they can't feel and for this reason have no potential for possession, except perhaps in science fictions (e.g., the computer HAL 9000 experiencing "fear" in Clarke and Kubrick's *2001: A Space Odyssey*).

The necessary qualifier for having minimal possession awareness is, accordingly, the feeling experience that elevates organisms from mere responders to volitional actors (goal-oriented and purposeful beings in a world made of affective values: pleasures, pains, envies). Possession awareness must co-emerge with feeling experience, both mutually necessary and co-defining.

Possession is therefore affective and emotional in origin, rather than cognitive in the etymological sense of consciousness *(con-scientia* or "with-knowledge"). If possession has anything to do with knowledge or cognition, it is with "hot" not cold cognition: what feels good or bad, what is pleasurable or not, ultimately what feels right and what feels wrong.

Children in their development, as I will try to show, demonstrate that the explicit conscious "content" of possession (explicit and conceptual awareness of ownership, entitlement, and ultimately property rights) rests upon and is eventually added to this basic pre-reflective and implicit affective process that distinguishes us from machines. But this implies major steps in brain and behavior development.

Within this theoretical framework, the question is: when can we say that an organism has feeling experiences, hence fills the criteria for having minimal feeling of possession? Do cockroaches feel? Are cold blooded species (fish, octopus, reptiles) and those which have not evolved a mammalian brain precluded from having possession experience? Do birds feel? What about human fetuses or young infants? When do we start to feel, and hence have the potential to have minimal experience of possession?

Looking at the brain, isolating neural networks and brain structures that are predictably associated in time with feeling experiences can help in determining whether an organism "feels" something and might be endowed with subjective experience, therefore qualifying for potential possession experience. Inversely, just looking at behavior and emotional expressions that are predictably associated with feeling experiences (e.g., pain) can do the same. But first, "peripheral" receptor systems (e.g., pain, auditory, vestibular, light, olfactory, or gustatory sensitivity) have to be functional and connected (projecting) to some higher centers of the nervous system for further processing and motor/vegetative responses.

Implicit versus explicit feeling experience

The feeling experience of pain in a fetus may be comparable to my experience of pain as it refers to an overall negative state (i.e., a state that puts the organism on sympathetic stress alert to be avoided and cancelled out as soon as possible). However, my own and a fetus's pain threshold are most probably not comparable, our subjective experience of pain quite different. Let's say that I get a finger caught in a slamming door. Aside from screaming, I would eventually look for a culprit, blame myself, search for sympathy by publicly feeling sorry for myself. My direct experience of feeling pain, the one I might share with a fetus, is quickly transformed and re-described via language and other higher self-conscious thought processes. From an implicit, direct experience, it becomes explicit and socially situated.

In the same way that it is important to distinguish implicit and explicit levels of pain experience, it is also important to distinguish between the implicit and explicit levels of feeling possession. This will be particularly relevant when discussing the psychology of possession from the perspective of development (Part II of the book).

As we shall see, the development of possession parallels the development of self and social (people) understanding. It fundamentally transits from a world of experience that is embodied and implicit to a world of experience that, in addition to being embodied and implicit, is also embodied and conscientiously *shared* with others via symbolic and cultural devices like language.

Implicit and explicit feeling experiences are ontologically different and emerge at different points in time during development, one preceding the other without strictly replacing the other. Implicit experience continues to play a central role in our adult conscious life. But in development, both come to co-exist and interact in complex ways. In other words, in psychological development, the child adds "layers" or levels of feeling experience, progressively adding layers of explicitness to primordial and deeply rooted implicit layers of awareness. There comes a point in development when both implicit and explicit awareness co-exist and interact in complex ways, our conscious mind transiting and voyaging through these layers of awareness. This may all sound very speculative but in fact there are numerous and increasing numbers of empirical studies that point to such co-existing levels of awareness: implicit and explicit levels of memory, concepts, thoughts, decision making processes, and social preference. These co-existing and interacting levels of awareness across the various domains emerge early in development, and certainly by the middle of second year, if not earlier. It is well established, for example, that implicit procedural memory exists in infancy, long before the child can explicitly reminisce about events and ways of resolving problems.[4] Some research even shows that 18-month-old children, surreptitiously presented with two dolls hugging one another, are subliminally primed to

[4] For an overview and more details regarding the development of implicit and explicit memory in early development, see Rochat, *The Infant's World*, and more specifically Bauer, *Remembering Times of our Lives*.

help an adult who has accidently dropped something on the floor![5] This remarkable finding demonstrates that various layers of mental processing (i.e., implicit and explicit experience) co-exist and interact very early in life, at least by the time children learn to speak, and possibly even earlier.[6]

Origins of feeling experience

A rich body of neuroanatomical as well as behavioral evidence points to the fact that it is reasonable to think that implicit feeling awareness, hence subjective experience, is already present at birth, possibly even in the womb. This is a rather revolutionary idea considering that, not so long ago, the idea of feeling-less infants (i.e., nonverbal children) was the default assumption.

Until fairly recently, the *Zeitgeist* was to deny infants any form of worthwhile feeling experience (phenomenal awareness). Proof of this is that in the 1940s and 1950s, surgery without anesthesia was routinely performed on infants and young children. Modern surgeons conveniently paralyzed squirming infants by injection of curare or similar paralytic agents. Under such circumstances, adults recalled excruciating pain during surgery. But patients were not believed and the practice went on for twenty years. As pointed out by Dennett: "The fact that most of the patients were infants and small children may explain this credibility gap."[7] Even today, local anesthetics are not routine in painful procedures on newborns such as heel prick and circumcision, even by pediatricians practicing in state of the art maternity hospitals. The *Zeitgeist* continues to be that infants have either no feelings or few feelings, or that feeling experience at this early stage may not be of any consequence because it is not remembered (infantile amnesia). Such a rationale raises questions when looking at the brain as well as behavior in prenatal and postnatal development.

Looking at brain development during the prenatal and postnatal period suggests that the necessary neurological prerequisites for feeling experience may already be in place by *8 weeks* after conception, meaning when the sperm met the egg! Here in a nutshell is what we know today about the emergence of the brain and neural growth from conception to birth. This emergence is astonishing in its pace and complexity, considering that the brain is probably the most complex system in the universe. It reminds us

5 Over and Carpenter, "Eighteen-month-old infants show increased helping following priming with affiliation."

6 For thorough discussions of implicit and explicit levels of conceptual awareness in early development, see Karmiloff-Smith, *Beyond Modularity*; Carey, "The origin of concepts"; Spaepen et al., "Number without a language model."

7 Dennett, *Brainstorms*, p. 201.

of the great biological forces behind development. It takes only 4 weeks from conception for the neural tube to be formed from layers of cells on the embryonic disc.[8] Only one extra week is needed for the basic five-part structure of the brain to be anatomically differentiated and clearly visible (i.e., telecephalon and diencephalon of the forebrain, midbrain, hindbrain, and the spinal cord). By 11 weeks of gestation (not 3 months after conception!), medulla, cerebellum, inferior and superior colliculus, as well as both cerebral hemispheres covering the diencephalon are also clearly visible.[9]

From then on and for a few years, both hemispheres grow in surface areas via folding grooves and convolutions. This growth reflects rapid and exponential connection networks among synapses as well as myelination of axons providing insulation (fatty "white matter") for better transmission of electrochemical nerve impulses. By 2 years of age, the child's brain already weighs 80 percent of its lifetime maximum weight.[10] Let's now look more closely at what we know about development at a more microscopic level: the level of the brain's building blocks, the neurons.

In terms of neural growth, between 10 and 26 weeks' gestational age, neurons are produced at a rate of 250,000 a minute, leading to overproduction. Beyond 26 weeks, more than half of the produced nerve cells are selectively pruned and die. The surviving 100 billion will eventually form the adult brain.[11] All of this development is indeed humbling. We should always keep it in the back of our mind when thinking about what it means to be present, alive, and having experience in this world.

Regarding connection between cells, there is also an overproduction of synapses that continues beyond birth, with peaking periods that vary across brain regions.[12] Synaptogenesis continuing after birth is not homogeneous and synchronous across brain regions. For example, post-mortem data indicate that synaptic density peaks earlier in the auditory cortex (3 months) compared to the middle frontal gyrus (15 months).[13] This kind of growth asynchrony is reflected, for example, in the sequential development of sense modalities in the womb and beyond (i.e., vision lag).

In short, these facts remind us that brain emergence, and the neural (sensory) machinery that necessarily underlies implicit feeling experience,

[8] Hepper, "Prenatal development."
[9] Carlson, *Human Embryology and Developmental Biology*.
[10] Kretschmann et al., "Brain growth in man."
[11] Oppenheim, "Cell death during development of the nervous system."
[12] Rakic, "Model of cell migration to the superficial layers of the fetal monkey neocortex."
[13] Huttenlocher and Dabholkar, "Regional differences in synaptogenesis in human cerebral cortex."

is fast, remarkably precise, and predictable in its unfolding. To the naked eye or through the lens of a microscope, it is an explosive and amazingly well-programmed growth. In relation to putative first feeling experience, brain development puts in place within 8 weeks the potential for fetuses to sense the world, hence also the necessary prerequisite to eventually feel it: the potential for first minimal, obviously implicit, and very rudimentary feeling experience. Let us not forget, however, that feeling experience rests on the prerequisite of an ability to sense the world, as machines do. What I have tried to show is that, in humans, such necessary sensory "machinery" matures within weeks of conception and long before birth. In its development and within the confines of the maternal womb, fetal research shows that this actually recapitulates the emergence order of the main sensory systems in the course of species evolution. The sensory machinery (sense modalities) of fetuses matures in the same sequential order as our ancestral species.[14] Somesthetic sensitivity (skin and body feelings) matures first. This sensitivity corresponds to tactile (skin pressure), vestibular (posture and balance), and pain stimulation (tissue damage). It is followed by the maturation of chemosensory sensitivity that combines olfaction and gustation (i.e., smell and taste), followed by audition (pitch, amplitude, and phrasing of sounds), and finally by vision (light and optic array). From this, we can conclude that the necessary sensory prerequisites of first feeling experience are in place at least by the third semester of gestation. But when can we say that first feeling experiences actually emerge in development? We shall see in more detail in the second part of the book, on the developmental origins of possession, that new ways of observing fetuses (three- and four-dimensional sonic echography and image scanning) suggest that already by the last trimester fetuses express emotions such as "happiness" via smiling and "sadness" via frowning of the eyebrows and lowering of the corners of the lips in the same way newborns express such mental states at birth and beyond.[15] More intriguing is the fact that nociceptive (pain) receptors appear first in and around the mouth area at around 7 weeks after conception. They rapidly extend to the palmar surface of the hands by 11 weeks, and the rest of the skin and mucosal surfaces by 20 weeks.[16]

[14] For further detailed discussion, see Gottlieb, "Ontogenesis of sensory functions in birds and mammals"; Lecanuet and Schaal, "Fetal sensory compentencies"; in relation to the development of pain responsiveness, see Anand and Hickey, "Pain and its effects in the human neonate and fetus"; Merskey and Bogduk, *Classification of Chronic Pain.*

[15] Hata, Dai, and Marumo, "Ultrasound for evaluation of fetal neurobehavioural development."

[16] Brusseau and Mashour, "Subcortical consciousness." See also Smith, *Commission of Inquiry into Fetal Sentience.*

In all, this suggests that in trying to find the roots of "feeling" experience, including possession, above and beyond sensing, we should probably already look in the womb for its embryonic stage.

On possessing oneself: implicit self-evidence

At some basic level, feeling experience carries with it a fundamental *self-evidence property*. It is that my feeling experiences of the world are mine, and can only be mine and nobody else's. This is true no matter what, and to the extent that I don't take drugs or show symptoms of schizophrenic autism or any other kind of psychosis. As phenomenological philosophers in the European tradition of Husserl, Merleau-Ponty, Sartre, and many others, but more recently Dan Zahavi or Shaun Gallagher, would claim, this self-evidence comes for free with any kind of feeling experience.[17] It is an implicit given. In the same way, James Gibson[18] in his ecological approach to perception proposes that perceiving the world always necessarily entails *co-perceiving* oneself as perceiver and actor in the world. One implies the other, no matter what, like the two sides of the same coin. This is a simple, yet powerful intuition that is theoretically helpful, accounting for much of what we see in the development of children and in devastating instances of psychopathology like schizophrenia. For these empirical reasons, there is good reason to endorse such implicit "self-evidence" that feeling would necessarily entail.[19] However, before presenting this empirical ground for siding with the phenomenologists, one should acknowledge other philosophical and psychological perspectives adopting radically different epistemological starting points. These views are that the mine-ness of experience is most likely an illusion and a cognitive reconstruction rather than a necessary given.[20] Accordingly, self-perception would be more the product of an inference and a mental representation rather than an implicit "direct" counterpart of any acts of direct perception as suggested by Gibson.[21]

[17] Gallaher and Zahavi, *The Phenomenological Mind.*

[18] Gibson, *The Ecological Approach to Visual Perception.*

[19] Note that contemporary philosopher Charles Taylor uses the concept of "self-possession" as an index of the new phenomenology and novel exigencies associated with emerging modernity (Taylor, *Sources of the Self*).

[20] In the tradition of David Hume, who claimed that self-perception was fundamentally not a given but rather an illusion, see a more modern cognitive science version of this view in Thomas Metzinger's recent book, *Being No One*. See also Rochat (*Others in Mind*) for a more succinct and simple presentation of these contrasted views in the philosophy of mind.

[21] See David Marr and all the Artificial Intelligence, machine-like simulation and model metaphors of perception in the realm of the cognitive and computer sciences that all share the idea that perception is piecemeal symbols-based reconstruction (see Marr, *Vision*, and Barsalou, "Perceptual symbol systems").

I would say simply that cognitive reconstruction views are untenable when considering very young infants, as well as adults suffering mental and other self disorders found particularly in schizophrenia but also in other psychotic symptoms.

Our own observations of young infants, together with many others that I will have the chance to review in more details in Part II of the book, point to the fact that we are born with the basic intuition of what belongs to our own feeling experience and what is not. Infants a few hours old show unambiguous discrimination between self and non-self touch. We were able to demonstrate that newborns root significantly more in the direction of another person's finger that touches one of their cheeks compared to when one of their own fingers comes spontaneously in contact with the same cheek. They discriminate between self-produced "double-touch" of simultaneous cheek and finger touching and the "single" touch of a non-self finger.[22] This simple observation tells us, among other empirical evidence found in neonates, that we are born with the potential for the implicit sense of exclusive mine-ness of experience, something that is probably the necessary phenomenal prerequisite of psychological development, its necessary subjective seed. That my feelings are mine is self-evident and does not have to be an indirect representational reconstruction. If that were the case, it is doubtful that neonates would show discrimination between double and single touch experience. Our observations imply that there is from birth the potential self-evidence property of feeling experience.

On being possessed

A look at the anomalous experience of psychotic adults who suffer from great cognitive disorganization and uncontrollable hallucinations within the schizophrenia spectrum demonstrates how fundamental and actually basic self-evident mine-ness experience is, the *sine qua non* condition of our sanity. It shows clearly that self-evident mine-ness of feeling experience is the cornerstone of the ways we create meanings and bring coherence to our experience of being alive in this world: something that is ineffable (hard to put words on) and pre-reflective (implicit) by nature.

Loss of self-evident mine-ness of experience can be pathological and long lasting, just as it can be temporary and provoked by drugs and trance-inducing rituals that are so pervasive across religions and cultures. Speaking tongues and other possessed states are symptomatic of

[22] Rochat and Hespos, "Differential rooting response by neonates."

self-evident feeling experience transmuted (mentally delegated) to a fictive entity that intrudes individual consciousness, be it the devil or a dead ancestor. Trance states can transform the implicit self-evidence typically accompanying feeling experience into the embodied *allo*-evidence of another. Possessed individuals are literally invaded and under the spell of another. There is experiential loss of self-control, until the individual snaps out of the trance state. Aside from religious rituals, hypnosis is a good, more secular example of a trance-like state. It continues to be successfully exploited in psychotherapy and psychoanalysis, in the footsteps of Charcot (1825–93) in his pioneer research on hysteria and other neurotic symptoms shown to be of psychological origin, as well as Freud in his early practice of psychoanalysis (*c.* 1895).[23] Such induced temporary disturbance and loss of subjectivity is similar in some fundamental ways to chronic psychosis like schizophrenia.

Refined examination of the subjective, first person perspective accounts of hundreds of schizophrenic individuals reveals that, first and foremost, schizophrenia and allied symptoms are disorders of minimal self-experience, including at its core the self-evident *mine-ness experience.*[24] It is typical for individuals suffering the atrocious ills of schizophrenia to report that although they rationally, thus explicitly, know that their thoughts originate from within them and are not hallucinations proper, these thoughts are nonetheless *not* felt as generated by them. There is no implicit sense of self-agency in thinking or generating thoughts, and they are thus somehow "possessed" rather than in possession as discussed above. It is a loss of thought "ipseity" (from the Latin word *ipse*, self), in other words the loss of the mine-ness of thinking one's own thoughts. Losing this basic and implicit sense of self is devastating, of almost unimaginable horror, as probably best conveyed by Elyn Saks's vivid, very personal, and detailed account of her own journey into schizophrenia:[25]

> This experience is much harder, and weirder, to describe than extreme fear or terror. Most people know what it is like to be seriously afraid. If they haven't felt it themselves, they've at least seen a movie, or read a book, or talked to a frightened friend – they can at least imagine it. But explaining what I've come to call "disorganization" is a different challenge altogether. Consciousness gradually loses its coherence. One's center gives way. The center cannot hold. The "me" becomes a haze, and the solid center from which one experiences reality breaks up like a bad radio signal. There is no longer a sturdy vantage point from which to look out, take things in, assess what's happening. No core holds things together, providing the lens through which to see the world, to make judgments and comprehend risk.

[23] See in particular Breuer and Freud, *Studies on Hysteria*.
[24] Parnas et al., "EASE: Examination of Anomalous Self-Experience."
[25] Saks, *The Center Cannot Hold*, p. 13.

Random moments of time follow one another. Sights, sounds, thoughts, and feelings don't go together. No organizing principle takes successive moments in time and puts them together in a coherent way from which sense can be made. And it's all taking place in slow motion. Delusions and hallucinations are an intrinsic part of the diagnosis of schizophrenia and its self-disorganization, including voices as running commentaries on the person's behavior or thoughts, some sort of inescapable hyper-reflectivity but from a third party perspective that invades the individual who has lost basic self-evidence and an implicit trust that subjective experience *belongs* to oneself, a feeling experience that is not self-specifying any-more but rather diffused and confused with a world that is chaotic: the forceful, uncontrollable voices and intrusive thoughts that have no overarching narrative structure, no meaningful organization.

Such psychopathologies point to the fact that to function and experience the world normally, self-evidence and the basic feeling experience that one's thoughts and perceptions belong to oneself is a necessity. It is indispensable, an absolute pre-requisite to avoid mental invasion and the loss of minimal self-reference. How easy it is for us to take for granted the fact that these gestures, this voice, this vision *belong* to no one else and no other source than *me*. Without this basic self-evident feeling experience, we are at a loss. Losing it is indeed devastating. We shall also see that this is the primordial prerequisite of psychological development that starts in the womb.

The me and the mine

William James, in his seminal discussion of the self as psychological construct states: "A man's Self is the sum total of all that he can call his, not only his body and his psychic powers, but his clothes and his house, his wife and children, his ancestors and friends, his reputation and works, his lands, and yacht and bank-account. All these things give him the same emotions. If they wax and prosper, he feels triumphant; if they dwindle and die away, he feels cast down."[26]

The question is, how do we come up with a "me" concept that includes a great number of things existing outside of our physical envelope, and therefore that are physically non-self entities, literally *incorporated* as parts of our bodily selves? The process of incorporation, when you think of it, is a rather curious propensity of ours. The question is even more salient and puzzling in light of William James's further consideration: "it is clear that between what a man calls me and what he simply calls mine the line is difficult to draw. We feel and act about certain things that are ours very much as we feel and act about ourselves" (p. 291). Here, James points to

[26] James, *The Consciousness of Self*.

the fact that the differentiation between self and objects can become blurry and eventually disappear with certain objects that are assimilated to the self via the elusive process of incorporation. By this process, some objects become part of the "embodied" self, an intrinsic part of the entity that feels and acts, the entity we perceive and conceptually identify as "me."

If we take this observation seriously, we can contemplate the depth of its psychological meaning. It is profound because mental sanity rests on the basic sense of where we stand in relation to things. Again, the mental suffering associated with psychotic bouts such as schizophrenia comes primarily from a blurring of the experience of what corresponds to the self and what corresponds to outside things. So, for example, in the midst of a crisis, a psychotic might hear voices in his head that he wrongly attributes as originating from outside his body, or he might perceive self-motion (own movements) as allo-motion (external, non-self movements). As we have seen, this is a source of great cognitive confusion associated with excruciating anxieties, and dramatic affective and existential consequences for the individual.

At both implicit and explicit levels of experience, the psychology of possession rests on a primordial process of incorporation to the embodied self: a literal process of projection and identification that leads to some assimilative re-embodiment of things to the self. It is a process of absorption and digestion into the embodied self, and eventually retention and expulsion as described by Freud[27] in his pleasure-related control experience of the anal stage in psychosexual development (i.e., pleasure of the sphincter as primary erogenous zone).

This primordial process of *incorporation* in the literal and etymological sense of the word refers to the combining of substances, the absorption into the *corpus* (Latin word for body) of something that is foreign to it. This process leads to the often illusory, but self-evident feeling that it is "mine." It is from incorporation that arises the feeling of "mine-ness" projected onto physical objects (my car, my toothbrush, my chair) or persons (my girlfriend, my mother, my husband, my teacher). It arises from the process by which things, objectified as external to us (a book, a glass, an individual), but also possibly things that we feel emanating from within us (a novel idea, a concept, the solution to a problem, a style, a gesture), become also experienced as *ours and nobody else's*. It is the bottom-line process of all propensities toward creating an exclusive world that enlarges the self with things possessed (i.e., belongings). As stated by William James, we do project and identify with things that become an intrinsic

[27] Freud, *Three Essays on the Theory of Sexuality*.

part of us and who we are for ourselves as well as the outside world. It is the process by which objects are somehow transmuted into belongings that become patently ours through our eyes but also the eyes of others.

Incorporation to the self is not limited to surrounding material entities. As everyone knows, especially divorce and other patent lawyers, it also applies to practices, styles, ideas, and manners, even people (my wife, my child, my maid, my priest). In fact the process of incorporation is what underlies *all* of our certainties about what belongs to us, and what we feel we are entitled to. Interestingly, at the group level, it is an analogous process by which laws induct companies, literally incorporating responsibilities and entitlements into institutions that become moral persons (Inc.).

Behind such incorporation to the self, there are two basic propensities emerging in development, especially exacerbated in humans, commonly referred to as *projection* and *identification*. The feeling experience of possession entails the complex processes of projection and identification, particularly when such experience becomes explicit and objectified, when the child grabs an object and claims to the world: "That's mine!" (see next chapter). Projection is a two-way, mutual assimilation of self and object. When claiming "That's mine!" the child in his words claims assimilation of the object to the embodied self, but also the reverse: the expulsion of self into the object, a dual phenomenon that Freud and followers like Ferenczi label respectively "exterojection" and "introjection" of the self to the object.

Freud in his writing insists that this dual process is characteristic of normal psychological functioning from the outset, and not just symptomatic of his patients' psychopathology. Rightly, Freud extrapolates the crucial contrast experience of what is inside and outside of the body afforded by the natural, instinctive inclination of infants to ingest and reject food.[28] Freud probably did not know at the time that this inclination is expressed already in utero.

It is now well documented that, by the last trimester of gestation, fetuses engage in much sucking and ingestion, as well as dejection of surrounding amniotic fluid. The potential of an implicit contrast experience of what is inside and outside of the body is therefore present very early on and is probably where the feeling of possession finds its budding, embryonic roots. But obviously, things develop and change radically. Their meanings change, from infancy and throughout the lifespan. The dual process of introjection and exterojection, the experience of ingestion and rejection,

[28] See also followers like Anna Freud and Melanie Klein who gave further thought to this idea in their own writings about early development.

inside versus outside of body, the implicit as well as explicit experience of things possessed, find different meanings in the history of individuals. Our relation to food changes with age as much as our relation to things and people. This relation is also context dependent. In Samoa being fat and big is associated with power and being served by others, not having to budge much in daily chores. In the industrial Western world, the USA in particular, it is associated with poverty. Some become health freaks, others compulsive junk eaters. Some become jealous individuals, others free spirits. Some try to get rid of superfluous things and others cultivate the hoarding of wealth and power. It all depends, but it all has in common the quest for a self-identity: trying to specify what is "me" in relation to others. In this common quest, what separates me from mine is elusive and forms the major grey area of self-psychology. This grey area extends from and separates embodied self and the world. It is the zone that is at the core of issues regarding the feeling of possession and the general process of incorporation. It is the grey area that arises from an intrinsic elusiveness in the determination of what individuates possessions that exist outside of the bodily envelope but are felt, and eventually objectified as being intrinsic parts of the embodied self: my house, my children, my car. It raises the fundamental question of what is the experiential demarcation between self and world. What determines the feeling of such demarcation and the point where me and mine are felt the same, thus experientially merging to become interchangeable like me and my face or my heart, but also my wife, my car, and my chair – at this point in time in this crowded restaurant: all felt as possessions of mine?

Are these shoes or these ideas mine? Yes, of course, but on what basis? Possession as self-experience is a grey area of psychology, dynamic and underspecified. The limits of entitlement and control over things, above and beyond our own subjective experience of entitlement, can only be socially negotiated.

Ooka Tadasuke was a Samurai turned judge during the eighteenth-century Edo period of Japanese history (1600–1838). He is legendary for his haiku type verdicts. Ooka Tadasuke's verdicts are much more than sanctioning sentences. Like haiku poetry, they open gates to deep reflections on essential issues, one of them being the limits and determination of possession. Best known is the legendary verdict pronounced toward a hungry and poor student who had only bland rice to eat. The student would eat his bowl of rice sitting on the steps of a restaurant, augmenting his diet with the rich odors escaping from the kitchen. The cook caught the student, accusing him of stealing the smell of his cooking. The case was brought to Ooka Tadasuke, whose verdict was for the student to pay back the cook with the sound of money passed from hand to hand. This verdict points to the elusiveness of entitlement and value equivalence. Indeed, is the water of the stream running through my property mine? What about the style of a drawing copied and reproduced in a magazine? Can an idea, the invention of a color scheme, or a signature character still be "mine" once it is public and reproduced with slight alterations? Who owns the air inside my apartment? What are good enough reasons for screaming "Thief!" and how should victims of theft be compensated? What is subjective equivalence (i.e., the perceived interchangeable value of things that are ontologically distinct like apples and oranges)? These questions are not only economic and political. They are first and foremost revealing of the complex psychology of feeling possession.

In William James's terms, the sense of possession is rooted in the conflation of the "me" and of the "mine." Questions remain, however, as to what might drive this conflation, and ultimately what might be gained from it since such conflation renders the limits that separate self and world blurry. The answer lies, I think, in the fact that ultimately the process of appropriation underlying possession is about social power but also – paradoxically – about the promotion of belongingness: the experience of social affiliation and ultimately the promotion of *social harmony.*

Envy and jealousy

In absolute solitude and with no potential aggressors, there would be no reason to experience possession. At the most basic level, possession is an experience that is grounded in the fear of a threat: the threat of being "dispossessed." It derives from and is the necessary counterpart of a fear of losing control over entities that are incorporated to the self, but also over one's own life and integrity. The experience of possession is thus, across species, in essence defensive *in relation to others*, whether others are conspecifics or not. The fear of losing control is therefore inseparable from the feeling of possession.

Social competition that is the evolutionary context of possession determines particular perceptions of mental states (feelings) and their public expression (emotions).[29] These are recognizable in the human affective spinoffs of possession that are envy and jealousy. If the drive and comfort of having control over things underlies possession, the loss of it

[29] See my earlier book *Others in Mind*, pp. 111–112, for a discussion and distinction between feelings, affects, and emotions, three concepts that are too often conflated and confounded in the literature. Accordingly, *feelings* are construed here as the perception of mental states, *affects* as the perception of general affective mood, and *emotions*, in the original Darwinian "expressive" sense, as the observable (public) expression of both feelings and affects.

determines and is a crucial and necessary counterpart of such experience. Indeed, aside from fear, it is when we actually lose control over an object of possession that we gauge the power of our attachment. Often, it is only when we lose something that we realize how much we cared for it, sometimes with devastating affective exaggeration as in the case of envy and jealousy.

Ancient Greek philosophers discussed envy as self-reproach, the reproach of not possessing what others have.[30] In this sense, and interestingly, envy is closely linked to guilt, a reproach to the self for having done something that could have been done differently, such as cheating on someone we care about, even love.

At some level, envy and guilt involve the sense of responsibility. Aristotle points to the fact that we tend to envy those who are close to us, live in our vicinity, and are of comparable age as well as social status. According to the ancient philosopher, we tend to envy those in whom we can recognize ourselves: "Envy pertains to the idea that we have of ourselves, what makes our difference, our identity, it touches us at our very core."[31] As we can see, envy as emotional spinoff of possession is a concept flying high in putative meaning.

Self–other comparison is what fundamentally underlies both envy and jealousy as psychological phenomena.[32] But upstream of such fundamental self–other comparison, there is the feeling experience of possession.

In envying others we tend to reproach ourselves with the fact that we do not own something we should have. We are frustrated by the incapacity of owning that same thing. Accordingly, envying is to mourn our own impotency at getting what we could have. In other words, it is the experience of disempowerment. Likewise, in jealousy, the fear of loss or of losing an object of love and devotion, there is the experience of a loss of something felt as owned and over which one had control. Therefore, attached to both envy and jealousy there is the basic feeling experience of entitlement and ownership, hence the feeling of possession.

In jealousy, we basically lose control over a loved one, typically to some rival who is real but often can be imaginary, a mere projection of our deep fear of a loss of control and command over our affective life. In many instances of jealousy drama, the delusion of rivalry is involved, as if the jealous person is objectifying causes to his or her ordeal. Such objectification serves the purpose of bringing some coherence in the chaos of irrationality and awful pain associated with jealous feelings. It is a desperate attempt at fighting pain, at alleviating the excruciating experience of

[30] See Moessinger, *The Paradox of Social Order* and *Le jeu de l'identité*.

[31] Moessinger, *Le jeu de l'identité*. [32] Rochat, *Others in Mind*, pp. 145–149.

rejection from the loved one, worst of all ordeals. In jealousy, the fear of rejection, mother of all fears, can take extreme forms of wrath, rage, and irrationality. Individuals can lose all judgment and codes of law grant extenuating circumstances to murderers proven to have acted under a jealous spell.

Passion and wrath aside, jealousy is inseparable from the experience of possession, the possession of something differentiated from the self but that one feels entitled to own. As we have seen, possession is the experience of assimilation to the self of things or persons that exist in independence of one's own body (process of incorporation). This process is in essence symbolic but can be embodied when the object of possession becomes a natural extension of the body as in the case of a tool (e.g., stilts, tennis racket, glasses, jewelry, hammer).

The same applies to envy, which consists in a claim of ownership of something that is missing to the self and needs to be incorporated or self-appropriated. Both entail *incorporation*, literally the assimilation into the body (embodiment) of external things, whether material (physical object) or immaterial (an idea, a style, a concept). As already mentioned, in many ways the psychological process of incorporation that underlies the experience of possession is analogous to the metabolizing of food by the body that incorporates and processes energy for its survival.

Such a process generalizes to immaterial things like objects of love and fantasies of control and seductive ascendance over people. At a psychological level, external things tend to be assimilated and end up fusing with the self. In a way, jealousy is the fear or the actual experience of the loss of something that ended up belonging to the self. It is the suffering arising from the wrench of someone's inner being. The fear of losing property and control over someone or something, losing proprietary and ownership "rights" over a lover or a portion of territory. The word "property" comes from the Latin word *proprius* which stands for "what cannot be shared with others."

Mundane examples of such remarkable psychological processes abound, most of the time expressed at an unconscious and implicit level of awareness. For example, it appears that many people invest a lot in their cars, both materially and emotionally. They groom them like they groom their own body. Cars are, in most instances, an extension of the self. People can recognize themselves in such material things that they carefully choose and groom. Like shoes and ties, cars are a non-trivial extension of one's own body. They are experienced as such, notwithstanding the fact that cars in particular do facilitate self-propelled locomotion. They also promote social affiliation by the public display of status and reputation.

Explicit laws aside, and at a basic phenomenal level, the feeling experience of "proprius" or exclusive possession that leads eventually toward envy and jealousy rests on three basic psychological ingredients. These ingredients account for the irrepressible need to incorporate as *ours* the things that exist essentially in independence of us, be it people or material things like cars, houses, clothes, or land.

The first ingredient is a sense of self, in particular a sense of self as *differentiated* from objects and other people.[33] The idea is simple: in order to incorporate something, the necessary prerequisite is to have something that comes from the outside. In other words, possession experience implies, at the most basic level, a differentiation between self and world: what pertains to the body and what does not. Once this requirement is fulfilled, the second necessary ingredient is the propensity to somehow *objectify* things and people as differentiated entities, to perceive them as such, and to consider them as objects of contemplation and exploration. This second ingredient is the ability of an individual to project, or *eject* outward, things that exist in independence of them. Contrary to the Freudian psychoanalytical meaning of projection considered as a major defense mechanism, projection here is considered as the propensity to eject outward and to create objects of thought, contemplation, and desire. Projection, in the sense proposed here, pertains to the objectification of subjective (self-evident) experience that is lived within the body.

But self–world differentiation and projection are not yet sufficient to explain the sense of possession and entitlement we are so inclined to experience, particularly when it becomes explicit ("That's mine!"). As third ingredient, there is the necessity to *identify* with the thing differentiated and objectified. Identification is the process of self-recognition in entities that exist outside of one's own body, entities that are differentiated and objectified.

Accordingly, the feeling of possession, at least in our species so ostentatiously prone to experience envy and jealousy, rests on the articulation and combination of these three basic ingredients. The model can be summarized in a simple equation:[34]

SENSE OF OWNERSHIP =
DIFFERENTIATION × PROJECTION × IDENTIFICATION

In subsequent chapters pertaining to the developmental origins of possession (Part II), this simple model will be useful in our discussion of how

[33] See Rochat, *Others in Mind*, pp. 145–149. [34] See Rochat, *Others in Mind*.

children develop a sense of ownership and entitlement. More importantly, it will be useful when considering the developmental origins of the various ways of relinquishing ownership via negotiation, rather than coercion (see Chapter 2).

If exclusive feelings of possession foster negative emotional spinoffs like envy and jealousy, they are also what afford *sharing* as the proximate mechanism of group and intergroup harmony.

At a much larger, societal and group level, behind the literal forceful, compulsive, and defensive feeling experiences of possession that are sources of devastating emotions like envy and jealousy, lies also – paradoxically at first sight – the seed of social harmony. The essentially selfish feeling of possession and the forceful appropriation of things to the self is the necessary counterpart of all the intricate pro-social ways, including institutions we have evolved to promote peace, cooperation, communal empathy, and social stability.

In humans, and possibly also in some other nonhuman primate species,[35] affiliation is promoted when shared feelings of possession become the bargaining chips of social peace. This is evident in the case of gift exchanges, when dispossession becomes voluntary and ritualized to promote social bonding.[36]

It is reasonable to view the experience of possession as the bottom-line engine of pro-social morality, in the same way that all economists could claim that possession and consumerism are the necessary conditions of any exchange system. In other words, without the feeling of possession, there would be no morality, just as there would be no economy.

Possession and morality

Controlling and feeling control over things such as food, progeny, territory, loved ones, or sexual partner is *de facto* the necessary prerequisite of any creatures living in an environment where resources are scarce and competition is high. Social animals are under the permanent threat of

35 There are empirical evidence and theoretical assertions regarding nonhuman primate propensities toward social "services" such as food sharing, grooming for sex, and cooperation in chimpanzees, even in humans' distant relatives like capuchin monkeys. The proximate mechanisms underlying such services would, however, be of various kinds: from simple tit-for-tat symmetry of exchanges, to actual mental score-keeping that only chimpanzees as well as humans seem capable of (see Brosnan and DeWaal, "A proximate perspective on reciprocal altruism").

36 Early modern anthropologists and ethnologies demonstrate the remarkable common denominator across various primordial cultures regarding complex gift exchange rituals that promote social peace among neighboring groups. See in particular Malinowski, *Argonauts of the Western Pacific*, as well as the seminal work of Marcel Mauss, *The Gift*.

losing what is under their control, including their own life. Morality, as explicit or implicit systems of social norms, evolved to regulate the basic propensity to possess, particularly potential conflicts over possession.

To survive as groups, each social species evolved particular buffers to alleviate inescapable conflicts over possession, preventing group extinction and mutual extermination. These buffering systems are necessary to bring harmonious group equilibrium, assuring some perpetuity of the species. In humans, these systems are incarnated in moral institutions like tribunals, books of laws, explicit legal codes, constitutions, etc., but also implicit social rules, tacit know-hows and "etiquettes" transmitted from generation to generation as ways of ruling conflicts and regulating group dynamic.

But each social species has evolved its own particular and complex ways of regulating inter-individual competition and conflicts, with tacit principles and inclinations such as cooperation (helping and collaboration), reconciliation (peace making), first possession (deference to first possessor), tit-for-tat exchanges (I give because you give me), or reciprocal altruism (I give because you gave me).

Morality emerged in humans, and also in other primate species,[37] primarily as a system of social rules and norms evolved to regulate recurrent conflicts over possession. One is hard pressed to conceive morality in independence of possession and conflicts necessarily arising from it because of competition over scarce resources. There is biblical evidence of this predicament when we consider that six of the Ten Commandments in the Old Testament pertain to issues of putative conflict over possession regarding object, life, wife, body, or truth.[38]

There is also ontogenetic evidence for such an assertion, as issues of ethics or codes of conduct arise first and foremost in the context of fights over possession: "That's mine!," "I want one too!," "Give it back!," "It's not yours!," etc. First social conflicts and rivalry tensions over possession are well documented from the end of the second year, when children become explicit claimers of what is theirs.[39] It is primarily in such conflict and rivalry contexts that adults are constrained to come up with explicit "deontic" rules of dos and don'ts. In such interventions aimed at fostering peace, children are exposed to the rulings and moral ways of their social niche. They will eventually internalize and transmit such cultural models

37 See the debate around the origins of morality in primate evolution in De Waal, *Primates and Philosophers*.

38 Thou shalt not covet, steal, kill, commit adultery, bear false witness, or have other gods. All six Commandments have something to do with protecting what should be one's own: life, wife, body, or truth.

39 See Dunn, *The Beginnings of Social Understanding*.

to future generations. This is another, simple way of stating that the feeling of possession is a necessary precursor, the experiential prerequisite for the evolution of any implicit or explicit ruling meant to promote social harmony, whether such a system rests on simple alliance, tit-for-tat exchanges, basic empathy, or higher-order explicit cultural and symbolic systems like the Ten Commandments.

Further evidence of the link between possession and moral obligations is once again evident in the pioneer works of early anthropologists like Marcel Mauss (1872–1950) and Bronislaw Malinowski (1884–1942). In the early twentieth century, these anthropologists established that gift systems or ceremonials of relinquishing possession are cardinal cultural institutions among pre-industrial societies from all latitudes. Gift systems are universal, identified as the cornerstone of social harmony within and between indigenous "primitive" human groups. The pioneer ethnographic works of Mauss and Malinowski, among many others,[40] demonstrate that, in human evolution, implicit feeling experience of possession is transformed into explicit and ritualized (symbolic) relinquishing of possession as "gift," within complex exchange practices fostering long-term harmonious inter-individual and inter-group relations via social debts and the strict obligation to reciprocate in an endless circularity of gift giving (e.g., the Kula circle described by Malinowski in the Solomon Islands of Melanesia).

If possession governs the social lives of all animals, in humans the experience of possession has unique features. If it shares crucial roots and aspects that are unquestionably homologous to those expressed in fish, birds, and all mammals, as in the case of the defense of progeny and territory, it is not strictly comparable. We belong to a species that is self-conscious, and particularly prone to caring about reputation. In this context, we develop a psychology and feeling experience of possession that has some unique if not awkward features, namely symbolic spinoffs not found in other animals (see Chapter 4). Among such spinoffs are humans' irrepressible animistic and fetishistic tendencies toward objects, projecting vitality into things and leading us to worship cult objects.[41] Such highly symbolic worshiping is not a trivial feature of the human psyche since it has recurrently led us to kill each other. We are taught that Christian Crusades were aimed at regaining possession of the Holy

[40] For further, more detailed discussion, see Godbout, *The World of the Gift*; Rochat, *Others in Mind*.

[41] Sperber, *Le symbolisme en général*: a cogent presentation of various accounts of the rational and irrational dimensions of human symbolisms, including the variability of its expressions across cultures and what would be its universal cognitive underpinnings.

Sepulcher in Jerusalem, the tomb of Christ: the reason for hundreds of thousands of deaths. In the meantime, as symbolic counterpart, we have also evolved cultural institutions like the International Tribunal at The Hague and the United Nations.

Other animals have also evolved complex ways and practices to promote social harmony and contain their forceful possession psychology (e.g., dominance hierarchy, alliances, instinctive regulation of aggression and defensiveness).[42] But unlike humans, this sedimentation of pro-social norms is not symbolic and not imbued with human beings' more often than not weird symbolic spinoffs, evident in fetishism, superstitions, and other animistic propensities. These are ontologically different.

Like any other social animal, we respond to threats of being dispossessed and losing control over possessions as if it were an attack on our own body. But in humans, it is often highly symbolic and abstract, removed from literal signals or signifiers to which other animals tend to respond automatically or in a predictable, conditioned manner. The reasons for human defensive aggression over possession are often far removed from the actual, literal situation. It tends easily to take some unpredictable irrational spinoffs with no obvious underlying adaptive reasons. We might resort to psychoanalytical concepts and other sublimation processes to account for them. How can we otherwise make sense of road rage and people pulling guns for a scratch on their car as if it was an integral part of their embodied self? How to make sense of devastating human crusades around sacred sepulchers and other sanctified objects? How to explain terrorist acts and other jihads pronounced against novelists or caricaturists for their ideas and ideological transgressions? How can the lives of young soldiers be so readily sacrificed for pieces of land that often are not even strategic but stand as purely symbolic in relation to elusive religious or political beliefs?

[42] See the seminal overview by ethologist Robert Hinde, *Animal Behavior*.

2 Claiming ownership

It is one thing to experience possession, but another to become public about it. This chapter focuses on the step that transforms the experience of possession (the feeling of possessiveness discussed earlier) into the explicit claim of ownership, the various levels and ways of advertising to others "That's mine!"

The explicit claim of ownership transforms the psychology of possession from intra- to interpersonal: from possession as an intrapsychic, intrapersonal phenomenon to an interpsychic, interpersonal phenomenon shared and co-experienced in reference to others.

Through this transformation, possession becomes *objectified*. It becomes an object of evaluation that can be assessed, negotiated, recognized, or challenged by others, and cherished and protected by its possessor. In the process, the experience of possession becomes object of desire calling for conquest and defense: progeny, territory, food, tribe, army, car, anything. This objectifying process begs at least two questions: What constitutes an object of possession? What are the personal and interpersonal mechanisms substantiating possession as an object that is socially recognized? This is what we want to discuss here.

Possession in action

After discussing the basic feeling experience of possession, we now add a new layer: the actual assertion of ownership of the thing that is felt as possessed and under the spell of one's own control. As discussed in the preceding chapter, to feel possession is a *sine qua non*, pre-reflective, and implicit feeling experience that we share with most animals. It is part of the minimal awareness experience of possessing a body that occupies space, has an inside and an outside, bounded and substantial, an operation center from which actions originate and are generated. We can assume that all feeling creatures, even fetuses, may minimally "possess" such subjective experience of possession.

Minimal subjective experience is the necessary counterpart of the feeling capacity, of having a psychology that is colored by some affectivity made of mental states and emotions like pain or possession. However, it is not yet an experience that is owned as such. Another general layer of self- and other-awareness, implicit or explicit, needs to be added. It is the extra psychological step that feeling creatures take to own something *by acting upon these feelings*: defending, asserting, and creating possessions. It is what leads creature to transcend the mere feeling of possession, the necessary but not sufficient condition discussed earlier.

Claiming ownership is *objectifying* feelings of possession. It is an active assertion of power and control over things, made public by the mere fact that it is enacted. The basic idea is that it is one thing to have feelings, and another to act upon them. The question is what might trigger such a step? Is it the result of a bootstrapping process within the basic feeling experience of possession, or is it caused by extraneous, higher-order factors?

In general, it is difficult to establish whether minimal, gut feelings of possession trigger the actions of taking ownership (defense, acquisition, assertion of possession that is objectified as mine), or the reverse. By analogy, the same conundrum was raised over a century ago by William James in relation to the nature and origins of emotions. James asked: Am I afraid because I objectively see a grizzly bear attacking me, or is it the reverse? Are emotions bottom up (from guts to reason), or top down (from reason to guts)? The debate goes on even if current theories tend to show that it is most probably a combination of both.[1]

In relation to possession, from the point of view of phylogeny (evolution) and ontogeny (development), we are going to assume that the experience of possession is a necessary, minimal, and *sine qua non* condition upon which the act of taking (claiming) ownership builds. We are also going to assume the possibility of a retroactive loop by which the claim of ownership might transform, reinforce, or re-describe the experience of possession. We do need to consider the extent to which possession as experience and the public claim of ownership modulate each other and are mutually conditioned. It is reasonable to think, for example, that degrees of possessiveness depend on multiple extraneous factors like the amount of social challenge encountered in the claim of ownership. High challenge can dramatically enhance feelings of possession via

[1] See the two-factor theory of emotions (cognitive–physiological interaction) originally demonstrated in Schachter and Singer, "Cognitive, social, and physiological determinants of emotional state."

struggles and frustration (see for example the Palestinian fight for land in the Middle East). Inversely, reduced resistance and obstacles can lead toward less inflamed feelings of possession.

Overall, reasons to feel possession and fight for it depend on relative resource abundance of the shared environment. The context of possession is indeed social and competitive. Obviously, the transformative process of possession from feeling experience to object of public recognition can have various levels of complexity. It can be literal and automatic ("instinctive"), but it can also be regulated in the context of highly complex explicit oral traditions and books of law. Let's reflect first on the most basic instinctive level of such transformation: the enactment of possession in gestures of defense and attack. The enactment of possession objectifies its experience. It makes this experience public and accessible to all, raising it to the realm of shared awareness.

Instinctive enactment of possession

At the most basic, implicit level, the objectifying of possession experience is evident in the instinctive defense by any animal against a predator, and vice versa, the instinctive chase of the predator. In instinctive actions and other fixed action patterns (e.g., growling of the dog, erected hair of the chimpanzee, fleeing and camouflaging of the octopus, hovering and plunging of the seagull), animals implicitly advertise and make public their feeling of possession via defense but also attack as in the case of the predator chasing its prey.

Prey and predators, the universal bipolar roles assigned to all animals in nature, enact their possession experience and objectify it, life for one and meat for the other. One could say, metaphorically, that in chasing each other, predator and prey "dance" to the tune of incompatible ownership claims. The chase objectifies for each protagonist their respective possession experience: envy and aggression for one, alarm (fear) and defense for the other. It is revealing of their mental states that are co-determined but also *co-objectified* in the chase. These mental states that are dormant or concealed become emotions in the sense of the Latin *emovere*, to move out or to render public.

As for everything else in nature, things evolve and develop because of adaptive pressures. They are here for their survival value and sometimes persist because they used to have survival values, like vestigial structures of ours such as the appendix or wisdom teeth, all dispensable ancestral relics. Similarly, there is an adaptive fitness to feeling possession, particularly when it comes down to taking ownership of such feeling. In simple behavioral terms, such fitness is easily measured against the permanent danger of predators, thieves, and competition over scarce resources within and across groups of conspecifics.

In the general context of natural selection, feelings, and all the coloring of affective life made of emotions and other mental states they bring to the animal, serve a basic motivational function *driving* behaviors that have been selected for their adaptive fitness. Among the most ancestral actions driven by the feeling of possession are antagonistic *fight* behaviors. These are in polar opposition, in terms of both autonomic nervous system commands and the functional meaning of *flight*, *freezing* and other *death fainting*, or *immobilizing* behaviors that most animals manifest in situations felt as fearful or threatening. The feeling experience driving such behaviors can be triggered by events or stimuli detected that are either distal to the body, caused for example by the vision, olfaction, or audition of a predator; or proximal as an actual physical touch or contact to the body.

In all cases, when animals act, whether by fighting, fleeing, threatening, fainting, or courting, the feeling (subjective) experience of the animal is de facto objectified or choreographed in action. It becomes public, on display for the world to watch and make sense of (threat, approach, fear, etc.). If that is true for all animals, in humans such objectification becomes quickly explicit and highly symbolic, mediated by language (e.g., "That's mine!"). It develops beyond the implicit automatism and fixed action patterns of other animals. However, across all species, including humans, the feeling experience of possession, hence the threat of losing possession, including the predator's fear of losing its prey, serves as a constant affective background, a vigilance system that puts the animal on alert, even when sleeping. The feelings can be materialized and objectified into defensive actions at any time. Again, this is true across all species, including humans, from the outset of development. What changes and can be vastly different are the ways that feelings become objectified into the action of *taking ownership*.

Evolutionary story

This movement from feeling to asserting possession is indeed pervasive in nature, where animals from fish to butterflies put themselves on all sorts of dramatic and very effective display for others to take note of and respond to. These are evident in the dog growling with raised hair resulting in bigger and stronger appearance, the peacock's tail transformed into a disproportionate colorful eye-spotted wheel, or chimpanzees' bounce and hoot with erected hair.

We, like other animals, spend a great deal of time in implicit posturing, displaying and advertising our own body for physical strength and health to scare off but also to attract. In doing so, we take ownership of our own presence in the world. We even deliberately decorate ourselves with makeup and particular kinds of clothing, something that is specific to our symbolic and self-conscious species. Self-promoting propensities by us tend to be much more suggestive and less literal compared to other animals, and certainly much more flexible and reaching higher levels of indirect symbolism, like defending and promoting one's ideas, styles, or inventions, but also taking ownership of one's responsibilities and commitments in front of a judge or a justice of the peace: "in sickness and in health, until death do us part."

The big question, of course, is how the feeling of possession eventually gets objectified in acts of taking possession. This process by which feeling experiences and emotions get transformed into patterns of action remains a fundamental and perennial question in the behavioral and brain sciences.

The process has deep roots in vertebrate evolution. Our gut feeling experiences with accompanying automatic actions (e.g., running or engaging in aggression when scared) are remnants of archaic non-conscious mechanisms that were selected, over thousands of generations, from one species to the next, because they allowed animals to survive by reflexively detecting dangers and threats in the environment. Those are – unquestionably – the underlying neurobiological foundations of the new layers of conscious ownership that we see unfolding in child development, for example. These are the "visceral," implicit origins of our feelings expressed in emotions that eventually lead the child to say, with all its heavy load of conceptual and symbolic meaning: "That's mine!"

William James and Danish neurologist Carl Lange proposed independently in the nineteenth century that the nature of emotions, including the feeling experience of threat or attack on possession, originates from our perception of visceral changes, rather than the result of higher, top-down processes. I have alluded already to this theory above. James[2] describes his theory, now referred as the James–Lange theory of emotions, in the following way:

> My theory ... is that the bodily changes follow directly the perception of the exciting fact, and that our feeling of the same changes as they occur is the emotion. Common sense says, we lose our fortune, are sorry and weep; we meet a bear, are frightened and run; we are insulted by a rival, are angry and strike. The hypothesis here to be defended says that this order of sequence is incorrect ... and that the more rational statement is that we feel sorry because we cry, angry because we strike, afraid because we tremble ... Without the bodily states following on the perception, the latter would be purely cognitive in form, pale, colorless, destitute

[2] James, "What is an Emotion?"

of emotional warmth. We might then see the bear, and judge it best to run, receive the insult and deem it right to strike, but we should not actually feel afraid or angry.

In James's account, there is a tight, implicit and automatic, hence *primordial*, coupling between visceral feeling experience of threat or fear and action. Emotion in general results from the perception of visceral changes recorded by the body (I feel scared therefore I am scared), rather than visceral changes resulting from higher-order perception (I am scared therefore I feel scared). In this account, there is a precedence of feelings leading to actions, rather than the reverse: action and reasoning leading to feelings and emotions.

More recently, and leaving aside many other theories of emotions that take an opposite stance to James and Lange,[3] researchers focused their attention on the kind of gut feelings we have evolved that make us detect danger and act upon it in a reflex fashion. A relevant and illustrative theory that has emerged in the recent comparative and developmental literature is one proposing that in vertebrate evolution, but particularly in mammalian and primate evolution, brain structures were *molded* to detect safety and assess risks in the environment, including threats to possessions (i.e., territory, one's own body, progeny, mother, food, sexual partner). These brain structures are implicated, since ancestral times, in the regulation of both defensive and affiliation (pro-social) behaviors, two polar opposite classes of action.

The *Polyvagal Theory* proposed by Stephen Porges[4] suggests that, in mammalian evolution, affectivity and fixed action patterns in response to these feeling states are tightly linked to different neural regulation of the heart (i.e., the vagus nerve surrounding the organ). Porges's theory distinguishes three major stages in the development of the autonomic nervous system in mammalian evolution. Each stage is tightly linked to specific adaptive behavioral strategies, from older to more recent: (1) mobilization (i.e., freezing responses), (2) mobilization (fight or flight responses), and (3) social engagement and communication (pro-social, affiliative responses). Upon assessing and detecting the risks of a loss of possession, one might indeed cling to it by freezing; fight for it or let go of it by attacking or fleeing; try to negotiate in peace. Of interest is the fact that such behavioral strategies are, chronologically, more or less ancient in their origins.

Immobilization, here by analogy clinging to possession, would be the oldest, emerging in early mammals responding to danger by feigning

[3] E.g., Schachter and Singer, "Cognitive, social, and physiological determinants of emotional state."

[4] For a succinct account of the theory, see Porges, "Neuroception." For more evolutionary and physiological details, see Porges, "The polyvagal theory."

death and behavioral shutdown (e.g., squirrels commonly observed in backyards moving from one freeze to another). These behavioral strategies appear to depend on the oldest branch of the vagus nerve that takes its origin in a specific and evolutionarily archaic area of animals' brain stem.

Mobilization, here by analogy fighting or actively defending possession, would depend on the later evolution of the sympathetic nervous system that increases metabolism and cardiac responses, boosting the organism toward attacking or fleeing.

Finally, and following the evolutionary chronology of species, *social engagement and communication*, here by analogy the negotiating of valued possession with others, would be linked to newer, more recently evolved vagus regulation mechanisms. These mechanisms would foster calm and attentive mental states, inhibiting sympathetic fight–flight impulses. They are linked to complex facial expressions, vocalization, and listening postures that are particularly prevalent in primates like us.

As we shall see in the second part of the book, on the origins of possession, it appears that children tend to recapitulate this gross evolutionary progression in their development: from taking ownership by clinging and rigid tit-for-tat, and eventually to the negotiation of values with others by complex trading, bartering, and other gift giving/receiving processes.

From an evolutionary perspective, the feelings of possession are thus linked to the development of particular behavioral propensities that objectify such feelings for both self and others. We detect proactive defenses of possession in others (clinging, threatening, bids to barter), as much as we detect threats over our own possession by detecting visceral changes sometimes coined and described as "neuroception":[5] the differential engagement of neural circuits we internally perceive that inform us whether the environment is safe or dangerous, the constant monitoring of whether we are in danger, or not in danger of losing control over what we feel attached to and rely upon – our possessions. Taking ownership is, fundamentally and at the origin, acting upon such private perceptions for which all animals, including humans, are innately prepared to perform in some basic adaptive ways.

Ingrained territoriality instinct

The threat of losing spatial possession is a deep, archaic fear that pervades nature. Arguably, it might be the most ancient of all feeling experiences. It led most animals to evolve complex ways of marking their territory, a

[5] See Porges, "Neuroception" and "The polyvagal theory."

portion of space that they feel is theirs, hopelessly trying to maintain control over it.

This is not just a tendency in dogs, birds, and fish. It is also what keeps us waging wars and dying for it. History is replete with what, for the most part, are pathetic, often on-going conflicts of control over a particular territory that antagonist parties feel is theirs. There is not one corner of this world that is not at the core of territorial issues. Situated in space, all "real" estate entails some physical and psychological markings, a recurrent source of sour and deadly conflicts.

What is remarkable, and cuts across all species, is the *anticipatory prevention psychology* that territoriality entails. It is forward looking, even if deeply instinctive and relying on evolved automatic gut feelings of possession. Territoriality is primarily mainly about protection, inseparable from the threat of attack and loss.

A good illustration is nesting. Animals, from birds to chimpanzees, do not randomly build their private quarters where they rest or breed. Nest building always entails remarkable planning, and the avoidance of various fears, the anticipation of attacks from potential predators but also dangerous natural risks like high winds and the choice of weak material. Nesting and creating safe space cut across species. They involve exquisite "instinctual" assessment of the potential risks of predators and other natural catastrophes. Exquisite preventive moves are objectified in the location choice, the architectonics, the material used to build the nest, but also in taking ownership of it in acts of protection, sometimes of "heroic" proportions, as often seen in the dramas of your typical Nature show.

Bird nests, for example, vary greatly in shape and size, and are all expressions of implicit (instinctual) prevention on the part of the breeder. They can be tiny (2 × 3 cm for hummingbirds) to huge (up to 11 × 5 m high for the dusky scrubfowl). They come in all forms and shapes. They can consist of holes, platforms, pendant structures, cavities, cracks, or burrows, depending on the species. Some involve intricate architectonics and techniques, while others are just a scrape, the digging of a shallow hole.[6] In most avian species females are typically specialized in nest building, but in some the male contributes to the task, this contribution at times being part of courtship display (e.g., weaver birds). There is intense preventive care and risk assessment involved in building nests, choosing location and territory to protect eggs and the future offspring from predators, particularly after hatching and during the period when the chicks are very vulnerable when temporarily left alone while the mother is busy gathering food.

[6] For much more details, see Hansell, *Bird Nests and Construction Behaviour.*

Some birds (e.g., auks such as murres) do not build nests, but lay their eggs on narrow rocky ledges of steep terrains or cliffs. However, they lay them not randomly but in an organized fashion, eggs pointing in one direction so that when disturbed they roll in an arc rather than dropping down the slope.[7] Even there, with no protective shelters built for the offspring, clear nurturing ways of laying eggs have been selected for their preventive value.

Protection, prevention, and the anticipation of predator threats for self and offspring are particularly evident in the pervasive propensity of most animals to mark their own territory: a portion of space, beyond the space of their own body, that they take ownership of, controlling and defending it aggressively against any intruders. Pet owners know how dogs and cats may react to strangers entering the secure space of their home.

Most animals are territorial, particularly against intruders of their own species. They precisely stake areas that extend beyond the nest or locations with accumulated food resources as a preventive system of deterrence from predatory attacks and other coercive raids. Territorial animals take ownership of these areas most commonly by scent marking or spraying, for example dogs urinating or big cats like jaguars rubbing their body against vegetation. Sometimes these protected and marked territories extend far beyond the nest or breeding ground, as in the case of some blackbirds defending feeding grounds away from the nest.

Taking ownership of spatial areas via acts of defense is found mostly in vertebrates, from fish to amphibians, birds, reptiles, and mammals, but also in some invertebrate species like ants, bees, crabs, even sea snails.[8] It all revolves, with great variation in levels of complexity, around the defense of food, mating, and offspring. There are as many specific expressions of adapted protective and preventive behaviors as there are territorial species. All, however, originate from some feeling experience of risks and vulnerability: some ingrained fear of losing what is under one's control.

Without falling into simple reductionism, we have to conclude that human possession psychology is not alien from this basic feeling experience that is shared by all territorial animals, despite the obviously great range of complexity across species. Some species mentioned here are probably borderline machine-like sensing mechanisms, hence not

[7] Ehrlich et al., *The Birdwatcher's Handbook*, pp. 228–232. Also, type "bird nest" as an entry into Wikipedia for a quick survey of the remarkable diversity of nests and nesting practices across avian species.

[8] Klopfer, *Habitats and territories*.

feeling proper, as in the case of the crab or the snail. For those territorial creatures that presumably experience mental states, and feel as opposed to just sense, it is in this ingrained, adaptive fear of losing what is under one's control, and the ingrained behavioral prevention of such risks, that we need to search for the roots of humans' own symbolic expression of possession: its feeling and the taking of ownership of such feeling via defensive actions like aggression and territoriality, but also via shared symbolic representations, the development of abstract notions like *property* that the laws and practices of all human societies try to protect. That is the unique human feat we turn to next.

The invention of property

"Property is theft," proclaims famously the nineteenth-century French anarchist Pierre-Joseph Proudhon (1809–65) in an attempt at promoting a more mutualistic and egalitarian and less authoritarian society, "an order without power," as he advocates. Proudhon's ideas regarding the necessities of human cooperation and fraternal (egalitarian) association find their roots in debates that raged in the previous century around the French and other revolutions of the Enlightenment that took Western civilization by storm.

Jean-Jacques Rousseau (1712–78) is often considered the philosopher and main ideologue behind the French Revolution of 1789 that toppled the centuries-old regime of French monarchy and aristocracy. His thoughts and ideas were certainly instrumental in rethinking societal values regarding political regimes, constitutions, and social contracts, but also education, and in general the place of individuals in the governance of society, their opportunity of becoming equal citizens. Rousseau was indeed a major figure of the French Enlightenment (the Age of Reason) of the eighteenth century that paralleled similar trends led by other intellectuals and philosophers in other regions of Europe, as well as in North America. Rousseau and other contemporaries, like David Hume and Adam Smith in Scotland and Immanuel Kant and later Georg W. Friedrich Hegel (1770–1831) in Germany, provided seed reflections that paved the way toward a new, modern way of construing and thinking about the individual rights of people as equal citizens, away from the elitist and absolute attitudes of the ancien régime that justified its power as God's will, not the power of equal citizens.

The Age of Reason led to the development of modern bourgeois ideology, and paved the way to the great industrial revolution of the mid nineteenth century and all the subsequent ideological turmoils of the twentieth century, including communist revolutions in most parts of the world and the more recent global cold war that started to dwindle with the fall of the Berlin Wall, and the beginning of our current "hypermodernist" era of global economic neo-liberalism.[9]

In the midst of all this rethinking of the place of individuals in society, their liberties as well as their obligations, *the right to own* became a central issue. All philosophers of the Enlightenment contributed to a profound reconsideration of what constitutes the nature of property: its origins and foundations, and ultimately what might be the right way to justify it in a new civilized society.

In probably what is the most well-known passage of his *Discourse on Inequality*,[10] also known as the "Second Discourse," Rousseau writes:

> The first man who, having fenced in a piece of land, proclaimed "That is mine," and found people naïve enough to believe him, was the true founder of civil society. From then on, how many crimes, wars, murders, how much human miseries and horrors could have been spared if this man by pulling up the stakes, or filling up the ditch, would have cried to his fellow humans: "Do not listen to this impostor; you are lost if you forget that the fruits belong to us all, that the earth belongs to nobody!"

Rousseau goes on:

> But from then on it all became obvious that things could not last the way they were: because this idea of propriety did not emerge at once in the human mind, but instead depended on many antecedent ideas that came about only in succession: much progress, industry, and enlightenment were needed for its emergence, for their transmission and augmentation over time, before we arrived at this final end of our original Natural State. (Author's translation)

In his discourse, Rousseau proposes that the idea of property that slowly emerged in human cultural evolution led us to leave an original natural state in which humans were equal with other animals, and by extension equals among ourselves, which was "our original natural state" in Rousseau's philosophy. The notion of property, and particularly its acceptance by all, is at the core of a civil society that promotes inequality and removes individuals from the fundamental egalitarianism of their natural state, except for health and strength.

Rousseau's basic assumption of an original noble nature of man is the polar opposite of the cynical or more precisely "disenchanted realistic" views of British philosopher Thomas Hobbes (1588–1679) on the

[9] Charles and Lipovetsky, *Hypermodern Times*.

[10] Rousseau, "Discourse on the origin and the foundations of inequality among men" (*Discours sur l'origine et les fondements de l'inégalité parmi les hommes*).

aboriginal brutish nature of man. For Rousseau, evil is not a state in nature but is linked to the creation of civil society in which the natural inclination of individuals' self-love, compassion, and perfectibility guided by natural self-preservation is transformed into envy, competition, pride, and jealousy toward others. In human cultural evolution, natural self-love turned into egotism and corruption made of alliances and power struggle, the societal corruption that is the source of all evils, from wars to inequalities. Social evil and corruption started when the aboriginal "noble savage" stopped minding his own business and working just for the sake of his own survival, like anybody else. For Rousseau and following the preceding quote, at the heart of this transformation there is the invention of the notion of property that created artificial, man-made divisions of the natural world into categorical kinds that are essentially arbitrary, serving certain classes of people to the detriment of others.

The invention of property generated and justified a new state of inequality in humans that did not exist originally. First came the division of the world between masters and slaves, between those people who were free to own themselves as well as others, and those people who were not. Then came the division into families that divided those who belonged and those who did not belong to a particular group. Finally came the division of land ownership that is pervasive in the constitutions of all human civil societies, whether these constitutions are oral or written. A crucial point in Rousseau's views on the origins of property, particularly his quote above, is the fact that it is not enough for someone to take ownership by claiming that is "Mine!," that "this" is my property. You need to have people around recognizing it, naïve or gullible enough to believe in such a claim. Indeed, property can only exist if the taking of ownership is *recognized and trusted* by others. Without it, it is void of any meaning. This is a crucial idea that goes to the heart of human ways of taking ownership. They rest on symbolic and cultural levels of inter-subjectivity (i.e., shared feeling experiences with others) that are unique to the species. These levels include mutual recognition, trust, reputation, and value negotiation, all of which are embodied in codes of law. These codes are human inventions, human cultural artifacts like the Universal Declaration of Human Rights that emerged from the bloody ashes of the French Revolution, which states in substance (Article 17): (1) Everyone has the right to own property alone as well as in association with others; (2) No one shall be arbitrarily deprived of his property.

Beyond such general statements, explicit codes regulate transactions, with a major focus on the claiming of ownership (property law). They rest on a wealth of implicit and explicit intuitions regarding the psychology of possession.

Human coding of property rights

Since time immemorial, human societies have tried to regulate the claiming of ownership. Among all the first explicit attempts in both Eastern and Western cultures (e.g., the Vedanic Indian philosophy or the ancient Babylonian King Hammurabi's legal code (1780 BC)), the Roman code is arguably the most detailed. It is foundational and continues to prevail in legal thought about property in many Western industrial societies. Of interest to us in particular are some of the basic assumptions, hence intuitions, behind explicit codes regarding the feeling of possession and the taking of ownership. The Roman code, for example, assumes that one owns something in absolute, not just relative terms. In Roman times, and even still today in codes of property laws deriving from the Roman code, immoveable objects like land, as well as moveable properties, were owned "absolutely," at least by certain individuals (i.e., Roman citizens as opposed to aliens or slaves). Behind the code is a conception of absolute ownership referred to as *dominum*. This conception is in contradistinction to the one behind the English and Germanic codes regulating property and that still prevail.

Compared to the Roman code, English and Germanic systems are based on a more relative intuition regarding the determination of ownership and the regulation of property. This relative intuition corresponds to "the better right to possession," the idea that what needs to be regulated and determined is how one might be more deserving of taking and claiming ownership *relative* and *compared* to somebody else.

This is a subtle, yet profound cultural difference. The Roman code presumes an absolute right to property. The British or Germanic codes presume the relative right to property (better right to own principle). In the same way, the British code assumes the presumed innocence of the accused until proven guilty. The reverse is true in the Roman code: guilt is assumed until the accused is proven innocent. These subtle contrasts correspond to profoundly different philosophical outlooks on social life and human behavior. They reveal collective variations across human cultures in views regarding the good versus bad seed of human nature, the perception of a bottle depicted as half full or half empty.

The Roman code on property was the legal system of the Roman Empire from the fifth century BC. It started – the story goes – with twelve wooden tablets written after consulting with ethicists and other legal ideologues of the more ancient and highly influential Hellenistic (Greek) civilization. The Justinian code of law (sixth century AD) was the foundation of legal practices (jurisprudence) for over a thousand years throughout continental Europe and all subsequent colonies in Africa, but also the Americas, including all the current post-colonial nations of Latin America. The intuitions contained in the Roman code of law regarding property are thus foundational to a large proportion of existing legal systems in the world. It is a sort of intuitive matrix, the historical sedimentation of ideas through consensual practices in the claiming of ownership. They reveal, like all other codes, the inter-subjective and deep negotiating nature of the human notion of property, what Rousseau emphasizes in his quote, namely the symbolic and consensual nature of ownership claims.

One of the main purposes of the Roman code is to give some explicit, formal, and consensual grounds to sealing deals on the transfer of property. Such sealing is by definition a public affair. It requires live witnesses and external markings that are recognized by and tangible to anybody. The code regulates and prescribes a formal ritual and induction of property right, a ceremony that is required to seal a property transfer, the official taking of ownership over something. The name of the ceremony, *mancipium* or mancipation, the formal taking of ownership, derives from the word *mancipatio* which means taking in hand, literally putting the thing in one's controlling hand. The public, official marking, in other words the public *objectification* and embodiment of the transaction, was the striking of a copper ingot into the thing over which ownership was transferred and which was newly owned. The code dictated a ceremony that involved, in addition to the two contracting parties, formal actors and props (i.e., five male Roman citizens as witnesses, two scales, and someone to hold these scales and tap the copper ingot marking the transaction).

Roman jurists introduce many distinctions regarding property, such as the regulation of rights to use a thing, labeled as "ownership," versus the rights to use *and* manipulate (modify) the thing owned, labeled as "possession" proper. The code reveals nuances in the way something may be experienced as possession and the various levels of control over this thing, depending on the object: a land, a slave, a house, or a moveable object. It has a complex psychology behind the feeling experience of possession. The code regulates the official, publicly recognized, and symbolically consensual taking of ownership of such feelings.

More specific to the culture and politics of the time, the code also discriminated among potential owners, namely who could own what and why. Owned and disposed of by their masters, slaves were not free to possess, nor recognized as owning their own *mine-ness* of experience. Slaves where objects of mancipation themselves and there was a special code that regulated the ownership for Roman citizens only (the quitirian code). All other individuals were under the rules and regulations of another (bonitarian) code. So, the code edicted "quitirian" and "bonitarian" ways of owning, but also discriminated between "quitirian" and "bonitarian" things to be owned. The quitirian properties, reserved to Roman citizens, were the soil (*commercium*) and its capacity for mancipation, but also its capacity for "usurpation and vindication." It also entailed "exemption from land-tax."[11]

In his seminal book (1776–88) on *The Decline and Fall of the Roman Empire*, Edward Gibbon (1737–94) comments on Roman views on property with the literary eloquence of the time and with clear connection to Rousseau's second discourse on inequality:

> The common rights, the equal inheritance of mankind are engrossed by the bold and crafty; each field and forest is circumscribed by the landmarks of a jealous master; and it is the peculiar praise of the Roman jurisprudence, that it asserts the claim of the first occupant to the wild animals of the earth, the air, and the waters. In the progress from primitive equity to final injustice, the steps are silent, the shades are almost imperceptible, and the absolute monopoly is guarded by positive laws and artificial reason.[12]

The Romans created the science of the law and allied law professions, the idea of a jurisprudence, a coherent system based on core, abstract, and public principles. As one of the earliest and often considered among the greatest of all Roman lawyers, Marcus Tullius Cicero (106–143 BC) writes with the legal conviction that we can assume motivated all human attempts at creating legal institutions to foster social harmony and justice: "Nothing is certainly more ennobling than for us to plainly understand that we are born to justice, and that law is instituted not by opinion but by nature . . . If the fortunes of all cannot be equal, if the mental capacities of all cannot be the same, at least the legal rights of all those who are citizens of the same state ought to be equal."

Note however a major caveat: these good principles were discriminatory, not applying to slaves and other non- Roman citizens (all the non-natives, rich or poor free people). Bloody revolutions happened to approximate greater social class inclusion, in particular the French Revolution and the rethinking of who owns what and why by Rousseau and the other philosophers of the Enlightenment. This reflection continues now with urgent immigration issues exacerbated by the global economy, from all directions in Europe, and north and south of the borders in the USA. Let us not forget

[11] Gibbon, *The History of The Decline and Fall of the Roman Empire*, vol. 2.
[12] Gibbon, *Decline and* Fall, vol. 3, ch. 44, p. 176.

that since the Greeks and the fifth-century BC era of Pericles – the "cradle of democracy" according to history textbooks – republican ideas have always been discriminatory, excluding slaves or labor classes.

If codes of law about property like the Roman code are clear expressions of the symbolic and inter-subjective nature of the human claiming of ownership, such codes do not need to be written. In non-literate cultures and societies where no writing systems exist or did exist, precise oral codes did and continue to prevail with analogous symbolic ceremonies and traditions marking consensual transfer and determination of ownership. Striking examples abound but let me refer to the primitive money used in some oral cultures in gift giving or the marking of property exchanges.[13] A good example is the stone money used in the island nation of Yap in Micronesia, the huge donut-shaped stones, sometimes weighing a few tons, that were used for gifts and payment of debts in land transaction and other rituals. Their shear size, enormous weight, and cumbersomeness represent dedication, effort, and work as compensation toward a debt that is more social and affective than economic.

Pleasure of owning

As already mentioned, Rousseau proposed that it was with the claim of ownership and the emergence of civil society that we lost our primeval egalitarianism, living on a par with other animals and among ourselves, sharing an environment that belonged to all, like the air, the trees, and the streams of water running. The corrupting emergence of property came slowly and dubiously over time according to Rousseau: "depending on many antecedent ideas that came about only in succession" (see above). With these corrupting ideas, we abandoned the aboriginal natural state in which humans were equal among themselves, as they were with other animals ("our original natural state"). Accordingly, Rousseau does not provide much of an answer to the question of what may have been the motives for our ancestors to leave their original state of nature, forging the civil society that fostered inequality and the creation of private ownership with all the associated evils of envy, jealousy, protection, and competition.

Rousseau's idea that possession is the source of our loss of a primordial unity with Nature is not just a Western idea linked to the turmoil of the industrial revolution that was starting to take shape in Europe. It finds some interesting though inverted resonance with traditional Eastern views. Buddhism has at its core the idea that self-preoccupation prevents

[13] For more examples, see Rochat, *Others in Mind*.

us from achieving wisdom, Buddha's wisdom requiring detachment and the renouncement of possessions, hence of the propensity to take ownership. Renouncing possessions as a way of achieving wisdom cuts across all religions, with a few chosen ones accessing sainthood by becoming ascetics and hermits, moving away from the envy and competition of earthly ownership. Saints, hermits, and ascetics, by giving up all the earthly pleasures associated with possession, give themselves to God, renouncing with their asceticism the owning of their own experience of being. The ascetic practices of all saints or aspiring saints in all religions (probably with the exception of most contemporary televangelists and other illustrious politicians) literally involve self-denial through stringent abstinence, typically voluntary seclusion as in the case of monastic life, or standing on top of a column in the middle of the desert as in the case of the ascetic Syrian saint Simeon Stylites. According to legend, in the fifth century AD Simeon spent thirty-seven years on a small platform atop a tall column in the desert in a quest for seclusion.[14]

In India, the birthplace of Buddha, Brahman theology (Vedanta) posits that the drive to take ownership is the expression of the deep illusion that we are separated from the universe. Close to the Buddhist view, Vedanta proposes that it is only when we manage to realize that the universe is one encompassing entity that we become liberated from the ills and illusions of taking ownership. Accordingly, our irresistible drive to take ownership finds its motivational roots in the vain attempt at reconnecting with the universe through possessions. As in Rousseau, the drive to own is associated with a loss of primordial truth.

At the time, Rousseau did not yet have all the conceptual tools that Freud came up with in his metapsychology two centuries later. For example, he was not influenced by the idea of an "id," the instinctive pulse deep inside our unconscious mind that pushes us toward a heightened, "pure" narcissism driven from birth by the pleasure principle (*Eros*) and in opposition to the principle of self-destruction and death (*Thanatos*).

With Freud comes the primordial idea of an insatiable, irrepressible urge toward immediate gratification, which needs eventually to be curbed and displaced via complex systems of defense mechanisms. But what is of relevance is the idea that from birth infants are pushed to acquire exclusivity over people and things: parents, nutritious objects, blankets, bowel movements produced by their own bodies. Following Freud's analytical grid, there is a primordial, instinctive quest for exclusive love and attention (*Eros*) from the primary caregiver (mother), a given propensity to compete

[14] See Luis Bunuel's movie *Simón del desierto* (Simon of the Desert) (1965).

for it with the parent of the other sex (Oedipus or Electra complex). In more direct relation to the claiming of ownership, there is also an ingrained urge from the outset to hold onto things for control, as is often the case in children's behavior during the toilet training that surrounds the anal stage of psychosexual development as depicted by Freud.[15]

A few decades before Freud, and a century after Rousseau, came the deep socio-economic changes associated with the first industrial revolution (1750–1850), and particularly with the second industrial revolution which took place in the later nineteenth century in Europe and North America, with enormous progress in the technology of producing manufactured goods. If the first industrial revolution is associated with the philosophical Age of Reason, the Enlightenment, and great colonial discoveries, the second revolution led to a novel conceptualization of the individual. It is associated in particular with the contemporary *Übermensh* philosophies of Friedrich Nietzsche, and not least the socio-economic analysis of Karl Marx in defense of the new proletariat that inspired the worldwide communist movement of the twentieth century. All of it revolved around novel revolutionary ideas about individual freedom: the spoiling of basic liberties by spiritual (Nietzsche) and economic forces of the past (Marx). But what is important is that all of these great intellectual changes revolved essentially around issues of who owns what and why, and, more importantly, in the footsteps of the French Revolution, who *should* own what and why. For Nietzsche, core metaphysical values should be re-owned (death to the monopoly of God). For Marx, the means of production should be re-owned by the workers (death to the monopoly of the bourgeoisie). The rationale for such momentum was the quest for individual strength and autonomy, and freedom from the tyranny of the Church and the enrichment of a few capitalists.

With the great economic transformation[16] of the mid eighteenth century, the landowners and peasants of rural England were forced out

[15] Freud, *Three Essays on the Theory of Sexuality*. See also Herbert Marcuse, *Eros and Civilization*, for a post-Marxist use of these Freudian ideas to explain contemporary exploitation of the working class and in particular the unleashed consumerism promoted by modern societies for the gain of a few.

[16] See Polanyi, *The Great Transformation*. In his book, Polanyi argues that the introduction of a market economy coincided with the first industrial revolution, where the exchange of goods happened, as in today's financial world, through complex price mechanisms (law of supply and demand, stock market, etc.). The introduction of a market economy dramatically changed the social order and the way people reciprocated in the transfer of possession. Polanyi's book captures this "Great Transformation" that started in England with changes in laws that brought to an end the world of the landed gentry, a particularly important social class in eighteenth-century England with its complex hierarchy of baronets, knights, squires, and gentlemen. It marked the end of an ancient world parceled in land titles. It also marked the beginning of the nation states that eventually

of the ways they had farmed from ancestral times. They relinquished the land, crops, and herds they had owned or rented, and that they had farmed for generations, to join the factories as wage labor.[17] Herding became primarily a monoculture of sheep supplying wool to large textile mills where agricultural workers became waged workers, while coal miners provided energy for the looms. Large dormitory towns were built around the mills and rural buildings were abandoned (many of them now converted into charming second homes so people can escape the city). With the industrial revolution began the modern experience of ownership, that has evolved in today's global industrial world that tries to foster maximum consumption of goods, hence maximum taking of ownership by individuals and groups.

The functioning of this new "hypermodern" and networked global world depends on the ever increasing fluidity of ownership transfer and the consumption of things owned and purchased for oneself: cars, houses, apartments, zillions of products, often built with so-called "planned obsolescence" to promote quick replacement, hence economic fluidity. Slight novelty introduced in products controls the wants and illusory needs of ever hungry consumers ready to sell out freedom for credit. Consumerism and the endless frenzy in taking ownership is not just brainwashing from the industry and the marketers. It taps into the indisputable lust, pleasure, and satisfaction in taking ownership. In it we find the delights of control, self-aggrandizing, comfort, and security. We also find social power: the power to hire, collaborate, share, exchange; the power of giving and building up a reputation for ourselves.

At the heart of the consumerism frenzy there is something psychologically important that marketers understand perfectly well, the bread and butter of publicists, but something that eluded Rousseau. It also hardly rang a bell with Freud, who was dealing with well-to-do patients in his research. Consumer frenzy points to the deep individual satisfaction and pleasure of taking ownership. There is an underlying affective process that is seemingly irresistible and that in the end is killing the planet. We can't help acquiring properties, obsessively expanding ourselves with ever increasing novel objects of possession that are irresistible and abundantly offered to us for ownership. The mixture is ecologically damning and seemingly hopeless. There is indeed deep comfort in taking ownership and owning. Consumption is irresistible.

contaminated the whole industrial and rural colonial world, starting in the nineteenth century, and was also the background for worldwide conflicts and tensions in the twentieth century.

[17] Karl Polanyi, *The Great Transformation*.

Carving space for self

Although a keen observer of nature, Rousseau probably did not pay enough attention to the pervasive territoriality of animals, as discussed earlier, not taking sufficient account of the deep psychological comfort of land, home, and shelter, the need to get one's own roof over one's head. This need can become symbolic, a desire for privacy and calm away from social threats and turmoil. This is often obvious in the struggle of urban homeless people all over the world, dragging their belongings in a shopping trolley and putting a makeshift roof of cardboard over their heads to sleep. As advertisers and consumer researchers know too well, there is deep comfort, often more symbolic than real, in getting under or inside an environment, under or inside the thing we take ownership of and which becomes a part of us. The makeshift roof, the prevention of lacking something, the irresistible need to own and control a thing or a product, to treat oneself with taking ownership over something ("I've got to have it"), all of it is in fact deeply engrained in Nature. It is rooted in the instinctive need for protection, control, and peace of mind, all deep motives behind taking ownership that we share with all animals, but that our species manages to elevate to great symbolic value.[18]

Carving out a safe space from public space is the name of the property game. It feeds necessary psychological illusions, the irresistible individualistic dream to control a portion of the environment for oneself, progeny, the group, the team, the culture, the nation we feel we belong to. It is embodied in the dream of pioneers who carved their land out of the wild to take ownership, explorers braving the oceans to set foot on a virgin land and claim its resources in the name of their king. Even if they only saw a place from the deck of a ship, maps were redrawn, new names given, colonies created.

It is also what drives us to purchase land and houses, private cars and all the numerous objects that we come to incorporate by signing deeds and getting receipts. It all gives us the necessary experience of control and autonomy, but also the accompanying illusion of incorporating the thing to the conception of who we are, as pointed out by William James. An attack on property becomes figuratively an attack on one's own body, a psychology that has deep roots in animal territoriality.

In human evolution, particularly in recent evolution, new objects of ownership were created exponentially. The production of artifacts

[18] See for example the last, poignant, and highly symbolic scene of Danish director Lars von Tries' 2011 film *Melancholia*, in which two adults and a child hug one another under the makeshift shelter of a few branches as a looming planet comes crashing against the earth at doomsday.

(jewelry, tools, and other utensils) and the creation of other objects of ownership (land, farms, animals, slaves) accompanied a proportional growth in the human need to possess: the propensity to project and identify with those objects. In this ratcheting production of objects that could be owned and recognized as such, the taking of ownership in human evolution became increasingly more complex and symbolic. Regulated by explicit laws, it became de facto more and more removed from the literality of the physical thing it pertains to, for its future exchange power or *fungible* dimension (i.e., its exchangeability as in a letter of credit, a universal commodity like salt, or a banknote). The taking of ownership also became psychologically more complex by becoming increasingly self-conscious, driven by what it represents in terms of wealth and stature in relation to others (e.g., a *make* of watch, the size and shape of a car, a flag, a totem). It all evolved to feed our individual values, our self-esteem and reputation in the eyes of others.[19]

The irresistible need to take ownership runs deep, forming the motivational core of property. Rousseau, like many other theologians, politicians, and philosophers, pointed to the great dangers of cupidity, ambition, and the hyper-narcissism they saw looming in their society made of self-aggrandizing and self-conscious proprietors. Rousseau writes with some premonition: "the savage lives within himself; social man lives always outside himself; he knows how to live only in the opinion of others, it is, so to speak, from their judgment alone that he derives the sense of his own existence."[20] In today's world, social man does live mainly in the pleasure of consumption and the incorporation of things to the self, the enlargement of the self in proportion to things owned and possessed.

In the current market economy and technological boom, there is an incomparable opportunity to feed the individual need of acquiring property and enlarging the self, in other words of engaging in a process of self-aggrandizement and self-love with no limits in sight. Market forces understand this psychology of possession too well, tapping into it with great

[19] David Hume in *A Treatise of Human Nature* (1739) notes: "Nothing has a greater tendency to give us an esteem for any person, than his power and riches; or a contempt, than his poverty and meanness . . . esteem and contempt are to be considered as species of love and hatred." Book 2, "Of the Passions," part 2, section 5, p. 231, ed. D. Fate Norton and M. Norton, Oxford Philosophical Texts, 2000. Hume, reflecting on the pleasure of taking possession and of seeing possessions in others, concludes on the social determinants of a universal pleasure of having and therefore taking possession: "Thus the pleasure, which a rich man receives from his possessions, being thrown upon the beholder, causes a pleasure and esteem; which sentiments again, being perceived and sympathized with, increase the pleasure of the possessor; and being once more reflected, become a new foundation for pleasure and esteem in the beholder," part 2, section 6, p. 236.

[20] Rousseau, *Second Essay on Inequality*, p. 136.

savvy. Self-aggrandizing needs and market forces are a marriage made in heaven. But this marriage is old, logically emerging with civil society and the ruling of exclusive property rights. The societal recognition of exclusive property rights allowed for the opportunity to enlarge the self with possessions that are recognized by others as exclusively *self-referential*. Self-aggrandizing needs could have become a psychological reality only once the civil society of men recognized exclusive property rights, providing rules, imposed or consensual, primarily to resolve property conflicts in a civil manner as opposed to merely by force. In his seminal book, not uncoincidentally written as the first phase of the industrial revolution was shaping up, Edward Gibbon notes: "The active insatiate principle of self-love can alone supply the arts of life and the wages of industry; and as soon as civil government and exclusive property have been introduced, they become necessary to the existence of the human race."[21]

Generalized greed

Public or group possessions like national parks, schools, military bases, the atmosphere, or the fish populating international waters are supra-ordinal property that transcends individual possession. Yet, although it belongs to us all, it is still a source of great conflict that calls for civil regulations to be tentatively resolved in relative peace. In order to work, these regulations need to be consensual, recognized by all, and this is the main difficulty and the source of great tensions that can bring us to the edge of war. Individual greed becomes group greed when nations cannot agree on air pollution quotas, allowing their nation to pollute more than their fair share. A river passing through a territory can be considered by the landowner to be under his exclusive rights and control. It is his prerogative if he wishes to dam the water and take all the fish, depriving all the other landowners downstream. But if all landowners show the same greed, the pay off will be zero to all, except maybe the owner of the river's source, way upstream. With this simple example, we see that to the extent that people sharing the same land are mindful of wars and endless bloody conflicts, some mutual agreements are a necessity and necessarily need to be reached. This is how civil society with its collective rules and obligations must have emerged: out of survival necessity, life or death significance, constrained in its emergence by dead end group sharing situations in which population density becomes too high and the resources too scarce to be loosely shared.

[21] Rousseau, *Second Essay on Inequality*, p. 176.

This general scenario is as simple as it is powerful in trying to comprehend the foundation of property when we consider, as first proposed by Rousseau,[22] that it rests primarily on a consensual group recognition of exclusive possession rules and rights that allow conflict resolution in a "civil" manner. It is this inter-subjective or shared dimension that elevates individual possession and the individual taking of ownership into property proper. But psychologically, under property and the consensual ruling of civil society, there is still the generalized individual greed to possess and the insatiable need for self-aggrandizing that possession allows, as well as all the strong associated pleasures of taking ownership. Generalized greedy motives constrained some ruling to avoid societal doom. They are the reasons behind the human invention of civil society expressed in various forms (e.g., the Roman code regarding property rights), hence the emergence of implicitly or explicitly *regulated* mutualism and civility in human evolution.[23] They are also the reason behind the human creation of property as a shared notion. In a way, generalized greed to own, the insatiable need for self-aggrandizing via the claiming of ownership, and all their deep associated pleasures, are the natural roots of property as an emergent, civil notion. These deep psychological motives naturalize the notion. The primordial dynamic of generalized greed constrained the emergence of property as a shared (social) notion. The shared notion of property became, by necessity, larger than the sum of its greedy parts, in the interest of all, with the caveat that property is by definition delineated: it is contained within limits.

This said, the containment of collective greed remains non-inclusive, only an approximation in the perennial context of special interests, continuing the tradition of the Roman elite making exceptions in their good-faith legal edicts by excluding foreigners (non-Romans) and the large population of slaves. It was the same during the "glorious antique times" of Pericles (the fifth century BC) in Athens, when democracy was invented, Plato's *Republic* was written, and Socrates voiced his revolutionary reasons for social justice that shaped all of our modern democratic constitutions replacing monarchy, but to the exclusion of slaves. It has

[22] "the first man who proclaimed 'that is mine,' and found people naïve enough to believe him, was the true founder of civil society" (complete quote earlier in the chapter).

[23] This logic is also what is behind most of the classic thought regarding the nature and origins of civil society, morality, and the spirit of the laws by philosophers of the Enlightenment including Hobbes, Rousseau, Smith, Hume, and Kant, but also successors like Hegel. Montesquieu (1689–1755), French philosopher and highly influential Enlightenment political thinker, writes pointedly in *The Spirit of the Laws* (1748): "Government should be set up so that no man need be afraid of another" (Book 11, chapter 6, "Of the Constitution of England").

never been global. Proof is the continuing deterioration of our planet via reckless industrial activities and overpopulation. Indeed, national interests keep prevailing and there are continuing failures in international agreements on global coercive environmental laws. The problem is that air and water cannot be fenced off.

"The population problem has no technical solution; it requires a fundamental extension of morality," proposes human ecologist Garrett Hardin (1915–2003) in his seminal article on "The tragedy of the commons."[24] Hardin warns of the inescapable doom of overpopulation and collective greed, the unleashed maximizing of special interests, regardless of whether these interests are individual or collective (familial, public, national). Hardin's article is a forceful call for the necessity of muzzling our irresistible greed in maximizing returns on possession. To make his point, he uses the metaphor of a pasture (the common) that is open to all herdsmen. Each herdsman is naturally and equally driven to maximize returns from the common by keeping as many as possible of his cattle grazing on it. But the bottleneck tragedy is of course that, as time goes by, positive returns eventually become negative for all. Overcrowded, overgrazed, the grass of the common fails to regenerate and all the cattle become unhealthy. Hardin uses this metaphor to show that the tragedy cannot be avoided unless rules are established as absolute necessity, strictly enforced to contain possession and its expansion. These rules have to transcend the rational, natural, and collective inclination to maximize gains (i.e., collective greed) to avoid the tragedy of the commons. As an ecologist, Hardin makes this point in the context of global pollution and the overuse of natural resources like water and fauna, calling for the need to control overpopulation via stringent rulings that run against *all* national interests. The apparent impossibility of ruling collective greed globally leads us knowingly toward an indubitable ecological bottleneck. As pointed out by Hardin: "the logic of the commons has been understood for a long time, perhaps since the discovery of agriculture or the invention of private property in real estate. But it is understood mostly only in special cases which are not sufficiently generalized."[25] Only in a brave new world can we imagine an all-inclusive United Nations kind of "anti-greed" charter against limitless ownership – a charter of "sustainable development," that would be strictly enforced with no favoritism nor any affirmative actions, including stringent ruling and enforcement preventing the damage that innocent actions by

[24] Hardin, "The tragedy of the commons," p. 1243.
[25] Hardin, "The tragedy of the commons."

individuals can inflict on the environment.[26] These innocent actions would include the seemingly innocuous and legitimate drive to live more comfortably, see more of the world, have a larger home, and build an whatever-you-please, multiplying family lifestyle: what amount to innocent, naturally irresistible dreams for all people, with the exception maybe of a few hardcore ascetics. But those are true exceptions. These are the generalized greedy dreams that are teased by commerce and fueled by technological progress. Needless to say that continuing to base our economies on the false premise of limitless growth will eventually burn down the house.

We do live the tragedy of the commons in full. However, the legislated notion of property will not resolve our dilemma, because at our stage of industrial development and greed, no borders, no fences, can contain polluted air and water, nor the global consequences of cutting trees in a private or nationalized estate. The only way to resolve the tragedy of the commons would be first to agree on what constitutes the commons, including the atmosphere and all connected waters. But this is probably a vain, if not absurd, quest considering that, to various degrees, we are all naturally driven by our own special interests, wherever we carve our space, and particularly when it comes down to protecting our children and improving our lifestyle.

It is doubtful by now that any decrees of stringent policies will ever control the rampant collective greed that fuels our economies to white heat, to the detriment of our global environmental commons. We can hope for technological breakthroughs that would alleviate some of the damage done, maybe giving some breathing room to the pasture we trample and feed off so recklessly.

Private versus common ownership

We are far from the time when philosophers and politicians were working out and debating laws and principles to try and define ownership, far from Hobbes, Rousseau, or Hume in our age of high technology and empowered technocrats. Trying to delineate what is private and common ownership (i.e., the commons) is incommensurably more difficult today, in an age of global media where *time and space have collapsed onto each other.*[27]

[26] Stuart Lavietes, "Garrett Hardin, 88, ecologist who warned about excess," *The New York Times* (October 28, 2003).

[27] I owe this depiction to a discussion with my insightful Aurora coffee shop friend Mr. Bideau, aka Dr. Laurent Oget.

Simultaneous televisual exchanges with anybody anywhere are now possible and widely used. At the press of a button, we can post an intimate childhood picture on the Web, instantaneously broadcasting it to millions, if not billions, of unknown viewers worldwide. Within hours a New Yorker can leave his office and be at the foot of a climb in Switzerland or in a desert in Mongolia pitching a tent.

Private and collective ownership become incommensurably more abstract and immaterial, hard to fence off mentally, revolving more and more around the ownership of ideas and creations. How can I clearly delineate the ownership of my ideas and putative inventions when information is so readily available and shared at the click of a few keyboard strokes. The possibility of ownership is fading, the private and the commons running increasingly into each other. Globalization is about efficacy through homogeneity. As a general consequence it blurs the private and the commons. What is the delineated private ownership that can be claimed by two individuals having lunch on Skype, while living on opposite sides of the globe? Where is the dining room? Is it the global network? Where is the locus of their time together? Skype? In the same token, what do we mean in our ecological jargon when we talk about "our environment"? Do we refer to everything everywhere that exists at the same time and surrounds each other? Does that include also the atmosphere of all the planets that surround ours? Where does it stop? Those are elusive and difficult if not unresolvable questions. They are far beyond the real estate, fenced pasture, or manufactured object metaphors used in past centuries to legislate and define property, be it private or common. The ownership of concepts and ideas is now at the forefront, what can or cannot be attributed to the self as agent and aboriginal "ur" source as in the case of copyrights and authorship issues.

That said, individually we hold a good, implicit and explicit subjective sense of what is ours, and what is shared with others. This is an existential necessity, as we have seen in our discussion of implicit self-evidence in possession psychology in the preceding chapter, in particular the devastating consequences for psychotic patients. However, claims of private and common ownership are profoundly subjective, elusive at best and logically fuzzy.

Claims to any trespasser that "This is my house!," "Get out of my house!" do not accurately convey the actual legal deeds and other papers delimiting the property in question that is co-owned by "my" wife, 80 percent being mortgaged, hence legally owned by "my" bank. The house is experienced as mine when de facto it is a distributed and therefore a collective property. We can generalize this example to most of our ownership claims, all elusive, as in assertions like "my city," "my soccer team," "my school," "my country," "my factory." These ownership claims are certainly useful communication devices, but they exist as fuzzy ideas that contrast with the strong subjective certitude that accompanies them. How can someone call any institution "mine," whether a country, an army, a soccer team, an ideology, or a bank? How can we defend an institution or a concept as if it were an embodiment of the self, often sacrificing one's own life for it? That is a central psychological question for which we still lack much in the way of answers, yet which determines major political events the world over.[28]

What is remarkable and probably uniquely human is the ability to scale ownership claims to spheres of possession that vary from the intimate microscopic (my cells, my genes), to the collective, highly distributed, and macroscopic (my people, my culture, my planet). At the core of the human psychology of possession there lie indeed this conceptual flexibility and these collapsible claims of ownership that are scaled to context, primarily the *social affiliation context* of belonging and belongingness.

Belongings and belongingness

The claim of ownership is made in relation to others, by definition and as pointed out over two centuries ago by political philosophers of the Enlightenment era. To claim "That's mine!" indicates also "That's not yours!" It is therefore asserting social power and control, rather than control of the thing itself (real estate or any other object or person). As emphasized by Rousseau in his reflection on the origins of property, the claim of ownership gains actual force only to the extent that it is heard, and, more importantly, *recognized* by others. An ownership claim is therefore to no avail if no one takes it seriously and respects it at face value. From this straightforward logic, we can see that the claim of ownership is inseparable from social posturing and the extent to which it echoes in an audience. If there are echoes and recognition, the claimer gains social power and ascendance. If it is not recognized, it is a blatant social dismissal, the claimer losing social ascendance and affiliation.

This is what is conveyed by images in the press of thieves and other criminals handcuffed and dispossessed, sitting in front of the things they illegally owned a short while before (stacks of money, jewelry, drugs). Everyday, everywhere, such destitution of ownership is put on display in the media. The fascination is about the brusque, sudden loss of power associated with wealth, the fall from grace, people suddenly ostracized,

[28] But see the recent, meaningful work of anthropological psychologist Scott Atran exploring the motives and mind of suicide bombers: Atran, "Genesis of suicide terrorism."

thrown into jail, deprived of their symbolic social capital in terms of credibility. What is fascinating to the public is the "joy ride interruptus," the power enjoyed moments ago pulled from under the feet. These images of falls from grace are what sells newspapers. They conjure a collective fear: the general fear of being debunked as an impostor (the basic and generalized impostor complex[29]), for example being falsely rich (scam), talented (plagiarism), or deceptive about our social ascendance (immorality and dishonesty).

At a group level, history shows that a power structure holds to its privileges (power, land, economy) as long as a critical mass of people recognizes their claim. The questioning of ownership eventually topples those in power. This has been the mark of political change all through history, from antiquity to the French Revolution erasing feudalism and monarchy, to the recent insurrections and dismissals of dictators throughout North Africa and the Middle East. These changes reshuffle privileges by redistributing power and creating new clusters of ownership claims.

Transfer and reshuffling of privileges are indeed history in the making. In this process, claims of ownership are not just expressions of a drive to control possessions, but ultimately claims of social power. Social recognition of ownership is a direct measure of social affiliation. Having belongings that are recognized as such is the measure of social power and group belongingness (relative affiliation). Possession claims, once socially recognized as belongings of the individual or group of individuals, become "principals" or capital of the owner. Against such capital, debts, social ascendance, and alliances can be generated. Over two thousand years ago in Greece and at the time of the Roman Empire, it was common for ultra-rich members of society to show great munificence, giving back to the people by building large edifices for games such as colossal theaters and other arenas, or throwing lavish parties and celebrations for other citizens. Such massive donations, some sort of indirect tax, a spontaneous payback to society, were apparently common and expected from the rich. Much has been documented and written on the sociological and psychological meanings of this largesse that archaeologists and historians have studied under the label of *evergetism*.[30]

As pointed out by early anthropologists, gifts and gift exchange systems foster social harmony and integration among human groups. The potlatch rituals of Native Americans and Melanesian Big Man societies with their

[29] Another central thesis of Rochat, *Others in Mind*, in particular the post-face of the book illustrated by the rise and fall of abstract expressionist Jackson Pollock.

[30] See the seminal work of Paul Veyne, *Le pain et le cirque* (Bread and Circuses), and also *The Roman Empire*.

lavish rites as ethnographic cardinal trademarks are direct expressions of the social "costly" display that is linked to the acquiring, claiming, and disclaiming of possessions.[31] In such rituals, possessions accumulated sometimes over years by an individual of the tribe are at one go lavishly distributed to the community, and in some instances even publicly destroyed and wasted in an ostentatious display of dismissiveness of the things once possessed. Marcel Mauss notes about the potlatch of American Northwest Coast natives: "In some instances, the point is not even to give and give back, but to destroy so as to give the impression to the recipient that you are not even interested in getting something back. Houses and thousand of blankets are burned, the most expensive copper pieces are destroyed, all that in order to crush, to flatten his rival."[32] By this kind of spontaneous, public, highly planned and choreographed act of *dispossession*, individuals gain social ascendance and respect. Ostentatious and recognized acts of dispossession are used to assert our social affiliation to the group. No need to visit exotic tribes to confirm this.

Gift exchange, prevalent in all cultures, is meant not only to generate pleasure in others (altruism), but to *please* (belonging, ascendance, and social affiliation). It is through gift and acts of generosity that we show our etiquettes, how we demonstrate our good will, create social debts, seduce and foster alliances with others. As I write these lines, through my window I can see people lining up in front of a flower shop on my street. It is Valentine's Day (February 14). Nine weeks ago, all the shops were mobbed for Christmas shopping.

The importance of gift rituals in our social lives, as well as our compulsive tendencies to ornament ourselves with all sorts of accessories, is a simple yet essential demonstration of how much belongings and belongingness are two sides of the same thing. They are intrinsic parts of the irrepressible need to connect, affiliate, and belong, to gain social power and ascendance in the eyes of others, to assert ourselves in relation to the social world.[33]

We have insisted that possession and being recognized as possessor is the prerequisite of giving and trading, hence of gaining social ammunition for affiliation and ascendance in relation to others. We now need to turn to the actual transferring of possession ownership: the kinds, forms, and meanings of possession exchanges, the alternating cycle of claims and disclaims of possession that is at the core of social life.

[31] Strathern, *The Rope of Moka*; Sahlins, "Poor man, rich man, big man, chief."

[32] Mauss, *The Gift*, pp. 201–202 of the French edition; translated by the author.

[33] The central thesis of Rochat, *Others in Mind*.

3 Possession and ownership transfer

Possession exists only in relation to the possibility of its reverse: dispossession. Possession and dispossession are terms that are co-defined, mutually exclusive, in the same way that light exists in relation to dark, life in relation to death, ying and yang: they imply each other. Possession and ownership imply the possibility of a loss. Discussion of such implication and associated psychology is the topic of this chapter.

We want to discuss the varieties and meanings of possession transfer, the forms and conditions of human dispossession experience. Once possession is felt, enacted, and claimed, eventually recognized, our focus is on the psychology of its transfer. What are the modalities of dispossession and repossession? What kinds of subjective experience are associated with the various modalities of possession transfer (gift, loss, theft, trade, exchange, etc.)?

But first, some basic, psychologically meaningful distinctions of possession kinds are in order. Each kind corresponds to varying degrees of attachment values driving the experience and claiming of possession (ownership). These attachment values also determine the extent to which ownership is transferrable or not transferrable. In this respect, different affectivities behind possession can be tentatively distinguished, in terms of strength but also in terms of forms. As we shall see, some possessions are *alienable* (can be easily transferred like a piece of bread or a house). Others are *inalienable* (like your child, your mother, your arm), or even quasi-inalienable or rarely alienable, like your kidneys in the case of organ traffic or transplant.

In general, it is useful to distinguish two primary kinds of affective value surrounding possession: *personal* and *interpersonal*. The first is intrinsic to the individual, depending on subjectivity (first person feeling experience). The other is extrinsic, depending on inter-subjectivity (co-experience in interaction with others). We start discussing this first, primary distinction. We then move on to a discussion of the distinction between alienable and inalienable possessions from an affective and psychological point of view. Finally, and more to the point, we discuss the psychology associated with the various modalities of possession transfer which is the main focus of the chapter.

Personal values

Possessions can have personal as opposed to interpersonal values. There is an ontological difference between possessions grounded in reasons that are intimate and personal, and others grounded in reasons that are social, under the influence of others. I can value a painting for reasons that are intrinsic to my person and my personal taste. "I like it" or "I don't like it" because it has a unique positive or negative resonance with my own aesthetic experience. Such experience is often immediate and based on gut reactions, as when we get caught in a museum by one particular painting among hundreds of others, for no obvious reasons: a light, a composition, or an expression that resonates with our particular sensibility. It is also at the origins of lingering attachments for reasons that are rational only for ourselves and we are hard pressed to articulate. Who has not been particularly fond of a decrepit object, a pair of jeans that have done their time, an old jacket full of holes. We resist disposing of them, often despite social pressure. We have an intimate relation with these objects of possession that defy social pressures and reasons. We are wedded to personal valuables, like a child to its grubby blanket, resisting all admonitions from parents experiencing it just at face value as a dirty piece of rag. But the child resists, because of an intimate relation to the thing that she has named and cares for. It provides her with comfort and security. It is her security blanket, imbued with strong affectivity, a "transitional object" that helps the child to self-regulate and sustain the stress of social separation.[1] It becomes the child's faithful companion when she is plunged in the dark to sleep.

The intimate connectedness we have with certain paintings, images, or objects, the sense of security that the blanket or the stuffed animal gives to the child, needs to be distinguished from and contrasted to objects of possession whose values are established in interaction with others, as in the case of a barter, a gift exchange, or any kind of reciprocal transactions. The personal values of possession provide possessors with stable and unique reference points. These values specify who we are for ourselves. They give us personal anchoring, the stable features we recognize as ourselves: our own personal "style" and sensible representation for ourselves.

[1] Winnicott, "Transitional objects and transitional phenomena."

We all own and have intimate rapport with our childhood memories: their smells, their music, and the faces we liked or disliked. We also all need to be surrounded by particular objects and pieces of furniture, a bed that has a certain firmness, a wall of a certain color, decorated with certain patterns and images that suit and sooth us, showing also who we are to the world as sensitive, public representations of self. The boundaries between personal and interpersonal values do indeed form a grey area, but they need to be distinguished and contrasted.

Probably the most important and consequential personal values of possession are those pertaining to the ideas we have about ourselves. Here I am talking about the reputation and self-esteem we hold for ourselves. This is expressed in common expressions such as "I own and earned my reputation; I hold on to my values; it is my pride!"

In an essay on glory feelings and reputation in the early Enlightenment period of the seventeenth and eighteenth centuries, Barbara Carnevalli[2] shows that the concern for and value of an intrinsic sense of reputation and self-esteem are a central dimension in the philosophy proposed by pioneer thinkers like Hobbes or Rousseau who forged the revolutionary ideas from which modern societies of the late eighteenth century were formed (i.e., the French Revolution and the first industrial revolution that transformed the relationships of the individual to society: the birth of the republican citizen and hourly paid labor that transformed the order of the Western world[3]).

Thomas Hobbes proposed that personal values, in particular our sense of reputation associated with the quest for glory, are core causal determinants of human nature that he bluntly described as brutish and selfish at its core. Accordingly, humans' quarrelsome, antagonistic propensities can only be tamed and controlled by formal laws and constitutional order, calling for the necessity of a civil society where all individuals submit to a social contract.

Hobbes, in his *Leviathan* (1651), sees three pillars to humans' quarrelsome state of nature: "in the nature of man, we find three principall causes of quarrell. First, Competition; Secondly, Diffidence; thirdly, Glory. The first, maketh men invade for Gain; the second, for Safety; and the third, for Reputation."

Hobbes proposed that beyond the quest for maximum utility in terms of food and sex, humans have also a basic need for self-esteem and signs of personal glory, hence a sense of their own reputation that they cultivate in

[2] Carnevalli, "Glory." See also Slomp, *Thomas Hobbes and the Political Philosophy of Glory*, as well as "Hobbes on glory and civil strife."

[3] Polanyi, *The Great Transformation*.

competition with others. Although the cultivation of reputation depends on others via competition, the end gain is a reinforcement and boost of personal values, the values one sees in oneself. Accordingly, the need for self-esteem and reputation, "a strategic fight for signs of honors,"[4] would be at par with utilitarian and self-maximizing needs like food or sex.

In the context of the history of ideas in Western philosophy, what is revolutionary in Hobbes's views is the idea that this is the property of all humans, not just a small elite of virtue-seeking nobles who in antiquity and all through the middle ages strived in measuring themselves against high standards and formal codes of honor reserved to knights of chivalry and other noble elites. In Hobbes's as well as Rousseau's more encompassing anthropological writings, it was now recognized, arguably for the first time in the Western history of ideas, that all humans, independent of class, have by nature the basic need to consolidate a capital of personal values, caring about their reputation and cultivating *pride in themselves*.

Personal values define *proud possessions*, possessions that echo who we feel we are, what defines us: ideas, creations, personal and family roots, traditions, past actions, moral rectitude, and principles we abide by as the foundation of our moral (idealized) identity. These possessions are abstract, symbolic, and for ourselves first (personal), although obviously there is some interference from evaluations from others. I have already mentioned that between the personal and the interpersonal sense of reputation, boundaries are porous. Yet, it is important to distinguish them. Personal reputation rests primarily on values (personal values) issued from a self-motivated and self-reflective value system that Hobbes captured as the search for glory, Rousseau as the urge for self-esteem (*l'estime de soi*). Interpersonal reputation rests primarily on social values derived from evaluative exchanges with others, in other words from inter-subjective value systems that are spinoffs of a basic need to affiliate with others – the central argument of an earlier book.[5] This is not an over-subtle distinction.

In short, regarding possession, there is a primordial distinction to be made between possessions that are personal and interpersonal. In the footsteps of Hobbes or Rousseau,[6] pioneers in the thinking of the modern "citizen and socially contracted" individual, I define personal value-based possessions as the stuff of our *individual identity* that is experienced from a first person perspective. Interpersonal value-based possessions are, in contradistinction yet with some overlapping regions, the stuff of our *social*

[4] Carnevalli, "Glory." [5] Rochat, *Others in Mind*.
[6] See Carnevalli, *Romantisme et Reconnaissance*.

identity[7] that is experienced as the integration of first, second (intimate), and third person perspectives.

Inalienable and socially binding possessions

We all understand that some personal possessions are more sacred than others, experienced as *inalienable* and by definition deeply non-fungible, like old family memorabilia, jewelry given by a loved one as a symbol of continuity. The cliché of gambling addiction and desperate moral transgression used in novels and films often portrays someone reaching the tipping point of irresponsibility and moral vacuity by bringing her wedding ring or ancient family jewelry to a pawnbroker for quick cash. Attached to a few "sacred" possessions are exigencies of maintenance and safekeeping: *possessio ad perpetuam* (forever possession). This is not the case for the vast majority of other possessions that, to various degrees, invite and are psychologically amenable for transfer.

At the level of values, there is thus a difference that needs to be drawn between "my head" and "my car." They are both mine but have profoundly different meanings for my own survival. My life depends on my head, not my car: my head is inalienable from my embodied self that depends on it. My car is alienable, without forcibly jeopardizing my own personal and social existence. In different ways and forms, this ontological difference is marked in most languages of the world.

The distinction between alienable and inalienable possession is not trivial, but is a basic and universal contrastive intuition finding various expressions across cultures. This is shown in comparative linguistics, but also in careful anthropological observations like those of Annette Weiner (1933–97)[8] and Marcel Mauss on the gift.[9] For example, expounding ethnographies, Mauss writes regarding the meaning of the gift in Maori culture: "The bond created by the transfer of a possession . . . is in fact a bond between persons, since the thing itself is a person or pertains to a person. Hence it follows that to give something is to give a part of oneself."

In Maori culture, and following Mauss's depiction, it appears that what is given is something that becomes inalienable: it cannot live outside of the

[7] See Dittmar, *The Social Psychology of Material Possessions*. In her book, the author discusses in depth the relation between possession and social identity, adopting a social constructionist view on the issue. Instead of focusing on individual experience, as is mainly the case here, Dittmar's social psychological view focuses primarily on the social, cultural, and group origins of possession psychology. These views are complementary and not contradictory, representing different takes on the issue.

[8] Weiner, *Inalienable Possessions*. [9] Mauss, *The Gift*.

circle of the bond it has created. Somehow gift giver and receiver become one moral person fused in the social obligation to reciprocate. The gift instrumentalises this fusion, becoming paradoxically inalienable from the bond it has created. We shall come back to this intriguing point later when discussing the gift as transfer of possession and the obligation to reciprocate that are typically tied to it

Based on fieldwork with the Trobriand Islanders of Papua New Guinea (now known as the Kiriwina Islands, on the eastern edge of this Melanesian nation), and in the footsteps of Bronislaw Malinowski who documented this culture in the early 1900s, Weiner shows that in the context of the Kula circle and gift reciprocation rituals, some objects are imbued with the spiritual force of the social bond between gift giver and gift receiver. By virtue of being a gift, the object cannot be removed (*alienated*) from this gift giver and receiver relationship. The gift cannot be sold or traded, and is not exchangeable outside of this narrow network. Inalienable possessions are marked by non-marketable properties: "What makes a possession inalienable is its exclusive and cumulative identity with a particular series of owners through time. Its history is authenticated by fictive or true genealogies, origin myths, sacred ancestors, and gods. In this way, inalienable possessions are transcendent treasures to be guarded against all the exigencies that might force their loss."[10]

Comparative linguistics provides further evidence of the ontological difference between alienable and inalienable possessions. Across languages, there are remarkable variations in the linguistic treatment of possession as separable or inseparable from its owner, but also from its context. Bernd Heine, a German cognitive and comparative linguist, notes for example: "The way inalienability is defined in a given case or in a given language is largely dependent on culture-specific conventions. In some languages, concepts like 'neighbour', 'house', 'bed', 'fire', 'clothes', or 'spear' belong to the inalienable category, while in other languages they do not. Languages do in fact differ considerably with regard to where the boundary between inalienably and alienably possessed items is located."[11]

Languages and the way grammar works within a language put emphasis on culture-specific delimitations of possession. These particular ways of delimiting possession can reflect deep contrasts in societal organizations and general mentalities around possessions and their norms. Each grammar affords relative emphases or accents on particular aspects in possessive predicates, putting relative emphasis and accent on either the

[10] Weiner, *Inalienable Possessions*, p. 33. [11] See Heine, *Possession*, pp. 1–44, at p. 11.

possessor or what is possessed (e.g., *John's car* versus *this car is John's*). Languages and their grammar afford cultural relevant distinctions. Tswana people of Botswana, South Africa, evolved grammatical means to mark collective as opposed to individual possession. In the Tswana language, the postfix syllable *-gao* allows its users to immediately differentiate, for example, between *our children* within the nuclear family and *our children* within the larger community (our children + *gao*).[12]

These nuances are subtle for novice linguists, but we can assume that they are psychologically relevant, evolving to facilitate communication among members of a community who share ways of life ways and values around the issue of possession. The possession values of the Tswana, because of their grammatical and vocabulary idiosyncrasies, are probably different from those shared by other linguistic communities that do not mark directly collective possession. It is the major task of anthropological psychologists to capture the semantics behind such differences, assuming that linguistic nuances in marking possession evolved for a reason, and are not just random, like variations in the universal marking of what constitutes alienable and inalienable possession. Each cultural community and each group of individuals has to develop norms – be they implicit or explicit – and shared collective sensibilities around possession expressed not only in language but also in moral intuitions about who should own what and why. Social harmony rests on such shared intuitions. Next, we review some of the intuitive priorities of ownership that exist and are more or less emphasized in development and across cultural norms, some with deep evolutionary roots.

Principles of ownership

The claim of possession (ownership), as expression of a basic need for the claimer to gain control over an object or a person, is not only the claimer's prerogative ("That's mine!"). As Rousseau writes in relation to private property, it is as much and more decisively the prerogative and decision of others, those who de facto are excluded from such a claim (not yours!). The legitimacy of such a claim depends on the recognition, acceptance, or submission of others. The question is: what makes a claim of ownership recognizable, acceptable, or submissive enough to make it legitimate in the eyes of others?

It appears that there are multiple *intuitive ownership priorities*. These intuitions correspond to implicit or explicit principles by which others

[12] Cole, *An introduction of Tswana grammar*, cited by Heine, *Possession*, p. 23.

recognize, accept, or submit to an ownership claim. These principles are powerful enough to overcome envy and jealousy, at least to control or repress these two basic possessive emotions discussed in the first chapter of the book. These principles are not trivial. They are the main ingredients of social harmony. Without them, we would most probably end up killing each other, echoing Hobbes's brutish and self-serving premises of Man in his *Leviathan*. The blind contest of ownership claims would certainly lead to social mayhem, as seen in crisis moments of looting during blackouts or following natural disasters.

Intuitive ownership priorities are multiple and depend greatly on context. We tend to use them interchangeably in our determination of *who should own what and why*, depending on who is the ownership claimer and what is the object of the claim. To these intuitive ownership priorities correspond *seven distinct principles*. We view these principles as constituting separate, implicit, or explicit rationales for the legitimizing, hence the social determination and recognition of ownership claim. Each principle has its own logic and internal consistency. They are, respectively, principles of (a) the strongest; (b) first possession; (c) labor; (d) creation/invention; (e) familiarity; (f) blood; and finally (g) luck.[13] I review them in turn.

Strongest and first possession principles

The *strongest* and *first possession* principles are to a large extent the simplest, "archaic" and most prevalent in nature among social creatures. They are also the two most archaic in the perspective of evolution, explaining why we consider them as a cluster, "the archaic principle cluster." That the *strongest* gets the lion's share predicts the resolution of conflicts over possession claims in most animals, and in most instances in all animals. The same can be said regarding *first possession*, i.e., that the first who gets

[13] Note that these principles do not include all the rights and juridical rulings surrounding rights of use, pre-existing ownership conditions, and all the complex principles and jurisprudence that fill books of property laws. Here we are talking about basic intuitive principles found in Nature and that children would develop long before they become aware of all the legal intricacies surrounding property in their own cultural context. However, as a disclaimer, we recognize that books of laws and explicit jurisdictions do interact with these basic intuitive principles. Legal codes influence children at some point of their development in the same way that they started regulating groups of humans when books of laws as cultural artifacts started emerging in human evolution like the ancient Hammurabi code of Babylon, or later the Roman code at the time of the Roman Empire. But such codes have a psychological foundation. What is constitutive of this foundation is a small ensemble of basic intuitive ownership principles. This is what we are discussing here.

hold of and enacts control over the object owns it; this is also a pervasive and archaic principle that predicts in many instances how conflicts over possession get resolve. This is true even in simple creatures like mollusks or crustaceans.

Conflicts of possession among conspecifics over prey, food, or any limited resources, in all social species be they vertebrates or invertebrates, reveal power hierarchy within the group. For many years, primatologists and other ethologists have used natural paradigms by creating conflicts, distributing quantities of desirable food in the midst of a group of primate or other animals to observe who gets what, and how conflicts peek and eventually get resolved. Such methods conjugated with careful observations reveal the power structure of the group, with, in principle, alpha males or females typically getting first choice and the lion's share of the resources, eventually trickling down the more or less stable dominance hierarchy of the group.[14] The *strongest principle* is unquestionably the most archaic of all principles, expressed in all social species, the bottom-line expression of competition for limited resources. However, there are different levels of power display attached to the strongest principle.

Patterns of power recognition across species involve more or less complex communication mechanisms: from the mere assertive snatching behavior of most reptiles, the colorful display wheel of the peacock, or the appearance of increased body size via erected hair in many furry mammals like dogs, to the more negotiated courting of food for grooming documented for example in chimpanzees.[15] There is also the power reputation that we are particularly good at memorizing and cultivating, constantly tallying it among ourselves. These obviously correspond to vastly different levels of complexity, yet they all boil down to the generalized sensitivity, perception, and assessment of power indices within the power structure among individuals within and across neighboring groups. In humans, evidence shows the remarkably early expression of the strongest principle whereby preverbal 1-year-old infants show marked surprise when a smaller, presumably weaker protagonist (animated puppet) has ascendance over a much larger protagonist, bowing to its power.[16] Infants are already attuned to the strongest principle, somehow prepared to detect power dominance and submit to it, like any other social animal at some basic level. The same can be said in relation to the *first possession principle* across vertebrate or invertebrate species. An interesting case is the hermit crab, a crustacean studied for its possession and ownership behavior.

[14] Kummer, *Primate Societies*. [15] De Waal, "The chimpanzee's service economy."
[16] Thomsen et al., "Big and mighty."

Hermit crabs are made up of an asymmetrical soft abdomen prolonged with a few claws (there are over a thousand different species with variations in size and shape). For shelter and protection, they scavenge and choose with care an empty sea snail shell of the right dimensions, clasping it from the inside and carrying it around as they move about and hunt for food on the seashore. As they grow, and become too large for the shell, they look for a larger, more suitable one for swapping. Once they have found one, they occupy the new shell, abandoning the former, making it available for a smaller conspecific. These successive moves among hermit crabs create a "vacancy chain." Research indicates that hermit crab ownership claims and competition over empty shells are astonishingly complex in terms of perception, principles, and even value determination. Careful observations show that hermit crabs do not compete for an empty snail shell only on the basis of its fitness as a shelter. They prefer a shell with no traces of sand inside it. A shell where some sand has been experimentally glued on the inside is significantly less preferred, and is associated with less defensive behavior and with less conflict over its possession.[17]

Hermit crabs tend to fight over shells and may sometimes even gang up to attack and try to dislodge a first possessor. However, typically, a crab that is first to occupy a shell tends to be left alone. Bigger competitors even show restraint toward smaller first possessors. First possession principle is nonetheless constrained by an energy factor. Dislodging a first occupant and engaging in a fight would be more costly than leaving the first occupant alone. But things are not that simple. Some researchers have shown that a shell that is artificially "devalued" with sand glued on its inside will tend to be not only less vigorously attacked, but also *less vigorously defended* by its occupant.[18]

This latter fact is particularly intriguing considering that the spoilage of a shell is information private to the occupant, since the sand in on the inside of the shell. Based on this information, research indicates that the occupant will manifest significantly more *pre-fight displays* toward an attacker. This surge of pre-fight displays is interpreted as a bluff to *increase* the chances of swapping shells. It is an attempt at faking the actual value of the sandy shell, the first occupant deceiving the attacker with a readiness to fight hard for its possession.[19]

In all, we see that both *strongest* and *first possession* principles of ownership are pervasive in nature. As archaic as they might be, closer inspection reveals complex mechanisms of social evaluation that are still major

[17] Arnott and Elwood, "Fighting for shells."
[18] Arnott and Elwood, "Fighting for shells."
[19] Arnott and Elwood, "Fighting for shells."

puzzles for scientists. The next four possession principles rest on higher abstract and conceptual levels of social evaluation for the determination of ownership.

Labor principle

The *labor principle* corresponds to the main criteria of ownership proposed by John Locke (1632–1704), the philosopher of the Scottish Enlightenment, in his *labor theory of appropriation.*[20] Locke, in his political writing on civil government, discusses what might be the civil way to decide on the values of resources that are by definition scarce and need to be rightfully shared beyond *strongest* or *first possession* principles, in ways that would be reflective of a just and democratic civil society.[21]

As a general principle, Locke proposes that *all wealth is the product of labor*. A man is justified in claiming ownership if he can show that he put physical effort into something. Property is acquired and would come about originally by virtue of the labor that an individual or group of individuals puts into natural resources (to plough a field, to pick a fruit, to plant a seed, to manufacture a tool from natural elements). Following the labor principle, ownership is justified primarily as an extension of work. When individuals *mix their labor* with an object in nature for which claims exist, by virtue of the labor principle that object comes under the absolute control and prerogative of the laborer. Carole Rose in her essay on possession as the origin of property[22] describes Locke's labor principle most succinctly as follows: "By commingling labor with the thing, establishes ownership of it" (p. 73).

An example often used to illustrate John Locke's labor view on property is the following. Let's imagine water running down a long stream and falling from waterfall to waterfall. The water that is running is nobody's particular property. However, if I scoop some in a cup to drink, the scoop belongs to me. What is scooped from the waterfall becomes mine by virtue of the caloric energy I spent laboring to scoop the water out of the stream and into the cup.

John Locke's labor theory continues to be debated, criticized, and reinterpreted. It does leave open issues as to how labor can be reliably evaluated and what determines the agent of the work produced, in particular in the most typical situation where labor is produced in collaboration with others rather than alone. It leaves open the question of who

20 Locke, *An Essay Concerning Human Understanding.*
21 Locke, *The Second Treatise of Civil Government.* See in particular chapter 5 on property.
22 Rose, "Possession as the origin of property."

contributed to what. Furthermore, as pointed out by the late political philosopher Robert Nozick (1938–2002), if one pours a can of tomato juice into the ocean, does it give natural right to this person to claim ownership of the ocean?

Despite the fact that labor as a principle or concept is highly abstract, it appears nonetheless that is an important intuitive principle that we use implicitly or explicitly to resolve ownership attribution conflicts as well as in developing ownership distinction in the social environment, intuitively or formally deciding who owns or should own. We are attuned to and somehow capable of fine social judgments and discrimination on the basis of labor merit, the relative energy (work) it took on the part of the ownership claimer in bringing the object of possession into existence, how much effort and calories was spent in maintaining that object. In certain contexts, and to a limited extent, it is from this highly abstract concept of effort and labor that we can infer implicitly or explicitly ownership attribution, deciding on the relative legitimacy of an ownership claim.

Ownership inference based on the labor principle is probably unique to humans, as it would entail, even at an implicit level, a proportional appreciation of effort, something that, to my knowledge, is not demonstrated in other animals. If nonhuman primates appear to collaborate and are capable of rewarding others for their help,[23] they do not show clear evidence that they would reward others in relative proportion to their effort. Humans are able and even have the strong propensity, at least in some circumstances, to decide on the relative legitimacy of ownership claims based on labor proportion, effort, or work merit.

Creation/invention principle

Nozick[24] proposes a theory of ownership that is an alternative to those closer to the egalitarian views of enlightenment philosophers like Locke, Rousseau, or Kant for whom affirmative action and equal opportunity were sacrosanct starting points. Those are the constitutive ideals proposed by these philosophers, as they thought about the creation of a post-monarchic civil society that modern states would embody. From these ideals were supposed to derive more just rulings regarding property rights. Putting into question these ideals, Nozick proposes instead a theory of property that takes as starting point the rightful entitlement individuals or collectives hold when their acquisition is not stolen or

[23] See for example De Waal, "The Chimpanzee's service economy."
[24] Nozick, *Anarchy, State, and Utopia.*

simply acquired by force. According to the entitlement theory, people who produce certain things and bring them to life (as opposed to just laboring on or maintaining them) have inalienable rights over them: "on an entitlement view ... things come into the world already attached to people having entitlements over them" (p. 160).

This entitlement theory rests on the creation/invention principle. According to this principle, the one who first creates it, thinks of it, or construes it, owns it. With creation or invention would come the rightful entitlement to own it as private property. For Nozick, this would be an inalienable right to individuals, above and beyond the egalitarian ideal of equal treatment and opportunity proposed by most contemporary moral philosophers, including the influential theory of justice proposed by John Rawls.[25]

The *creation/invention principle* of ownership attribution is becoming particularly prominent as the foundation for intuitive ownership priorities in today's hypermodern and cyber-connected global world.[26] This principle is unique to humans. No other animals seem to feed on and strive for the joy of self-creation and inventiveness. No other animals would feel crushed if the originality of their creative imprints were somehow contested. It is not part of their reputation repository or symbolic capital as it is for humans.

Information technology promotes individual creations and inventions that are source of exponential entitlement claims, including patent claims on designs and other artistic productions. Copyright issues on concepts, ideas, voices, looks, melodies, and even styles have become a major source of ownership conflicts. Cumbersome protective actions are implemented, but often to no avail, as in the case of the endemic illegal duplication of music and movie productions. There is an increasing mayhem of ownership claim liability in our rich industrial corner of the world. Everybody is entitled to their own creation, now afforded by the clicking of a few computer keys and highly formatted as well as pre-hashed commercial software programs like Facebook or Photoshop. With progress come inflated liability, entitlement, and ownership issues. Any slightly computer-literate individual can feel that he owns what he created and feels that he invented: ideas, concepts, reshuffling of ideas, reshuffling of concepts. Claims quickly slip into of the infinite regress of ownership and entitlement disputes. Most often these disputes remain unresolved, leaving much room for narcissistic, egomaniac delusions about who owns the original rights to what. Does such and such a songwriter own the rights to

[25] Rawls, *A Theory of Justice*. [26] See Lipovetsky, *Hypermodern Times*.

the tune or words he is known to have ripped off? Who owns a distinctive painting style, line of furniture, trademark voice of a singer?[27]

Ownership attribution based on the creation and invention principle has become prevalent, yet incrementally elusive from a normative point of view. It is commonly "felt" today (my idea, my production), but not easily recognizable from a third person perspective. Regulating intellectual, artistic, and other property rights has become a major headache for lawmakers in our cyber age. It resembles politicians' vain attempts at regulating pollution or the use of clean, fresh water. Both are still unresolved, probably never to be resolved conundrums of planetary proportion. This is the trade-off of our post-industrial hyper-individualistic and self-proclaimed entitlement age. Copyright conflicts grow at the exponential pace of technological and cyber progress.

Familiarity principle

The feeling of ownership and entitlement is often based on the distinctive intuition that one has more rights to own if one is more familiar with or has more presumed intimate relations to the object of possession. A house where one grew up, associated with decisive experiences, a place that is full of memories, tends to be thought of as exclusively owned, an inalienable possession: a family estate, an old chest, a jewel, a geographic place, a country. This holds even if the house, land, painting, or any other affectively charged artifact has changed hands multiple times and may have been radically transformed or changed as in the case of a renovation.

To find a family relic, by chance, at a public auction, a pawnshop, or a flea market can be very upsetting. Linked to a sense of nostalgia and deep identification, the familiarity principle is also tied to the social phobia recurrent in the face of immigration, the all too common xenophobic feelings and contempt toward nationals who have recently acquired their citizenship. First or second generation citizens of any country are likely to feel or be made to feel like second-rate citizens among others having the same passport. A black person with a Swiss passport is still looked down on by many Swiss citizens and the source of uneasy feelings to most. Deep down, there is greater national entitlement felt by all those US citizens ostentatiously claiming to be of direct descent from the 102 Mayflower immigrants who landed on the coast of Plymouth, Massachusetts, in

[27] A highly publicized liability suit initiated by Tom Waits ended up in a ruling adjudicating the artist's ownership of his voice's deep raucous timbre, which a German car firm imitated without permission for a TV ad (see "The great Tom Waits wins a court case against VW-Audi," *The New York Times*, February 4, 2006).

1620 – which should have been a much larger flotilla considering all the presumed descendants.

The feeling of entitlement toward possession is thus linked in part to an elusive, albeit in some cases measurable, sense of seniority. Familiarity is a gut feeling, probably the most difficult to articulate in words. Time and personal history is of the essence. At the explicit level, it is probably the most contentious of all the principles, a perennial source of conflicts and hard-earned peace accords, like the perennial multifaith and political fight over the ownership of a city like Jerusalem. History and roots, and hence familiarity, are evoked by all feuding parties, but to no avail. With no end in sight, the archaic principle of the strongest prevails, bringing with it countless horrors of human sacrifice and insane behavior. It is the perennial cause of major enduring conflicts: the Middle East, the Balkans, Kashmir, Tibet, Chiapas, Congo, Myanmar. Worldwide, wars and conflicts tend always to boil down to feuds around the familiarity principle, feuding factions justifying their antagonistic moves on the rationale of familiarity and other historical ascendance. It is the deepest yet most elusive and irrational of all ownership and entitlement rationales. It is also the most devastating, considering that it is mainly what is behind most wars, even when caused by pure hegemony as in the case of Nazism invasion, fed by the cleansing ideology of Aryan entitlement and ascendance.

The familiarity principle is a spinoff of the first possession principle, with an open-ended addition of personal, collective, often highly ideological memory and construal of the past as rationale.

Blood principle

Nepotism and cronyism refer to a transmission of privileges, in particular possession privileges, with no regards to merit: meritless acquisition of property based on favoritism, acquaintanceship, the "old boys" network, but more importantly family ties, direct descent, or blood line. Etymologically, the word nepotism derives from the Latin word *nepotem*, accusative of *nepos* which means *nephew* or *grandson*.

Nepotism as a concept involving favouritism, in contradistinction to a merit-based transmission of privileges, comes from medieval practices in the Catholic Church. Popes and bishops who had no children of their own because of their chastity acquired the habit of designating nephews as successors. Cronyism stands for the same transmission of privilege and power, based on the general principle of acquaintance favoritism. Etymologically, "cronyism" comes from the Greek word *chronos*, meaning *long standing* according to the *Oxford Dictionary*. Cronyism thus stands for long-term social bonds constructed over time and projected into the future as favors to old friends and acquaintances, any close circle of friends and family ties, whether it pertains to the transmission of political privileges, or rights to land, monies, durable goods, or family estates. Blood rights and other forms of favoritism are probably what make the concept of "fairness" most elusive.[28] In all human societies, inheritance based on blood and direct lineage is at the core of privilege transmission, the transmission of private possessions from generation to generation.[29]

Inheritance and the designation of inheritors, successors, or heirs to possession assure sustainability of values and goods among close kin as individuals face death, the inescapable fate. Inheritance (blood) transmission of possessions is often a source of sore disputes among designated heirs, painful family feuds, envy and jealousy among siblings who tend to measure their bond to the deceased with what is contained in a will, reviving old rivalries, notwithstanding greed, envy, and jealousy.[30]

A paradoxical yet most telling example of the complex affective connotation of inheritance and bereavement that most often finds outlet in painful possession conflicts is the way Manouche people (a French branch of the Roma gypsies) tend to resolve the universally thorny and often highly conflictual issues of inheritance among descendants. It was reported to me

[28] See the recent book by S. T. Asma entitled *Against Fairness*, trying to embrace our unavoidable favoritism inclinations, particularly toward close ones.

[29] In this respect, the work of French sociologist Pierre Bourdieu is most insightful regarding the larger social dynamic surrounding the maintenance and legitimizing of the blood principle, in particular via education. Here is a relevant quote taken from Bourdieu, "The forms of capital": "Because the question of the arbitrariness of appropriation arises most sharply in the process of transmission – particularly at the time of succession, a critical moment for all power – every reproduction strategy is at the same time a legitimation strategy aimed at consecrating both an exclusive appropriation and its reproduction. When the subversive critique which aims to weaken the dominant class through the principle of its perpetuation by bringing to light the arbitrariness of the entitlements transmitted and of their transmission (such as the critique which the Enlightenment *philosophes* directed, in the name of nature, against the arbitrariness of birth) is incorporated in institutionalized mechanisms (for example, laws of inheritance) aimed at controlling the official, direct transmission of power and privileges, the holders of capital have an ever greater interest in resorting to reproduction strategies capable of ensuring better-disguised transmission, but at the cost of greater loss of capital, by exploiting the convertibility of the types of capital. Thus the more the official transmission of capital is prevented or hindered, the more the effects of the clandestine circulation of capital in the form of cultural capital become determinant in the reproduction of the social structure. As an instrument of reproduction capable of disguising its own function, the scope of the educational system tends to increase, and together with this increase is the unification of the market in social qualifications which gives rights to occupy rare positions" (p. 258).

[30] There are rumors that one third of all last wills and family successions in France end up contested and ruled by a tribunal.

by a friend[31] who researched the Manouche ways of life that at the death of a community member, aside from the person being buried, all personal belongings of the deceased, including car and trailer, are burned to the ground "so they can be remembered as a person."

Blood principle as legitimate grounds for the transmission of possession, with its inherent favoritism that defies fairness in terms of egalitarianism, is universal. Some political regimes have tried to control it, but in no time novel forms of "apparatchik" systems emerge, reshuffling the cards of inescapable cronyism and, in general, our deep-down "limbic" propensities to favor blood kin and a close circle of affiliates. This is a built-in fact of nature that is a major determinant in the transfer and hence acquisition of possession. Favoritism is not just a human propensity. We find it in the maternal instinct of most animals toward their young. It has deep evolutionary roots.

Luck principle

No one would dispute the right to sudden wealth for the lucky winner of a lottery jackpot. Luck is probably the most legitimate, most acceptable principle in everybody's mind, across cultures. Unless accused of cheating or misreading his lucky number, the legitimacy of ownership claim by the lucky winner is undisputable.

In the stochastic midst of a lucky draw one can inherit from pure chance. Here there is no blood link, no labor, no other merit than the idea, impulse, maybe persistence in purchasing what eventually came out to be the winning ticket, maybe also the effort of paying attention and monitoring the lottery result on radio or TV, or in the newspaper. Rationales to explain luck are superstitions or rest on the elusive alchemy of winning algorithms. Chance, hence luck, can only be described a posteriori, not explained a priori or predicted. This is what luck is about. By definition, if chance is pure, no algorithm, no magic tricks, nor any kind of memorized tallying can account for it.

In pure chance, the probability that the tossed coin will end up showing head or tail is unpredictable, even if the preceding eighteen tosses were heads. In the next toss of the coin there is still a 50–50 chance that the head will show up, even if most of us would bet to the contrary. This is very hard for us to conceive, always prone to find regularities and predictive "winning" algorithms. With each throw, if the coin and its thrower are not fraudulent,

[31] François Bertrand of Paris who interviewed and documented the life of Manouche people communicated this to me in one of our many intellectually charged lunches while I was writing this book, in the spring of 2013.

we are in fact back to a 50–50 chance. No memories of the preceding throws can be involved, no possible predictive probability algorithm can be generated. This fact is difficult to grasp for we have the ingrained cognitive instinct to project causal explanations to all events, the proclivity to assign intelligent design behind any kind of random occurrence.

In relation to luck, we are quick to consider what might have been the merit of a lucky draw. Casino winners rarely consider that their winning streak was purely due to chance. Professional croupiers at roulette, unless instructed otherwise by the gambler, leave the lucky bet on the same number, giving the winner his bet times 33, not the bet itself, deliberately leaving it on the table for the next spin, out of superstition. Raking the bet times 34, which would be legitimate according to the rules of the game, is considered "bad luck." It also hides the false intuition and cultivated superstition that the same number will come up again in the next draw, a tradition among gamblers.

A lot of false assumptions and superstitions are involved in chance gambling. In a sense, luck is counter-nature, as we seek for merit and intentions at all cost, for reasons behind wins but also for their reverse: losses. Luck, whether good or bad, doesn't boost much of our ego or reputation. This fact is universal in the context of games of absolute chance like roulette or lottery, but also in the context of games not of absolute chance, like trading on the stock market or betting on horses. But there are some exceptions for experts who have a better chance at winning. The odds of winning for someone knowledgeable about horses, particularly horses involved in one race, are certainly greater than for a novice picking out his horse on the basis of its name, the jockey's color scheme, or his astrological sign. The point is that there are always grounds for finding merit where in fact there is very little to none.

Luck is a fact of life. It is always a factor, if not now, then in the chain of events that led to the "now": the luck of becoming heir, a creator, the strongest, or ending up the most familiar by virtue of the lucky or unlucky draw that constitutes our birth circumstances, no matter what. The merit in all this is, at close inspection, rather slim. Yet we have the instinctual inclination to magnify its role and proclaim merit to justify our present situation, our present state of wealth or poverty of possessions. But in earnest, how does a king justify his inheritance of a throne without invoking either luck (rarely done) or divine choice (typically the case, whether explicit or not)? Is there merit in being born in a rich family? Certainly not, but that is the way we tend to think about it.

Even in a pure case of luck, like a jackpot win, we tend to rationalize some merit into it. The fact is that the lives of jackpot winners are known often to fall apart after the win. Not only because zillions of salesmen come suddenly knocking on their door, but because of a lost sense of merit.

Below is a direct account by a lottery winner I found in a British newspaper article entitled "My lottery win is making me miserable,"[32] apparently a common experience for those who hit the jackpot, in an all too legitimate fashion.

> I won nearly £1m in the lottery nine years ago and . . . I gave up work, thinking I'd spend the rest of my life enjoying my money. I was a lorry driver and lived on a council estate, so the win was a dream come true. I spent three years on holiday until it hit me – I was bored. I needed some direction, so I set up a business. *I wanted to feel I had earned my money*. Now my company turns over £1m a year, and I work harder now than I ever did. *I don't even touch my lottery money*. (italics added)

This testimony is common in lucky punters who tend to search in vain for merit in their win. Many of them end up in support groups. Some psychologists describe sudden wealth acquisition as a grieving process.[33] The paradoxical grieving that follows chance winning, as many accounts from lottery winners show, is primarily linked to a vain quest for a *merit* where there is none. How can someone recognize herself in something she cannot, in earnest, claim merit for? Grief is the realization that chance is involved and not particularly self-elevating, not a good ground for the merit-based recognition we all tend to strive for. Lottery winners tend to express their frustrated need to project an image of legitimacy and deservingness regarding their sudden, albeit legitimate, wealth.

To be perceived as an impostor is one of our biggest fears. The impostor complex is the curse of the "nouveaux riches" perceived and labeled as such by old-money people to emphasize skepticism and suspicion about and in the end contempt for lesser deservingness and entitlement to wealth. Why would they otherwise be called "nouveaux riches"? What is wrong in being newly rich, considering that wealth, like anything else, has to start with somebody, somewhere, sometime. The derogatory connotation of new money is just an indication of how classes are formed and social stratification is reinforced by clique cultures. In this context, social mobility is not a smooth, continuous ride. It is a movement through social classes that are strata of various thickness and "density." It entails obstacles and initiations, a passage over generations through layers of

[32] M. Brudenell, L. Boswell, and S. Wolfson, "My lottery win is making me miserable," *Health Panel, The Guardian–The Observer*, Sunday, January 7, 2007.

[33] R. Friedman, "Winning the Lottery: instant millionaire or instant griever?" in *Broken Hearts: Exploring Myths and Truths about Grief, Loss, and Recovery*. *Psychology Today*, August 17, 2009.

exclusive group cultures, each with its own merit value system and inclusive criteria. All these obstacles can be viewed as essentially driven by the preservation of class privileges. It is also what underlies snobbism and associated "habitus," the social etiquettes and practices systematically passed down to children.

Three basic kinds of ownership transfer

Ownership transfer is the process by which possession changes hands in a more or less reciprocal or unilateral fashion. This is how ownership tends to be constantly at stake and redefined. With the exception of possessions created by the owner, there is a limited number of ways possession can be acquired, retained, and eventually transferred: either by theft (i.e., stealing), gift (e.g., inheritance), or exchange (e.g., trade or any forms of barter transaction). Psychologically speaking, we can see that there are essentially only three basic kinds of ownership transfer, which we can categorize in broad psychological terms as *violent*, *generous*, or *by agreement*. The first kind is forceful, the second kind corresponds to gift and giving, the third kind covers transfers based on negotiated agreement or trade.

Each kind forms a general experiential category at both the subjective and the inter-subjective level, each corresponding to a social practice that is ontologically different, with a radically different mind frame attached to it. We want to capture the specific psychology around these experiential categories, with the caveat that none is pure and impermeable, and they often overlap and interfere with each other. For example, a generous kind of ownership transfer might not be so generous in the end but rather self-interested as in the case of indirect reciprocity. Likewise, an agreed transfer can end up being a steal in disguise (a scam or deliberate swindle). Nonetheless, from a psychological perspective, there is some mutual exclusivity among these categories. They are conceptually helpful in our discussion on the origins of possession, particularly if we want to uncover the largest array possible of all the psychological processes that hide behind such phenomena. We review them in turn.

Violent kind: theft and usurpation

There is intrinsic violence in seizing something without preliminary rightful agreement, or to be suddenly dispossessed of something by malice. It is malevolent at its core. In this kind of ownership transfer, there is always a victim and an abuser, as good and "Robin Hood" as the cause might be. Ontologically of a violent kind, the psychology behind it is no less than rape-like: the forceful, intentional, and malicious removal from others of liberties and prerogatives to which they feel entitled, whether this entitlement is judged legitimate or not by either party. It always corresponds to the taking over of control outside of any negotiated consensus or preliminary agreements. It is fundamentally a one-way forceful dynamic between protagonists, whether or not this dynamic is part of a rightful redistribution or sudden reappropriation, often looting of wealth following the fall of oligarchs. Whether appropriate or not, from the perspective of the dispossessed it is always experienced as a basic abuse of power.

We have all experienced theft or heard from victims of theft. Coming back home to find the mayhem of a burglary, with open and empty drawers, possessions scattered around the floor, the experience is typically a very deep sense of infringement into personal space, a rape of one's own order and control over things that are an extension of the self. My own experience is something like a sense of dirt and spoilage, as if there were a contamination by dirty hands of my belongings, an experience acknowledged by many. There is a sudden sense of insecurity, a deep feeling of loss of control. Helplessness tends often to turn into anger and a blind, often very risky drive to catch the thief, not only to re-own lost possessions, but also to punish and get even. As a case in point, it is common to hear that the number one rule in cases of mugging is to give up your wallet without hesitation and resist chasing your perpetrator.

By analogy, and while keeping a sense of proportion, it is the experience of someone coming back to her trailer home after a tornado,[34] finding the home in a shambles and possessions that were contained in the private space of the trailer spewed out all over the front lawn. The homeowner's experience at this point is despair and disempowerment, a profound sense of insecurity. It is the experience of having been overcome by curse and bad luck. In the case of theft, the fact that we can actually personify the malicious cause behind it changes the nature of disempowerment of the victim. It allows for a redirection of anger into seeking revenge and retribution, the opportunity to be proactive in winning one's possessions back and getting even with the perpetrator.

[34] I use trailer home rather than regular home in my analogy because over all the years I lived in the southern United States, TV reports of the frequent tornadoes hitting the region always seemed to show destroyed trailer homes, as if Nature was targeting the poorest among us. In fact, the damage is most visible in dwellings made of thin walls, reporters getting more visual impact for their bucks by documenting the damages caused by twisters in trailer parks.

From the thief and usurper's perspective, the temptation to steal and get away with it is the central core of the experience, driven by the desire to create a gift for oneself, acquiring possession at no cost, the potential thrill of overcoming the fear of being caught, the intense excitement of getting away with it.

But there are various levels of violent ownership transfer, multiple degrees in the stealing of properties. Some are physically more harmless than other, pickpocketing versus mugging for example. The degrees of physical harm may vary greatly, but the fundamental process of violence and a victimization process remains: the basic abuse of power and authority over another party, the bottom-line psychological force behind such transfer of ownership. The affective coloring of experience on the part of the victim is violence, rape, and disempowerment. On the part of the thief or usurper, thrill, fear of getting caught mixed with the unquestionable excitement of getting away with it, with possibly the post-mischief guilt and depression commonly reported by recovering criminals relieved to pay their debt to society, as they say. All the experiential aspects give this kind of transfer its specific affective flavor, corresponding to a particular subjective and inter-subjective "phenomenal category" of ownership transfer.

There are, however, many interesting legal nuances that tend to give varying weight to different psychological consequences in reference to theft and usurpation. *Mischief*, for example, in the United States criminal law, stands specifically for any direct damage toward property. It is what captures the *direct* offense against property in the broad legal sense. Yet, in the language of law, there is a difference between mischief and what is called *criminal conversion*, another kind of theft and usurpation against property but one that does not entail its malicious destruction or total disappearance, for example tapping into someone's water line, freeloading on my neighbors' wireless connections or stealing a car for a joy ride with the intention of returning it at dawn as if nothing had happened. In law terms, and in contradistinction to mischief proper, criminal conversion does not include the intention of depriving the owner of the possession and control over property. It is considered a lesser offense. We can see again how much the notion of intentionality is at the core of who owns what and why. These nuances are important because, psychologically, they correspond to different levels of theft and usurpation experiences, from both the victim's and the thief or usurper's perspective. As in the case of mischief versus criminal conversion, the levels of experience are incommensurable, at least in terms of subjective and inter-subjective intensity. The language of the law and its jurisprudence reflects precisely such varied degrees of experience.

Generous kind: giving and obliging

Once again, transferring ownership via gifts, as an outward gesture of generosity, is central to all cultures in various expressive forms, following different, often intricate norms and rituals. Birthdays or other religious celebrations like Christmas or Hanukah are examples of such rituals. All are centered primarily around individual members of intimate circles, typically family and friends. Yet, in a lot of group cultures that promote more collective ways of living, birthdays tend to be ignored, not a cause for individual celebration and gift giving.[35]

This is the case for example in most traditional, insular societies of the South Pacific where Kula circles and gift giving happened at a group level, playing a central role in creating group ties and alliances, resolving conflicts, and maintaining long-term social harmony between families, villages, and island communities, typically around funerals, weddings, and other large celebratory events. In these cultures, some objects are specifically meant to be gifts, and only gifts, like straw mats in most regions of Oceania, particularly Polynesia, in island nations like Samoa that are still very traditional. The gift value of a mat is commensurate with its size and the fine density of its weave, which meant more time and effort to create it. A fine mat can take a few years to make, and the same mat can circulate as a gift for generations, gaining history, with woven marks of past exchanges adding to its value. But these long-term circulating gift currencies are also accompanied by vast amounts of food and money, with the recurrent goal of overwhelming gift recipients, with a typical, well-staged choreography of gestures that emphasize the absence of hesitation in giving. In Samoa, the gifts are publicly pushed forward one by one, piled up, and thrown in front of the receiving party sitting there passively witnessing the event, but tallying carefully every single gift received for future celebratory reciprocation, a reciprocation that is expected and part of deep cultural and collective etiquettes. In Samoa, everybody knows what is given and received, among families and villages, all stored in the collective memory for generations. The same basic gift rituals are observed in all regions of Polynesia, Melanesia, and Micronesia, but also in various forms and with different choreography all over the world.

[35] In many regions of the world, like traditional regions of Melanesia or Polynesia, it is not uncommon to meet people who don't know exactly when they were born. In general, all people know where they were born, but not always when (personal field observations, for example in Vanuatu and Samoa where we encountered major difficulties in collecting the dates of birth of children tested in these regions).

A common trait in the generous kind of ownership transfer is a typical display of disinterest that is only a veneer hiding long-term, more selfish motives. It is always a mark of seduction and ultimately a major instrument for reputation build-up, social binding, and social maintenance creation. Businesses know that well when they shower their clients with gifts at the end of the year.

The primary function of gifts is to create social ties. It is an investment in social capital and reputation. It also creates an obligation to reciprocate. There may be some exceptions, like anonymous donations, but these are either rare or suspiciously pure. Typically, gifts are tied implicitly or explicitly to a circle of reciprocation, a gesture either for getting even or for creating *social debts*, as exemplified in the Kula described by Malinowski and Mauss. There is always a debt or an obligation to reciprocate tied to the gift, hardly the one-way process or expression of pure generosity. Pure generosity is either rare or does not exist, its purity always hard to measure, never completely eliminating any suspicion of being self-serving. Ulterior motives can always be viewed as a mix of self-serving determinants like reputation maintenance, social debt creation, or even self-image boosting in the case of anonymous donation. To be pure, generosity would need to be automatic, with no traces of intentions, something that is hard to find aside from instinctive, heroic moves like jumping into icy water to rescue a stranger, a mother sacrificing her life to save her child. These heroic instances of life giving do exist. Typically, however, they tend to be dictated by strong environmental demands and adrenaline-filled circumstances, as on the frontline of a war where in the midst of great exhaustion and fear, instinctive, more limbic responses take over from volitional and calculated decisions. It is not uncommon to hear individuals decorated and recognized for their bravery reporting that they do not feel like heroes.[36] Their account is that they could not have done otherwise, but responded "instinctively," leaving no room for hesitation. Those instinctive acts of total donation would be exemplars of pure generosity.

Are they *disinterested gifts*, gifts that would entail no expectation of social recognition on the part of the donor? The question of pure gift is an open question. On the contrary, it is fairly easy to measure the relative "impurity" of generosity. For example, there is a clear difference between donations that do or do not include the donor as beneficiary. There is a difference in picking up the bill after eating with friends or picking up the bill of another table unbeknownst to them; between leaving a tip in a

[36] See the interesting work by Walker and collaborators exploring the personality of identified heroes, e.g., Walker, Frimer, and Dunlop, "Varieties of moral personality"; Walker and Frimer, "Moral personality of brave and caring exemplars."

jar while being seen by the bartender or while the bartender is turning his back fixing your drink. Although pure generosity is elusive, it can be more or less anonymous or ostentatious, more or less directly contributing to the public construction of our moral character and reputation. However, never mind the various degrees of "impure" generosity, what cuts across gift giving and treating others is always the creation of social obligations and debts in others. Gifts are never socially innocent, as the ethnography of the Kula by Trobriand Islanders shows, but a general feature of the generous kind of ownership transfer.

Gift is giving as much as it is obliging others to eventually reciprocate. Social ingratitude is not well regarded across cultures, a universal taboo that preserves long-term group cohesion and harmony, just as the incest taboo prevents the genetic damages of consanguinity. Gifts and their obligations tend to be universally experienced by individuals and groups as crucial instruments of social harmony.

Agreed kind: negotiating and exchanging

The violent kind of possession transfer (theft and usurpation) and the obliging kind that is tied to gift giving are both ontologically different from the process by which possessions are traded on the basis of explicit and voluntary agreement, in the context of some sort of a mutual negotiation among traders of possession. This is what constitutes the third, *agreed kind* of ownership transfer. It is "agreed" because it is based on some agreement among protagonists on the terms of a transaction. Furthermore, it is distinct because, unlike violent or generous kinds, agreed transfer of ownership can be accepted, refused, or contested until an agreement is reached. This is categorically not the case for the former two. In the generous kind of transfer, it would be an insult to refuse a gift. In the violent kind, refusing the imposition of the strongest would be worthless. In the agreed kind of transfer, it is not an insult and nor is it worthless to refuse or contest the transfer. It is instead the currency of the transaction after negotiation and until an agreement is reached, when parties have reached some inter-subjective level of mutually recognized "win–win" situation, a reciprocal agreement.

The nature of the agreement enabling the transfer of possession can vary greatly in forms and levels of complexity: from simple, direct, and concrete as in instances of "tit-for-tat" bartering of possessions (you give me this object against that object, OK?), to complex, *indirect*, and abstract transactions involving money and other complex market valuations (e.g., auctions or stock exchanges), including more or less intricate long-term strategies involved. These levels presumably map onto the relative reciprocity expressed by children in their development and what can be observed across animal species. The theoretical debate is ongoing as to whether some levels of reciprocity are actually unique to humans or shared with other species.

Obviously, we are the only species trading stock and participating at art auctions, agreeing on highly abstract values, notwithstanding the use of totally fungible currency of reciprocation that is money. However, empirical evidence suggests that our close evolutionary relatives like chimpanzees, and even more distant relatives like capuchin monkeys, engage in some forms of indirect, not straightforward tit-for-tat reciprocal exchanges such as food for grooming[37] or food for sex.[38] This would mean that we are not the only species able to find some equivalence among disparate goods or possessions, be they material things or favors. Chimpanzees as well as capuchin monkeys can indeed be trained to equate the quantity and quality of non-edible tokens varying in color and shape (small colorful plastic objects) with the quantity and quality of food (a grape that is considered as a treat versus regular food). This ability is used by researchers to document the relative symbolic capacity in nonhuman species,[39] as well as the hotly debated question of the evolutionary roots of a moral sense in terms of fairness sensitivity[40] and signs of an aversion to inequity.[41] Signs of inequity aversion are typically measured by the behavioral reactions of captive animals that are paired in the same cage or adjacent cages, to whom a human experimenter distributes unequal amounts of preferred food. When the distribution is unequal, monkeys do react with apparent stress resembling jealousy and may retaliate following a lesser treatment.

In all, it seems that we are not the only species capable of engaging in reciprocal exchanges, including exchanges where mental score keeping of past interactions plays a role.[42] However, as a species, we have brought the propensity to negotiate values in reciprocal social interactions to levels that are unmatched in Nature.

[37] De Waal, "Food sharing and reciprocal obligations among chimpanzees."

[38] Gomes, Mundry, and Boesch, "Long-term reciprocation of grooming in wild West African chimpanzees," as well as Gomes and Boesch, "Wild chimpanzees exchange meat for sex on a long-term basis."

[39] Addessi, Crescimbene, and Visalberghi, "Do capuchin monkeys (*Cebus apella*) use tokens as symbols?"

[40] Proctor et al., "Chimpanzees play the ultimatum game."

[41] Dubreuil, Gentile, and Visalberghi, "Are capuchin monkeys (*Cebus apella*) inequity averse?"

[42] "There are sound evolutionary reasons to expect chimpanzees to be sensitive to unequal outcomes. They routinely cooperate by defending territory, form coalitions, hunt in groups, share food, and engage in reciprocal exchanges that suggest mental scorekeeping. For example, chimpanzees are sensitive to unequal outcomes in experiments, refusing to

Debating and trying to agree on the value of things is unquestionably a human trademark. This is evident in the human evolution of material possession trading (market economy), but also in the uniquely human proclivity to exchange non-material possessions like ideas, constantly trying to agree *ideologically*, at abstract and symbolic levels. From a comparative perspective, this fact is inescapable, calling for some non-reducible qualitative distinctions among various levels of reciprocity, even if such distinctions remain highly controversial in the comparative and evolutionary biology literature.

Levels and forms of reciprocity: direct, indirect, and strong

It is important to remember that the bottom-line principle of the agreed kind of possession transfer is that all protagonists necessarily understand, implicitly or explicitly, that the transfer can be refused before being mutually concluded, and that each will get something out of the trade. The background context is a win–win deal. If I go to the market to purchase something, I expect to get something against my money and the merchant expects some money or something against his merchandise. Mutual expectation of a trade is the bottom-line reciprocal principle of the agreed kind of possession transfer. However, this principle can be expressed in various ways, corresponding to psychological processes that are incommensurate both quantitatively and qualitatively. For example, I can expect an analog, symmetrical, one-to-one, tit-for-tat transaction between me and another possessor in a simple barter transfer. In such a transaction, the same amount of two things are traded in the *here and now* of the market place.

In contrast, I can expect a non-analog, asymmetrical, and complex negotiation with the other possessor that would project our commercial and interpersonal relation into the future. That would be the case for any credit-based transactions, automatically entailing some tallying of scores, and assessment of mutual trust and reputation. I can expect my current income, collateral, credit history, and references to be checked. My overall reputation is assessed in terms of credit rating, solvency, and trustworthiness, themselves at stake for future transactions. A contract that would include price and compound interest is eventually

participate when a partner earns a better reward for equal effort, and occasionally even refusing a better reward when a partner receives less. The ability to recognize and be sensitive to unequal outcomes would theoretically help them establish beneficial partnerships. Additionally, chimpanzees pay attention to intent, reacting more negatively to a partner deliberately stealing their food rather than one giving their food to another. They also show 'targeted helping,' which requires recognition of another's needs and goals" (Proctor et al., "Chimpanzees play the ultimatum game," p. 2).

proposed, agreed upon, and signed, guaranteed by the law in case of transgression. Direct and indirect kinds of reciprocity are psychologically incommensurate. The degree of complexity of indirect reciprocity is unmatched in our species, particularly in recent history.

Historically, and from a sociological point of view, the forms and degrees of complexity of indirect reciprocity grew exponentially with the first and second industrial revolutions of the eighteenth and nineteenth centuries. These revolutions changed the way possession was transferred in a new modern market organized around a capitalist economy. These changes were linked to great technological advances in the means of production, hence a sudden surge of material wealth, but also new forms of proletarian poverty that led to the communist and fascist revolutions of the early twentieth century.

These great socio-economic transformations promoted indirect rather than direct reciprocity, removing exchanges from simple and concrete barter of goods, making them increasingly removed from socially embedded exchanges via fictitious and highly abstract financial operations.[43] Psychologically, this transformation promoted what Karl Marx termed *commodity fetishism*, whereby social relations come to be expressed primarily in terms of economic relations, such as credit score, debt level, relative investment, and purchase potential. In the process, subjective economic values like purchase power, or abstract concepts such as commercial reputation and trust, become objectified, as if they had real intrinsic value (hence the terms fetishism coined by Marx).

In the *direct reciprocity* prevailing in archaic societies prior to the modern economy, the trade equation tends to be unilateral and simple. It tends to be analogical as well as symmetrical, happening here and now, with little to no projection into the future or the past. This is the case, for example, when people trade seats with strangers on an airplane so friends or a couple can travel together; when unacquainted children meeting by chance at a playground trade shovel for rake in the sandbox; when capuchin monkeys share the same reward of preferred food after cooperating in pulling a heavy tray toward them, not influenced by previous successful or failed interactions.

[43] In his seminal book *The Great Transformation*, Karl Polanyi discusses the historical co-occurrence of modern nation states, modern market economies, and the new concentration of the means of production in large factories in nineteeth-century England that created a mass exodus of traditionally self-sufficient peasant families from rural areas lured by daily wages at industrial sites. Polanyi shows that with the modern free market economy, money, land, and labor became increasingly fictitious, disconnected from simpler more embedded social exchanges based on symmetry and self-sufficiency, closer to principles of simple barter and direct reciprocity as discussed here.

Direct reciprocity thus captures trade or cooperation where there is no long-term memory, nor any clear score tallying and planning into the future, no accounting of past interactions. In game theory jargon, it corresponds to non-iterated, one-shot-deal anonymous transactions.

Indirect reciprocity, in contrast, entails the tallying of past exchanges, the planning of future potential exchanges, and also partner choice based on reputation as well as the co-construction of mutual trust over iterated trades with same partners. It is the basis for cronyism and nepotism, but also what is sometimes called *strong reciprocity*: the propensity to punish freeloaders and cheaters even at one's own cost, what is also termed "costly punishment" (costly in the sense of self-sacrifice or spending of one's own resources).

In *strong reciprocity*, partners are sensitive to the abidance to fairness principles (e.g., equal distribution, no freeloading, abiding by rules, no cheating, etc.). Those "moral" principles have priority and override any economic rationale for self-maximizing. So, in a transfer of possession, one might step out of a deal even if it were a crucial and lucrative opportunity because it violates agreements and defies set principles. An act of strong reciprocity would be to sacrifice what would otherwise be lucrative, turn down a deal because it is sketchy and unethical. In strong reciprocity, economic power and advantage are sacrificed to take an ethical stance by which principled points are made to express moral rectitude and to project moral integrity, inside and out.

Clearly the reciprocity that can be expressed within the agreed kind of possession transfer corresponds to very different levels of psychological complexity, from symmetrical and reverberated (*direct reciprocity*) to reputable (*indirect reciprocity*), and eventually in relation to moral norms (*strong reciprocity*). Each of these levels entails different cognitive and social capacities that children express chronologically in development, as we shall see in the second part of the book. From an evolutionary perspective, these capacities are differentially expressed depending on the relative mnemonic as well as self-reflective abilities of the species: the ability to construe oneself in relation to others projected into the future and in reference to past transactions. Signs of such ability exist in humans from approximately 3 years of age, even possibly earlier, as discussed in the second part of the book on the ontogenetic origins of possession.

Homo negotiatus

Like no other species, humans excel in the agreed kind of possession transfer. This tendency is the necessary by-product of an exacerbated concern for reputation and unique levels of self-consciousness, the inescapable propensity to find explicit consensual values in things and find closure on disputed prices or ideas. Human language and communication, for that matter, cannot be considered outside of an exacerbated drive to *agree upon things*. This drive, as some sort of human-specific urge, is itself associated with the necessary process of negotiation: the bartering of values until an agreement is reached. Presumably, all social species evolved various mechanisms to maintain social harmony, a prerequisite for group survival. This would include the creation of alliances, and empathic or other feelings of concern, as well as an inclination to cooperate, all phenomena that are arguably reported in nonhuman species, from rats to monkeys and great apes. Evidence for such phenomena now abound in the comparative literature. However, there is no equivalence in nature to the human propensity to refuse, brand, debate, argue, barter, maneuver, seduce, or strategize until some sort of inter-subjective agreement is reached. These agreements can pertain to just about anything, from the price of a painting to the logic and soundness of a political argument, from the beauty of a piece of music to the relative guilt of a criminal. In human affairs, as in the affairs of no other animal, it all boils down to the tentative reaching and sealing of agreements. This is an ongoing process that feeds our social lives, regardless of cultural diversity.

Across human cultures, agreements are reached and sealed either amiably or lawfully in case of unresolved conflicts, following the authority of cultural norms and law arbitration under the guidance of established and consensual cultural institutions (chief hierarchy and tribunals in oral cultures; books of law and trade agreements in literate societies). From a psychological perspective, *Homo sapiens sapiens* is also *Homo negotiatus*: a species that evolved a uniquely agreed kind of psychology. This psychology revolves around the concern for reputation, partner choice in cooperating with others, and in general an exacerbated propensity to sense oneself through the evaluative eyes of others. *Homo negotiatus* is indeed a species that, by necessity, is uniquely self-conscious, uniquely prone to feel shame and to produce shame in others.[44]

The psychology surrounding the agreed transfer of possession via negotiation requires complex mindreading, something at which humans excel. In a barter of possession, one has to figure the other possessor's wants, beliefs, and strategies in owning and sharing, let alone the

[44] See further discussions in Rochat, *Others in Mind*; Rochat and Passos-Ferreira, "Becoming *Homo negotiatus*: ontogeny of the unique ways humans own and share; Rochat, "The gaze of others."

assessment of the other's relative attachment to her possession, the reading of verbal or nonverbal cues as to whether an agreement is close, or on the contrary far from being concluded. The art of the deal is a human art, an ongoing exercise, not only when we bargain goods or trade possessions, but also when we try to convince and seduce each other, argue about who is right and who is wrong until some conclusions are eventually reached. The process underlying the art of the deal rests on the human proclivity to create inter-subjective values, the sense of shared values in the experience of things, always trying to find agreements regarding their worth, particularly the worth in the eyes of others of what we experience as *possessions*. An inseparable process, the value of possessions established in negotiation with others serves to establish our self-worth.

As noted by John Dewey: "The *Me* cannot exist without the *Mine*. The Self gets solidity and form through an appropriation of things which identifies them with whatever we call my self . . . Possession shapes and consolidates the *I*."[45]

Likewise, and elaborating on Dewey's comment, the inter-subjective value of possession arising in negotiation also contributes in a major way to shaping and consolidating our own worth and social power.

[45] Dewey, *Human Nature and Conduct*, p. 116.

4 Symbolic spinoffs of possession

The psychology of possession revolves around three basic urges: the urge to acquire, the urge to protect what is acquired, and the urge to accumulate. The backdrop of this psychology is a generalized self-protective *threat* experience. There is fear at the core: fear of being deprived and the *fear of losing.*[1]

This fear leads to behaviors and motives that are essentially protective in nature. The child screaming "That's mine!," the marking of a territory, political borders, bills of sale, signed deeds, all are expressions of an attempt at sealing control over possession, a preventive move against the threat of competition. It all means the same: a psychology fundamentally built around the binary anxious matrix of either *not having* or *being deprived of.* But it is also a matrix from which compulsions arise: the uncontrollable urge to own and accumulate possessions.

As already mentioned and discussed, all social animals express possession psychology, but in ways that are not comparable to humans. In humans, it takes symbolic forms of unmatched complexity. It becomes indirect and abstract, way beyond instinctive defense of or attack on territories, progeny, food, sexual partner, or stature maintenance within a group hierarchy. The experience of possession is re-described to become signified rather than literal fear expressions. In humans, possession urges are transformed to become sublimated expressions of desires and fantasies that are channeled through tortuous, devious, often obsessive behavioral outlets: stinginess, kleptomania, overboard generosity, collecting, hoarding, fetishism, gambling, and many more. In the human process of symbolic re-description, the basic possession psychology expressed in all

[1] Along the same lines, Aung San Suu Kyi, the Nobel prize winning opposition leader of Myanmar, once said about power and corruption in her acceptance message for the 1990 Sakharov Prize for Freedom of Thought: "It is not power that corrupts but fear. Fear of losing power corrupts those who wield it and fear of the scourge of power corrupts those who are subject to it" (July, 1991).

animals is somehow cultivated to become phantasms, sublimated phenomena, and compulsive obsessions. This is what we call here *human symbolic spinoffs of possession*, the focus of this chapter.

Affective investment into things

At the origins of the psychology surrounding possession, there is the propensity to invest feelings into things, literally falling for them like falling in love. There are deep pleasures and satisfactions underlying the experience of possession that explain much of our avidity to acquire and consume, falling prey to advertising and other branding effects. The inclination to prefer and orient our attention to individuated things and phenomena, like preferring one thing over another, is a built-in feature of any sentient beings that by definition possess feeling experience. Again, affectivity is what distinguishes us and other sentient animals from machines. Machines don't feel and have no emotions. We do. Machines may select by following algorithms. We can do the same but the difference is that we are selective with *feelings*. Our selective process is not simply mechanical. It is also affective. This is a fundamental difference: machines select, animals prefer.

Preference is selection plus an affective investment from sentient beings, those creatures that feel and are not just machines. Selective affective investment corresponds to the emotional pushes or pulls of feeling attractors, leading the animal's attention and causing it to fall for one particular object and not another. Exclusion is the necessary counterpart of such "fall."

Possession experience thus rests on feeling attractors. What determines such attractors is the big question. For example, what makes one person feel drawn toward a painting that makes another indifferent or repulsed by it. Likewise, what creates aesthetic unanimity around Vermeer or Da Vinci paintings? Siri Hustvedt writes in her 2005 essay on painting:

> Why do some works of art, even very old ones, continue to seduce viewers who know nothing or little about art theory, a work's provenance, or its cultural history? In museums, I have repeatedly seen men and women transfixed by a painting, and I presume not all of them were professional art critics. In my reading of writers as diverse as Diderot, Van Gogh, Proust, and Baudelaire, I've discovered a remarkable uniformity of emotional response to painters such as Vermeer, Chardin, and Goya. Some pictures elicit similar emotions in many viewers.[2]

At a more mundane level, an enduring mystery is why every lover discovers his incomparable princess "Dulcinea del Toboso," always finding

[2] Hustvedt, *Mysteries of the Rectangle* (Introduction, p. xx).

the right match for his own taste without too much competition. It is evident that the match made in heaven is not an elitist process, but a reality regardless of physical or mental attributes. Mutual attraction happens to the ugly as much as it happens to the handsome. In diversity, everybody ends up finding the right size shoes for their own feet.

The process of affective preferences leading eventually to the experience of possession and associated feelings of exclusivity (i.e., the fear of losing control) is a direct spinoff of feeling attractors. The question is what determines such attractors that have both universal (La Gioconda by Da Vinci) and individual characteristics ("my" woman or "my" man that I love)? In all cases, it rests on affective resonance between the sentient individual and the perceived object becoming possession. The object resonates back and forth to the perceiver creating deeper echoes, hence causing greater feeling experience compared to other objects. But it still begs the question: what determines feeling attractors?

In trying to capture what constitutes selective preference it is hard to escape circularity, describing the phenomenon by another phenomenon still begging the question. Using the sonic metaphor of affective resonance we are just moving by a notch the conceptual approximation of what selective preference and affective attractors might entail. At a sensual level, it is the experience of something that is rewarding like calm (e.g., stress reduction) or on the contrary like boosted excitement (e.g., enhanced engagement or infatuation). This experience maps on to physiological states that fuel selective preference. Whatever these rewarding states might be within the *affective grammar of the sentient individual*,[3] once attention is captured and sensual mobilization of the individual occurs, it automatically opens up a privileged interactive field between object and perceiver.

The back and forth, "bouncing" or resonating relation between object and perceiver accompanying the typical sustained attention and the perceiver's sensual mobilization creates an area of awareness enabling exclusive learning and memory. More importantly, this area allows for the growth of special bonds between perceiver and object. It enables *affective growth* between perceiver and object giving rise to exclusive preference.

[3] The nature and origins of "the affective grammar of the sentient individual" have multiple levels and are deeply rooted in the evolution of adaptive behavioral (instinct) systems that determine basic trends toward approach and avoidance responses. These responses are instinctively selective, guiding exclusive preferences for particular perceptual features of the environment (e.g., attraction or repulsion to certain rotten or appetizing tastes or smells). But beyond this basic instinctive level, humans have evolved complex (indirect and symbolic) affective syntaxes that are not comparable to what other animal species evolved, even close primate relatives, all unfolding in ontogeny with the psychological development and maturation of each child.

In common language, we often say that something or somebody "grows" on us. This is exactly what the resonating process of special bonds creation between perceiver and object is meant to capture: the growth of the object on to the person. But selective preference and special resonating bonds creation is not enough to account fully for possession and the experience of possessiveness. An extra ingredient is needed. This ingredient is *projection.*

The phenomenon of projection is the process by which perceivers not only manifest selective preference for an object, but also tend to confound its existence with their own. The object, which is objectively perceived as individuated and differentiated, begins to participate in the intimate (embodied) self-experience of the perceiver. With projection arises intimacy and fusion between perceiver and object. It is in the projective process that self and object become *confused* – in the etymological sense of blending, mingling, or mixing – and that exclusive attachment comes to life: the mark of possession psychology.

It is thus in projection that humans excel, showing deeply entrenched, compulsive propensities to project intimacy and generate obsessive, devious attachments to material things but also to animate things like pets and people they can deeply fall for. Regarding material things, humans have furthermore the strong inclination to see patterns of intentions and designs in events and things that are occurring by chance or things moving randomly like branches of a tree animated by strong wind. We tend to perceive intentional forces and causality like pushing, pulling, or lifting, inferring weight and projecting effort where there is none. In the 1940s, perception researcher Albert Michotte as well as social psychologists Fritz Heider and Marianne Simmel, in seminal studies[4] involving animated two-dimensional geometric figures like circles, squares, or triangles moving on a screen, showed that naïve adult participants spontaneously perceive and describe such events as involving protagonists "chasing," "pulling," "attacking," "dragging," or "running after" each other. All these interpretative, presumably deliberate actions are expressions of irrepressible projective propensities. They do not exist in reality, but are somehow obligatorily fantasized by the perceivers to make sense of the events as if they were necessary illusions. In the kinds of experiments used by Heider, Simmel, and Michotte, perceivers tend to feel and have irrepressible intuitions of forces and intentions where there are none. It would explain at least in part the human obsessive tendency to generate superstitious beliefs regarding ghostly intelligent designs presumably guiding what are de facto random happenings.

[4] Michotte, *The Perception of Causality*; Heider and Simmel, "An experimental study of apparent behavior."

It is hard for us to perceive and relate to things directly, without projection. Our mind is full of *necessary illusions.*[5] Human psychology is indeed not just literal and direct. It is hard for us to see without interpretation, without going beyond the information given, as in the case of shapes moving on a screen. We tend to attribute forces and intentional movements in our compulsion to make sense and create meanings. In short, for humans there is a force of evocation in what we perceive because we are non-literal and symbolic beings. This characteristic is particularly evident in human possession psychology.

Literal versus non-literal (symbolic) experience of things

Individuals across cultures demonstrate "the urgency of meaning."[6] This urgency is not simply an epistemic urge to know.[7] It is also the untamed drive found in all societies, for individuals and groups, to specify who they are. There is an obsessive urge for self-specification, the drive to distinguish oneself, to identify and recognize who we are in relation to others, the drive to specify what is our own and ultimately our worth in relation to others. The study of human cultures points to remarkable similarities in this propensity, despite great variability of material circumstances and ways of sharing values.

The incomparable syntactic power of language maps on to profound changes in subjective experience. Human unique symbolic endowment is evident in the way we communicate compared to other animals. Our communication is unmatched in its richness, creativity, and indirect (non-literal) expressiveness. It is extensively referential and intentional. From an evolutionary perspective, but also from the perspective of child development, communication is transformed from being direct and literal to become indirect and semantically infinitely connoted. The same applies, a fortiori, for subjectivity in general and the way children develop the experience of their own existence, how they relate to the world.

The subjective transformation, inaugurated by the evolution of communication into language proper, is the change from a *one-to-one* correspondence between a feeling experience and its singular cause (e.g., sensing injury corresponding to a sharp object) and a *one-to-multiple* possible causes and meanings (sensing injury caused by an object identified as a nail left behind

[5] This concept is borrowed from my friend Michael Heller. See Heller, *Body Psychotherapy*.

[6] "l'urgence du sens"; see Augé, *Le sens des autres*.

[7] Rigo, *Conscience occidentale et fables océaniques* (see the chapter on the problematic of meaning, and p. 126 in particular).

by an unscrupulous co-worker who intended to hurt me or who maybe dropped it accidentally, etc.).

The symbolic/linguistic endowment that is a special adaptation of our species changed the phenomenal experience of being in the world. It made this experience unlike the experience of non-symbolic, non-grammatical, and non-syntactic animals. Language renders the phenomenal experience of being alive in this world infinitely more complex. In relation to possession, the symbolic endowment associated with language opened the symbolic floodgates by which we, like no other animal, let objects participate in our lives, and how we are inclined to possess them and, in turn, how we let them *possess us*.

The symbolic functioning underlying syntactic and creative language changed the way our ancestors started relating to things, in the present, but also in the past and in the future. It also changed how our ancestors started relating to one another. Let it be clear that human symbolic capacity expressed in syntactic, intentional, and referential language is profoundly different from the complex and highly adaptive signaling systems other animals evolved in their communication. The latter is in essence automatic, instinctive, and direct; in other words rigid, for the most part non-creative and non-conventional.

Human language, in contrast, is no rigid communication, but allows for the reference to all possible things in the world, material or immaterial like ideas or beliefs. Human language, as opposed to any other forms of communication, is in essence *intentional*. It requires the basic understanding that others have intentions: whether the intention is to help, to convert, to agree, or to do harm. By "intentions" and "intentional" (thorny concepts) what is meant here is the representation of plans for actions that are projected into the future and can be reflected in reference to the past. Communication in other animals, in principle, does not require such an *intentional stance*.[8]

Vervet monkeys in the wild emit different alarm calls when threatened by a snake, an eagle, or a lion. Con-specifics are observed responding appropriately, hence adaptively, to the kind of predator by either climbing a tree or hiding in a bush.[9] We could argue that in such instances nonhuman creatures grasp the referential meanings of the calls. It is possible, and researchers are still debating this possibility. However, the remarkable

[8] The intentional stance is a concept coined by philosopher Daniel Dennett, trying to capture the abstract levels we tend to perceive in the behavior of animate or inanimate objects in terms of mental properties (intentions, beliefs, moods, etc.). See Dennett, *The Intentional Stance*.

[9] Seyfarth, Cheney, and Marler, "Vervet monkey alarm calls."

communicative skills of vervet and other monkeys, although referential, do not necessarily entail intentionality. It would be a long stretch to consider that the monkey that sees an eagle does indeed engage in calling with the intention or internal representation of the goal to alarm the others. The individual probably does it instinctively and its companions respond to the call in the same way. It might be construed as referential semantic communication, but it is unquestionably, by and large, rigid and automatic. Human communication is not, because is it is both semantic and referential as well as intentional: it is intended to have meaning for someone "about" something. It is in essence triadic (me–other–object). The "aboutness" and the intentional stance defining human language are a major constraint on the special ways we relate to things. They are also at the roots of the human "urgency of meaning."

Without both referential (semantic) and intentional communication, the experience of the world is literal. It is literal in the sense that a chair is a chair that affords sitting and a carrot is a carrot that affords feeding. With human combined referential and intentional communication, a chair becomes much more than an object affording sitting or a carrot an object affording feeding. With human language and symbolic endowment, objects can stand for any other things, sometimes the most abstract concepts. A carrot can become the symbol of a club (rabbit owners) or of a rally against genetically engineered crops. A chair can become a stylish statement with particular political and economic connotations (e.g., the throne of a king or the Popemobile). Plural representations or polysemantics attached to things obviously change the way we experience them. A good example is art.

For a novice eye or an inexperienced ear, most contemporary art is noise with basically no other meanings than being, boring, irritating, and not even funny, a presumptuous, useless nuisance. Like wine, it is an acquired taste. It does take education and exposure to distinguish and debate values about Bordeaux. It takes practice and learning to capture harmony and coherent meanings in modern jazz, serial music, or conceptual sculptures. There is typically more than meets the novice ear or eye, if we trust that most recognized artists are not just impostors, but rather highly sophisticated individuals.

The point is that the experience of things changes as a function of the *layers of meanings* we are able to detect. A first layer is literal, the direct, implicit perception of the thing as a thing, the way it looks or feel, but also what it affords for action. This is the experience of the world of non-linguistic, non-referential/symbolic beings. Obviously, this experience is sufficient for beings to adapt in remarkably sophisticated ways and survive in their niche.

Literal beings perform exquisite actions and other social feats, migrating in flocks over huge distances (birds), reconciling and making peace (chimpanzees), or building and operating collectively shelters that are more like highly efficient factories (bees and their hives). Also, it does not prevent them from anticipating and expecting things to happen that they learned would happen from past experience. There is memory and some expectation expressed in most literal beings. However, the world of things is experienced in a straightforward and rigid manner compared to the non-literal, symbolic, referential beings we humans evolved to be. Our subjective experience of possession is a reflection of this added symbolic sophistication.

In ontogeny, we are literal at the outset. Human children develop to become symbolic and to relate symbolically with things in the world. By the second year, with the emergence of conventional language that is learned quickly with an explosion of new words for things, children take off from the literal approach to the world. They pass a symbolic threshold that profoundly changes their outlook on things, the fact that a thing can stand and represent something else. It is a world of dual representations where a thing is a thing but can also be above and beyond it, something else. A stuffed bundle of material standing for a real baby, some marks on a physical piece of paper standing for the map of a country. With the emergence of multilayered and encasing representations, things come to be experienced simultaneously as what they are in the here and now of perception, and the multiple ways they can signify and *re-present*.

It is true that our close relatives like chimpanzees can learn very quickly to search for food in their compound that they have seen being referred to on a video screen, for example.[10] We could argue that they possess a dual representational capacity in the sense that they can refer the image on the screen to the real space of their compound. In this sense, they would detect "aboutness" in what they see on the screen, drawing an analogy between the virtual and the real. However, if chimpanzees can quickly detect the referential aspects of things, this is very limited. In the same way, chimpanzees like many other non-primate species may behave by pretending, with the apparent intention of deceiving a competitor (e.g., hiding food at various "pretend" locations), but such actions remain very rudimentary and non-generative of open-ended meanings, as is the case in the pretense of young children from their third year.

Although this issue remains highly controversial, it is hard to argue that nonhuman animals, even our close primate relatives, are not showing the degree of reality suspension one can typically witness in children from 2 or 3 years of age, as they begin to be generative not only in their pretense, but also in their teases, lies, cover ups, and budding humor. The intentional

[10] See for example Poss and Rochat, "Referential understanding of videos in chimpanzees (*Pantroglodytes*), orangutans (*Pongo pygmaeus*), and children (*Homo sapiens*)."

dual representation and symbolic conventions developed by children to communicate are also a major determinant in and inseparable from the unique ways humans *possess* and ultimately *get possessed* by objects: their symbolic spinoffs, as we shall see.

Within the context of human communication, objects become symbolic vehicles of non-literal meanings, in addition to how they appear in the here and now of perception. As articulated by pioneer linguist De Saussure (1857–1913),[11] there is a differentiation between the *signifier* (the essence or materiality of the thing itself) and the *signified* (what the thing might stand for or mean). With a dual representational capacity, the experience of a sound by the individual endowed with this capacity is more than meets the ears. It is a sound that has the potential for an infinite range of meanings, not only in relation to the context in which it is uttered and heard, but also in relation to previous sounds (i.e., in relation to a "grammar" of sounds like words in a sentence). With this capacity in place, at the level both of comprehension but also of production via intentional speech acts, the sound is now experienced in its limitless potentiality for meanings. It is limitless in relation to other sounds, other things, and other contexts. More importantly, from a psychological and phenomenal perspective, the experiential nature of the sound changes.

The symbolic step taken by children from around 2 years of age is not only a major cognitive step in their development, it is a phenomenological revolution. It explains our unique ways as a species of accumulating possessions, adorning things, worshiping inanimate objects, or collecting. All these very human propensities are linked to the fact that we are symbolic experiencers, knowers, and communicators. In our human minds, a rose is not just a rose, it is a Pandora's box of meanings. It is a fragrant, colorful, and thorny thing that can stand for beauty, passion, or threat. It can also stand for freedom and solidarity in the context of socialist movements from France to Poland. The same applies to possessions: a car is a metallic colorful object on wheels that can stand for much more than the object it is and its functionality as a vehicle: it becomes a dream and part of the individual's deliberate construction of self-presentation in society.

Objects' peculiar participation in our lives

Human subjective experience of the world is thus special, in many ways not comparable to the experience of other animals. This is of course hard to prove empirically, but we can speculate. In all probability it is a true

[11] Saussure, F. de, *Ecrits de linguistique générale*.

statement because we, unlike any other animals, communicate with each other with intentions, constantly inventing new ways of conveying *meanings* about things, which in themselves become objects of thoughts, ideas, and feelings. The intention in humans is not only to convey information, but also to negotiate meanings: to convince, and eventually agree on things that are abstract like the values or prices of things or their relative beauty. This changes the ways we experience the world of things compared to other animals. It is what can be called a *great symbolic transformation.*

Intentional communication determines a public or collective experience of the world, a world made of things that have open-ended meanings to be shared, but more importantly to be negotiated with others. This collective experience of the world determines, I propose, the peculiar ways objects participate in our lives. No other species adorns objects and worships them. No other species accumulates and fights over objects the way we do.

When dealing with objects in a literal way as all animals tend to do, the character of experience is essentially functional and mainly utilitarian. It is linked to the use of the object in relation to direct functional goals (dominating, feeding, mating). The phenomenal experience can be construed as direct, in the same way that we experience the racket we hold while playing tennis or the obstacle we maneuver around while hiking so as not to lose balance. It entails little or no contemplative reflection or inner deliberation, no elbowroom for thinking.

When objects are experienced not only in the stream of functional actions but also potentially in the stream of intentional communication, the phenomenal experience is transformed in radical ways. Things are now objects of communication, in addition to being associated with the experience of personal use, personal action, personal protection, and covetousness: they become represented in a triadic way with *others in mind.*[12]

The human experience of the communicative potential of things profoundly changes the way we relate to them as a species. This change is both cognitive and affective. It has also transformed our sensibility to non-self entities (things) in deep cultural and historical ways. Cases in point abound, some more glorious than other.

During the crusades, the sepulcher of a prophet in Jerusalem (Christ's tomb) became an obsession for generations of medieval antagonistic believers. Thousands died voluntarily or were massacred for what literally is a burial site. In Santeria and other voodoo cults, a chicken or a doll is magically transformed into a powerful source of social spells and individual healing. At a more mundane level, collectibles are endlessly hoarded. We

[12] For further discussion, see Rochat, *Others in Mind.*

surround ourselves with decorative objects. We collect memorabilia and other nostalgic relics of our past that we experience as intimate "belongings." There is an insatiable human propensity to invest in objects as reminders of our own roots and of who we are: totems, flags, wealth, food, outfits, and other costumes adorning our bodies. Objects and artifacts stand for impressions we project. They are part of our public (visual and sensory) identity. We use them to advertise our taste and aesthetic experience.

The Holy Sepulcher in Jerusalem is endowed with prophetic symbolic power. Bones became the symbol of a group affiliation around a spiritual identity, an enormously consequential leap of faith and meaning. Such a symbolic leap is linked to intentional communication, itself inseparable from how objects participate in our lives – the main source, I would suggest, of our peculiar cultivation of and attachment to things, including people.

In worshiping relics or collecting objects, possessors become possessed. The physical object, once transformed into a cult or a collectible thing, comes to possess the individual. There is compulsion associated with it, like millions of worshipers kneeling daily in front of a crucifix, or orienting to kneel and pray twice a day toward Mecca, the place in Saudi Arabia where lies the small black cubic building which is the Holy Kaaba. More mundane are the irrational resources sometimes invested to add missing items to a collection: paintings, stamps, shoes, butterflies, any imaginable physical object. Some even collect lovers. There are endless examples of the uniquely human ways by which items become objects of contemplation, worship, and obsession. With the human great symbolic transformation, objects gained "psychic power," reaching new, incomparable controlling influence over individuals and collectivities. From a historical and sociological perspective, obsession with material objects and their accumulation was further amplified with the rise of consumer society during the second industrial revolution of the nineteenth century.[13]

The basic idea, once again, is that when things begin to be experienced potentially as representations of other things that can be shared with others, the relation we have with these things changes. We begin to project representations into them, representations that we intend to be shared with others: the symbol of a particular relational alliance or group affiliation as in the case of the shared representations associated with a flag, or with the totem poles of small traditional societies all over the world. They can also be symbols of social status or reputation, as in the case of an expensive car or a particular type of garment. The fact is that the environment we grow in is filled with objects such as totem poles, flags, and bow ties. They all have an

[13] See the book by consumer analyst and theorist R. W. Berk, *Collecting in a Consumer Society*.

indirect symbolic function attached to them. We can climb a totem pole or blow our nose on the bow tie of our neighbor, but this is not the norm and what they stand for. There are shared meanings or representations invested in these things, and this is what children learn. In development, we all had to learn the shared meanings of things in addition to their literal affordances. We learned to detect representations that, over generations, evolved to be collectively recognized as semantic norms. In this process, the physical reality of the object is transformed into a social one, one that is identifiable and shared with others. A baby raised alone on a hypothetical plentiful island could not be subject to any such symbolic transformation.

One could argue that attachment to things and what they represent is not peculiar to our species. After all, dogs have their favorite toys and baby monkeys prefer a substitute mother that is soft and warm to a machine that feeds them *ad libitum*.[14] All mammalian pups latch to their mother's breast and younglings of most species get imprinted with the stamp of a compulsive attachment to their mother. In this sense, things in the environment can participate in obsessive ways in the life of other animals.

However, the nature of human attachment to things and our obsessions are profoundly different. It is different because there is the element of open-ended *intentionality* in the way we communicate and learn from others. This particularity is inseparable from the human capacity for conventional, referential, or triadic language. It is inseparable from the capacity to contemplate things with the intention to communicate about them, or to read intentions in them.

The dog may be protective and "jealous" of his squeaky rubber duck but it would be a long stretch to impute the dog with the capacity to represent that it is a playful thing *meant* to stand for a real bird. Dogs do not make the ontological distinction between toy and non-toy artifacts. They don't possess a concept of toy versus non-toy objects. They chew the rubber ducky as they would the sofa or a bone. For the dog, these things are literally chewable artifacts that are more or less pleasurable in texture and noise. Children quickly learn to make the difference between natural objects and artifacts, beyond their literal affordances. By at least the second year, they get attuned to and discriminate the culturally shared meanings attached to artifacts, beyond their physical characteristics. We would be hard pressed to claim that dogs and other animals do the same, even if human pets may be pushing the limits by virtue of the necessity that they depend upon, and hence have to adapt to, the cultural environment of their intentional and symbolic human "masters."

[14] Harlow, "The nature of love."

Pet owners cannot resist talking to and interacting with their animals in referential and intentional ways. In return, their pets adapt to a human, intentional environment and, in their adaptation, pick up intentional cues, giving an impression that they themselves are intentional in their communication. But these are arguably only subjective and projective impressions on our part. Dogs, as for all other nonhuman animals, do not experience the same urgency of meanings. They may be tricked and scared by fake (pretend) artifacts standing for real predators like scarecrows, but they cannot construe the actual *intent* behind the design of such fake artifacts (the intentional pretense design of scaring off scavenger animals).

In summary, objects participate in human lives beyond their direct functional utility. They become endowed with symbolic connotations that are far, sometimes very far, removed from literal physical appearances or potential uses for straightforward survival. These connotations are social and intentional, socially learned and intentionally shared. Shiny red high-heel shoes or bottled water from the remote South Pacific island of Fiji purchased at a fancy food market in New York are not just shoes to walk or water to drink. Advertisers know this too well, intentionally signifying elusive concepts such as lust, glamour, or purity. They know it and they are right because we are universal suckers for such indirect messages, under the spell of the "urgency of meaning" and the urgency to respond to things beyond their literal sense: for what they symbolically connote as phantasms of our desires and the projections they call for in our fertile imagination. This contributes to the peculiar ways objects participate in our lives, the propensity to impute vital and intentional forces to material things. With this propensity, we bring physical objects to life and tend to endow unintentional creatures with intentions. At a social level, objects as possession also tend to become an intrinsic part of the symbolic capital that defines our status and reputation in relation to others.

Symbolic capital

Objects as possession do participate in the construction of our social renown and reputation. Through education, networking, and resources, we build not only wealth and material comfort, but also a symbolic endowment that is part of our social prestige and positioning in relation to others. To capture this phenomenon, sociologist Pierre Bourdieu (1930–2002)[15] introduced the concept of *symbolic capital.* He writes:

[15] Bourdieu, "The social space and the genesis of groups."

The position of a given agent within the social space can thus be defined by the positions he occupies in the different fields, that is, in the distribution of the powers that are active within each of them. These are, principally, economic capital (in its different kinds), cultural capital and social capital, as well as *symbolic capital*, commonly called prestige, reputation, renown, etc., which is the form in which the different forms of capital are perceived and recognized as legitimate. (p. 724, italics added)

The symbolic capital of individuals and groups is measurable and does not simply correspond to subjective experience. It is inter-subjective by nature as it refers to how someone is evaluated by others, or might imagine she is. It materializes in various marks of distinction such as manners and tastes, but also in physical possessions like medals of honor, or symbols of wealth and social ascendance signified by particular houses, cars, clothes, club memberships, and other socially acknowledged badges of particular social standing. Referring to the nineteenth-century novels of Jane Austen, Bourdieu talks of symbolic capital as collections of "legitimized impostures."[16] These impostures are legitimized by whoever is recognized as the incarnation of absolute authority, typically some incarnation of the state. The state is recognized by all, as the legal usurper of an authority to perform what amounts, following Bourdieu, to the "symbolic violence" of sanctioning merits of ownership, deciding who should be honored, who should have, and in general who has social ascendancy in a hierarchy,[17] as in the case of the nomination of judges, magistrates, educators, and other pivotal positions in society. It is also on the basis of such recognized absolute authority that the symbolic capital of individuals and groups materializes and can accumulate as publicly recognized marks of distinction such as titles and diplomas.

The symbolic capital possessed by individuals in a society (i.e., what is considered more or less reputable and enviable in that person) remains

[16] "A woman must have a thorough knowledge of music, singing, drawing, dancing and the modern languages, to deserve the word, and besides all this, she must *possess* a certain something in her air and manner of walking, the tone of her voice, her address and expressions, or the word will be but half deserved": Caroline Bingley defining an "accomplished" woman in Jane Austen, *Pride and Prejudice*, chapter 8.

[17] Bourdieu writes: "The state, which produces the official classification, is in one sense the supreme tribunal to which Kafka refers in *The Trial* when Block says to the attorney who is to be one of the 'great attorneys': Of course, anybody can say he is 'great', if he likes to, but in these matters the question is decided by the practices of the court ... The legal consecration of symbolic capital confers upon a perspective an absolute, universal value, thus snatching it from a relativity that is by definition inherent in every point of view, as a view taken from a point in social space," in "Social space and symbolic power," p. 22. Along the same lines, Bourdieu writes: "The President of the Republic is someone who pretends to be the President of the Republic, but unlike the mentally insane who pretends to be Napoleon, he is *recognized* to have ground for it," in *Raisons pratiques*, p. 122 (no italics in original; translated by the author).

relatively stable from generation to generation. The probability that the son of a chief will become a chief is high. Bourdieu's empirical work on French society demonstrates clearly, for example, that the state laws and social practices (i.e., education) preserve the reproduction and transmission of class habitus, from distinctive ways of holding a fork to the *cursus honorum* (course of honors) that is the acquisition of schooling and of educational qualifications. Symbolic personal possessions like medals, diplomas, or any other selective badges of honor and recognition are warrants of rites of passage that are socially recognized (e.g., finishing high school or getting a diploma from an elite school). Such symbolic possessions are a source of social recognition and class distinction, the main source also of our ways of parsing and thinking about the social world.

The transmission of habitus as social-cultural predispositions occurs at the level of the individual over developmental time, but also at the level of the group over historical time.[18] It is the enduring source of social class stratification in terms of rich versus poor, educated versus less educated, affluent versus less affluent, etc., becoming the source not only of injustice, but also of our cognitive categories by which we, as social agents, think abstractly about our social surroundings.

The work of Bourdieu demonstrates that family and birth circumstances determine the inheritance of practical as well as cognitive predispositions to navigate the social world. This inheritance rests on the transgenerational transmission of habitus that tends to be maintained and even reinforced by institutions like schools.

The actual value of each individual item of symbolic capital (titles, diplomas, experience, curriculum vitae and other résumés, exploits, talent, economic wealth) is actually for the most part circumstantial. It is relative to each society's particular stratification and where possessors of such capital fall within the stratum of their sociocultural circumstances. What is symbolically valuable as possession and what constitute a symbolic capital at one social level often is not so at another level of society. Reputation and prestige tend to have different meanings depending on social class and economic circumstances, some emphasizing pride in diplomas and educational achievements, others emphasizing pride in becoming an excellent independent worker or productive artisan. It is not uncommon that the working classes look down on the intellectuals and vice versa, an expression of categorical habitus that is determinant of tastes and distinctiveness, hence variable values and variable relevance of symbolic capital, what makes someone reputable and renowned within his group.

[18] See in particular Pierre Bourdieu's 1984 book *Distinction: A Social Critique of the Judgement of Taste.*

Taste, aesthetics, and what is considered a valuable possession are determined in great part by inter-subjective agreements that are negotiated within a particular social stratum. Popular art is distinct and deliberately maintained as distinct by intellectuals who protect their elite status by marking their distinctive, educated taste, often spoofing or looking down at what they see as vulgar and uneducated art, even if they pretend to love it.[19]

It is a fact, well demonstrated by Bourdieu, that possession carries with it a symbolic capital, the complex mark of individual as well as class prestige and reputation, all of which is sanctioned by institutions and norms that are recognized by all. Symbolic capital is the complex referential veneer that is inseparable from human possession. The fact is that what we own and feel we possess is not just what we have and control in exclusivity, but also the prestige and reputation it represents in the eyes of others. When I buy a lamp, it is not just to get more lights in my apartment. It is also to shed light on my style and taste in furnishing my place. A major symbolic spinoff of possession is the complex prestige connotation, the symbolic capital that it stands for.

Rituals of possession transfer

In the United States, it is striking to see that when someone purchases a house, becoming a homeowner, she tends to be systematically congratulated by whoever knows about it. In this culture, becoming a homeowner is initiatory, an achievement, a major step forward in someone's life toward the fulfillment of the American Dream, an elusive symbolic spinoff in that culture. For a foreigner who grew up in rentals, it is strange even if he could afford it. Here is what tends to happen in the European mind: why would you congratulate someone who has probably contracted an enormous mortgage and burdened herself with a major debt load for many years to come? But to have your name on a real estate deed is a rite of passage in American culture.

These kinds of ritualistic and symbolic connotations in economic transactions of possession are evident, sometimes in ostentatious ways. Ethnographies of pre-industrial societies are replete with examples of complex symbolic and cosmological rituals surrounding possession transfer. These rituals clearly demonstrate that in human cultures possession and its transfer entails much more than an economic transaction and commercial motives.

[19] See for example the work of the highly successful artist Jeff Koons, beautifying cheap popular balloon dogs by making them huge and of shiny bronze, ironically placing them in the most aristocratic and culturally distinguished environment, the château of Versailles, paradigm of the French monarchic *ancien régime*.

The German sociologist, philosopher, and political economist Max Weber (1864–1920), in his study on the origins of capitalism as an economic system based on loans and compound interest, showed that forms of human economic systems are rooted in religious beliefs, esoteric affinities, and derived ethics. In his opus on the Protestant ethic and the spirit of capitalism,[20] Weber details the link between the emergence of market-driven capitalism alongside modern nation states (still dividing the world today) and the rise of ascetic Protestantism (reformist movements) of sixteenth-century Europe promoting Christianity outside of the Catholic Church and papal authority. Weber shows how sixteenth-century German Lutheranism and French Calvinist movements shaped new banking and economic (capitalist) practices.

As a broad thinker, Weber was also interested in other religions of the world (i.e., China, India, and ancient Judaism), showing why, compared to the West, other forms of non-capitalist economic exchanges evolved in these cultures, despite radically different forms of social class organizations such as the caste system in India. In a nutshell, and relevant to human symbolic spinoffs of possession, Weber shows at a macro level that forms of human economic exchange, hence possession transfer and acquisition, are always rooted in particular cosmologies and beliefs, and the specific cultural affinities, world-views, and aesthetics expressed in religions. Human forms of economic exchange are never just rational, legal, and utilitarian, but always *symbolically transcended*, standing for deep collective intuitions regarding our place in the universe.

Prestige, honors, and the constitutive principles of our reputation, what corresponds to our symbolic capital, are also part of collective cosmologies finding major expressive outlet in rituals of possession transfer. Possession transfer across human cultures is rarely just direct and matter of fact. It tends to be highly ritualized and symbolized, as in the flamboyant and extremely lavish commercial trade shows which take place in our own industrial corner of the world, where businesses meet in vast compounds to engage in extravagant branding of their products, accompanied by lavish ritualized corporate entertainment. All of these rituals connote the symbolic capital of prestige and reputation.

The ethnographies of the Gunvinggu Aborigine people of northern Australia (Western Arnhem Land) demonstrate the extent to which human possession transfer and the bartering rituals of goods among neighboring communities are complex and intertwined with prestige and reputation symbolism. Ethnographies of the 1950s show that these

[20] Weber, *The Protestant Ethic and the Spirit of Capitalism.*

people engage in so-called Dzamalag rituals in which the bartering of goods (tobacco in particular) is accompanied with singing and dancing, but also sexual favors and the swapping of women. During these exchanges of goods, women approach males of the other group, seducing them publicly for quick copulation in the bushes (bush sex).[21] Once again, clearly, what is expressed is not mere commercial profit and advantage in the transfer of possession, but much deeper social transactions.

Anthropologist David Graeber describes this phenomenon in his 2011 book on the human evolution of debt as the fundamental process by which social bonds are asserted, constantly created and re-created at a symbolic and representational level, through gift exchange and elaborated expressions of *general sociability* via dances and other sex rituals. This symbolic spinoff of possession transfer corresponds also to the ritual gift exchanges found in Polynesian and Melanesian cultures, as well as in the Potlatch celebrations of Native Americans of the Pacific Northwest that are described in the pioneer ethnographies of Franz Boas (1858–1942).

Another, most telling example is the symbolic group rituals performed by Toraja people, a group of about half a million people living in the mountains of South Sulawesi in Indonesia.[22] Until roads were built and the tourist industry invaded the region in the early 1980s, the life of the Toraja revolved naturally around very elaborate funeral rituals. There were and still are lavish days of celebration and gift transactions surrounding the burial of the dead. These celebrations take months, sometimes years to prepare, the corpse being kept in the family house until the funeral and actual burial are set, the deceased is prepared for his journey to the afterlife, and enough wealth is accumulated. The burial preparation entails a major accumulation of highly valuable goods, in particular water buffaloes, pigs, and chickens. Meat among the Toraja is the most valuable commodity and its possession is a measure of wealth.

Funeral celebrations are for family members rare occasions for massive donations and exchanges of meat as gifts. During these celebrations, sometimes tens of buffaloes and hundreds of pigs and chickens are sacrificed, their blood being drunk in an impressive and sudden orgy of throat slitting and stabbing. The village main square is typically soaked in blood. Among the sacrificed animals, some are brought by guests as gifts. After the killing, the meat is carefully distributed between villagers and guests, every single piece being accounted for in a precise and systematic

21 Ethnographies of the 1950s by Australian anthropologist Ronald Berndt, referred to and discussed in relation to barter in Graeber, *Debt*.

22 Thank you to my friend Pierre Masson of Librairie des Alpes, rue de Seine in Paris, for pointing out this ethnographic fact.

recording for future gift reciprocation. The exact amount and quality of meat donation is noted all through the celebration among much singing and dancing.

The celebration ends with the actual burial of the dead in dug-out caves on the face of a cliff, a sort of vertical cemetery. At the entrance of each cave are carved wooden human effigies lining up on a balcony, representing the dead, dressed and exposed, looking out to the land with one arm reaching out to receive from the gods, the other to give.

What is of interest to us is the remarkable juxtaposition of a major possession transfer with highly symbolic rituals around a whole cosmology. It is another great example of the symbolic spinoff of human possession psychology.

The same juxtaposition of highly symbolic, lavish funeral rituals and carefully recorded possession transfer in terms of gift exchange are observed all over the South Pacific, in Micronesia and Melanesia but also in Polynesia, particularly Samoa, which is still very traditional and continues to be a major fieldwork area for anthropologists since the seminal work of Margaret Mead in the 1920s. The main function of such juxtaposition is to mark the social obligations of future gift exchange, in an endless circle of reciprocation. Death and the mourning of the dead become an opportunity to create social debts, assert social bonds and foster alliances outside of the village and the immediate family circle. In these cultures, rituals of possession transfer in the context of funerals, but also births and weddings, are a major source of social harmony.

If across cultures possession transfer tends to be symbolically ritualized, such ritualization varies greatly. In today's global economy, it continues to vary, divorced from the mere rational profit logic and consequences that economists continue to consider as the driving force, the *invisible hand* of the market first evoked by Adam Smith (1723–90) in his book on the theory of moral sentiments.[23]

Evidence for this assertion is the recent fieldwork of Mayfair Mei-hui Yang on the societal changes accompanying the rapid introduction of capitalism in a coastal region of Wenzhou, Zhejiang Province, on the southeastern coast of China. It appears that the capitalist transformation of this region leading to sudden and dramatic wealth improvement actually caused some revival of ancient economic rituals that are obviously not economically rational from a purely profit-driven perspective. Here is what Mayfair Mei-hui Yang concludes from her recent study:[24]

[23] Smith, *The Theory of Moral Sentiments*.
[24] Yang, "Ritual economy and rural capitalism with Chinese characteristics."

There is an intriguing linkage between the current rural economic development of Wenzhou, Zhejiang Province, on the southeastern coast of China, with Chinese popular religiosity. Once this linkage is made, we can see that what has been taking place in this area of coastal China is not merely another penetration of capitalism, but the hybrid reconstruction of a ritual economy whose genealogy can be traced back to the late imperial Chinese commercial culture of the common people. This ritual economy involves not only the profit motive and material production based on the household unit, but also heavy investment in the cosmic ledger of merits, the sacred world of the gods and ancestors, and the Underworld of ghosts, demons, and the dreaded courts and officials of Hell . . . Here, the emphasis is not just on material investment, but also on investments into the non-productive realms of community welfare, ritual consumption, and conversion of material wealth into the currency of transcendent divine worlds. In rural Wenzhou, the local culture exerts pressure on capitalism to conform with the outlines of an ancient ritual economy, where rituals must be financed and performed, the gods must receive offerings, and wealth must be diverted from this temporary world to other more powerful and lasting realms of the cosmos. (Chapter 23)

As we can see, once again, human economics is always mixed with the veneer of esoteric representations, always tainted with superstition and various forms of *animism*. We discuss this curious phenomenon next, another cardinal feature of human "symbolic" possession psychology.

Animism

The propensity to impute vital power to physical objects is universal across cultures, arguably a human trademark. With this propensity, at the level of experience, inanimate objects but also other animals start to participate as interacting life partners. They become animate in the sense that they are experienced equally as mindful and agentive as we are, often endowed with supernatural power. Stones can become magical and endowed with the power to change the weather or cast evil spells. This is what a shaman on the island of Tanna in Vanuatu will try in all sincere credulity to convince you of. A dog becomes often the equivalent of a human companion for its "owner."

Animistic inclination changes radically the nature of attachment to and dependence on physical objects, a core aspect of possession experience. By one year, a child can already show compulsive attachment to a particular object, a favorite toy or security blanket that becomes a substitute for primary care. It is seen as helping the child to cope with separation from the mother, as psychiatrist and psychoanalyst Donald Winnicott (1896–1971) proposes, terming this kind of invested and endowed object *transitional*.[25]

[25] Winnicott, "Transitional objects and transitional phenomena."

Predilection and attachment for particular objects is pervasive in nature, but humans take it to another, exacerbated and incomparable symbolic level. The first mark of it is the representation and experience surrounding infants' transitional object experience. Likewise, it is fairly common that dogs have their favorite toy or that great apes in zoos have their favorite tyre to swing on or blanket to cover their head as they nap, as in the case of orangutans. Habits and object infatuation are indeed pervasive in the animal kingdom, but humans beyond infancy take it to another symbolic and experiential level that includes *animistic* propensities.

Etymologically, the word animism derives from the Latin word *anima*, meaning *soul*, and also from *animus* which means *principle of life*. The words *anima* and *animus* themselves have an Indo-European root (*ane*, which stands for "vital breath"). They derive also from the Greek word *anemos* which means *wind*. Figuratively speaking therefore, and based on the etymology of the word, animism is the phenomenon by which we tend to *breathe life* into physical things and events, endowing them with vital power. In the animist mind, objects come to have a life of their own.

As opposed to being mere passive objects of infatuation or affective investment, with animism objects are transmuted into interactive partners, magically becoming agents in the life of individuals. It is the psychological phenomenon by which mental states and intentions are magically infused into otherwise inanimate things. Coffee grounds or sticks of wood drawn from a bundle can be read as oracles from invisible forces; relics can protect and dispatch divine messages; ancestors can manifest themselves in mineral and wooden artifacts; stones can capture invisible energy that can be used by medicine men to heal or cast evil spells onto others. This is not just a primitive inclination. It is pervasive in our modern existence.

Superstitious and obsessive–compulsive behaviors in relation to objects are rampant across human cultures, in small traditional, pre-industrial, "primitive," or "archaic societies," but also in today's hypermodern world. People cannot help but read horoscopes, or engage in all kinds of implicit or explicit superstitions whereby objects and artifacts are experienced as endowed with invisible power that can determine individual and group destinies. Our animistic propensities are pervasive, regardless of culture and education. They persist more than ever in our global, hypermodern era. Tokyo businessmen turn off their hi-tech cell phones to go to the Shinto shrines, communicating with their ancestors and praying for the protection of their business. They ring bells and burn incense, just like businessmen in Moscow attending services bathed in thick odorous smoke at their church, high-tech people continuing to engage in communion by eating a small piece of bread and drinking a sip of wine, that in the context of the church ritual is magically transmuted into the body and blood of Christ.

Animism is indeed pervasive at all levels of human life, from individual superstitions and projections, to elaborate group rituals, traditions, and collective beliefs. As suggested earlier, what humans have in common and what is putatively the cardinal trademark of the species is *communicative intention*. As a probable by-product, we cannot help reading intentions into things. There is a pervasive tendency in humans to *animate the inanimate*. As French anthropologist Marc Augé says:[26] "One must animate to make sense." We need to breathe life into things to capture their meanings in our lives, and, inversely, the meaning of who we are in relation to them. Augé shows how *obligatory* the representation of God into metal and wooden objects is for native tribes of Benin in Africa. He concludes that this kind of animism is obligatory to the extent that "these people think." Again, the idea is that the projection of meanings into material things is a natural human way to reflect on our situation in the universe, but also in the society of people we end up living with. Humans are indeed a uniquely self-conscious and reputable species.[27]

Totems or flags serve as collective rallying points. Mundane and pervasive items become ostentatious objects of adornment in every human society to signify status, for example fancy shoes, jewelry, makeup, or stretch limousines. The meaning of these objects is more than the expression of comfort, beauty, or utility. They help individuals to think their situation in relation to others. They are vehicles of reputation, empowered with such representations as a symbolic capital. As objects of desire, objects of envy, or trophy objects, they become agents in our lives. Particularly in our modern consumer societies, objects become a central focus of individuals' worship, replacing the more collective relics of pre-modern, traditional societies.[28]

With the rocketing progress of technology and social networking, objects clearly play an increasing interactive role in our lives (i.e., the recent global invasion of screens, from smart phones to tablets across cultures). In many ways, animism is not replaced but is gaining momentum in our hypermodern times. As machines get "smarter," we experience them increasingly as agent entities in our lives. We have created great

[26] Augé, *Le sens des autres*. [27] This is the premise of my previous book, *Others in Mind*.

[28] Guy Debord provides a decisive critique of merchandise and commodities as fetishes and bizarre objects of desires. Merchandise dominates the life of the post-industrial individual who is essentially reduced to consumption, a consumer, a person alienated to the logic of an explosive free market economy, who lives and adapts to exponential abundance of products and media appeals, surviving in a society of consumption: Debord, *The Society of the Spectacle*.

technological dependencies, affective attachments to our numerous tools, ending up finding meanings and directions in our lives through them.

All human societies have fabricated cultural institutions that imbue objects with power that could be functionally channeled by special people in the group (priest, shaman, medicine man, sorcerer or sorceress). Once mastered and channeled, this power could be used to cause good or evil, predict and plan future events within the group, or tame supernatural powers (with offerings and animal sacrifices, for example). In the same way, we could say that in our modern high-tech societies, objects such as smart phones, software programs, cars, or computers are imbued with a power that impacts our lives for a handful of money and no shamanic mediation. The cult of objects and animist trends are alive and well in modern consumerism, in some respects growing exponentially with the high dependency on new technologies.[29]

One could argue that, contrary to stones, skulls, and feathers attached to wooden sticks, computers, software, smart phones, and other modern artifacts have measurable power. This is probably correct from an engineering perspective. It is certainly incorrect from a phenomenal and psychological viewpoint. The force of human beliefs is incommensurable from the deterministic perspective of engineering theories, for example the belief system of the shaman manipulating stones to control the weather or tame the eruption of a volcano on his island (heard from a shaman on the island of Tanna in Vanuatu, during the author's multiple visits to the island between 2003 and 2010). Such a belief system is collective, shared by all members of the group, as real and powerful in its societal impact as the growing capacity of electronic machines in our high-tech societies. Shamanism and consumerism are both expressions of human animistic propensities and both are equally real and potent in the life of individuals.

From the general human propensity toward animism, the process by which we endow material objects with vital power, derives another major human symbolic spinoff of possession: *fetishism*.

Fetishism

French psychologist Alfred Binet (1857–1911) is best known for putting together the first quantitative assessment of mental capacities (i.e., the Binet-Simon IQ test still used today in updated versions). Less known is the fact that Binet was much more than the engineer of a tool to differentiate and sort out individuals based on their ability to solve abstract

[29] Again, for more elaboration, see Debord, *The Society of the Spectacle*.

problems or think logically. He was an eclectic thinker, with passionate curiosity about a wide range of psychological phenomena. He wrote about chess masters, but also on fetishism in sexuality.[30]

Fetishism is a concept widely used in a range of disciplines, from psychoanalysis, psychiatry, and the anthropology of religions, to economics (i.e., Karl Marx's idea of "commodity fetishism" in his critique of capitalism[31]). In the realm of psychology, the term as relating to human sexuality is attributed to Alfred Binet, later picked up by Freud and followers. Binet was in fact the first to identify and think in detail about the psychological process underlying the phenomenon. He describes fetishism as the creation of a sign that serves for a whole, complex, and compulsive representation laced with intense emotions. These emotions are often linked to irrepressible sexual desires and excitement. After identifying the phenomenon, Binet provides compelling individual cases as illustrations that all have in common the fixation and *appropriation* of one element as standing for a whole complex system of intense erotic representations.

Isolated body parts such as feet, breasts, or hair, or objects that are physical negatives of body parts like shoes, bra, or panties, become objects of intense sexual desire, representing the whole. In fetishism, one becomes compulsively enthralled with these objects, conflating their perception (visual, tactile, or olfactory) with sexual urges and desires. Fetishism is some kind of abstract reduction of the whole to one of its part, a smell, a shoe, a lump of hair, an anonymous rub of the body against another body in a crowd. Following Binet, it is a phenomenon by which a singular object or individuated aspect of a whole experience becomes a *thing* of sexual fixation and desire. In relation to possession, the fetishist might be compelled to collect things pertaining to his or her fixation. If these things are of a straightforward sexual nature, they become substitutes for sexual partners, orgasm being achieved through them or in contact with them. Fetishists are described as becoming exclusively

[30] Binet, "Du fétichisme dans l'amour."

[31] Karl Marx coins the term fetishism to capture how social relationships among people somehow become *transformed* or reified into economic commodities and exchange values, everything becoming linked to production and trade relationships. Commodity fetishism is the curious process by which social relationships are transformed and objectified into economic, trade value. Marx writes: "fetishism ... is therefore inseparable from the production of commodities": *Capital*, vol. 1. Capturing the same fetishistic process as some sort of subjective reification of value (value production and objectification), Carl Menger, another economist of the nineteenth century, writes: "Value is, therefore, nothing inherent in goods, no property of them, but merely the importance that we first attribute to the satisfaction of our needs, that is, to our lives and well-being, and in consequence carry over to economic goods as the exclusive causes of the satisfaction of our needs": *Principles of Economics*, chapter 3. I call this the fetishism which attaches itself to the products of labor as soon as they are produced as commodities.

aroused by such substitute objects, leading them to behave and be compelled to behave in eccentric ways relative to social norms. This eccentricity can be for individuals a source of guilt and much suffering. Binet describes for example in detail the case of a respectable and distinguished Latin professor who, on his way to give a class, is suddenly compelled to follow a red haired woman in the streets of Paris, enthralled by her smell. This erotic compulsion leads the dignified professor to the point of kneeling and putting his nose under the door of the woman's apartment after she has disappeared behind it.

In fetishism, things or part of things (a smell as in the case of Binet's Latin professor, a hair color, a shoe) become *cult objects*, objects of fixation in the animist sense of being endowed with psychic power and uncontrollable attraction. There is an urge to endow them with the power of sexual desire, taking individuals to the brink, and strong enough to derail them from habitual, socially accepted ways of behaving.

The word "fetish," and its derivative "fetishism," comes from the Latin word *facere*, literally meaning *to make*, *to do*, or *to fabricate*. The etymology of fetishism points to the psychological act of creating objects or symbols that stand for other things. In the case of fetishism, things stand for a whole complex of desires and strong affective (i.e., sexual) arousal. As indicated by the title of his article "Du fétichisme dans l'amour" [Fetishism in love], Binet dealt with the issue exclusively in the sexual realm. But the psychological phenomenon can be enlarged to encompass the compulsive process by which we tend, in general, to invest strong affective values into material things that we possess, but that also possess us in the way we compulsively hold on to them.

Fetishism as a concept and a psychological phenomenon goes far beyond paraphernalia and other deviant sexual behaviors. It captures something fundamental about human possession, ultimately the human sense of property and entitlement. There are at least three reasons to draw an analogy between the clinical approach to fetishism and possession in general.

The first and major reason is the *symbolic creation* by which an object can come to stand for a complex and overwhelming affective experience: strong sexual arousal in the cases studied by Binet where objects are objectified, eventually collected (e.g., shoes or any other paraphernalia hoarded and accumulated).

The second reason is the *compulsive aspect* of fetishism as process of symbolic creation. Both clinical fetishism and possession have a compulsive component. Both share this obligatory aspect. We tend to experience ownership and entitlement in the same intense and compulsive way we might get sexually aroused by a particular part of the body or a particular kind of artifact.

Finally, the third reason is the *animism* attached to both clinical fetishism and possession in general. In both instances, things are endowed with participatory power in the life of individuals. Things come to possess us as much as we possess them. They define who we are and what we do. For example, a medal is a medal, a piece of metal with a ribbon, until it is ceremoniously placed on the uniform of the soldier. From then on the medal possesses its symbolic meaning, a thing that stands for an act of bravery. It becomes part of a symbolic capital defining the soldier. Inversely, a general who is stripped of his medals feels naked, and loses his pride and reputation. Medals, once endowed with the symbolic meaning of bravery and recognition, do come to be charged with social power. It becomes part of a symbolic capital, a powerful source of personal pride or shame, but also compulsive attachment and entitlement.

Centripetal and centrifugal pathologies of possession

Extreme animistic and fetishistic tendencies linked to possession can become pathological, spinning out of control for the individual. They can translate into compulsive and obsessive behaviors that are uncontrollable, putting individuals at risk of bankruptcy and social exclusion. People lose job, family, and freedom as they spiral down into their various forms of compulsive and obsessive behaviors like gambling, stealing, hoarding, unreasonable generosity, gullibility, excessive consumerism, and debt accumulation. These are human pathologies, the "extravagances" of possession: various forms of possessive excess, some sorts of "material obesity." Mild signs of such pathologies can be seen in propensities to collect or buy to excess. Inversely, they are visible in those opting for material denudation: the vows of poverty taken by monks or nuns entering an order, hermits choosing a frugal, solitary life. All are human possession extravagances.

These spinoffs of possession can affect the mental health and social life of people, as in the case of gambling addiction, compulsive hoarding, or kleptomania, often co-morbid symptoms of bipolar disorders.[32] Clearly, pathological spinoffs of possession can have varied personal and interpersonal consequences, depending on severity but also on kind. There are, however, overarching commonalities among possession pathologies and extravagances, all sharing a *compulsive* and *obsessive* character.

[32] As a case in point, legal systems prevent such compulsive-obsessive spinoffs of possession. In France, any transfer of possession (from small to big) can be voided within two weeks, if one is shown to have purchased something under the spell of obsessive-compulsive urges associated for example with clinical depression or manic episodes.

Obviously, this account does not constitute a new diagnostic tool for clinicians, unlike the Diagnostic and Statistical Manual of Mental Disorders (DSM) that helps sort out symptoms falling into the spectrum of obsessive-compulsive disorders for therapeutic purposes. Our characterization helps us to grasp the psychological meaning of human pathological and extravagant spinoffs of possession, regardless of their clinical severity and specificity.

In general, there tends to be always a *compulsive* and *obsessive* character in possession pathologies, in the sense that they tend to be uncontrolled (compulsive) and recurrent (obsessive). Hoarders, gamblers, and kleptomaniacs all feel the untamed pressure to do it repeatedly over time. In many ways, it is like an addiction that is hard to kick, bringing people to the edge of personal and interpersonal bankruptcy.

There are two major kinds of obsessive-compulsive pathologies and extravagances of possession, each corresponding to fundamentally different psychological dynamics. They map onto Freud's account of the anal stage of psychosexual development, in particular the contrast Freud draws between anal *retentive* and *expulsive* personalities in adults. From the vantage point of psychoanalysis, Freud construed such personalities as resulting from issues surrounding toilet training in early childhood, typically around 2 years.[33]

Without endorsing Freud's interpretation, or his etiology, there are two general classes of possession pathologies and extravagances. One is characterized by an inward, *centripetal* dynamic, like hoarding, compulsive buying, collecting, or kleptomania, the other by an outward, *centrifugal* dynamic, like gambling or excessive generosity and gullibility. Closer to Freud's depiction, one dynamic is indeed retentive and the other fundamentally expulsive. However, in the context of possession, these dynamics need to be construed much more broadly than what can be derived from sphincter control and other bowel movements during childhood. That does not mean, of course, that issues surrounding toilet training are not an important opportunity for children to learn about their own bodies, how much they control their bodily functions, the limits of what is inside and outside of their bodily envelop, notwithstanding the assertion of control and obedience in relation to others, all things we shall discuss in a later chapter.

Compulsive and obsessive gambling and stealing (kleptomania) are in this respect paradigmatic of the polar opposition between *centrifugal* and *centripetal* kinds of dynamic in the pathologies and extravagances of

[33] Freud, *Three Essays on the Theory of Sexuality*.

possession. In pathological gambling, individuals are unable to control impulses to bet and gamble resources, typically leading in the long run to disastrous personal and social consequences (family, work, friendships). In the psychiatry jargon it falls into the umbrella diagnosis of impulse control disorder that resembles, but with some nuances, substance abuse and addiction. Psychologically, it displays a behavioral pattern that leads toward the untamed centrifugal (outward) distribution of possessions (money, assets, etc.) with the illusion – but only illusion and that is the core of the problem – of high returns that are always redistributed (gambled) in a vicious circle that typically ends up in material and social bankruptcy. The same pattern applies to behavioral habits, not exclusively psychiatric, characterized by extreme patterns of generosity, trust, and gullibility. These correspond to a compulsive "splurge" of possession pattern, the obsessive attempt at seducing and capturing the attention, approbation, and affectivity of others via untamed spending and donation. It is the case, for example, in the behavioral pattern of individuals throwing lavish parties in absolute denial of great financial difficulties. They often do so to cover up such difficulties, entertaining a vicious circle of personal and interpersonal delusions until it all falls apart (e.g., the Madoff pyramid scam syndrome).

In the case of religious people and other hermits taking the vow of poverty and frugal life, answering a call to dedicate their life to prayer and meditation, the dynamic is also centrifugal in the sense of breaking the possession circle by giving it all away. The difference from the extreme pattern of generosity described here is that, albeit not always, vows of poverty and frugality are regulated and validated by the norms of a cultural institution that is recognized by the larger society, such as a temple (Buddhist monks) or a monastery (Catholic orders of monks and nuns). This normative validation sets them apart from individual centrifugal patterns that often enter the realm of psychiatry.

In polar opposition, the retentive dynamic of hoarding, collecting, compulsive consumerism, or kleptomania reveals paradigm patterns of *centripetal* kinds of possession extravagance, all oriented toward an excessive inward movement of retention, accumulation, and self-incorporation of possessions. The issues associated with such extravagance become pathological in the case of obsessive hoarding. In hoarding (also called *Diogenes syndrome*) people end up suffocating under the possessions they accumulate by pathologically removing them from the normal cycle of exchanges. This is what happens when people (compulsive hoarders) keep newspapers and all sorts of trash, or, in the most extreme cases, collect their own body fluids like, reportedly, the millionaire inventor Howard Hughes who is famous for keeping the urine he produced over the years in small jars carefully labeled with time and date, stored in a room like a museum archive of organic self-production.

In the same kind of centripetal possessive compulsion, kleptomaniacs cannot help but appropriate objects for themselves, breaking the normal commercial cycle of possession transfer. Obviously, some end up being sanctioned by society, while for others, like Howard Hughes, retentive ways are regarded as simply awkward yet socially tolerated private *retentive* possession extravagances. As for the opposite, centrifugal kinds of possessive compulsion, the same applies regarding the tolerated vow of frugal life and societal exit of hermits, as opposed to the often reprehensible, debt-prone *expulsive* compulsion of gamblers. What appears to be the overarching trait of both centripetal and centrifugal kinds of possessive compulsion and obsession is the *break* in the fluidity of the normal circle of balanced (reciprocal) possession transfer. A breach in the normal reciprocity of exchanges, be they gift and counter-gift as in Kula-like circles, reciprocal commercial labor or money for goods exchange, or any other forms of barter transactions. All of them entail some sort of interpersonal reciprocity that promotes possession equilibrium over time among people, exchange reciprocity being universally a main source of social harmony across human cultures. In general, the centrifugal and centripetal dynamics of retentive or expulsive possession patterns are anomalies because they break reciprocal circles of possession transfer.

At a more intra-individual and motivational level, all these anomalies can be seen as spinoffs of the universal tendency we have to explore the limits of our control over possession. With gambling or stealing propensities, whether they remain at the level of temptation or they materialize in risky actions, we actually *conjure our basic fear and threat of losing control*: losing control over possessions in the case of gambling, losing control of our moral integrity and freedom in the case of stealing.

Linked to this conjuration, there is the basic need to specify the limits separating the experience of control from the experience of a loss of control over things, including the control of our own capacities as social agents. We always need to explore what separates the state of holding on to things from the state of letting go of them, sometimes in ways that become pathological and extravagant, breaking the normal circle of reciprocal exchanges that tends to be a source of social harmony.

In the end, the conjuration of the fear of losing control over things is universal, the true bedrock of possession psychology. In turn, this fear is itself a spinoff of the larger existential conundrum that all sentient individuals, but particularly members of our self-conscious species, have to grapple with while alive: the contrast between attachment and detachment, me and not me, mine and not mine, life and death.[34]

Decoration, ornamentation, and costly signaling

Another important aspect of the human symbolic spinoffs of possession is the unique way possessions tend to be decorated and ornamented, including one's own body. Across cultures, we put makeup on, dress up, pierce our ears, and get our skin tattooed; we paint and decorate objects we own and acquire as possessions, arrange them, and in general cultivate their visual presentation. A legitimate question is why and for what? The decoration of possession is another ostentatious way, unique to our species, of claiming ownership over things, promoting attachment and packaging values for ourselves as well as for others. It is also our unique way of specifying personal and group identities, in general our way of enhancing the symbolic capital attached to objects we own and claim control of.

There is no equivalent symbolic propensity or similar open-ended cultivation of possession in other animals. No other animals deliberately decorate their eggs, shelters, territories, or dress up for occasions and put makeup on to conceal their age. Animals are adorned as part of their fixed natural inherited attributes, selected through evolution for their adaptive fitness. The mind-boggling camouflage abilities of certain animals are part of this genetic endowment, like colorful wings adorned with eyes that scare off predators in many butterflies, or the remarkable camouflage of octopuses that change color to disappear visually, fusing with the rock beneath them. All of this is part of literal appearances to which predators respond literally by missing their prey or by being deterred from attacking. None of it is self-conscious and intentional; none of it is symbolic as such.

In contrast to other animals' decoy and inherited deception devices, the adornment we put on ourselves or on our possessions is symbolic, done deliberately in reference to the self-conscious image we have of ourselves and that we deliberately (intentionally) want to advertise and project into the mind of others. It is an intentional act of communication by a self-conscious creature, communicated to other self-conscious creatures for recognition and evaluation (social seduction and deterrence).

[34] Related to the general topic of selfhood and consumerism, see the collection of interesting and relevant chapters in the volume edited by A. L. Benson, *I Shop, Therefore I Am*. See in particular the chapters by Russell Belk, "Are we what we own?" (pp. 76–104), and Helga Dittmar, "The role of self-image in excessive buying" (pp. 105–133).

Through possession and its embellishment, we tend to assert and assess who we are, particularly our self-worth in relation to others. It is part of our symbolic capital: more or less rich, more or less refined, more or less educated and affluent. The barriers surrounding properties, for example, are highly connoted and most telling of social stature as well as social intents, from wooden slats to chain links, from brick, concrete, or stone walls, to gilded gates and fancy crafted iron fences. All represent different ways of delimiting and protecting property with much symbolism attached to them. The same deliberate style, taste, signs of distinction, and status symbolism exist and are readable for other objects of possessions, from mailboxes to furniture, clothes, and shoes. Shoes, for example, are well-known markers of wealth and status that doormen of fancy clubs often use to select patrons and guests. Shoes can be mass produced or hand made, varying in price and quality. Fitting close to the body, visible to all and worn by all, shoes stand for their owner's taste, class, style, originality, social power, and ultimately relative wealth.[35] As for any other possession, their decoration contributes to the symbolic capital of the individual or the group. It is through possession decoration that individuals and groups assert their own identity. The effort to specify who we are in relation to others is done through style and sensory projection (hair color, perfume, makeup, clothes, or ties).

Over a century ago, the economist and sociologist Thorstein Veblen (1857–1929) pointed to a new "conspicuous consumption" in non-aristocratic people ("nouveaux riches bourgeois") who had accumulated new wealth during the industrial revolution at the turn of nineteenth century and formed a new social class.[36] In today's economics jargon "Veblen goods" correspond to what are also called "position goods," a category of commodities that are conspicuously luxurious and which, beyond comfort and aesthetic appeal, have the primary function of signaling wealth and social, often sexual, fitness.

In more operational economics terms, Veblen goods are commodities for which appeal increases as their price increases: the more expensive, the more desirable. They have the peculiarity of having a demand. From an evolutionary perspective, all positional goods are *costly signaling* of social ascendance and sexual fitness. They are also the public assertion of group identity in terms of social power as belonging to a higher social rank. They are costly in the sense that they are somehow superfluous from a purely rational perspective of energy and risk expenditure. Conspicuous

[35] For further evidence and discussion from consumerism research, see in particular the interesting short article/essay by Russell Belk, "Shoes and self."

[36] Veblen, *Theory of the Leisure Class.*

signaling, Veblen goods, and costly signaling are not limited to wealthy or high socio-economics individuals or groups of individuals. They cut across all social classes.

It is common, for example, that emigrant workers from impoverished countries come back to their village for vacation conspicuously signaling wealth, with larger than necessary cars and other "Veblen goods" that more often than not are tied to costly loans. The aim is to gain prestige and recognition at home: to improve their symbolic capital among native peers, show off their economic success.

Costly signaling is not purely a human phenomenon. It is pervasive in nature, but is not cultivated and deliberate as it is in our species. Evolutionary biologists have pondered the costly design evolved by some animals, such as the encumbering peacock tail. Such an appendage is costly of energy for the male to develop, and is cumbersome, making it more vulnerable to predators. Amotz Zahavi, an ornithologist, proposes that animals evolved such encumbrances as signals of strength and sexual potency to females and predators. According to Zahavi's *handicap* theory,[37] the more handicaps (costly encumbrances) a creature shows, the more strength (i.e., energy to grow such encumbrances) is signaled. This, in turn, deters predators and enhances sexual attractiveness in courtship with females.[38] Zahavi shows that in evolution, across many different species, reproductive benefits outweigh the cost of fluffy encumbrances, selected for their adaptive fitness.

In nature, the forms of costly signaling have emerged over evolutionary time to become part of the animal's repertoire and constitution. Humans, in contrast, evolved the propensity to be self-conscious. They are deliberate in cultivating and creating their own costly branding via adornments, accessories, decoration, tattoos, body building, and other Veblen possessions, all constitutive of a symbolic capital they actively construct through the lifespan and interaction with others.

We do advertise and deliberately build symbolic capital for ourselves in what we wear and what we possess. We do so with others in mind. Body builders advertise health and strength by deliberately bulging their muscles, taking steroid drugs to help them in the branding of themselves, with the risks of dangerous side effects. This is another form of costly signaling whereby one's own body becomes another kind of Veblen good,

[37] Zahavi and Zahavi, *The Handicap Principle*.

[38] The concept of handicap apparently comes from horse racing and betting. To increase the odds and make a race more competitive for the punters, it is customary to place a weight under the saddle of a horse on the basis of past records and performances, in other words its perfomance portofolio from which race commissioners infer natural odds of winning the race, leveling the playingfield of betting odds by adding weight to the horse.

now becoming increasingly common in our hyper-narcissistic era, of ever more costly signaling.[39]

Decoration of possessions is also a collective cultural expression. Group styles in possession ornaments and arrangements are clearly visible in all cultures, from houses to clothing, and collective color schemes: planters with red geraniums on window sills in the Swiss Alps, straw tatamis in Japanese homes, tiled frontages of houses in Portugal, red and white gingham tablecloths emblematic of the traditional rural French restaurant, all corresponding to stylish decoration reproduced by groups and cultures. It is through possession ornamentation and style that groups assert themselves and their own specificity in relation to other groups, as it is also the case at the individual level within a group. It is through costly decoration and ornamentation that individuals as well as groups assert their own individual or collective symbolic capital.

At the level of the group, an interesting example is the evolution of the style and size of pottery of the Lapita civilization that originated in southern China, spreading south and eastward through the South Pacific over the past 3,000 years. The first settlers of the islands of Polynesia were Lapita people who produced a particular kind of clay pottery with geometric dentate-stamped ornaments that was discovered first in New Caledonia ("Lapita site"), but also later on islands in the northeast of Papua New Guinea and the Solomon Islands, as well as various islands of Vanuatu in Melanesia, and spreading farther east into Fiji, Polynesian Tonga, and Samoa. In recent years, archeologists have found pieces of this style of pottery to be the unique remnant clues to this aboriginal South Pacific culture and civilization, apart for linguistic clues (the Austronesian family of languages that spread from east to west over three millennia).

In relation to Lapita pottery, what are remarkable are the changes in the size and richness of its decoration as the migration progressed east, away from the rich demography of Papua New Guinea. Archeologists find that the closer the Lapita sites are to neighboring islands populated with earlier settlers of different cultures (e.g., Papua New Guinea), the richer and more *conspicuous* the ornamentation and size of the Lapita pottery are.[40] Lapita pottery found on more isolated islands of Polynesia, like Tonga or Samoa, is markedly simpler in design and ornament. Archeologists interpret this simplification and minimization of design as an expression of

[39] For further historical insights on human costly signaling revealed in accessories (position goods), fashion, self-presentation, and other objects of possession decoration, and design, see for example the illuminating, cleverly entitled book by Hebdige, *Hiding in the Light*.

[40] Clark, "Specialisation, standardisation and Lapita ceramics."

diminishing costly signaling requirements, as the Lapita civilization moved farther away from other competing cultures.

In other words, as Lapita people migrated away from the more densely populated Melanesian islands of Papua New Guinea, reaching the widespread islands of Polynesia approximately 1,200 years ago, the necessity to assert cultural identity in the decoration of possession (i.e., pottery) diminished. This kind of archeological evidence suggests that at the level of the group, there is the evolving constitution of a symbolic capital asserting group identity in ways that are analogous to what we discussed at the level of the individual.

Coins and cultural identity

The decoration of possessions is conspicuous in human cultures. Even *money* is decorated, the most abstract and fungible (i.e., exchangeable and substitutable) of all possessions. Money is the possession of all possessions, consisting of coins, banknotes, and other artifacts designed to stand for the value of just about anything: from food to sexual favors, the life of a person (hit man), even real estate on the moon.[41]

Cast copper coins were found by archeologists in a tomb dating back 13,000 years during the Chang dynasty. In the West, the first coins seem to have appeared in ancient Greece some 2,500 years ago, made of gold, silver, and copper alloys. Sometimes rectangular, coins tend to be made of rare metals and are almost always round, of graspable size, for easy exchange and transport. However, there are noticeable exceptions such as the stone money used on the island of Yap in Micronesia, mentioned already in the first chapter.

> Huge donut shaped stones, sometimes weighing a few tons, were used for gifts and payment of debts in land transaction and other rituals. As artifacts, these stones are carved out of one particular quarry in the island of Palau, a few hundred miles east of Yap, and transported perilously on fragile wooden outrigger canoes to their destination. Once given, these heavy gifts were laid to rest and sunk against the house or on the land of the addressee. When you travel on this island today, you can still see these huge stones lying there on display. Part of the landscape, like abstract repetitive sculptures, they are memories and stand as public reminders of past gifts and transactions. This money, by its size and weight, its encumbrance, is a constant reminder of indestructible interpersonal ties among the Yapees.[42]

Each token of Yap stone money is a unique gift, recognizable only by an invariant round donut shape. The stone money is purely symbolic. It is money with fungibleness removed from it because of its physical

[41] See in particular www.moonestates.com. [42] Rochat, *Others in Mind*, p. 148.

encumbrance. It stands for social recognition more than economic value. The treacherous journey from Palau on frail canoes and the great weight of the stones are symbolic or conceptual measures of the social ties among the Yap people. Its value is represented by dedication, effort, and work as compensation toward a debt that is more social and affective than economic. Its symbolic shape is highly conceptual, carrying with it the abstract notion of a sociality that is shared only by those living for generations on the island of Yap.

In history, since their first appearance in eastern and western history, coins have always been decorated, typically with effigies of the ruler or those representing the region's authority: emperors, kings and queens, forefathers and national heroes of the independence, symbols of national identity and justice, and more recently, particularly on banknotes, outstanding national inventors and creators exalting recognition and pride. Coins, the most fungible of all possessions, from the time they appear in human evolution, added to the fungible value, the symbolic capital of the collective authority, those who ruled, the moral values that are supposed to rally members of the group like the three mottos that can be found on dollar coins: *In God we trust*; *Liberty*; and *E pluribus unum* in Latin which translates *One from many*, the abstract notion of unity and power that money makers express in this symbolic ornament.

Clear evidence of the intention to specify and assert identity by coin ornamentation is the euro, the unified European currency. Most European nations share this currency, in value, but not in style or decoration. If the currency is unified, the design of the coins is not. While keeping the same identifiable size and weight, representations engraved on them are different. If you look carefully, they vary across eurozone countries, each carrying its distinctive style and character. Spain, France, Italy, Greece, etc., all have their own symbolic representations expressing some mark of their own identity, their own symbolic capital.

Before the economic unification of Europe, however, the money decoration of each independent European nation was significantly more colorful, distinct, and flamboyant, in the same way Lapita people displayed costly signaling in their pottery design as they lived in closer proximity to other cultures. Possession style and decoration matter, as a way of asserting group- and self-identity, above and beyond commercial or utilitarian values. It is part of human unique self-conscious psychology.

Part II

Development

Human ontogeny of possession

5 First possession

In this opening chapter of the book's second part, on development, the primordial subjectivity of infants is considered: what they feel and live as sentient creatures, the early experiential context from which first feelings of possession would arise. The aim is to lay down what may constitute the origins and development of possession as a *feeling experience*.

This chapter is the developmental equivalent of the first chapter which considered the feeling (subjective) experience of possession from an adult and general psychology perspective. Here, I try – as concisely as possible – to discuss what is meant by subjectivity, a loaded term. The goal is once again to assert the fundamentally non-reducible, private or personal possession aspect of feeling experience, but now with a particular focus on its early signs in human ontogeny.

Two questions drive the chapter: what is it like to be a newborn and how does it determine the dawn of possession as a feeling experience?

Personal possession of feeling experience

Minimally, subjectivity refers to what feelings creatures (human and non-human) necessarily experience privately, from a first person perspective, as they live, perceive, go about, and act in the world. At a more elaborated level, and for some species like ours, it may also refer to what the feeling creatures understand, objectify, and explicitly *reflect upon* via thinking, language, and any other communicative exchanges with others. But minimally, subjectivity refers to a psychic (mental) experience that all feeling creatures necessarily have by the mere fact that they are aware and living. Basically, this necessary experience is direct, implicit, and literal. At maximum, it can be symbolic, indirect, and intentional as discussed in earlier chapters.

It is in this sense that subjectivity pertains to something that is personal and private, although, more often than not, subjectivity depends upon and is determined in relation to external events that are in essence public (i.e., people, scenes, and other events). Yet it is an experience with privileged access to the embodied self. Minimally, it is direct self-experience that has authority over any other person's empathic feelings, simulation, or attempts at reconstructing what such self-experience might be. The bottom line is that we do have privileged access to what we feel. This is an irreducible fact.

It is reasonable to think that even the most empathic, in love or in hate, one individual toward another, will never be able to fully experience what this other person or group of persons feels from within his or her own sentient body. By nature, there will always be some *degrees of experiential separation* among us, even when sometimes we tend to feel the reverse, as for example in intense fusion and impressionistic comprehension of the other while sharing orgasms, when finding ourselves falling in love or at the height of love, when someone helps with evident self-abnegation as in instances of heroic rescue when the individual overlooks personal risks to save suffering others. Although much empathy may be on display, experiential separation always remains, by the simple, inescapable fact that the feelings I experience cannot exist outside of my own body: they are necessarily *self-embodied.*

The feeling experiences constitutive of subjectivity and from which it emanates, like smoke from fire, are *personal possessions* in the absolute sense of the term. They are personal because, once again, we do have, like any other feeling creatures, privileged access to an awareness of them. Yet, these feeling experiences are not exclusive to the self. They do not form inalienable possessions per se, since we share them, or at least try to, in inter-subjective exchanges with others who can simulate our feeling experiences, show empathy, and approximate such experiences via inferences and other hypothetical theories. However, those are only tentative approximations, never an absolute grasping or mirroring of mental states by others. This is necessarily true, when considering that the subjective experience of each of us, and all those personal feelings that we hold for ourselves, will inescapably forever disappear with our individual death. Even if we believe in an afterlife, they will not remain in the same embodied form. This absolute personal dispossession is an inescapable fact, an unsharable personal feeling experience. It is the bottom-line exclusivity of each and every one of us as discrete embodied feeling creatures.

Dawn of human feelings

In the first chapter of the book, I discuss what may constitute the criteria qualifying any creature as "feeling organism," an organism that feels and experiences as opposed to just sensing. The difference between sensing and feeling determines whether subjectivity exists or not. A machine can sense but cannot feel; it has no emotions and no affective life. It is by definition "cold," with no reference to mental states and experiential values like pain or joy. Machines have no affective life. They can sense risk threshold and trigger alarm and shutdowns of a system, like thermostats, but they do not feel dangers or risks to the system. This is their main ontological difference.

A machine – by definition and in contradistinction to a feeling organism – has no qualms, no frame of mind, nor anything that is analogous to feeling states or mental states. We might project some affective life and moods into a machine, when for example we indulge in qualifying computers as friendly or unfriendly. But this is a metaphor. Computers cannot be friends or enemies. They are what they are: cold, more or less performing tools we depend on, "smart" screens we carry around that become extensions of our thoughts and memories. But they are no companions proper because they, in themselves, have no mental states. They just store and transform signs of ours in their cryptic software codes and hardware circuits for further decoding by other feeling and intentional creatures via their own screen machines.

For a long time, infants were seen essentially as sensing machines, incapable in particular of experiencing pain. We have mentioned already, in Chapter 1, the fact that until fairly recently (1940s and 1950s), infants and young children were routinely operated on without any anesthesia. Medical teams would paralyze squirming infants by injection of curare or similar paralytic agents. We also alluded to the fact that, even today, local anesthetics are not routine in painful procedures on newborns (heel prick and circumcision), even in ultramodern, state of the art maternity hospitals. There is a continuing overtone in the adult mind, around the world and particularly in certain cultures, that infants have either no feelings or fewer feelings, or that feeling experience at this early stage may not be as consequential through lack of memory (infantile amnesia).

Whatever intuition we hold on the issue, the question is how do we determine whether an organism, any kind of living organism, and a fortiori an infant or a human fetus, *feels* something as opposed to just sensing? In other words, how can we determine whether an organism has a subjective, hence affective life organized around mental states like pain, joy, sadness, or anger? When do organisms, a fortiori human fetuses and infants, begin to have mental and affective states expressed in emotions – begin to have feeling experience and subjectivity? When do they begin to manifest emotions in reference to such mental states, not just manifesting machine-like surface physiological responses?

There is a hard and a soft way to answer these crucial questions regarding the dawn of subjectivity. The hard way is to show that the basic neural hardware normally associated and supposed to minimally support any kind of emotions and feeling experiences is in place and functional. The soft way is to show that signs of emotional life and the expression of what is typically associated with the experience of particular mental states like fear, hunger, anger, pain, and joy are unmistakably recognizable in the behaviors normally associated with and supposed to minimally stand for such feeling experience (e.g., smiling, frowning, crying).

A propos the hard way, in humans, it appears that what is typically recognized as the necessary neuroanatomical underpinning of feeling experience like pain is already in place by the third trimester of gestation, even possibly much earlier (8 weeks). For the soft way, it is also by the third trimester of pregnancy that fetuses demonstrate unmistakable facial expression of pain or joy (smiling), with corresponding heart rate and other expressions of overall behavioral states like wakefulness or sleep.[1] In human ontogeny, it is thus reasonable to think that by at least 31 weeks of gestation, almost 3 months before term birth and 6 months after conception, minimal feeling experience and subjectivity is de facto in place. From this point on of prenatal development, and probably even earlier, it is not farfetched to be ethically concerned about the comfort and potential suffering of fetuses.[2]

The extraordinarily fast pace of brain development and its complex organization during the first 2 months of gestation puts in place within 8 weeks the hardware potential for fetuses to sense the world, and eventually by the third trimester of gestation also to feel it, hence to have the potential for minimal subjectivity. In general, feeling experience, and therefore subjectivity, rests on the necessary prerequisite of an ability to capture a sensible world via systems that are in place and functional. Recent research documents the emergence before birth of this necessary sensory prerequisite of subjectivity.

Next, we review some of the empirical evidence documenting emerging sensibility in fetal development. We envision these facts as first signs of feeling experience in epigenesis.

1 See for example: Prechtl, "Assessment and significance of behavioural states"; Hata, Dai, and Marumo, "Ultrasound for evaluation of fetal neurobehavioural development"; Hepper, "Prenatal development."

2 See Chapter 1 for more details and references regarding the mindboggling rapidity of brain growth in prenatal development.

Prenatal dawn of feeling experience[3]

Fetal sensibility matures sequentially depending on the modality.[4] In epigenesis, it appears to recapitulate the evolutionary order of the main sensory systems.[5] Somesthetic sensibility (skin and body feelings) matures first. This sensibility corresponds to tactile (skin pressure), vestibular (posture and balance), and pain stimulation (tissue damage).[6] It is followed by the maturation of chemosensory sensibility that combines olfaction and gustation (i.e., smell and taste), followed by audition (pitch, amplitude, and phrasing of sounds), and finally by vision (light and optic array). Below are some relevant empirical facts regarding this prenatal dawn of feeling experience.

Skin and body

Tactile and somatic sensibility is already expressed by 8 weeks gestational age. Eight-week-old, externalized fetuses display head movements away from an object touching their lips.[7] Nociceptive (pain) receptors appear first in and around the mouth area at around 7 weeks post conception. They rapidly extend to the palmar surface of the hands by 11 weeks, and the rest of the skin and mucosal surfaces by 20 weeks.[8]

Taste and smell

Fetuses are documented swallowing amniotic fluid by 12 weeks of gestation when chemoreceptors already pave the inside of the nose and the oral cavity. Chemosensation (sensibility to taste and smell combined) is evident when a sweet substance (sugar) is injected into the amniotic fluid, and swallowing increases. It decreases with the injection of a "noxious" (iodinated poppy seed) substance.[9]

Different studies[10] demonstrate that newborns manifest not only taste and smell discrimination, but also chemosensory *preferences* (preferential

[3] These facts were originally put together and elaborated in relation to the origins of self-awareness in Rochat, "The self as phenotype."
[4] Lecanuet and Schaal, "Fetal sensory compentencies."
[5] Gottlieb, "Ontogenesis of sensory functions in birds and mammals."
[6] Merskey and Bogduk, *Classification of Chronic Pain.*
[7] Hooker, *The Prenatal Origin of Behavior.*
[8] Brusseau and Mashour, "Subcortical consciousness"; Smith, *Commission of Inquiry into Fetal Sentience.*
[9] Schaal, Orgeur, and Rognon, "Odor sensing in the human fetus."
[10] Marlier, Schaal, and Soussignan, "Neonatal responsiveness to the odor of amniotic and lacteal fluids"; and "Bottle-fed neonates prefer an odor experienced in utero to an odor experienced postnatally in the feeding context."

postural orientation of nose and mouth) that have been learned in the womb (e.g., smell of maternal amniotic fluid), a preference that perseverates days after birth.

Sounds and voices

Fetuses display bodily movements in response to sounds from 22 to 24 weeks. These movements reflect a complex auditory sensitivity to variations of sound's frequency and intensity, as well as duration.[11] From 30 weeks gestational age, fetuses display heart rate acceleration at the onset of external airborne sounds they hear through the uterine wall, as well as vibroacoustic stimulations applied against the mother's abdomen.[12] Based on habituation/dishabituation paradigms with extra-uterine speakers placed close to the mother, fetuses learn from approximately 32 weeks to discriminate structure characteristics of speech sounds. Changes in the order of two syllables composing a word like "babi" and "biba" are correlated with heart rate deceleration indexing an orienting response of the fetus.[13]

The womb is not soundproof, sounds travel through the amniotic fluid, with the voice of the mother particularly amplified. In their niche, fetuses learn and develop preferences for familiar noise configurations. Based on an operant sucking paradigm, newborns a few hours old are shown to discriminate and actively prefer to hear their mother's voice compared to another female's uttering the same phrases with the same intensity. This preferential discrimination is based on what infants have heard and eventually learned in utero regarding their mother's voice characteristics.[14]

Light and dark

Light experience being greatly limited in the darkness of the womb explains the maturational delay of vision. However, fetal eye activities are recorded from 13 weeks gestational age, starting with downward movements of both eyes (12.5 weeks), slow eye movements (16 weeks), eye closing (20 weeks), rapid eye movements (23 weeks),

11 Hepper and Shahidullah, "Development of fetal hearing."
12 Kisilevsky and Hains, "Exploring the relationship between fetal heart rate and cognition"; Lecanuet, Granier-Deferre, and Busnel, "Fetal cardiac and motor responses to octave-band noises as a function of central frequency, intensity and heartrate variability."
13 Lecanuet et al., "Perception et discrimination foetales de stimuli langagiers, mise en évidence à partir de la réactivité cardiaque, résultants préliminaires."
14 DeCasper and Fifer, "Of human bonding."

and conjugate lateral eye movements by 24 weeks.[15] From approximately 26 weeks, changes in heart rate and overall bodily movements are recorded in the fetus when a bright light is flashed on the mother's abdomen.[16]

Compared to audition, which is almost adult-like at birth, vision is noticeably poor in comparison. Babies are born with poor visual acuity and contrast sensitivity, in need of the rich illumination and much larger view outside of the womb to develop. Vision improves dramatically in the weeks following birth, and within 6 months becomes close to adult-like, with detection of colors' full spectrum, sensibility to movement parallax, contrast sensitivity, convergence, and accommodation for objects at far distances.[17]

Mental states in the womb

By 30 weeks gestational age, fetuses display marked changes in their habituation to acoustic vibrations and coupling of movement to heart rate, as well as some indications that they may begin experiencing pain.[18] Such changes suggest a budding minimal experience of "what it is like" or phenomenal (P) consciousness.[19]

We read pleasure and pain in others, perceiving as well as eventually inferring feeling states. We do so primarily by perceiving organized patterns of outward bodily movements (e.g., facial expressions), either directly or by linking them to perceived circumstances or events in the environment such as loud sound = startle = fear; needle prick = cry = pain; or tickle = giggle = pleasure. Warm blooded animals evolved patterns of such recognizable bodily movements (emotions) rendering their feeling states public, accessible to others in communication.[20] There is indeed an inherited equation between particular feeling experience and the expression of specific bodily patterns. This equation is directly perceived in communication (e.g., threat or fear bodily expressions as signs of aggressive or avoidant feeling states), but can also be inferred and made explicit in conversation at more advanced stages of development (e.g., the typical content of old wives' tales and other folk theories that furnish our social lives).

[15] DeVries, Visser, and Prechtl, "The emergence of fetal behavior."
[16] Hepper, "Prenatal development."
[17] Kellman and Arterberry, "Infant visual perception."
[18] Anand and Hickey, "Pain and its effects in the human neonate and fetus."
[19] Block, "Consciousness, accessibility, and the mesh between psychology and neuroscience."
[20] Darwin, *The Expression of the Emotions in Man and Animals.*

In relation to the issue of subjectivity in development, the question concerns when emotional patterns emerge in epigenesis that are readily perceivable as standing for particular feeling states. What might be the actual origins of emotional patterns that we perceive as standing for particular feeling states like pain, fatigue, or pleasure, all of which could be linked to minimal self-awareness? Newborns do cry when in pain or physically hurt and smile when satiated, but what about fetuses?

New technological progress in real-time sonographic imaging of fetuses (2D–4D ultrasound)[21] allows us to study with great precision facial expressions that are universally recognized as standing for basic mental states. Ultrasonic imaging demonstrate that from *30 weeks* gestational age, fetuses display highly organized facial expressions that stand unambiguously for what we perceive as experiences of pleasure (smiling), displeasure (scowling), and fatigue (yawning). These patterns of emotional expressions are also readily observable immediately after birth.

When newborns fuss before feeding or smile away following a feed, we can assume that they are feeling either pain or intense pleasure, not just "on or off" hunger sensations that would set off some sort of thermostatic responses. Mental states and affective values most likely motivate newborns' behaviors, not just sensation as I will try to show next. Newborns do experience the world, including themselves, beyond the raw "proximal" sensations transduced on the surface of the sense receptors. They are not *just* stimulus bound.

If clear, unambiguous emotional expressions can be detected in fetuses in the same way that they are readily observable in newborns, the inference of feeling states is not too far fetched, particularly in light of the abundance of data showing the remarkable behavioral continuity of prenatal and postnatal development.[22]

Recent use of fine-grain 4D ultrasound graphic recordings confirms that no movements observed in the fetus during the last trimester of pregnancy (from at least 30 weeks) are not also expressed by neonates.[23] These include also, aside from unambiguous smiling and scowling, isolated eye blinking, hand and finger movements, tongue protrusion, and all reflex responses displayed by newborns with the exception of the Moro reflex that requires space for the spreading of arms.[24]

[21] Hata, Dai, and Marumo, "Ultrasound for evaluation of fetal neurobehavioural development."

[22] Prechtl, *Continuity of Neural Functions.*

[23] See Prechtl, *Continuity of Neural Functions.*

[24] Andonotopo and Kurjak, "The assessment of fetal behavior of growth restricted fetuses by 4D sonography"; Andonotopo et al., "Assessment of fetal behavior and general movements by four-dimensional sonography."

Furthermore, by 36 weeks fetuses also show four well-defined grouping of behaviors (Sleep–Wake behavioral states) that would correspond to distinct levels of consciousness (levels of "feeling" experience). These patterns are stable and show clear transitions, respectively: *Quiet Sleep* (stable heart beat, no eye movements); *Active Sleep* (eye movements, body movements with heart rate acceleration); *Quiet Awake* (eye movements, stable heart rate); *Active Awake* (eye movements, unstable heart rate, and bouts of tachycardia).[25]

These patterns of behavioral states are observed in newborns and beyond via applicable electro-encephalographic (EEG) recordings. Starting a trend that will continue beyond birth, the proportion of time fetuses spend in an *Active Awake state* augments significantly during the last 4 weeks of gestation (from 6% to 9% of the time). This developmental trend continues in the weeks following birth, infants spending an increasing amount of time in an active and awake behavioral "feeling" state.[26]

Finally, sensory evoked potential recorded in infants born premature, 10 week before term, indicates that minimal level of phenomenal consciousness might be present already by 30 weeks of gestational age as thalamocortical connections become functional,[27] although continuing to develop markedly through adulthood, with documented changes in childhood and adolescence.[28]

Some researchers suggest that cortical–subcortical interactions must play a role in "the shift from reflexive, stimulus-bound behavior in childhood, to the goal-directed and more flexible functioning found in adulthood."[29] However, cortical–subcortical interactions remain scarcely mapped in the perspective of fetal and infant development. However, as we shall see next, early behavioral signs of such shift clearly exist in infancy, with precursor signs possibly manifested already by 32 weeks gestational age (see discussion above).

In this context, noteworthy is the observation that the significant increase of full-range emotional expressions and facial movements observed in the fetus from 32 weeks of gestation is associated with a

[25] Prechtl, "Assessment and significance of behavioural states"; Nijhuis et al., "Are there behavioral states in the human fetus?"; Hepper, "Prenatal development."

[26] Wolff, *The Development of Behavioral States and the Expression of Emotions in Early Infancy*.

[27] Klimach and Cooke, "Maturation of the neonatal somatosensory evoked response in preterm infants."

[28] Fair et al., "Maturing thalamocortical functional connectivity across development."

[29] Fair et al., "Maturing thalamocortical functional connectivity across development," p. 2.

decrease of overall movements.[30] This growing expressive specificity is consistent with the normal neurological development of the fetus.[31]

In summary, recent progress in fetal psychology research suggests that there are prenatal signs of feeling experience. The well-organized emotional expressions combined with the remarkable continuity of prenatal and postnatal development support the idea that first feeling experience, therefore the potential for minimal self-awareness, might emerge 8–10 weeks before birth (30–32 weeks gestational age). Keeping in mind the striking continuity of behaviors observed during the last 10 weeks of gestation and what can be readily observed and tested after birth,[32] what can be seen in the newborn could stand also for what is not readily testable in the womb, from at least 32 weeks when fetal behaviors show all the aspects of what is observed after birth.

Another demonstration that at least from birth infants feel and are not just sensing the world is the fact that what characterizes their behavior is much more than simple automatic responses triggered by particular stimulations. Much more than simple reflexes, what infants manifest from birth are complex action systems oriented toward particular resources with *affective values* that they perceive and feel rather than just sense in some sort of on/off switch or trigger mechanism. From birth, infants are actors and feelers rather than responders or just "sensors." Newborns are best described as active explorers of a world that has values they feel and experience in reference to particular mental states: satiety, hunger, pain, comfort, pleasure, fear, surprise, or curiosity. What follows is a presentation of what characterizes behavior at birth.

Acting and feeling by neonates

Behavior at birth and in the first months of life can be divided into two basic kinds: autonomic *reflex systems* and *action systems*. Reflex systems correspond to what pediatricians probe immediately after birth to assess the neurophysiological health of the infant, performing typical neurobehavioral tests to see if there are any neurological red flags. Action systems, in contrast, correspond to behavioral patterns present at birth that are much more than triggered responses to specific stimulations. They correspond to actions that are oriented toward functional goals and particular resources in the environment: food, protection, comfort, etc. The first

[30] Hata et al., "Ultrasound for evaluation of fetal neurobehavioural development"; Andonopo et al., "Assessment of fetal behavior and general movements by four-dimensional sonography."

[31] Prechtl, *Continuity of Neural Functions*.

[32] Prechtl, *Continuity of Neural Functions*.

kind entails mere sensing and responding, the other feeling and meaningful perception proper. Yet both are expressed immediately after birth, covering drastically different capacities.

The beating of the heart, the movements of the lungs in breathing, the shaking of the whole body under a cold spell, the knee jerk response, or the blinking of eye lids in response to an air puff, all belong to the first kind of triggered (sensed) bodily movements. They are autonomic and reflex responses of the organism. The control of such movements is endogenous and self-contained. These movements consist in highly predictable stimulus–response loops or tight circuits. They are in essence automatic, triggered by particular stimulations. Following the first account by physiologist Charles Scott Sherrington (1857–1952) of this kind of bodily movement, the control is encapsulated and rigidly prescribed within the organism as reflex arcs. It involves low-level, subcortical neural networks, as surgically decorticated animals continue to express such movements.[33] What control such movements are closed feedback systems like thermostats controlling for constant temperature inside a house. Those mechanisms are machine-like sensing and closed control systems. They are simple when considered in isolation, but they are complex when considered in interaction with each other, each calibrated to respond to particular ranges of stimulation from the environment that are internal as well as external to the body. Each system controlling for a particular autonomic/reflex response is also adapted to interact with myriad other similar systems that, in concert, maintain the integrity of the organism as a whole living and adapting system. But they do so in a very mechanistic way, with no reference to any sorts of mental states, controlled by closed loop feedback systems (i.e., autonomic reflexes) insuring basic physiological functioning: like breathing, digesting, or swallowing. They keep the individual organism alive but such movements do not involve any perception, or any particular higher-order treatment of basic physiological signals or sensations that are, like a machine, sensed but not felt in reference to mental states. The infant regurgitating an object that obstructs the wind pipe, does it automatically, not feeling the danger but sensing the obstruction, in the same way that a thermostat senses automatically the crossing of a temperature threshold, without feeling temperature change. In a way, this kind of bodily movement is sensitive but psychologically blind to the environment it responds to. Such movements are triggered by non-specified circumstances.

[33] Sherrington, *The Integrative Action of the Nervous System*.

Action systems, in contrast, correspond to bodily movements that are more than autonomic or reflex responses. Also expressed from birth and prominent during the first 6 weeks of life, they are distinct on two basic grounds. For one, they are movement systems consisting of actions that are oriented toward specific functional goals. These systems are by definition adapted to tap into available resources that exist outside the individual organism, in the surrounding environment: food, surfaces, objects, or people. For two, these movements are organized into systems that are *flexible*, capable of changing based on previous experiences, and adjusting to novel circumstances. They allow room for learning, controlled by open feedback loop systems. Action systems do entail perception (feelings) and learning. Contrary to reflexes, they entail some psychology and meaning making (perception), presumably higher-order cortical involvement. In support of this second kind, much research indicates that infants at birth show more than autonomic/reflex arcs.[34]

For a long time, newborn sucking, grasping, stepping, rooting, or head turning were construed merely as reflexes or automatic responses triggered by non-specific stimulations. Multiple studies now exist showing in fact that such movements need to be construed as actions rather than reflexes, actions that are already oriented toward particular features and resources in the environment, such as faces or objects with a certain shape, texture, consistency, or smell. Newborns, immediately after birth, track with their eyes and even show attempts at reaching toward objects that move close by in their field of view. More impressive is the fact that they do so preferentially when the object consists for example of a schematic face-like display. Old research, validated multiple times since then, indicates that newborns tend to track more canonical face-like displays (two adjacent dots for eyes above vertically aligned two dots for nose and mouth) compared to non-canonical face-like displays with the same features but scrambled.[35] Similarly, newborns tend to suck differentially on pacifiers that are more or less mimicking the biological nipple of the mother. They suck less and tend significantly to increase oral exploration as a function of the eccentricity of a pacifier compared to the biological nipple in terms of texture and consistency.[36]

We found the same kind of results when recording newborns' grasping of objects varying in texture and consistency that are placed in one of their

[34] For a general review, see Rochat, *The Infant's World*.
[35] Morton and Johnson, "CONSPEC and CONLERN."
[36] Rochat, "Oral touch in young infants"; Rochat and Senders, "Active touch in infancy."

palms.[37] In more recent years, researchers have even established that newborn infants are significantly more inclined to orient their face toward gauze impregnated with their own mother's amniotic fluid or breast milk as compared to gauze impregnated with the amniotic fluid or breast milk of another women who has just given birth.[38] If newborns orient and root to smells or face-like displays, if they suck and grasp at objects introduced in their mouth or in their hands, they do so with discrimination and preference.

This kind of movement is not made of autonomic, reflex responses triggered by non-specific stimulation. It is under the control of previous experiences (learning) and intrinsically oriented toward particular environmental resources. It calls for some psychology engaging more than sub-cortical structures. Even if we cannot qualify these movements as being intentional (another loaded term), it is reasonable to qualify them as arising in the context of adaptive actions generated in relation to objects infants perceive, hence feel, and not simply sense. Such feeling experience is the personal possession of the child by which minimal, implicit self-awareness is expressed, based on evidence presented next.

Minimal self-awareness in newborns

Infancy research of the past four decades has changed our views on the starting state of mental life, namely what it is like to be a newborn. Until then, developmental theorists tended to endorse the view, in their own ways, of an initial state of confusion with the environment, the famous initial "blooming buzzing confusion" proposed by William James (1842–1910).[39] Neonates were presented as stimulus-bound, sensing but not feeling the world, their behavior primitively reduced to ready-made, evolved automatisms (reflexes or pulsions). Newborns were thought to experience a world that was not yet objectified or differentiated, subjectivity and objectivity confounded and in need of progressive integration through experience (e.g., cognitive distancing and construction in the case of Piaget,[40] ego development in the case of Freud's pulsion theory[41]).

More recent research shows that, in fact, healthy newborns do perceive the world objectively and are not in a state of subject–object confusion. From birth they express a difference between what pertains to their own

[37] Rochat, "Mouthing and grasping in neonates."
[38] Marlier et al., "Neonatal responsiveness to the odor of amniotic and lacteal fluids."
[39] James, *The Principles of Psychology*.
[40] Piaget, *The Origins of Intelligence in Children*; Piaget, *The Construction of Reality in the Child*.
[41] Freud, *Three Essays on the Theory of Sexuality*.

body and what pertains to the world "out there." Within the proposed framework, infants at birth do not just sense and respond based on reflex-like mechanisms. More than thermostats functioning on the basis of on/off closed loop feedback, they also feel and act on objects that they experience as *differentiated*, *distal*, and *situated* in relation to them. This research demonstrates that infants from birth are capable of "feeling" not just "sensing" the world, demonstrating the potential for minimal embodied self-awareness. Here is a sampling of empirical evidence.[42]

Although babies are born with poor contrast sensitivity and grading acuity,[43] infancy researchers investigating newborn vision demonstrate that despite the obvious developmental lag of the modality, active perceptual processing does take place at birth. For example and relevant to our discussion, using habituation and novelty preference paradigms, researchers have established that newborn infants, only a few hours old, when awake and alert, perceive the real (distal) size of objects, not the varying (proximal) sizes projected onto the retina. Newborns perceive size constancy of objects,[44] most likely via visuo-proprioceptive convergence cues from both eyes as they line their gazes and focus on the distal object.[45]

What is particularly relevant to our discussion is that this kind of empirical evidence suggests that newborn infants have feeling experience, and are not just limited to sensing what is recorded at the proximal level of the receptors (i.e., the retina). But what does it say about self-awareness? If feeling experience is required for minimal self-awareness, what kind of evidence is there that newborns actually express such awareness?

From birth, infants are capable of perceiving their own body as an entity among other entities: an entity that has unity, is differentiated, occupies space, and is substantial. In addition, from at least 2 months of age, there is good evidence that infants have a sense of their own agency on objects, aware of themselves as embodied agent in the world.[46]

For example, we were able to show that newborn infants do discriminate between self-stimulation and stimulations coming from the outside world, suggesting that they are not in a state of confusion with the world outside. They root (i.e., orient head and mouth) significantly more toward the finger of an experimenter touching their cheek than toward their own

[42] For more evidence, see Rochat, *The Infant's World*.
[43] Banks and Shannon, "Spatial and chromatic visual efficiency in human neonates."
[44] Granrud, "Size constancy in newborn human infants"; Slater, Mattock, and Brown, "Size constancy at birth."
[45] Kellman and Arterberry, "Infant visual perception."
[46] See Rochat, *The Infant's World*.

hand spontaneously brought in contact with the peri-oral region of the face.[47] We also showed that 2-month-olds are attentive and systematically explore the auditory consequences of their own action while sucking on a sound-producing pacifier.[48] They differentiate between sounds that are perfectly contingent but that are either analog or non-analog to the physical pressures they apply on the pacifier. In the context of our research, from 2 months of age (not at birth) infants show clear signs that they perceive themselves as *agent* of what they hear.

Other empirical observations demonstrate further the minimal subjectivity of neonates who seem to experience the world with an implicit differentiated sense of themselves as embodied perceivers. For example, there is some evidence that from birth infants differentiate movements of their own body (ego motions) from movements of objects and things in the world that occur independently of the self (allo-motions). Newborns pick up visual information that specifies ego motion or movements of their own body while they, in fact, remain stationary. This kind of observation points to the fact that from birth infants are endowed with the perceptual, qua inter-modal capacity to pick up and process meaningfully *self-specifying* information.

Overall, all these observations suggest that from birth infants possess minimal, implicit self-awareness, hence subjectivity in terms of first person perspective. We are not born in a state of confusion with the environment, but rather possess a sense of ourselves as differentiated and situated entities among other entities in the world. Newborns perceive objects as distal and distinct from their own body, thus showing the potential for engaging in object relation, *the capacity to exert control over them*. It is thus reasonable to posit that, from the outset, all conditions are in place for the development of first feelings of possession. Next we consider the active context in which feelings of possession might actually emerge, consolidate, and grow from birth on.

Embodied centrifugal and centripetal forces at birth

From the outset, infants show signs of being implicitly aware that they themselves are exerting actions on things. If we look at these primitive actions, we can see that they are essentially organized around *centrifugal* and *centripetal* attractor forces taking their reference point in the body. These forces are, I will propose, the primary embodied experiential

[47] Rochat and Hespos, "Differential rooting response by neonates."
[48] Rochat and Striano, "Emerging self-exploration by 2-month-old infants."

context in which first feelings of possession emerge in epigenesis: the active source of their first emergence.

Experiencing their own body as differentiated, situated, and agent in the environment, newborns interact with objects and people according to adaptive action systems that, we have seen, are more than reflexes. These systems include feeding, calming, maintaining postural balance, maintaining close contact for temperature regulation, seeking protection and care, exploring and orienting toward novelty in the environment.[49] All systems have in common the fact that, at a dynamic level, infants from birth are pushed and pulled by *two* opposite attractor or motivational forces in relation to their own body. One is a *centripetal* force, orienting actions toward and inside of the body. The other is a *centrifugal* force, orienting actions away and outside of the body. These forces can be construed as opposite attractors or action "magnets." They take the body as a reference point, and in relation to this point they are in geographic polar opposition with different overarching goal orientations: one to import or incorporate inside and within the body's realm, the other to export or ex-corporate outside and out of the body's realm. These two opposite motivational forces are enacted from birth, even probably prior to birth, at least during the last trimester of pregnancy when fetuses are shown taking their hands in and out of their mouth.

Centripetal and centrifugal forces correspond to two ontologically different, i.e., polar opposite, dynamics, each presumably with specific motivational and psychological underpinnings. Mutually exclusive because they are polar opposites, these forces are co-defined, like the two sides of a coin: one can exist only in relation to the other, although they do not have to co-exist with equal strength. Centrifugal forces may dominate the centripetal, and vice versa, depending on development but also on the individual: some taking in (importing into the body) more than they tend to give out (exporting out of the body), or vice versa.

What I propose here is that it is fundamentally in the interplay between centrifugal and centripetal forces in relation to the body that infants, from the outset, develop first feelings of control over things, what constitutes and is meant by possession feelings: *the perception of having exclusive self-control over things*.

Concretely, first feelings of possession grow out of actions on things that afford to be taken in or out of the mouth, or that can be manually grasped and released, swallowed or expelled from the oral cavity. It is in the self-generated interplay of polar activities such as latching on to the

[49] See Reed, "An outline of a theory of action systems."

breast, releasing it, and latching at it again that a newborn develops feelings of possession, hence control over maternal nipples that are the source of his feeding.

The same would be true for any recurrent objects in the life of babies, such as particular nipples on bottles, soothing pacifiers, or any other sort of security object, toy, blanket, or textured and scented thing that infants tend to get attached to and want to exert exclusive control over.

These opposite forces that orient and organize actions in relation to the body, in particular in relation to the mouth – main gravitational center of perception and action in early infancy – give rise to first feelings of possession and control. Again, they would arise from the primitive dynamic created by the interplay of these two opposite forces. To use a simple physiological metaphor, "breathing" is a process that arises from the inhaling and exhaling of air in and out of the lungs (centripetal and centrifugal forces). Likewise, feelings of possession would be an experience arising first from the enactment of centripetal and centrifugal attractor forces around the body. This interplay represents a primitive dynamic of *give and take exchanges*, first implicitly enacted in relation to the embodied self.

Oral and manual capture in early development

Looking at newborns awake and active in their cribs it seems that all of their actions gravitate around the mouth, oriented toward oral contact and stimulation. They bring hand to mouth, and suck and orient toward anything that can be brought into contact with the oral region. They open their mouth in anticipation of their hand touching the oral region and they root toward a touch on one of their own cheeks with mouth open, protruded tongue, and anticipatory sucking. Anatomically and neurophysiologically, mouth, lips, and the oral cavity form the surface region of the body that concentrates the highest density of tactile receptors. Combined with the olfactory and gustatory sensory systems of the mouth, this bodily locus represents from birth a complex and incomparable *perceptual hot spot* orienting infant actions from birth, and even probably also prenatally since fetuses demonstrate hand–mouth coordination and engage in much swallowing of the amniotic fluid in utero.

The mouth continues to be the terminus end point (*tertium quid* as Bruner described it some years ago[50]) of most actions beyond birth and

[50] Bruner, "Eye, hand and mind."

well into the first year. Infants begin to reach and grasp objects systematically and successfully from around 4 months, but even when they begin to grasp objects, it is to bring them to the mouth for further exploration. When presented with an attractive object within reaching distance but with both arms constrained to the side by an experimenter holding them down, 6-month-old infants will tend to bypass their bodily constraints by launching head and trunk forward in order to capture the object with the mouth.[51] This kind of oral capture demonstrates the primary goal orientation of early reaching: contact with the mouth, which is, as Freud accurately suggested years ago, the primary bodily locus attractor in development: a primary source of erotic pleasure, perception, and action (exploration[52]). But what happens when an object, including own fingers and hands, reaches the mouth under the general centrifugal force that is reaching and grasping?

Objects are introduced in and out of the mouth: licked, sucked, bitten, chewed, sometimes swallowed or spat out. All these oral activities are at the interplay of centrifugal and centripetal forces, what would be the primary source of acquired feelings of control and possession in relation to own body. Inversely, this interplay specifies for the infant her own body parts (i.e., mouth, arms, and hands) as agentive entities capable of perceiving and exerting actions on objects. Both become objects of first feelings of possession and control, emerging and being consolidated in the interplay of centrifugal and centripetal motivational forces: in, out, and around the mouth and its cavity early in development.

In relation to food, particularly when infants are introduced to solid food, the mouth is the primary locus of actual object incorporation, once it is swallowed and landing in the stomach for digestion. It is from a very early age the privileged and probably prototypical or paradigmatic source of possession feelings, the point where, unless food is regurgitated, the interplay of centrifugal and centripetal forces relative to the body actually *ends*. The experience of possession comes to absolute closure by physical incorporation, the object of possession literally digested by the infant's own body and ending up fusing with its substance.

Object manipulation via early reaching and grasping is also organized around centrifugal (reaching out and grabbing) and centripetal (pushing out and dropping) motivational forces. Infants typically engage in much holding then repeatedly dropping things on the ground, like balls, toys, food, or spoon as they eat in their highchair or elsewhere, caregivers having each time to pick the object up. Infants certainly capture attention and

51 Rochat and Senders, "Active touch in infancy."
52 See Rochat, "Oral touch in infants"; Rochat and Senders, "Active touch in infancy."

care from adults with such actions, but they also consolidate the control and possession feelings, by once again enacting the interplay between centrifugal and centripetal forces relative to their own body.

Freud depicts something that is similar in relation to the anal stage in his theory on infantile psychosexual development. We have already mentioned in the preceding chapter, in relation to the pathologies of possession, that toilet training revolves around the child's learning and exploring control over bladder and sphincter. In the reverse of food or any other external objects that might be incorporated to the body, bowels and urine as objects originating from within the embodied self can also consolidate feelings of possession in the interplay of centrifugal (expulsive) or centripetal (retentive) motivational forces.

Possession and control of others' attention

There is a peculiar evolutionary context to human childhood that we should never forget when considering any aspects of human psychology, especially from a developmental perspective. This context is defined by the basic fact that human childhood is first and foremost incomparably *protracted* in duration. Compared to any other primate species, humans are born too soon, greatly immature, and markedly dependent on others to survive. As a species, we are both "precocious" (born early) and "altricial" (in need of extended intensive care from others to survive).[53] It is useful, even indispensable, not to lose track of this basic context when thinking about the origins of human possession psychology, in particular the emergence of first feelings of possession.

To make a long and certainly much more complex story short, let's say that the human precocious birth and "external gestation"[54] evolved under the combined pressures of a proportionally larger brain and the narrowing of the female's birth canal that is associated with the emergence of bipedal locomotion.[55] The narrowing of the birth canal in human evolution led to a precocious birth, and, in turn, shaped the unique ways we are brought up and cared for over a uniquely protracted period of dependency, what can be described as *human prolonged immaturity*.[56]

The prolonged immaturity and dependence on the care of others that characterize human childhood gave rise also to a unique existential conundrum: the conflicting pressures of maintaining proximity with

[53] See Gould, *Ontogeny and Phylogeny*.
[54] See Montagu, "Neonatal and infant immaturity in man."
[55] See in particular Trevarthan, "Human birth"; Konner, *The Evolution of Childhood*.
[56] See Bruner, "Nature and uses of immaturity."

those dispensing the indispensable care, and a growing, insatiable need for infants to roam the world independently of others, away from the secure base of the mother or other attachment figures.[57]

All healthy children are faced with this basic existential conundrum that is particularly exacerbated in humans. Such a conundrum enters the psychological landscape of the child from around *8 months of age* on average, the typical onset of independent locomotion that is operationally defined as the child's ability to creep or crawl a distance of 4 feet in 1 minute.[58] Coincidently, it is at the same point in development that infants are known to show first signs of strangers and separation anxiety (the eighth month "anguish" described by René Spitz some years ago[59]), as well as first signs of joint attention with social partners,[60] a crucial development that is the first major source of reciprocal exchanges of point of views with others. As we shall see in more details in Chapter 7 (on the origins of sharing), in joint attention, children engage others in their object exploration, checking back and forth whether others are attuned to and in visual alignment with their own object of exploration. Although it is rarely thought of in this way, I have proposed elsewhere that joint attention is probably the basic process by which children resolve the "proximity maintenance versus independent roaming" conundrum.[61] With joint attention, children de facto incorporate the gaze of others, hence the social attention or third person perspective on themselves that they feel they control and possess, integrating it into their own free roaming and object exploration. They manage, at a distance, to be alone but together, "alone in the presence of someone" to quote again Donald Winnicott, who perceives this frame of mind as a major achievement in human development.[62]

Construed in this way, joint attention would be the expression of children's deliberate attempt at controlling and possessing the gaze of others. In doing so, they promote feelings of possession, bringing others' attention toward them, while roaming and exploring the environment away from their close physical proximity. Once again, they do so in the interplay of opposed centrifugal and centripetal motivational forces in relation to their own embodied self.

57 Rochat, "The gaze of others."
58 See Bertenthal and Campos, "A systems approach to the organizing effects of self-produced locomotion during infancy"; Benson, "Season of birth and onset of locomotion."
59 Spitz, *The First Year of Life*.
60 Scaife and Bruner, "The capacity for joint visual attention in the infant."
61 Rochat, *The Infant's World*; Rochat, "The gaze of others."
62 Winnicott, "Transitional objects and transitional phenomena," pp. 47–48.

Via joint attention, children thus gain *tele-control* (control at a distance) of others' attention, constantly chasing it, always trying to possess and control it. Early on, long before the end of the first year when infants typically begin to locomote and roam freely on their own, they try to control and possess the attention and care of others in the primordial context of face-to-face inter-subjective exchanges. From 2 months of age, infants show distress, in a very robust fashion, when someone surreptitiously interrupts a joyful, mutually attentive exchange with them, when for example adopting a sudden frozen "still face" while continuing to stare straight ahead through the child's gaze, or suddenly looking away and being distracted by something else. Young infants pick up subtle changes in their social partners' affective attunement, when they demonstrate that they are temporarily "off" (less contingent) in their emotional responses. Infants react strongly to a person who ceases being engaged, someone with whom they lose the feeling of possession and control.[63] This is a primary and crucial social source for the consolidation of early feelings of possession and control, feelings that, as before, arise in the interplay of centrifugal (gaining and maintaining the attention of others) and centripetal forces (losing the attention and attunement of others).

First object of love and jealousy

Among all the existing speculations on what might animate the psychic life of newborns, assuming that there is one prior to language, which was not easily accepted until fairly recently, ideas emerging from Freud's psychoanalytical approach have been the most prolific as well as the most controversial. Freud was the first to place desire in the instinctive behaviors expressed by newborns, and the first to identify early embodied sensory experience as being the cradle of the person, with its often debilitating characteristics emerging in development. To introduce the notion of infantile sexuality was a revolutionary act of courage at the time, and still is to a large extent.

Freud's "pulsion theory" of psychosexual development outlined in *Three Essays on the Theory of Sexuality* (1905) was a paradigm shift. With it he took on the taboo idea that infants from birth might be driven by erotic desires that quickly expand and transcend survival instincts evolved by the species. In the history of ideas, Freud offered with his pulsion theory certainly the most comprehensive account of what might drive behavior at birth, aside from conditioning.

[63] See for example the large collection of research compiled in Rochat, *Early Social Cognition*. See in particular the chapter by P. Rochat and T. Striano.

Obviously, Freud's theory was not the first published account on the question of early experience and what it might be like to be an infant,[64] but Freud's account was the most thorough and inquisitive to be proposed on what might constitute the psycho-affective forces driving behavior at birth. This account opened a whole new vista on what might be the constitutive elements of subjective life.

Although Freud's pulsion theory and the theoretical concepts inferred continue to be criticized, to his credit it was the first to ground subjective life, from the outset, in the experience of the body as we perceive and act in the world, an "embodiment" of psychic life, its somatic grounding that is now routinely vindicated by current research in the cognitive and affective neurosciences.

The important contribution of Freud's pulsion theory is that it grounds psychic life in the feeling of the body, particularly certain bodily regions (oral, anal, genital) invested successively by the young child in his or her development. At the core of this theory, there is the pleasurable quest for bodily feelings (excitability) and its control (search and suppression): a drive reduction account that remains a powerful causal account of what might motivate psychic life at the outset. There is also the general, rightful intuition that, at birth, the body is the primordial locus of exploration and meaning making. It is also, as proposed here, the primordial locus of first feelings of possession that progressively gets objectified in things, and very early on in people with the universal propensity of infants to develop *exclusive attachment* and imprinting to their primary caregiver, typically the mother.[65]

In *The Family Idiot*, his biography of nineteenth-century writer Gustave Flaubert, Jean-Paul Sartre (1905–80) speculates at length and in remarkable depth on the early mother–infant bonds that arise from essential care, the origins of the primordial dependence that is the source of attachment and its necessary counterpart: the fear of losing. In the first part of this long

[64] For example, over sixteen centuries ago, in what is often considered the first self-narrative in the history of Western thought, Saint Augustine in his *Confessions* reflects and speculates on the origins of what he feels and knows about himself, and where he learned the possibility of communicating these feelings to others. He concludes that it must be learned in infancy, from others, particularly women because of the primal maternal bond and care: "I give thanks to you, lord of heaven and earth . . . For you have granted to man that he should come to self-knowledge through the knowledge of others, and that he should believe many things about himself on the authority of the womenfolk. Now, clearly, I had life and being; and, as my infancy closed, I was already learning signs by which my feelings could be communicated to others" (*Confessions*, 1.6.10).

[65] See the seminal work of John Bowlby on early affective attachment and the cross-cultural validation of the concept in the more experimental work of Ainsworth: Bowlby, *A Secure Base*; Ainsworth, *Infancy in Uganda*; Ainsworth et al., *Patterns of Attachment*.

essay ("the constitution"), Sartre describes at length the initial experiential state of total abandon to the care of the mother. Sartre writes: "The newborn, molded everyday by dispensed cares, internalizes the maternal activity of his own passive 'being there', in other words the infant internalizes the maternal care activity as the passivity that conditions all the pulsions, and all the internal rhythms of desires, speeds, accumulated storms, schemas that reveal at the same time organic constancies and unspeakable wishes – in brief that his own mother, buried deep into that body, becomes the *pathetic* structure of affectivity" (p. 58).

Sartre insists on the inescapable determinant of the mother as a whole person who determines the affective core experience of nurtured newborns. Maternal constitution, relative sensitivity, and life story are inescapably reflected in the kind of care, attention, and gestures mothers are able to dispense to their infant. Indeed, in the experiential life of newborns that revolves primarily around the passive reception of care molded by others, there is more than the serving of basic survival needs such as food, warmth, and hygiene. There is also, as Sartre points out, the transmission of unique trans-generational idiosyncrasies or family truth: "when the mother breastfeeds or cleans her infant, she expresses herself, like anybody else, in her personal truth, which, naturally, sums up in it all her life, from her own birth; in the meantime, she realizes a rapport that changes depending on circumstances and people – for which she is the *subject* and that we can call maternal love . . . But, at the same time, by this love and through it, by that person, skillful or unskillful, rough or tender, the way her history made her, the child is manifested to himself" (p. 57).

From Sartre the philosopher, at the end of his life, wearing the hat of psychoanalysis that for years he tended to dismiss, these reflections depict the mutual transmission of affects arising from recurrent and necessary care. This would be the context in which first exclusive attachment arises in early development: from the affective molding of the infant to the mother, and the molding of the mother to her infant in the dispensing of care. By analogy to the dialectic bond of master and slave, but with love added: the newborn would extract a sense of imposed passivity and submission, the mother would extract a sense of duty and fulfillment in the instinctive call for maternal love and protection. First deep exclusive possession feelings could arise from such a universal and necessary care transaction.

Instinctual imprinting of the young on the mother and strong attachment to the primary caregiver is an adaptive feature found across species. In avians, imprinting and attachment to the mother, source of food and protection, can take only a few minutes, as shown by the pioneering work of ethologists like Konrad Lorenz with goslings and other chicks. Among primates, and particularly in humans, attachment develops over time and is more protracted. In humans, attachment to the mother lasts for months, if not years, typically shared with multiple siblings of various ages, cause of inescapable rivalry, conflicts, and competition for attention, the source of the seminal fear of being abandoned, left out, ostracized, and banned from the group.[66]

However, before the first documented signs of jealousy, when for example the mother is attending to another infant (6 months),[67] or the first signs of wariness of strangers that an infant shows by clinging to its mother and burying its face in her (8 months),[68] there are signs of innate selectivity. Exclusive feelings are expressed and learned from the outset.

Built-in addictive pleasures

Newborns orient to things in the environment that are highly rewarding such as food smell or the scent of the mother that is quickly associated with comfort and care. As already mentioned, newborns tend to orient preferentially toward an object impregnated with the smell of their own mother's amniotic fluid, but they also prefer a sweet taste that is associated with high nutritient content and intense built-in sources of pleasure, endorphin rushes from the engagement of *opioid* (pleasure) pathways that are highly functional in the young brain. The satiety of newborns after a good feed is as unmistakable as the rush of heroin addicts after getting their fix: the eyelids get heavy and the eyes roll back into the head.

Pleasure orientation is a built-in feature that is the basic source of subjective contrasts: to have or not to have pleasure, to have more or less of it in relation to others. Pleasure orientation is indeed the foundation of what will eventually become claims of injustice and rejection in sentences like "She got more than me!" In a more extensive fashion, it is the foundation of all the jealous and envious clamor that surrounds rivalry, power, and competition, the main stuff of social life in general.

From birth, intensely addictive built-in pleasures are associated with particular features of the environment: eyes and facial features, food, mouth-able objects, breast, people specified by particular smell, temperature, skin texture, ways of moving, talking, holding, reacting, responding, and interacting. Quickly, privileged sources of pleasure are objectified and differentiated by the young child, particularly the mother and

66 Fear of rejection and the quest for recognition is a basic premise of human psychology, the thesis I developed in a former book, *Others in Mind*.

67 Hart and Carrington, "Jealousy in 6-month-old infants."

68 Spitz, *The First Year of Life*.

whoever provides food and comfort on some regular basis. This discriminatory process also feeds infants' anticipation of pleasure satiation. The child implicitly expects food when seeing and feeling the maternal breast. Hungry, it displays agitation, fussiness, and vital excitement in anticipation of food. Food itself is associated with intense pleasures, and eventually leads to the built-in craving for sweet things and calories. This pleasure addiction is part of the system we and other animals have evolved. It is the essential motivational (energetic) source that guides behavior from the outset. Subjective pleasure is a feature selected for its survival value. It is also the source of what tends to lead us astray beyond infancy.

The origins of our untamed propensities toward envy and jealousy, our insatiable thirst for power and self-assertion, are to be found in the addictive pleasure experience of newborns. It all boils down to an original contrast of pleasurable versus less pleasurable or unpleasant experiences, with all their complex associations that go rampant, becoming exponentially more intricate and indirect (symbolic) as a function of development.

At birth, the association between the experience of embodied pleasures and features in the environment are not yet objectified. Newborns habituate to and learn to detect as well as to anticipate pleasure-associated features of their environment based on mechanisms that can be functionally and superficially described in terms of classical and operant conditioning.[69] At a deeper and more meaningful level, however, it is more accurate to describe the behavioral "phenotype" of newborns as revolving around the strong subjective experience of more or less pleasurable categorical values, in terms of both quality and intensity.

Daniel Stern, in an unusual 1991 book entitled *Diary of a Baby: What Your Child Sees, Feels, and Experiences*,[70] took on the developmental task of imagining what it is like to be a young child from 6 weeks to 4 years. Stern writes from the perspective of the child and reconstructs what it must feel like to be hungry, to wake up, or to stare at a moving spot of light. Stern infers the world of feeling experience of a fictive newborn (named Joey), informed by what we now know about perception, learning, and affect regulation in infancy. The world of Joey at 6 weeks is for Stern a world of sensations, in the sense of feelings described above in reference to mental states. Although this world is nameless and non-objectified, not yet explicit or conceptualized, it is a world rich in motion and moving impressions, where pieces of space are contrasted, detached,

[69] See all the pioneer works of Lewis P. Lipsitt; for an overview, see Rochat, *The Infant's World*.

[70] Stern, *The Diary of a Baby*.

move, meet, overlap, vanish. It is a world made of rhythms and changes of pace in which the infant detects forces expressed in movements: acceleration, deceleration, shrinking and looming of forms and shapes that are more or less capturing the attention of the child like magnets of various forces that wax and wane. The world that Stern describes has phenomenal "qualities." It is experienced from a particular embodied point of view, the first person perspective that Stern tries to capture from the first weeks of life. The assumption behind this approach is that the world of sensations and associations with pleasures and displeasures of the newborn (her feeling experience) is not just undifferentiated or diffuse like the initial blooming buzzing confusion proposed by William James. It is a world of experiences with distinct qualities and values that are anchored in the body, lived from within, and therefore carry with them a subjective perspective.

Pleasure and need to control

In the course of the first months, this subjective experience is quickly projected into things (objects or persons) and associated with the control of these things in interaction with them. By 6 weeks, infants universally begin to smile back at smiley faces. They engage in socially elicited smiling, the beginning of reciprocal affective exchanges in which emotions are produced and co-constructed in face-to-face interactions. By 6 weeks also, infants begin to instrumentalise their body to deliberately produce specific consequences on objects: sounds or movements that they explore and discriminate. In this context, the feeling of control over objects and people, the mastery of particular self-produced effects on things and people, are the roots of the first feelings of possession: the embodied sense of possessing control and efficacy over things from which exclusive attachment grows.

Control over things, including one's own body, is a feeling of power that materializes first in the direct (non-symbolic) embodied experience of self-efficacy. From the outset, the feeling of embodied self-efficacy appears to be *self-elevating* and *self-aggrandizing*, as Hume had already proposed in the eighteenth century,[71] the source of great pleasure and comfort as we shall be discussing next. Inversely, being *dispossessed* of the power to control and experience self-efficacy is universally and from the earliest age a source of profound discomfort, even despair (e.g., crying and protest when forcefully unlatched from the breast or the bottle in the middle of a feed).

[71] Hume, *A Treatise of Human Nature*, see chapter 2.

The pleasures and need to control expressed from the outset in humans have deep evolutionary roots and are shared by most animals. For example, there is a well-established animal model of learned *helplessness*: the paralyzing and deleterious feeling associated with the experience of being dispossessed of the ability to control and have predictive power over events in the environment. Animal learning, at the most basic level of classical or operant conditioning, entails some predictive ability: the learned anticipation that certain events, good or bad, will follow a signal (classical conditioning) or that certain self-produced actions will be followed by certain consequences, good or bad (instrumental or operant learning).

Ancient roots of subjectivity

The detection of regularities in the environment as well as the detection of the effects an organism has on the environment are the necessary endowment of every organism to feed, avoid predators, reproduce, and ultimately spread their genes. It is the endowment of every animal that has a nervous system, from invertebrates to vertebrates, insects, fish, birds, rodents, and primates like us.

Linked to such endowment is subjective experience made of feeling states that have embodied *values and qualities*. These drive the organism, pulling and pushing it while it learns, acts, perceives, decides, and memorizes, all of it forming an experience of the world that is fundamentally meaningful in terms of resources and perceived affordances.[72] At an affective level, this experience of the world refers to mental states that are categorically organized along polar opposite built-in value systems such as pleasure versus displeasure; flight versus fight; pain versus no pain; stressful versus calm; safe versus unsafe. These built-in value systems correspond to a primordial experiential semantics, what can be called a *primitive grammar of feeling values* that we share from the outset with most animals.

One could strongly object to the attribution of subjective feeling experience to fish, even more so to invertebrate like crustaceans, insects, or mollusks (e.g., the hermit crab we discussed in Chapter 3). It is indeed

[72] This view resonates with the general approach taken by James J. Gibson in his book *The Ecological Approach to Visual Perception*. Gibson introduces the concept of affordances, what an environment offers to a particular animal for action. Affordances are values for action that are co-defined by the mutual relation linking the animal to its environment. Ceilings afford walking for a fly, but not for most other terrestrial animals like cows. The environment of the fly is made of different affordances, hence has different values in terms of action and its control.

hard to draw the line but there is now strong evidence that feeling experience is very ancient in the evolution of living systems. However, recent research has shed new light on the issue, providing hard facts on the feeling states of ancestral species. As a case in point, I will briefly review some convincing structural and functional evidence suggesting that rainbow trout, in all likelihood, do feel pain.[73]

Specific pain receptor systems are now described in the nervous system of the trout. They fire in the same way as pain receptor systems in our human brain fire as we experience pain. Ours and fish pain systems are homologous. Behaviorally, when bee venom, a source of pain for us, is injected into the lips of a rainbow trout, the fish responds by rubbing its lips along solid surfaces, like stones or the wall of their tank, in the same way we rub ourselves to alleviate local pain. These responses appear to persist over time and are variable, not straightforward rigid reflex responses, rather resembling genuine engagement of more flexible pain relieving action systems. In the same vein, other research demonstrates that goldfish previously injected with morphine show less avoidant (escape) behavior to heat stimulation.[74]

Zebrafish, a species that is among the most evolutionarily primitive vertebrates, actually display a nervous system that in many ways is homologous to the mammalian brain (including ours). The zebrafish is endowed with a structure that is homologous to our amygdala, which sustains our emotional engagement in the world. This is what researchers concluded after reviewing the large body of recent research on the neuropsychology of learning and memory in this fish of the teleost group:

> recent developmental, neuroanatomical, and functional data indicate that the evolution of brain and behavior may have been more conservative than previously thought. Experimental data suggest that the properties and neural basis of learning and memory are notably similar among teleost fish and land vertebrates. For example, lesion studies show that the teleost cerebellum is essential in classical conditioning of discrete motor responses. The lateral telencephalic pallium of the teleost fish, proposed as homologous to the hippocampus, is selectively involved in spatial learning and memory, and in trace classical conditioning. In contrast, the medial pallium, considered homologous to the amygdala, is involved in emotional conditioning in teleost fish. The data reviewed here show a remarkable parallelism between mammals and teleost fish concerning the role of different brain centers in learning and memory and cognitive processes. These evidences suggest that these separate memory systems could have appeared early during the evolution of vertebrates, having been conserved through phylogenesis.[75]

[73] Sneddon, Braithwaite, and Gentle, "Do fish have nociceptors?"
[74] Nordgreen et al., "Thermonociception in fish."
[75] Salas et al., "Neuropsychology of learning and memory in teleost fish," at p. 157.

For our purposes, what we should retain from all this is that, from a neuroanatomical (structural) and behavioral (functional) standpoint, it is not farfetched to impute emotions, feelings, and hence basic subjective experience to simpler, more primitive animals at both the evolutionary and the epigenetic scale. They appear to possess the equipment to act, perceive, memorize, and learn in a world specified in terms of feeling values (e.g., dangers and safety; pleasures and displeasures), showing evidence of *emotional conditioning*. Whether the analogy should stop there, or possibly could go down further into the invertebrate order, is an open question. A line certainly has to be drawn at some point and strict criteria that would be recognized by everybody may be difficult to find, like the criteria for the beginning of subjective life in fetal development, hence the implicit self-awareness discussed earlier. Here, for the zebrafish and other primitive vertebrates, as well as for the human fetus, the criteria are both structural and functional, strongly pointing toward primordial subjectivity and implicit self-awareness in these creatures.

6 Ownership in development

Central to the book is the construal of possession as a feeling experience and ownership as the public expression of such experience. In this chapter, we consider how ownership, hence the public expression of possession, develops. As for all domains of child psychology, this development unfolds from being first implicit and non-conceptual, to becoming explicit and conceptual or symbolic. In the broadest developmental sense, the development of ownership captures a transition from obligatory and inescapable, to more intentional and deliberate, public manifestations of possession. The goal of this chapter is thus to map this development. We shall do so in reference to various levels of *general awareness* that appear to unfold between birth and 5 years. To these various levels of general awareness would correspond different ownership kinds, different putative processes, and differences in meaning regarding ownership. The main point of the chapter is to drive the idea that this development prepares children to become moral individuals among other moral individuals. The main feature of this development is that the public expression of possession (i.e., ownership) eventually becomes moderated by ethical principles that can be articulated, understood, and negotiated in explicit terms with others.

The question is: how does this development unfold and what leads children to eventually reason about ownership in relation to values that are collectively shared and recognized, as in the highly conceptual notion of property with all the abstract rights putatively attached to it? What leads children from the implicit feeling of possession, to the highly abstract and explicit sense of property?

In order to deal with these crucial questions, we need to place them in the larger context of general awareness and its development, in particular what might constitute our awareness of things and how such awareness develops to become conscious, ultimately co-conscious and collectively shared with others, like the notion of legal property. To do so, I use a simple *onion metaphor* to capture what amounts to various constitutive layers of general awareness.

Layers of wakeful mind states in development

In the most general sense, there are different ways of being awake and alive in the world, hence different ways of feeling possession and of expressing such feelings in public displays of ownership. We shall see that these ways build up in development to form layers of awareness corresponding to different general mind states that are important to distinguish from both a developmental and an ontological point of view. If we look at children in their development, we can extract a natural taxonomy and filiation of mind states or awareness levels.

The constitutive layers of an onion that grow from and around its core provide an apt metaphor of mind states in development.[1] At the level of awareness, there is a centrifugal growth starting from a minimal experiential core. This growth would map onto the rapid brain growth that is visible and clearly described in embryogenesis. We briefly alluded to it in the first chapter. We now tentatively draw a parallel, albeit superficial, between brain and mental state development.

By 4 weeks post-conception, the neural tube (brain core) forms from layers of cells on the embryonic disc attaching to the mother's uterus wall, from which the main brain structures rapidly differentiate (spinal cord, hindbrain, midbrain, and forebrain), each differentiating further into macrosystems like the medulla, the cerebellum, the inferior and superior colliculus, and the two cerebral hemispheres.[2]

At a psychological level, the developmental growth of awareness and wakeful mind states corresponds also, by analogy, to the centrifugal growth dynamic of the onion and the brain from a coarse anatomical perspective and at a very coarse scale. From a basic core, layers build up on top of each other. The end product is a system as a whole that is constituted by these various, distinguishable layers that can interact with each other in various, more or less complex ways. The interaction between the constitutive layers of an onion is essentially one of support, like the physical pressure on bricks forming a building. Obviously, the interaction among the constitutive layers of the brain or the adult mind states is incommensurably more complex. However, the onion, the brain, or our

1 However, note that a more apt metaphor would be that of a "blooming" onion, each layer expanding not only in circumference but also exponentially in thickness or depth. A new layer opens vastly larger, more open-ended meaning-making horizons, in the same way that the emergence of language, recursive thinking, and referential (symbolic) functioning exponentially expands children's communication, apprehension, and meaning making of the world.

2 See Carlson, *Human Embryology and Developmental Biology*; Hepper, "Prenatal development."

wakeful experience of being alive can similarly be envisioned as complex systems constituted by added, distinguishable layers forming a whole.

In relation to mind states, in our existence and encounters with the world, we do oscillate and navigate through layers of relative awareness, from sleep to wakefulness, from unconscious to various conscious states. In development, we add layers of possible awareness. The emergence of a new, possibly more powerful and encompassing layer of awareness does not radically eliminate or replace others. What is proposed here is that a new layer adds a new possible mind state through which the individual tends to navigate in the dynamic oscillation between mind states that is the character of phenomenal awareness in the broadest and general sense. It is the stream of consciousness William James accounted for in his seminal depiction of being aware and alive in the world.

A new layer of awareness in development does not restructure and re-describe the experiential landscape as a whole, eliminating former experiential landscapes. Development would just produce new layers of awareness and mind states, novel dimensions to *the* (only one) experiential landscape in general, in the same way that polarized glasses can give you temporary access to a third spatial dimension (depth) of a two-dimensional screen surface at a movie. *Development would enhance our experiential potential of being alive and aware in the world.*

Describing these layers or ways of being mentally alive in the world allows us to establish some sort of developmental *blue print map* that can serve as reference and illuminate ownership from its origins and in development.

Six mental states as they unfold in development

There are at least six mental states that can be distinguished from a phenomenal standpoint, spanning from non-conscious to co-conscious mind states. These ontologically different mental or mind states would emerge chronologically in development. They correspond respectively to (1) *non-conscious*, (2) *unconscious*, (3) *aware*, (4) *co-aware*, (5) *conscious*, and last but not least (6) *co-conscious* states of mind. There follows a summary description of these different mental states in the putative order of their emergence in development.[3]

(1) *Non-conscious states* correspond to the state of being alive, yet absolutely oblivious of being, like a comatose person in a vegetative state. It is a state of the mind by negation, like a cosmic black

[3] These six mental states are described and discussed in detail in chapter 3, "Variety of self-reflective mind states," in Rochat, *Others in Mind.*

hole of antimatter, a thing of nothingness. It is as difficult for us to construe non-consciousness while conscious as it is to construe death while alive, nothingness while being in the world. However, non-consciousness does exist as a reality that is necessary, if not by direct inference from experience, at least by logical deduction.

(2) *Unconscious states* correspond to another kind of oblivious state of the mind with no traces of explicit awareness as in the preceding state of "comatose" non-consciousness. Yet, it is clearly distinct from it, because contrary to a non-conscious, comatose state, in being unconscious one can eventually become aware and conscious of it. For example, through a psychoanalytical cure or mere self-reflection and mental inference, one can bring to explicit awareness subliminal phenomena like subconscious desires or influences that are shown to pull and push us in our feelings and decisions. Advertisers are fully aware of such phenomena in planning commercial and other branding campaigns. Likewise, individuals can retrospectively and prospectively become aware of these unconscious states.

(3) *Awareness* is an implicit state in which one is neither conscious, non-conscious, nor unconscious. It is a state in which one is aware of being alive in a sentient body in the world. It corresponds to what phenomenologists like Husserl or Merleau-Ponty capture as the sense of being present in the world: "le sentiment de sa présence au monde" (the feeling of one's own presence in the world). To be aware is ontologically distinct from being conscious. It is different because awareness is by definition implicit as it does not have to be conceptual. It is preconceptual or implicit. To be aware of something is different from conceiving, thinking, objectifying, or being explicit about this thing, just as I am doing now writing about it. One is aware of something typically prior to being able to communicate about it to others via language or any kind of *intentional* gesture. In awareness, no intention is involved. Note that any explicit account of the awareness of being alive is very difficult since it is an experience that, in essence, is implicit and preconceptual. As adepts of phenomenology insist, it precedes and is the foundation as well as the necessary condition of any explicit experience of the self in the world.

(4) *Co-awareness* is an extension of the awareness state presented above. As for awareness, it is not an objectified, intentional state of mind, nor is it non-conscious or unconscious. It is experientially accessible. Yet, it is ontologically distinct because it is a mind state that is in essence social. It is an awareness projected outward toward the presence of other individuals. It pertains to the sense of being aware of one's presence in the world with others, not alone in a solipsist way. Co-awareness is

the awareness that our presence in the world is communal rather than individual, a presence that is simultaneously shared with the presence of others: that one's presence in the world is not alone but rather together with the presence of others. As elusive as it might sound, it is crucial to emphasize *co-awareness* as a specific state of mind, distinct from either awareness per se or any other conscious state. It is for example the implicit awareness that there are other tenants in my apartment building, even if I don't hear them or don't know explicitly who they are. They represent an implicit presence that explicitly determines my behavior (e.g., not making too much noise with my stereo, shushing my friends if they are too loud during a late party).

(5) *Consciousness* is the state of mind where one knows that one knows, and that what one knows knowing is not just transparent, but rather opaque in the sense of being objectifiable. It can become explicit in terms of propositions, predicates, or any other kinds of mental representation, be it simulation, pretense, or memories. These representations are for oneself but also eventually for others, when formatted in words, in texts, or in any other public formats. Consciousness is a mental state in that it is the result of a process that depends primarily on the individual's self-reflection and thinking, as exemplified in Descartes' famous *cogito*: "I think therefore I am." It acknowledges the fact that there is a state of mind where we can think primarily for ourselves, making discoveries on our own and for ourselves in the privacy of our embodied self, and not primarily for others. Consciousness does entail a self-reflective loop and an introspective process dealing with mental objects or objects that are re-presented. The nature and format of these mental objects is the main topic of today's abundant cognitive science research. Some claim that these mental objects are mainly symbolic and propositional in nature. Other researchers claim that they are mainly embodied simulations. Whatever these mental objects may be, they are considered mainly as mental objects generated by the solitary conscious individual, and not often enough as mental objects co-constructed and elaborated in interaction with other individuals.

(6) *Co-consciousness* corresponds to the mind state in which, not only do we know of knowing, but more importantly, we know of sharing knowledge with others. Here the knowledge of knowing is not just individual as in the case of consciousness, but is collective. In contradistinction to the Cartesian, solipsistic conception of consciousness, the knowledge of knowing co-exists in multiple minds, and in a way transcends the individual who becomes only one part of a whole. The knowledge that the individual knows is not of the conscious kind described previously. Why? Simply because it will survive individuals.

> This knowledge will eventually be retained in the mind of other surviving persons as well as in institutions (marriage, justice, schools) that the transient individuals helped in shaping during their lifetime, whether by abiding by it, by transgressing it, or by rebelling against it. Rather than embodied in the individual, this meta-knowledge is embodied in the group, including the family, the society, and the culture where the individual evolves. Furthermore, the mental objects or re-presentations of co-consciousness are not within the individual, but rather *outside.* In particular, they are between the individual and others, not in one of them taken separately. They exist in the social transaction. The mental objects of co-consciousness are at the interface between an individual and other individuals with whom he or she is sharing the experience of being in the world.

The development of ownership needs to be referred to the emergence of these mind states. They represent constitutive layers of experiential awareness. It is the phenomenal soil in which we can find the expressive roots of ownership, its budding layers of meaning in development, from the latching of the newborn to the breast, to the claim of ownership of a 2-year-old screaming "Mine!," or the bartering negotiation of an object in a commercial transaction. All are expressions of ownership within the various layers of mind states just outlined. The idea is that various ways of expressing possession, hence various kinds of ownership, correspond to the successive layers of mind states aggregating in development.

Again, following the onion metaphor, what characterizes ownership in development is the deployment of multiple ways of expressing possession, not the emergence of a new way that would eliminate all the others. An astute property or patent lawyer capable of reasoning and expressing possession in very abstract ways is also capable of falling under the spell of implicit and seemingly irrational expressions of exclusive possession, in jealousy or in the experience of uncontrollable envy often leading individuals of public stature to take unfathomable risks.[4] Instances of powerful politicians and highly educated business people engaging in clearly fraudulent and irresistible acts of possession (e.g., embezzlement or sexual predation) are common occurrences. What develop are multifaceted, often conflicting expressions of possession corresponding to various ownership kinds.

[4] See for example the fall of Dominique Strauss-Kahn, ex-president of the International Monetary Fund and favorite French presidential candidate in the 2012 election, or more recently the French budget minister Jérôme Cahuzac, caught over blatant lies regarding a Swiss bank account he opened to evade French taxes, all the while implementing stringent new tax laws to fight tax evasion of the riches. Both Strauss-Kahn and Cahuzac are officially left-leaning politicians.

Birth: first inalienable ownership by clinging and binding

At birth, infants first cling and latch to things, the breast and the nipple in particular. They systematically manifest discomfort and scream with much agitation when forcefully dispossessed or deprived of the breast in the midst of a feed. A newborn lacking such responses might raise a red flag on the child's health and neurological integrity. Universally, the epitome of a healthy newborn is not a passive recipient, but an infant feeding avidly, latching to the breast with much energy and determination. All of it is measured against both the force in possessing but also, inversely, the force of the newborn's protest in being unwillingly dispossessed from the breast or any other feeding sources.

From a psychosocial perspective (i.e., the vantage point of the individual infant in relation to others), the public "latching" expression of possession of neonates and their typical, "healthy" blind protest of dispossession when unwillingly unlatched from the breast demonstrates that the primordial form of ownership is of an *inalienable* kind.

At first, the expression of possession is fundamentally "autistic" from the infant's perspective, a one-way phenomenon with no obvious psychological reciprocity or volitional value exchange involved compared to what takes place within a few weeks of development time. In the case of feeding, there is pre-adapted physiological reciprocity and mutual co-design between maternal breast and the infant mouth. There is also remarkable pre-adapted behavioral co-design between mother and child. The mother tends instinctively to facilitate her infant to feed with particular positioning and support of the breast (or the bottle for that matter) and the child is equipped with appropriate action systems (rooting, sucking, etc.), adapted to what is offered by the mother. If there is reciprocity, it is mainly the product of the mother's projection and strong empathic feelings toward her infant that is the central psychological "command" core of the basic care and bonding infants depend upon for their survival.[5] If feeding at birth is de facto the meeting of the infant with her caregiver, it is never

[5] For Colwyn Trevarthen, Vasudevi Reddy, and colleagues, two-way shared experiences taking place in face-to-face interaction, what Trevarthen first coined as "primary inter-subjectivity," would happen from birth. What is proposed here is different in that two-way affective reciprocity would emerge unambiguously only by 6 weeks of age, indexed by changes in behavioral states, levels of attention, and more importantly the universal emergence of socially elicited smiling in the context of face-to-face exchanges. All of this forms a constellation of what we view as reliable indices of primary inter-subjectivity. Prior to 6 weeks, evidence of active affective co-construction between infant and mother is not clear, or at least hard to operationalize.

simply a one-way exchange between an active mother and a passive child, but it is nonetheless an exchange that starts off with a major mutuality gap.

Psychologically, nothing indicates in newborns' primitive possessive behavior that they are unambiguously aware of the mother or any caregiver as *agent* of nurturing actions, nor that they are the agent of such actions. They may discriminate nurturing actions and orient to particular features of feeling experience, whether these features are innate or quickly learned, like particular tastes, smells, even gestures. Newborns do show innate and learned preferences, orienting and latching preferentially to breasts or artificial nipples that have certain smells, tastes, density, or texture.[6]

2 months: first inalienable ownership of agency and effects

By 6 weeks post partum, things change as infants start to become significantly more often awake and alert, being less stimulus-bound in their response. In general, they begin to adopt a more *contemplative stance* toward objects and people.[7] It is also by this time that infants start to engage unambiguously in mutual exchanges of smiles and all sorts of affective bids in the context of face-to-face interactions with others. It is in this context that infants and others become mutual agents, co-constructing affective meanings in mutual interactions. Infants begin to smile back, but, more importantly, they begin also to expect others to smile back at them, hence to express mutual, matching feelings via particular gestures and facial expressions. They react negatively to the sudden still face of a social partner, crying, protesting, and displaying negative emotions.[8] From approximately 2 months, infants begin to expect mutuality in affective exchanges, above and beyond specifically utilitarian needs such as food or temperature regulation that seem to guide newborns' behavior. They become increasingly sensitive to the pragmatics and narrative envelops of face-to-face exchanges initiated by caregivers, reacting negatively to sudden changes or disorganizations. For example, a peek-a-boo game initiated by an adult is at once engaging to the infant, particularly from 4 months of age. However, if the adult suddenly

6 See Rochat and Senders, "Active touch in infancy"; Rochat, *The Infant's World*, for more details and discussion.

7 See Rochat, *The Infant's World*, regarding what is described as the "2-month revolution" in infant behavioral development.

8 See the original work by Tronick et al., "The infant's response to entrapment between contradictory messages in face to face interaction"; Rochat and Striano, "Social cognitive development in the first year"; Rochat, *The Infant's World*, for a review.

scrambles the sequence of the game, the infant reacts with negative affects and avoidant gazes.[9]

In developing social expectations within the pragmatic context of face-to-face exchanges and the co-construction of joyful experiences that are shared, young infants from 2 months of age begin to experience their *own sense of agency* via the amplified impact they have on others, often at a distance with no actual physical contact. In response to the infant, adults tend irresistibly to reinforce the child's sense of social agency with exaggerated contingent emotional responses in the form of systematic affective mirroring, including the production of high-pitched vocal responses, so-called "motherese," or infant-directed speech. This is universal, observed in all cultures, albeit sometimes under different disguises and modality (predominantly tactile and gestural, in addition to vocal).

In this emotional nurturing of contingent mirroring responses from caregivers and a new contemplative stance, infants manifest a new kind of ownership: the "mine-ness" of self-produced actions and their effects (e.g., smiling). The sense of this new ownership kind rests on an awareness that is implicit and non-conceptual: the embodied feeling of producing effects on people and things, the possibility of developing expectations in the social but also in the physical realm, as they encounter physical objects and discover novel situations in their physical environment.

By 2 months, for example, but not at birth, infants discriminate and explore systematically the auditory consequences of the pressure they apply on a musical pacifier. If the sound they produce (pitch variation) corresponds and is commensurate to the pressure they apply on the pacifier, they suck very differently compared to when the sound is equally contingent but not analog to their sucking.[10] These observations demonstrate that by 2 months infants begin to explore the consequences of their own actions (i.e., sucking), modulating and controlling their auditory consequences (analog or non-analog pitch variations). We can say that in doing so they manifest possession: the feeling that they have control of the means to produce effects that they own. Since this is not observed in neonates, it appears that from 2 months infants begin to manifest the implicit awareness of the *inalienable mine-ness* of self-produced actions and the ownership of the effects they cause on people and things. But this awareness would emerge first and is primarily built in face-to-face interaction with the caregiver, who in her care of the infant tends

[9] Rochat, Querido, and Striano, "Emerging sensitivity to the timing and structure of protoconversation in early infancy."

[10] See Rochat and Striano, "Emerging self-exploration by 2 month-old infants"; Rochat, *The Infant's World.*

spontaneously and compulsively to mark with amplification the emotional impact and effects of the infant's own affective bid via mirroring, in particular in relation to smiling, but also in the active display of other emotions like disgust, anger, interest, or sadness, all part of the child's innate affective repertoire.

From an early fascination with and privileged focus of attention on faces and people, from approximately 4 months of age infants become increasingly engaged with physical objects that they systematically try to reach and touch. With the emergence of the systematic, well-documented eye–hand coordination, an infant's motto becomes "Touch all at all cost." As mentioned already in a preceding chapter, reached and grasped objects are first predominantly brought to the mouth for further inspection and appropriation (oral capture), often with repetitive transports in and out of the oral cavity.

In the emergence of these new behavioral patterns, that are once again universal and systematic from the fourth month with nascent forms observed already in the first month in so-called "pre-reaching behaviors,"[11] infants further consolidate the mine-ness of their own control and agency over things, expanding this feeling experience to physical objects without the active building, affective mirroring, and hence reinforcing encouragement of an interactive adult. The infant is now compelled to do so of his own volition. We see this transition as a crucial step toward the objectification of ownership proper, the roots of what it will become in a few months' developmental time: explicit (that's mine!) and potentially alienable ownership kind through bartering, donation, and negotiation. But the question is how do infants get there? How do they go from actively developing an implicit awareness of their own control over people and things that they unambiguously perceive as differentiated and situated in relation to them, to the explicit notion of owning something that is either alienable (can be brought to a zone of exchange with others as in the case of food or a toy) or inalienable (absolute, exclusive, and immutable ownership like the mother or the effects of one's own actions)?

9–18 months: the differentiation of alienable ownership

It appears that this developmental transition begins to operate by 7–9 months, once the infant has firmly established the necessary awareness of having exclusive (inalienable) ownership of the effects of their own actions

[11] See von Hofsten, "Eye–hand coordination in newborns"; Rochat, *The Infant's World.*

on people and objects: their mine-ness. Importantly, this transition also operates in relation to postural development, in particular the infant's rapidly developing mobility to explore the environment away from the secure base of the mother (scooting, crawling, and eventually taking first steps). As infants become more independent from the postural support of others, they can feel and bring their insatiable curiosity to touch and manipulate objects to a dramatically new level. Postural maturation and the accompanying development of autonomous mobility, as well as the general capacity to maintain basic bodily balance while acting in the world, open up new horizons with significantly novel access to much larger portions of the physical and social environment. From approximately 9 months, infants' degrees of behavioral freedom explode, expanding also the realm of their subjective experience with more reasons to claim ownership and entitlement over things.

With increased mobility, infants have suddenly infinitely more reasons for being envious and jealous, infinitely more reasons to compete with others and control what they experience as their possession. By analogy, children become king of a much larger kingdom. As emperors of an empire that includes more and more distant lands, they need to police, i.e., assert power and ownership, in new ways. The new existential conundrum arising by the end of the first year is the following: How can one render compatible the irresistible need to explore and get physical access to an ever expanding universe of objects, compulsively and imperialistically asserting physical control over them, while at the same time maintaining close contact with the secure base of the mother that is still needed for survival.

This basic, novel existential conundrum for the infant, in general the major human conundrum that infants taste unambiguously for the first time starting at 9 months, is the source of new claims of ownership, not only in number but also in kind. It is also probably the major source of morality in general, since most human conflicts pertain to issues of possession and ownership, as is biblically exemplified by at least six of the Ten Commandments inscribed on two tablets that Moses received from God on Mount Sinai.[12]

At this new developmental juncture, many novel patterns of social behavior emerge, in particular new manifestations of possession that are associated with the first implicit signs of a new major kind of ownership: *the ownership of something that is alienable*, the expression of a possession feeling that can be undone via a reverse process of dispossession.

[12] See Rochat, "Possession and morality in early development."

This new kind of ownership thus emerges in contradistinction and by differentiation from a primordial inalienability of the objects of first possession and first public manifestations of ownership. We have seen that this primordial inalienability of things possessed and controlled, eventually publically manifested as implicit ownership, is illustrated by prototypical forceful latching at the mother's breast, the quick protest of newborns dispossessed from things they are attached to, the early selective attention to the primary caregiver, the mine-ness experience of self-produced actions, and, more to the point, the inalienable, hence exclusive, expression of ownership of own actions' *effects* on things and people starting at 2 months of age.

Interestingly, the differentiation of alienable from inalienable ownership kinds is most evident when considering two opposite facts emerging at around 9 months and rarely considered together by researchers. These facts are that on the one hand infants begin to manifest exclusivity, hence inalienable ownership, for familiar people. On the other, they begin to enjoy offering and bringing to the attention of others objects they grasp, control, and explore of their own volition.

Regarding the expression of inalienable ownership and exclusivity, it is well documented that, by 8–9 months, infants typically start to demonstrate so-called "stranger anxiety."[13] Up to 6–7 months, infants tend not to be bothered when picked up by a stranger who wants to play and interact with them. By 9 months, however, things change drastically. The sight of a stranger, whether the infant is outgoing or not, drives the 9-month-old to cling, hold tight, and often to bury its face into the familiar caregiver in an excess of apparent wariness and search for protection. These are expressions of a generalized "proto" social phobia (the fear of social novelty), but they are also the expression of an assertion of ownership toward the familiar person. This assertion is unmistakable and oriented toward that novel, scary individual (the stranger). It is the assertion of an inalienable sense of owning exclusively the person the child is clinging to (i.e., the mother or familiar individual). Clinging and holding on to someone else, burying one's face into her, is always more than simple comfort seeking like getting closer to a source of heat or affective warmth seeking. It is, possibly in addition, always an assertion of control and exclusivity over something that is outwardly claimed to be inalienable, in the sense that separation would be the source of major protests like tantrums and other signs of outward despair and suffering.

Signs of stranger anxiety are, in the social context, a clear assertion of exclusive ownership of the person the child clings to and with whom he seeks

[13] Spitz, *The First Year of Life*; Rochat, *Others in Mind*.

refuge. By analogy, someone rushing toward a shelter to escape a danger makes it de facto his *own*. He will defend with teeth and nails any attempts at dispossession or destruction of what now is, in the face of danger, an inalienable possession and, with its public defense, the social manifestation of inalienable ownership. It is in this context that attachment and the importance of first bonding is probed by clinical psychologists interested in what might be the source of inter-individual differences in personality development. Attachment theorists can sometimes predict future personality outcomes and provide rich personality descriptions based on how infants, children, and even adults express ownership and exclusivity of significant others in the face of separation (death or abandonment) or in the context of trying to establish and regulate new intimate (love) relationships.[14]

Parallel to this novel explicit expression of exclusivity over people, infants by 9 months also begin to play with the control and risks of being dispossessed: dispossessed of caregivers' presence and devoted attention as they gain independence and start to reach and grasp objects increasingly on their own. The repertoire of infants' manipulation and actions on objects also grows exponentially, starting to include first signs of tool use and other means–end coordination, like pulling a blanket in order to bring closer an object for grasping and exploration. Infants start spontaneously piling up objects and bringing them in contact. They engage in increasingly fine manipulations and enjoy playing dispossession and repossession, regaining control over things after spontaneously pushing them away or dropping them, often involving others to pick them up and bring them back for further manipulation. These games can be construed as "alienation exercises," where the child probes and enacts the possibilities of controlling and losing control over objects, owning, disowning, and eventually re-owning them. This is a recapitulation of what infants manifest during the first months with the systematic oral capture of objects they grasp, bringing them in and out of their mouths, but always in physical contact with them. The kind of alienation exercises that start to become prominent from 9 months involve episodes in which the child experiences spontaneously total loss of contact and control over the object only to eventually regain possession over the object: pushing away or dropping objects, then regaining control. When others are involved, picking up an object the child systematically pushes away or drops on the floor, there is the first enactment of a give and take exchange. It prefigures the spontaneous transfer of possession, hence the idea of an object that is alienable, like a ball in a game of table tennis that transits from one possessor to another.

[14] See Bowlby, *A Secure Base*; or for example Fonagy, Target, and Gergely, "Psychoanalytic perspectives on developmental psychopathology."

From 9 months, infants clearly show that they systematically explore the possibility of objects' alienability that can be more or less temporary, and sometimes even forever when the object is destroyed, eaten, or thrown away. The learning and exercise of this possibility is in contradistinction to the exclusive feelings of possession and the inalienable kind of ownership infants manifest toward their mother and other familiar caregivers, often including objects like security blankets and other favorite dolls or stuffed animals, "transitional objects" young children invest in and use as a reminder and comfort substitute when coping with temporary separation from the mother.

In his 1922 book *Beyond the Pleasure Principle*, Freud reports the alienable exercises he noticed in an 18-month-old child. It is a good illustration of the early propensity to explore the conundrum of gaining and losing control over things, exploring the transition from feeling possession, to losing possession, eventually regaining it. It appears that this kind of alienable exercise that children transform into joyful games is an important aspect of play from the outset. Between 9 and 18 months, the games become more complex and sophisticated as children develop new possibilities for action. Yet the general psychological meaning or theme remains the same: conjuring loss and re-appropriation of control over things. Here is what Freud writes about this child's favorite game, in which his own separation anxieties were conjured by being spontaneously and joyfully acted out.

> Occasionally, however, this well-behaved child evinced the troublesome habit of flinging into the corner of the room or under the bed all the little things he could lay his hands on, so that to gather up his toys was often no light task. He accompanied this by an expression of interest and gratification, emitting a loud long-drawn-out "o-o-o-oh" which in the judgment of the mother (one that coincided with my own) was not an interjection but meant "go away" (*fort*). I saw at last that this was a game, and that the child used all his toys only to play "being gone" (*fortsein*) with them. One day I made an observation that confirmed my view. The child had a wooden reel with a piece of string wound round it. It never occurred to him, for example, to drag this after him on the floor and so play horse and cart with it, but he kept throwing it with considerable skill, held by the string, over the side of his little draped cot, so that the reel disappeared into it, then said his significant "o-o-o-oh" and drew the reel by the string out of the cot again, greeting its reappearance with a joyful "*Da*" (there). This was therefore the complete game, disappearance and return, the first act being the only one generally observed by the onlookers, and the one untiringly repeated by the child as a game for its own sake, although the greater pleasure unquestionably attached to the second act.

2–3 years: conceptual inalienable ownership

The terrible twos is the period most parents struggle with, when their child begins to claim ownership over things. The emergence of the infamous

"Mine!" which de facto means "Not yours!," source of major conflicts and probably the origin of moral invectives from the social surrounding intervening to appease tensions and regain social harmony. Inalienable ownership changes in kind, becoming explicit and conceptual. It is now objectified and the expression of consciousness and self-consciousness proper.

Children become explicit and conceptual in their possession by the time they also begin to recognize themselves in a mirror, literally beginning to own explicitly their specular image. Based on the well-documented mirror mark test, from around 21 months toddlers reach for a mark surreptitiously put on their faces that they discover while looking at their mirror reflection.[15] In the meantime, by 21 months, as children become proficient speakers and as the volume of their vocabulary explodes, their mouth also becomes full of personal pronouns and adjectives like "Mine!," "I," or "Me."[16]

Beyond attachment and explicit exclusivity expressed toward familiar persons, including "transitional" objects, from 2 years of age children, particularly in industrial Western cultures as we shall see in Chapter 8, start to claim possession of most things they feel threatened to lose, particularly in a situation where they have to compete with playmates or siblings. These new explicit and forceful claims epitomize a period marked by frequent tantrums and fights over the possessive control, protection, and appropriation of things. It is part of a new stubbornness with common inclinations to escape control, the child taking off to assert his own autonomy, running faster as adult's invectives to come back become more pressing and loud. The child enacts and enjoys newly acquired mobility and behavioral freedom. This marks the opening of a crucial transition in development toward a novel period of defiance in which the child is now actively probing and exploring the limits of others' attention and cares, actively gauging her own situation in relation to others.[17]

In relation to ownership, what is new at this developmental juncture is that the child explicitly projects herself into the object, identifying with it. "That" object is now publicly recognized as an extension of the "Me" that is recognized in the mirror. Ownership is now explicit and conceptual. The feeling of possession is explicitly objectified, publicly recognized, and identified as an extension of the self. Because it is recognized

15 Amsterdam, 1972; Lewis and Brooks-Gunn, *Social Cognition and the Acquisition of Self*.
16 Bates, "Language about me and you"; Tomasello, "One child early talk about possession." See also Haye, "Yours and mine."
17 See Rochat, *Others in Mind*, for a more detailed discussion.

and publicly identified, possession is now elevated to a concept that is socially shared. However, this new public assertion of possession corresponds to an inalienable kind of ownership that progressively will be brought into a zone of exchange and transaction, primarily through social pressures and adult invectives in their arbitration of conflicts over possession, the primordial source of moral exposure for children. It is in the context of adults' and older peers' explicit arbitration and enforcement from others and the explicating of moral norms that specify a space of dos and don'ts, right and wrong, in which the child evolves and has to build an identity that defines his own *perspective* in it.[18]

It is only progressively that the child will develop the central notion that objects that are possessed can gain additional social power by being brought into a space of exchange. This is the major next step transforming ownership from inalienable to being actively used and envisioned by the child as *alienable* commodity in relation to others. This step is a major development in the conceptualization of ownership, a conceptualization that is social and by which ownership starts to be conceptualized as an instrument of social power and social ascendance. Ownership becomes an instrument by which children manage and gauge their own social situation. This emerges unambiguously by the fourth year.

3–5 years: reputable concept of alienable ownership

Until the fourth year, children tend to be unbashful in their typically "rude" assertion of exclusivity and control over possessions. An adult intervention is necessary to resolve conflicts among peers, eventually managing to convince 2–3-year-old children that it would be "nice," "kind," "normal" to let go of selfish clinging and latching on things possessed. By 4 years, children increasingly come to terms *on their own* that it is not such a good idea to cling too much to possessions. They realize that much can be gained from letting go of possessions, aside from adult praises.

From this point on, typical children come to the realization that people do remember and keep track of what they do. Aside from realizing that there is possible retaliation for the immediate gratification of maintaining absolute control over possessions, inversely they also come to grasp that

[18] The notion of moral space is borrowed from the philosopher Charles Taylor, who pointedly states in his long essay on the emergence of modern identity in Western culture: "What we are constantly losing from sight here is that being a self is inseparable from existing in a space of moral issues, to do with identity and how one ought to be. It is being able to find one's standpoint in this space, being able to occupy a perspective in it": *Sources of the Self*, p. 112.

people tend to reciprocate to the unlatching of possessions. Because it is generally acknowledged, recognized, and typically publicly approved by adults, but also by peers, children are quick to realize that much social ascendance can be gained by not showing too much defensiveness, competition, and fear of losing control over possessions.

By 4 years, children finally realize that it pays to let go of possessions, that there is much social gain and empowerment in letting go of ownership. At this juncture, ownership starts to become what it will remain all through the lifespan: the main instrument of social ascendance and recognition, because of the possibility it gives in terms of bartering power and reputation enhancement by being generous and lenient toward others. But what accounts for such transformation? Aside from obvious encouragement and reinforcement from adults, children also develop by 4 years new abilities in reading the mind and intentions of others. It is for example established that between 3 and 5 years children develop an understanding that others have emotions and desires. They anticipate accurately what people will do next based on this knowledge that is not all directly accessible but sometimes has to be mentally inferred or possibly simulated or imagined.

Much research shows that by 5 years, across cultures, children construe that people have beliefs and that sometimes these beliefs are false. In the classic false belief task, they anticipate that a person will look for a treat at a wrong hiding place if they have been surreptitiously tricked with a change of location. Accurate predictions of others' behavior based on the inference of their wants and emotions are even expressed earlier than false belief understanding, but in general it is now well established that psychology and mental state understanding develop markedly and gain much sophistication between 3 and 5 years.[19] What this development indicates is that children grow a capacity to construe secondary representations of what people hold in their mind, able progressively to suspend the primary, experience-based representation they hold for themselves.

In relation to possession, this representational progress means that, as children claim ownership, they become capable not only of experiencing the direct control they exert by claiming possession, but also of conjecturing and probing what others might experience about such a claim: how they feel about it and the extent to which they trust it; whether for example they believe in it, take it seriously – in other words "buy" it or not. At this developmental juncture, what emerges is a new propensity to take into

[19] See the meta-analysis by Wellman, Cross, and Watson, "Meta-analysis of theory-of-mind development"; or the cross-cultural study by Callaghan et al., "Synchrony in the onset of mental-state reasoning."

account what might be the experience of others experiencing possession from a second (intimate) or third party perspective. Considering whether a possession claim might trigger envy and desire in the minds of others, as children assert ownership they may start conjecturing what should happen next, be it a fight, subjugation, a negotiation, or an invitation for exchange. The child also can begin to assess changes in the mind states of others in the course of a negotiation about ownership, whether they understand that a possession is inalienable, or on the contrary alienable and negotiable, and the extent to which the possession claim is taken seriously or not.

Parallel to all this, between 3 and 5 years children develop a sophisticated sense of their own reputation and how others might perceive them as possessors: whether for example possession claims are perceived as more or less fair, more or less generous, whether they are signs of good intentions or bad intentions. The child shows increasingly complex evidence of self-consciousness, representing and fearing the evaluation of others, developing a sense of guilt and shame in parallel to new capacities for help and empathy toward others.[20] During this period, children become flexible and prone to take the perspective of others as third party judges and potential scolders or praisers of them, but also as potential sufferers and future partners in exchanges. Overall, during this period of development, children become better abiders by the *golden rule* by which one should treat others as one would want others to treat oneself. They begin to gain, lose, or maintain ownership, factoring what others might feel and think about it, not just guided by a blind, protective fear of losing control over possession. From this point on, children care about their own reputation. They could be said to become distinctly human, if, aside from language, to be human is to care about reputation.[21]

5 years and up: normative and ethical ownership

Beyond their new concern about reputation, how people might feel in relation to their possessions and possessive behaviors, children from 5 years of age and beyond start to act and think by "principle," according to norms and ethical rules they can articulate and argue about. Ownership becomes part of a conceptual self-identity that is based on more than how people might perceive and evaluate, the simple concern for reputation. It is also based on standards of moral rectitude (what one holds as right or more rightful), standards that are individual but that also become collective.

[20] See Rochat, *Others in Mind*; but also Lewis, *Shame*; Lewis and Brooks-Gunn, *Social Cognition and the Acquisition of Self*.

[21] Rochat, *Others in Mind*; see also Rochat, "The gaze of others."

Abiding by these standards becomes part of a moral identity that children develop from their sixth year, adding a new layer of meaning to ownership, above and beyond mere concerns for reputation. Questions of merit start to play a central part in the child's determination of ownership for self and for others. From who owns what and why, children begin to consider the question of who deserves what and why, reasoning and deciding. In case of conflicts, they become increasingly capable of referring to a consensual third party authority the decision of who should own what and why. In case of fights and competition, they will learn to resort to the larger context of institutions and their ruling, calling for adult authority or invoking collective laws ruling public properties, like school or playground. The child's mind develops to become "institutionalized" in addition to socialized. Outside of the intimate family environment, as they enter school and meet new peers, children have to act, decide, and assert themselves in relation to a larger and more abstract context, dealing with new individuals in public institutions outside of the close family circle of intimate relatives. This reality constrains children toward greater considerations of the rational and putative principles underlying ownership, the reasons why one should own what and why. These considerations result in more or less conformism or more or less questioning of authority, depending on the child's own character but also on the culture surrounding the child that tends to promote more or less individual initiatives in children, as discussed in the final chapter of the book.

From 5 years, ownership becomes increasingly normative and ethical in the sense that it now refers more specifically to what governs and is implicitly or explicitly consensual in the group. Children now progressively appropriate for themselves the norms of their group, calibrating their own personal moral compass in reference to these norms that, paradoxically, also define the child's potential for moral autonomy and the questioning of the authority of these norms. Moral independence and identity can only be determined in relation to norms that exist and that the child can more or less endorse and own.

The quintessence of normative and ethical ownership is what pertains to legal property defined in relation to a code that represents the social, consensual norm. By 5 years, the child begins to include this normative and ethical group perspective in his claim of possession and how he might argue and reason about it, referring to past use and rules, past ruling and judgment, like a form of jurisprudence. In a sense, from this point on and as he will continue to do throughout the lifespan, the child learns to *own the norm* by which he now can also possess and calibrate the relative alienability of his possession: whether or not to donate or exchange for example, and how much to fight, compete, or sacrifice to maintain control over things possessed.

The sensitivity to rule and abiding to implicit norms is evident in children younger than 5 years: 2–3-year-olds will tend to protest if a peer or even an adult violates some pragmatic rules in a game, that for example it is not right to destroy gratuitously someone's artwork or transgress the rule of a game outlined by an authority.[22] But these protests are not yet ethical and moral in the sense discussed above, nor in relation to the new normative layer of meaning surrounding ownership that emerges in 5-year-olds. Prior to this age, protests about norm transgressions are indices of mere conformity to rules of behavior established by an authority, typically adults or older peers. It is a reaction to a transgression of obedience to an authority, with no clear signs of an autonomous decision resting on the child's own moral compass. This compass is best assessed in terms of the ability to *question authority* rather than to obey and conform to it. As discussed by moral philosophers, but also empirically demonstrated by sociologists or developmental psychologists like Piaget or Kohlberg, morality develops in contradistinction to blind obedience, and is measured in terms of relative autonomy and independence from rigid conformity and the norms imposed by an authority.

From 5 years, children start to forge their own moral identity, in part by owning the norms that calibrate the moral compass governing their decisions to claim possession, but also to recognize (or not recognize) the possessions of others. They develop the potential to experience ownership as something that is analogous to "legal" property. What develops from this age is an ownership that is normative and ethical in essence, governed by consensual group rules, the rules of cultural institutions like schools, club activities, birthday parties, group games, and other peer activities. The context of this development is an enlargement of the primordial family environment that constrains children to situate themselves in a more public and less intimate moral space, the moral space defined by larger institutions like schools and peer groups. In this context, children need to recalibrate their moral compass in reference to public, extra-familial norms that are more formal and less lenient, like the rituals and order of the classroom that resemble public institutions like tribunals, hospitals, or libraries where things are basically shared, temporarily owned, or borrowed (e.g., justice, health care, books), things that are owned by everybody for anybody according to strict, consensual rules.

[22] See Haun and Tomasello, "Conformity to peer pressure in preschool children"; also Rakoczy, Warneken, and Tomasello, "The sources of normativity." See also Rossano, Rakoczy, and Tomasello, "Young children's understanding of violation of property rights," demonstrating in 3-year-olds the early signs of pragmatic rule violations regarding ownership from a first but also a third person perspective (when self or third party is concerned).

The normative and ethical kind of ownership adds a new and final layer of meaning to possession claims.

The developmental emergence of this new layer of ownership kind coincides with the first signs of social conformity with peers, linked to new affective needs outside of the close family circle to affiliate and create alliances with friends. This is what happens and becomes the core of children's affective life when integrating public spaces like school, as they discover new group norms and a new, typically more rigid and less tailored order than the safe base of home.

In this new context, children conform selectively with groups of peers, creating alliances and spending much of their energy trying to find some social bearing in the public, extra-familial environment that can quickly become cruel and brutal. Bullying is indeed a phenomenon that is universal and pervasive from 5 years of age.[23] Paradoxically, and by contrast, bullying is revealing of its polar opposite: friendship and popularity that form the holy grail of all children. If the envy of popularity and friendship is universal from the outset, particularly in relation to parents and siblings, it becomes prevalent when children enter preschools and the extra-familial, public context.

The extra-familial, public context of schools and playgrounds is a major source of burgeoning social prejudices that become both implicit and explicit. Children from 4 to 5 years show, like adults, a tendency to hide explicit evidence of prejudice ("I am not a racist"), but are caught up in implicit prejudice reflexes as measured via reaction times in implicit attitude tests. From 5 years, children start to show the same prejudice trend.[24]

Children by 4 years start to display tendencies toward social conformity when interacting with peers. They adopt majority beliefs and opinions even though they know that they are untrue. In conforming, children are ready to defy what they know as true just for the sake of affiliation, reputation, and the gain of social recognition to avoid their biggest fear: social rejection.[25] However, as in the case of objectified and reputable ownership, this early conformity trend is not yet normative and principled proper. It corresponds first to an expression of abidance by and obedience to majority views for the

[23] See the thorough review and meta-analysis of bullying as a pervasive and universal phenomenon from the preschool years in Berger, "Update on bullying at school." More specific to young children and early onset: Alsaker and Valkanover, "Early diagnosis and prevention of victimization in kindergarten."

[24] Cyencek, Greenwald, and Meltzoff, "Measuring implicit attitudes of 4-year old children." See also the concise overview on the dissociation between explicit and implicit social attitudes by Dunham, Baron, and Banaji, "The development of implicit intergroup cognition."

[25] Main thesis of Rochat, *Others in Mind.*

mere sake of feeding the basic need to create affiliation and integrate with the group. There is no necessary ethics in social conformity. In early conformity, children try to avoid suspicious attention from others that could lead to ostracism and prejudice, something that is a prevalent threat from this age on. Autonomous decisions within a group often entail courage and assertiveness, an ethical engagement developing beyond 5 years.

The development of autonomous social decisions parallels the emergence of normative and ethical ownership. It leads the child toward a conceptualization of possession as *property*, a formal and ethical idea of ownership formed around codified and socially recognized rules, in other words around cultural institutions established to prevent and resolve recurrent conflicts regarding who owns what and why.

From 5 years, children begin to integrate this new formal layer in their experience of possession. It is last to emerge but keeps developing throughout the lifespan as it relates to larger institutional and cultural belief systems like religion and political ideologies. It is in this last normative layer that moral identity grows, the source of individuals' more or less autonomous attitudes and political decisions toward others and in their society in general.

Reasoning about ownership in development

With the added layer of normativity and ethics to ownership, children begin to articulate cogent reasons as to why one should own, but even, at a more ontological level, who is endowed with the capacity to own or who is not. Can a worm own? Does a foot own the shoe it wears? Can a person in a coma, asleep, paralyzed, or with hands tied up own something?[26] They develop ideas and concepts regarding who might own what and why?

In recent years, child psychologists have started a new body of research on these cognitive questions. In general, this research demonstrates that, from at least 5 years, children begin to have strong, systematic, increasingly autonomous abstract and ontological thoughts underlying their intuitions about ownership. They begin to articulate systematic, cogent responses and decisions to ownership questions, revealing some normative and ethical reasoning about the legitimacy of possession either for self or for others. Like adults, from 5 to 6 years, children have unambiguously strong abstract and conceptual intuitions regarding who can own and who deserves to be proprietor, in other words who can or cannot experience possession.[27]

[26] Noles et al., "Children's and adults' intuitions about who can own things."
[27] Noles et al., "Children's and adults' intuitions about who can own things."

Research shows that from 5 years children begin to use an ontological boundary to determine and reason for themselves who can own and who cannot. As for adults, this boundary guides children in their third party judgment of ownership as they are asked whether, for example, it is possible for a dead person to own something or whether a thumbtack can own the wall it is attached to or, vice versa, whether the wall owns the thumbtack. However, children begin to express an ontological boundary separating potential owners from individuals or entities that are not endowed with ownership potential, hence legitimate rights to own.

Against the idea that the reasoning around ownership (i.e., ontological boundary) originates in development by an associative process where owner and property are simply connected because of their high temporal frequency and spatial contiguity,[28] changes occurring beyond 5 years support the idea that the concept of ownership and property is rather made of an amalgam of necessary conditions. For legal theorists, this amalgam corresponds to a bundle of independent property rights.[29] In development and beyond 5 years, children appear to solidify this bundle of rights that become explicitly shared with others, the foundation also of all the social and cultural institutions surrounding the child and understood increasingly in their *normative* dimension, beyond strict and forced obedience (rituals, games, schedule, rule of loans, borrowing, and appropriation, ways of being in a group depending on context like church, school, playground, etc.). Indeed, research shows that the concept of owners and the reasoning behind ownership does change and develop in the childhood years, but also throughout the lifespan in the realm of politics. For example, it takes some years (only by 8–10 years of age) for children to attribute ownership potential to people described as being asleep, having low IQ, or being paraplegic. Here is an excerpt from some of the conclusions from a recent developmental study where children and adult participants were asked to determine ownership of property with simple questions in the format of "can a little baby own a blanket?":

> Children and adults uniformly agreed that an individual who was awake owned property. In contrast, there was developmental shift in their judgments about individuals who were asleep or tied up. A significant proportion of adults, 10- and 8-year-olds determined that simply falling asleep did not break the owner–property bond, but only 35% of 6-year-olds reported that Bob still owned the ball after he fell asleep. Similarly, in the Tied-up condition, many

[28] Rudmin, "To own is to be perceived to own."

[29] See Hofeld, *Some Fundamental Legal Conceptions as Applied to Judicial Reasoning*, cited in Noles et al., "Children's and adults' intuitions about who can own things."

children reported that Bob no longer owned the ball after he was tied up, but older children increasingly attributed ownership to tied-up Bob. Both the Sleep and Tied-up conditions exhibited significant Age effects; more children attributed ownership to sleeping and tied-up actors as age increased … children and adults made different ownership attributions. If humans lacked the ability, even temporarily, to exercise their property rights, then children judged that they were not owners. In contrast, adults attributed ownership to humans even when they were unable to exercise most of their property rights.[30]

But what are younger children's ownership "rational" intuitions prior to 5 years and where do they come from?[31] Two and three-year-olds already show that they have reliable intuitions as to what belongs to whom. However, these intuitions seem to rest primarily on prior superficial visual associations between object and person: that for example this sweater belongs to "daddy" because the child saw it frequently and only as worn by her father. By 24 months, children may reliably point in the right direction or act appropriately when asked "Whose sweater is it?" or "Can you give the sweater?" but these responses depend first on the here and now of tangible visual information linking possessor and possession. Research shows that it is only a few months later, starting at the end of the second year, that toddlers are able to abstract ownership based on verbal information, in situations where objects and potential owners are visually absent.[32]

Learning ownership through language rather than through direct visual information is more demanding for the young child. However, at this young age, learning about ownership does not yet rest on systematic conceptual thinking and reasoning about possession, nor apparently on any explicit "theories of mind." It is qualitatively different from the norms and ethics underlying the concept of property that children 5 years and older begin to express.

Study of spontaneous ownership conflicts among same-age toddler peers or siblings reveals that from 24 months children understand and de facto are mentally assimilating (memorizing) the designation of ownership established by the authoritative donation of an adult. In research where pairs of 23–25-month-old children received various toys from an adult, each designated specifically as recipient, resolution of later conflicts over the toys tended to be resolved in reference to the adult's original designation. Designated owners within the pair were, for example, significantly more inclined to maintain and successfully regain possession of

30 Noles et al., "Children's and adults' intuitions about who can own things," p. 277.

31 For a good review of the current research addressing these questions, see the 2011 special issue edited by Ross and Friedman entitled "Origins of ownership of property."

32 Blake and Harris, "Early representations of ownership."

the contentious toy compared to non-designated owners.[33] Interestingly, longitudinal observations of young siblings and same-age peers during play dates indicate that North American middle-class parents tend to resolve conflicts over ownership by not following strictly what young children intuitively reason as their rights to own property (e.g., first or originally designated ownership, gift, etc.). Typically, parents are primarily driven toward teaching their child to share and be nice to others, at all costs, particularly if they are friends. Young children's intuitions regarding the right to own are often violated by parents, constraining the child to articulate ethical reasoning that questions adult authority.[34]

There are now many developmental studies documenting evidence of reasoning about ownership from a third person perspective in children younger than 5 years (i.e., when not directly recipient or owner of the object, just judging others' relative rights in case of conflict).[35] From age 2, children identify owners in some systematic ways based on familiarity, basic default rules that are part of the learned pragmatic of exchanges, or that are explicitly enforced by an authority, typically an adult. In the third year, children show evidence of inferring ownership based on *first possessor principle* (first person to control an object is its owner) or who labored to create it.[36] They begin to understand rights of ownership transfer, although it will take some months and years for children to understand the transfer of ownership rights across multiple contexts (birthday party, purchase, theft, or illegal appropriation).[37] This is where the consolidation of normative and ethical understanding of ownership that emerges by 5 years brings the reasoning about ownership to new abstract levels. These new levels open wide the door to the notion of a consensual legal property ruled by formally recognized communal principles. Interestingly, however, as proposed by Friedman and colleagues,[38] it appears that such formal progress is from the outset built around a better consideration of object history: where it comes from, who made it, who had it first, etc. From early childhood to adulthood, in the thinking of legal

33 C. L. Conant, "The influence of toy ownership on toddler peer interaction," unpublished doctoral dissertation, cited in Ross, Conant, and Vickar, "Property rights and the resolution of social conflict."

34 Ross et al., "Property rights and the resolution of social conflict."

35 Rossano, Rakoczy, and Tomasello, "Young children's understanding of violation of property rights." See also the recent doctoral dissertation of Gabalda, "Development of the sense of ownership," which provides a good review of existing literature.

36 Friedman, "First possession"; Friedman and Neary, "Determining who owns what"; Kanngiesser, Gjersoe, and Hood, "The effect of creative labor on property-ownership transfer by preschool children and adults."

37 Blake and Harris, "Children's understanding of ownership transfers."

38 Friedman et al., "Ownership and object history."

practitioners and global geopolitics (land ownership, repartition and exploitation, who own fish in the ocean, etc.), such historical considerations remain at the core of ownership reasoning and determination.

Three matrices of ownership in development

There are different matrices or lines of development in relation to ownership as public claim of possession. Three at least can be distinguished: (1) the development leading the child from a preconceptual (implicit) to a conceptual (explicit) sense of possession; (2) the development leading the child progressively toward an objectification of possession; (3) the development toward the explicit differentiation of alienable, as opposed to inalienable, possessions. We discuss these three lines separately, trying to capture the essence of developmental changes in ownership values and the issue of their articulation and integration in development. The latter consideration will serve to reintroduce the onion metaphor presented at the beginning of the chapter regarding the various layers of wakeful mind states in development. Here I want to reassert the basic premise of this metaphor to describe ownership in development.

(1) From preconceptual to conceptual ownership

When infants latch on to the breast, they do not have any implicit theory, nor any abstract concepts of breast, food, or mother. These kinds of representation are sometimes projected into the infant's mind. But those are indirect and speculative reconstructions. A good example comes from psychoanalyst Melanie Klein (1882–1960) whose theory of personality development gives a central role to representations of "good" and "bad" breast from the outset, and even early representations of "good" and "bad" penises through a neo-Freudian reinterpretation of the Oedipus complex.[39]

All these speculations presuppose that infants from birth are actively representing a person's character present in their social environment, even if it is via the parts of a person like the breast. By extension, infants from the outset would objectify these characters via complex processes of projection and introjection, each of them presumably an innate given. Although this theory might be useful in helping adults to alleviate and make sense of the symptoms that lead them to seek therapy, it is most unlikely that it does not correspond to what it is like to be a neonate.

[39] Klein, *The Psycho-analysis of Children.*

In the perspective of what develops and changes, the early experience of being alive is in essence preconceptual. At birth and in the first few weeks of life, this experience does not yet include the autonomy of abstraction and representation. It does not carry the capacity to conceptualize "objects" like good maternal breast or bad paternal penis. Looking closely at infant behavior, abstraction and conceptualization emerge and change in development. Ownership is no exception as an intrinsic part of this development.

Theories and abstract reasoning about ownership develop well into childhood and even throughout the lifespan, once such reasoning is shared and negotiated with others in the fertile soil of social conflicts over possession. In early infancy, possession conflicts are implicit and preconceptual, arising mainly from obstacles to the neonate's inborn drives: food, warmth, comfort. The resolution of these conflicts is always temporary, until new obstacles are encountered. However, we have seen that the innate action systems underlying the earliest forms of possessive behavior, such as sucking, grasping, food ingestion, or object transport to the mouth (i.e., hand–mouth coordination), operate in a matrix made of vectors or force dynamic. This force dynamic is a given and works in the context of polar oppositions: centripetal versus centrifugal force; approach versus avoidance motives.

In this context, the motivational engine of early possession rests on preconceptual and implicit values already expressed at birth. As already discussed in the previous chapter, these values represent an *innate affective grammar* made of predetermined feeling experiences of good versus bad tastes or smells, more or less attractive objects like face versus non-face entities. Behaviorally, all of these values are innately expressed and measurable in terms of more or less sustained attention, more or less avoidant responses, more or less orientation and attraction.

From this starting state of affairs, we have seen that infants expand rapidly their range of possession experience as they gain active control of their body as agent of changes in the world, combined with the gain of control over posture and mobility that allows them to explore objects in the environment on their own, at ever greater distances from the secure base of their mother.

The incorporation of others' gaze in the exploration of the environment, via joint attention or social referencing, allows the young child to resolve tentatively the perennial human conundrum of being "alone together," a major achievement as Donald Winnicott proposes. It is also instrumental in rendering public objects of desire in the environment and therefore to construe them explicitly in communication with others, pointing toward them and sharing them in joint attention. The child begins to objectify these things as potential possessions in triangulation with others. This is one of the steps leading young children toward a mental re-description and the first conceptualization of the potentiality to own and have control over an object *in relation to others*. This conceptualization is unmistakably expressed from around 21 months when the child starts to utter "That's mine!," meaning also "Not yours!" It marks the transition from preconceptual and innate propensities to *intentional and conceptual theories* of ownership (i.e., third party reasoning about ownership). This transition opens up a new developmental landscape that extends way beyond childhood with the perennial issues of ethics and politics surrounding property.

(2) Toward the progressive objectification of ownership

When infants by 2 months begin to adopt what we have described as a contemplative stance, exploring the consequences of their own actions and showing signs of "owning" the effects they produce on things, these are the first signs of an implicit objectification of their embodied experience. This does not entail yet a re-cognition (literally "knowing again" or explicit conceptual representation) that they themselves are the agents of the effects they produce. All of it is embodied and implicit, not reflective proper. It is progressively that infants and young children begin to explicitly re-cognize themselves as agents. The same applies for the ownership of objects and people in development.

Ownership of possession is progressively re-cognized by the child when he begins to objectify it as an extension of self via a dual process of projection and identification. This process starts to emerge by the end of the first year, when infants begin, for example, to discriminate and prefer to attend to someone imitating them, compared to someone else who is just behaving contingently but not mimicking them.[40] It is also evident when by 18 months the child begins to engage in true imitation, as opposed to mere emulation, reproducing not only the effects of the action performed by a model, but also the ways the model performs this action leading to the effects.[41] In doing so, the child is de facto demonstrating an ability to project into and identify in the other, able to get into her shoes and under her skin. The child displays the budding ability to hold two perspectives or representations in her mind: a self-perspective and the representation of the perspective of somebody else. This multiple representation ability is also an important aspect underlying ownership in

40 Agnetta and Rochat, "Imitative games by 9-, 14-, and 18-month-old infants."

41 Meltzoff and Moore, "Early imitation within a functional framework."

development, from being implicit to becoming explicit and conceptual as we have seen. The emergence of this ability is at the origins of further objectification of ownership from around 21 months as the child starts to utter "Mine!" (first person perspective) and the necessarily inseparable, inverse negative assertion "Not yours!" (second or third person perspective). As for self-consciousness, the objectification of ownership is the actual integration of these projective perspectives on the object. It is the same, parallel process that leads children from not recognizing to recognizing themselves in a mirror: from the direct experience and exploration of the perfect contingency between embodied self and specular (mirror) reflection, to the projection and identification of self on the polished surface of the mirror as object of reflection.

When starting to show embarrassment in front of the mirror which coincides with mirror self-recognition, children begin also to objectify themselves by integrating first person perspective (that's me in the mirror), with second and third person perspective (that's me in the mirror as seen and evaluated by others). Thus the development of ownership and self-consciousness is parallel and in many ways analog. Both rest on an integration of multiple perspectives (of the embodied self and of others). It also rests on the progressive emergence in infancy of a propensity to identify and project onto people and things. This propensity ultimately leads the child toward the objectifying of self as person, and likewise, the progressive objectifying of possession as ownership and property.

(3) *Toward the progressive differentiation of alienable ownership*

Infants at birth express ownership by latching and binding. When encountering an obstacle to their latching propensities, they manifest distress and caregivers read such distress as protest. Maternal breast, bottle, or food in general, as object of possession for the neonate is like the bone of a growling dog that feels threatened and defends it. The early experience of possession and its claim is absolute and somehow blind. It corresponds to what we described as the *first inalienable ownership by clinging and binding*. By the second half of the first year (approximately by 9 months), things change. Infants begin to show first signs of a differentiation between the original, preconceptual sense of inalienable ownership and an emerging preconceptual sense of *alienable* ownership: a control over things that is not absolutely exclusive to the self but can be shared with others.

The new alienable sense of ownership does not replace the primal inalienable sense expressed by newborns. Rather, it *complements* it. By 9 months, infants begin to manifest stranger anxiety and a renewed clinging to their mother as they encounter novel faces and are placed in new social situations. In the meantime, they also begin to enjoy new degrees of behavioral freedom (i.e., independent locomotion) allowing them to explore the environment on their own, away from the secure base of the caregiver. As we have seen, the child resolves the tension between clinging and exploring by sharing with the adult objects of interest via solicitation of joint attention, starting to present and offer objects for mutual inspection. This would constitute the precursor signs of an ability to transfer ownership and, by the same token, enables the child to learn about the social power attached to giving and exchanging possessions.

By the end of the first year, signs of an alienable sense of possession and alienable ownership remain essentially preconceptual in the sense that they consist in concrete actions happening in the here and now, via offering gestures, or games of losing then regaining control over an object. By the end of the second year (approximately 21 months), at a conceptual level and in parallel to major linguistic progress as well as emerging signs of self-consciousness in front of mirrors, children's sense of inalienable possession regains prevalence. Absolute and inalienable claims now dominate, with imperatives like "That's mine!," meaning "That's not yours." It appears that the differentiation of alienable possession observed at 9 months at a preconceptual level is recapitulated at a conceptual level between the second and the third year. It is somehow conceptually "re-described" as children become proficient speakers and begin to care about their own reputation.[42]

From then on, at a more abstract and conceptual level, children rediscover the social power attached to alienable ownership. Beyond 5 years, they also discover the moral and ethical power attached to owning and sharing. At an abstract and conceptual level, the reasoning about ownership and sharing (who *ought to* own what and why) becomes central to children's construction of a moral identity. From this point on, inalienable and personal values versus alienable and exchangeable values become a crucial dichotomy. The child becomes selective in bringing objects of possession into a zone of exchange. He starts engaging in increasingly complex negotiation and bargains with others.

In the systematic transfer of ownership, the topic of the next chapter, children become increasingly the agent of their own social affiliation, gaining social power by giving and bartering. They also begin to grasp the meaning of shared social norms, abiding by and starting to enforce

[42] See the general representational re-description model of cognitive development proposed by Annette Karmiloff-Smith in *Beyond Modularity*.

rules governing games and other collective activities,[43] including notions regarding shared versus private property.

The onion metaphor and the values of ownership in development

Another way to capture ownership in development is to consider changes in the meaning and subjective values that are apparent in the claim of possession at various points of development. At birth, the meaning and value of ownership is inseparable from innate perception and action systems. At this primal stage the value and meaning of ownership is essentially *biological* and pre-adapted. By 2 months, a new layer of meaning is added with the value of the child's sense of its own agency. Infants discover and contemplate the direct impact they have on people and objects in the environment. With this second layer, they add a *control* value to their sense of ownership. By 9 months, with the differentiation of alienable ownership and the emergence of joint attention, a third layer is added, what can be described as the *shared* value of ownership. By 18 months, at a conceptual level now, a fourth value of ownership emerges: the explicit inalienability and what can be described as the explicit *exclusive* value of ownership. Finally, with the sense of reputation and the development of moral identity, from 3 years of age ownership gains its last "veneer" value, which can be described as *normative* or *exchange/reciprocal* value.

As for the onion metaphor presented at the beginning of the chapter in relation to the *layers of wakeful mind states in development*, the successive values of ownership emerging in development are not simply replaced; rather these values would add up like geological strata. Once constituted, at any time and depending on circumstances, the individual could instantiate any of the values corresponding to each particular layer. Following the onion metaphor, these layers would lie against each other, individuals continuously navigating through them depending on circumstances. For example, a judge can condemn a thief based on abstract ethical and legal principles, but a few hours later can revert to contradictory, more primal values with his wife while under the spell of jealousy.

One developing layer of meaning does not cancel the other. Grown up individuals express alternatively all of the ownership values that are progressively constituted in development: from biological, to shared, inalienable, alienable (exchangeable), to ethical and normative. This expression

[43] Rakoczy, Warneken, and Tomasello, "The sources of normativity."

depends on circumstances and varies between people, as we shall see in the final two chapters of the book.

In general, the onion metaphor accommodates to the multifaceted, often paradoxical and contrary values we can simultaneously hold regarding ownership, like the judge in relation to the thief and, moments later, in relation to his wife, a phenomenon that is at the core of human nature. What is progressively constituted in development would be a panoply of ownership values from which one can choose depending on circumstances.

7 Sharing in development

Different kinds of sharing emerge in development: from the implicit sharing of feelings manifested in face-to-face exchanges, to the much more abstract and explicit sharing of things that emerges from approximately 3 years, as children start to engage in distributive justice, splitting birthday cakes as equitably as possible or protesting about what they see as an unfair distribution of resources, for example in instances where adults ask children to "share with friends." Sharing in this latter case implies the elusive notion of *fairness*. This notion is not implied in the earliest forms of affective sharing. Fairness in sharing is not just a social issue that children come to grasp and resolve in their development. They learn that fairness needs to be negotiated with others and that equity in sharing is always an open social issue.

In the last section of the preceding chapter we described how ownership values change from birth and in the course of development. With this chapter, we aim at doing the same in relation to sharing, discussing how the ability to relinquish control over things comes to children and where such ability might originate. Things possessed and owned should not, once again, be limited to physical and material objects. They encompass both material and immaterial things like ideas and feelings: land, cars, and money but also political beliefs, admiration, pride, love, or hatred. Claims of possession (ownership) pertain also, and maybe more importantly, to points of view, feelings, love, or aversions: my views on this issue, my feelings for that person, my repulsion about this or that situation that I can share or not share with others. All of it is always negotiated with others, a major activity and trademark of human social life.

We are interested here in how children come to voluntarily accept to be *dispossessed* by sharing with others. The adverb "voluntarily" is added because sharing as dispossession exists in opposition to the forced, unwilling dispossession that happens in the case of theft, accidental loss, or usurpation. The act of sharing is, by definition, a willful dispossession for someone else or in reciprocal exchange with others, a voluntary act of relinquishing control that one once had over something, be it material or immaterial. In the case of sharing, even if obvious, the voluntary act of relinquishing control over something always presumes an *addressee* taking over this control. Sharing is by definition social, always oriented toward another individual, a group of individuals, or an institution (e.g., relinquishing time for volunteering or money to pay taxes). This definition implies that sharing in development is about social cognitive development. It is inseparable from the question of how children develop an understanding of others as *addressees*, whether these addressees are individuals, groups, or institutions.

From a first person (self) perspective, sharing is also about how children perceive and construe themselves in relation to others as actors as well as recipients of sharing acts. Sharing in development also pertains to how children learn gratitude. When something is relinquished to them, how do they understand such acts? How do they learn to reciprocate and acknowledge gifts of time and affection, all the food and material warmth, the volunteering of time and care they require from birth in order to survive?

Sharing in development is thus about both social acknowledgment and social acknowledging. In general, it is about social recognition: how children develop the experience of being recognized as well as of recognizing others in voluntary and reciprocal acts of dispossession.

Onion metaphor *redux*

The onion metaphor is helpful in trying to capture important features of sharing in development. Again, the intuition behind this metaphor is that children in development accumulate layers of meaning forming strata around a basic biological core. Together, these strata form the multilayered semantic field we navigate through as adults by constantly crossing through its layers as we take social decisions, control our behavior, and in general make sense of the world. As already mentioned, the major advantage of such a framework is that it accounts for the multiple standards all people tend to hold, the general and universal potential for profound transgressions and apparent lies from one moment to the next, the universal ability we hold to be civilized at one point (educated, thoughtful, and ethical), regressing and being anything but civilized at another (violent, cruel, and deceptive).

The onion metaphor is an attempt at accommodating the inescapable fact that we all share the capacity to oscillate between being highly ethical and moral, for example in relation to close relatives and in certain official circumstances, and being the exact opposite. The model accommodates the crucial fact that we all live with the capacity to juggle radically different standards that are compartmentalized in the way we make decisions and deal with each other. If to be human is to care about reputation,[1] it is also to have the remarkable flexibility of switching ethical standards, to transgress these standards while keeping face, often in denial or not even noticing such transgressions.[2] In this respect, there is something fundamentally multifaceted and paradoxical in human nature that we have to account for, especially dealing with the issue of sharing in development with all its ethical connotation.

Dynamic core of gaining and losing control

Sharing in development grows out of a generic motivational core that is universal, a major source of pleasure across species. This core is the interplay of tension between gaining and losing control, first for self, then for somebody else. Arguably, this core drives humans as it does other animals that learn to control food, sexual partners, or progeny in their environment. This is particularly evident in animal play: the cat tossing around the dead mouse it has just killed, as if it were still alive. Puppies roughhousing or the dog tirelessly fetching the ball to bring it back to its master for another throw. Likewise, human ball playing like soccer is all about control: losing, gaining, transferring, and regaining control.

What human evolution added to this basic core are strategic goals of domination and winning in the context of explicitly organized competition. Our species transformed play into game institutions made of rules and trophies, the invention of war made of uniforms, rituals, and specialized technology like guns and gunpowder. We invented trophies and medals for the public recognition and objectification of merits and virtues (i.e., courage, sacrifice, suffering, success), all of which grew out of a basic core we share with all other animals engaging in social play. This core is a highly engaging and pleasurable propensity to gain and relinquish social control over things: to give but also to take and to regain possession. This core is determined by endless and necessary utilitarian exchanges with others, but also by the basic need of individuals to affiliate with others, to gain social power and reputation.[3]

[1] A central thesis in Rochat, *Others in Mind.*

[2] It is always striking how close acquaintances, family members, and neighbors of violent terrorists, serial rapists, or murderers tend to see them in a way that rarely matches their crimes. They always seem flabbergasted, portraying them in a radically different light: good father, quiet, trouble-free individuals, attending the same church, etc. This is revealing of the multiple standards we tend to hold, criminals or not.

[3] See Rochat, *Others in Mind.*

Underneath the complex symbolic veneer of human play, there is the same basic psychological and motivational core found in all animal play: the generation of a tension between gaining and losing control, source of intense pleasures and thrills. Look at young children running after a ball, kicking, dribbling, and trying to keep it under their own control as long as possible. They resist attacks and assaults from others who try to take over its control, all of it for "the kick of it." No rules or goals are needed but simply the intense drive to maintain control over the ball, as long as possible. Watch the same young children playing tag, running after each other, switching roles from being chaser to being chased. All are paradigmatic and revealing of the motivational core of play in general. It essentially focuses on the intense pleasure attached to gaining, maintaining, relinquishing, losing, transferring, and regaining control over things.[4] This constitutes the motivational core of sharing in the most generic sense, an expression that is pervasive in the animal kingdom. Sharing in human development could just be a spinoff of this generic motivational core. However, compared to the younglings of other animals, the human child in his development novel quickly adds layers of meaning that culminate, as we shall see, with sharing that is principled (rule based) and normative (morally constrained).

Sharing games in development

We can distinguish two ontologically different subjective contexts in which sharing occurs, in general. These contexts are either *utilitarian* or *playful*. The utilitarian context pertains to sharing that occurs in ordinary life, as part of the daily chores and activities allowing individuals to survive, such as feeding, competing, or cooperating for resources. In

[4] This construal would arguably capture the absolute, bottom-line core of play in general and the source of sharing as construed here. However, many other theoretical takes on the essence of play exist in the literature. For example, and by no means least, in a book entitled *Man, Play, and Games*, French essayist Roger Caillois (1913–78) describes what he sees as the five constitutive characteristics of play activities: *freedom* (no obligation); *separation* (circumscribed in time and space); *non-productive orientation* (not geared toward a specific production of goods); *rules* (includes conventions regarding the suspension of reality); and finally *fictitiousness* (entails an awareness of a reality that is different from ordinary life). In his essay, Caillois also proposes that play activities fall invariably into one of five basic types: plain agitation and production of laughter, like children's noise and gossips (*Paidia*); play of competition, like soccer (*Agon*); play of chance, like lottery (*Alea*); play of simulation, like pretend and disguise (*Mimicry*); and play of dizziness, like swinging or climbing (*Ilinx*). Following this taxonomy, all play activities would fall into one of these five categories, with particular weights and specific expressive forms depending on age and culture. This taxonomy of play may not be exhaustive, but it is an interesting alternative account of the psychological essence of human play in general.

contrast, the playful context pertains to sharing that occurs with no direct apparent utility other than enhancing the pleasure of gaining, losing, and competing for control. The playful context gives ways to more gratuitous, not strictly utilitarian subjective experience (i.e., not indispensable or "vital" for the individual). The motivational core of the playful context is the control of self-agency in games of chance, competition, challenge, thrill, exploration, or pretense. This context dominates childhood, becoming increasingly compartmentalized as a function of age.

A first, fundamental change in development is indeed the relative place of utilitarian and playful contexts as a function of age. As children grow, introduced to institutions outside of the family environment (schooling) but also as the demands from adults become more pressing (work, chores, and other labor contributions), utilitarian and playful contexts become increasingly compartmentalized. Obviously, the place of play and work as well as adult demands on children can vary greatly across cultures.[5] If sharing in the playful context tends invariably to dominate in early childhood, with age it becomes "normative," constrained by the demands of social and institutional rules, children under the pressure of cooperative and collaborative norms.

In general, sharing games is a better appellation than just "sharing." It better captures the exploratory dimension and a pleasure-oriented motivation driving the activity, not just reducing sharing to utilitarian motives like teaching, cooperating, or helping others, as is too often implied by evolutionary and other developmental psychologists with a strong cognitive bent.[6] In this view, sharing would be primarily motivated by the pleasurable propensity and universal need to explore one's control and agency over objects and people.

In a seminal 1938 book entitled *Homo Ludens* (Man the Player),[7] Dutch historian and cultural theorist Johan Huizinga (1872–1945) considered play as a distinct marker of human cultures in general. First, Huizinga shows that, although most animals play, human playing is distinct from the play behavior of other animals, adding a new layer of self-consciousness. As Huizinga writes: "We play, and we are conscious of playing: we are therefore more than rational beings, because play is irrational."

[5] In traditional subsistence living societies of Polynesia and Melanesia, for example, children's chores and adult demands on school age children are not comparable to the demands typically placed on same-age middle-class children in Europe or North America. In the South Pacific, children from an early age have to care for younger siblings and are supposed to help in domestic and sometimes heavy chores like fishing, collecting fruit, vegetables, or gardening, aside from cleaning and cooking.

[6] See for example Tomasello, *Why We Cooperate*.

[7] Huizinga, *Homo Ludens*.

Following Huizinga, human play is in general a deliberate and self-conscious expression of freedom from ordinary life, freedom from bare survival and utilitarian existence. In humans, play corresponds to a fundamental *liberation* from ordinary life, from the purely functional and utilitarian aspects of existence. It pertains also to sharing games from the earliest age, as we shall try to show.

In human cultures and from a very early age, play is temporally and spatially marked, as for example the timely recess periods and playground locations assigned to children's play at school. The same is true for recurrent group rituals and celebrations across human cultures, all having temporal and spatial markers, with fixed schedules and locations. Human games, as opposed to other animal play, can become a source of order and absolute (supreme) rules regarding competition. It is within this created order that there is the promise of surprise and unpredictable outcomes, as in a soccer match, the main source of drama and joy associated with play. Particular forms and kinds of play activities obviously dominate each culture and each developmental age, but they hold some universal and invariant features, all arising from a main motivational core: the probing of mastery and control over things, arguably the psychological essence of play in general and the primal source of the pleasure that drives people from birth, including sharing games.

In play and games, there is a basic freedom, as Huizinga proposes, the freedom to explore and to deviate, the *freedom to test possibilities*, in itself a source of universal pleasure driving all animal play. It is a freedom expressed by children from birth. Mixed with the utilitarian needs to survive by feeding, reproducing, and the protection of progeny, there is *ludic* pleasure driving what amounts to "gratuitous" activities with no other apparent purposes than to suspend the necessary chores of ordinary, purely utilitarian and adaptive life. Compared to basic survival activities, play and games serve only indirect and satellite functions, yet they are central in the life of young animals, particularly human children with their protracted childhood and their inability to survive on their own for the first few years of life. These uniquely human circumstances give children much room to explore and play, hence to cultivate the ludic pleasure of gratuitous activities that play and games embody in contrast to ordinary life.[8]

From the seminal work of cultural theorists like Johan Huizinga or Roger Caillois (see note 4 above) on human games and play, but also the original discussion of animal play by Karl Groos,[9] we can infer that

[8] See Bruner, "Nature and uses of immaturity."

[9] Groos, *The Play of Animals*. This book includes an interesting preface by the great James Mark Baldwin who discusses the role and place of imitation in play behavior.

across ages and cultures, play and game activities are generally dictated by the basic need to *probe the limits of our own existence*. An important driving force behind sharing games would be the need to probe the limits of our own existence and situation in relation to others.

In his 1898 book *The Play of Animals*, Groos already emphasizes the universal pleasure of being a "cause." Groos suggests that there may be an innate instinct shared by all playful animals to dominate and overcome obstacles, a source of intense pleasure. Likewise, play and games give children privileged access to their own limits and possibilities as agents in their environment, in particular in relation to others. Of all the playful activities children engage in, sharing games provide a fair gauge of the own situation in relation to others: their social impact and the recognition children get from others. It is primarily in affective, face-to-face playful exchanges (sharing games) of gazes and smiles that infants first gauge their social situation: the impact they have on others, the quality of social attention they are able to generate and receive from others. All of this primordial subjective experience happens in the context of reciprocal exchanges and mutual affective attunement (i.e., affective mirroring and primary inter-subjectivity in face-to-face exchanges).[10]

But the context of this primordial form of emotional sharing games is enlarged in the course of the first months, as we shall see next. This enlargement follows a path that parallels and echoes the development of ownership reviewed in the preceding chapter. It also parallels and echoes the development of self-consciousness. In this development, the content of and apparent reasons for acquiring, transferring, and exchanging control over things change, children adding new layers of meaning to sharing.

This development leads children on from the exchange of gazes and smiles to the sharing of attention toward objects, the actual offering and request for physical things, ultimately the negotiation of material and immaterial values in reciprocal exchanges. This development is nonetheless open-ended when it comes to the normative and legal issues surrounding the ownership of property, linked, as we know, to never ending negotiation and tight competition in adult life. This is most evident, for example, in the frequent conflicts surrounding inheritance and family estate succession, a common source of bitter legal fighting among heirs and kin.[11]

[10] Trevarthen, "The foundations of intersubjectivity"; see also Rochat and Striano, "Social cognitive development in the first year"; Rochat, *The Infant's World*.

[11] It is said that in France, for example, but also probably in most other Western industrial regions of the world, approximately one-third of all wills and inheritances from parents to their descendants end up in court, requiring ruling by judgment.

Sharing and mental states in development

From a psychological, hence subjective and inter-subjective perspective, there are different kinds of sharing, each paralleling the chronological unfolding of the six mind states discussed in Chapter 6 on ownership in development. These are respectively *non-conscious*, *unconscious*, *aware*, *co-aware*, *conscious*, and *co-conscious*. We describe basic kinds of sharing mapping onto these mind states in the order of their emergence in development. Once again, this approach allows for a developmental roadmap of sharing in relation to the various layers of general mental states unfolding in development. These would correspond to basic sharing kinds that we distinguish as (1) *biological*, (2) *inter-subjective*, (3) *referential*, (4) *intentional*, (5) *co-conscious*, and finally (6) *negotiated and ethical.*

Following the onion metaphor, each of these unfolding kinds of sharing adds a layer of meaning[12] around the basic motivational core that is the instinctive, innate, and pleasurable propensity children have to control, relinquish, and eventually regain control (agency) over things in their environment: physical objects but also people and eventually immaterial things like ideas.

(1) Biological sharing (birth and up) A primeval kind of biological sharing is expressed at birth between infant and mother. This is evident in feeding activities whereby a mother instinctively shares her breast with her infant, and reciprocally an infant instinctively shares its mouth with its mother. Premature infants are often incapable of such active reciprocation, and have to be kept alive by gavage tube feeding. Even if they may show some early rudiments of sucking engagement, they do not have the strength and are not mature enough to engage in active co-regulation with the mother.[13] Healthy newborns are ready to suck and display complex action systems oriented toward feeding. Mothers, on the other hand, display *intuitive parenting.*[14] They instinctively and viscerally coordinate care responses, gently tending to their newborn, accompanying, supporting,

[12] Again, the onion is a "blooming" onion, in the sense that each new layer of meaning increases exponentially the meaning-making potential of the child. Metaphorically speaking, each added layer increases not only the circumference, but also in depth or "thickness." It opens up new meaning-making potentials in the same way that language, recursive thinking, or symbolic functioning do as they emerge in child development. As these potentials (new layers) emerge, they open up new ways of making sense of the world that are exponentially more complex. Our task as developmental psychologists is primarily to account for these various ways, their emergence, and the putative mechanisms behind it.

[13] Rochat, Goubet, and Shah, "Enhanced sucking engagement by preterm infants during intermittent gavage feedings."

[14] Papoušek and Papoušek, "Intuitive parenting."

and facilitating infants in their behavioral propensities. This instinctive parental support includes, in addition to providing food and facilitating feeding, affective mirroring, empathic responses, postural reorientation (e.g., positioning the infant in relation to the breast or bottle), systematic tactile (caresses and massages), auditory (clicking sounds, lullabies, and infant directed speech), vestibular (rocking and shaking), visual (face presentation), taste and olfactory stimulation (food and nipple rubbing in the perioral region of the child). Most mothers discover these skills and gestures spontaneously, pushed and pulled by their infants, anticipating and responding to their needs.

Newborns' innate behavioral organization and intuitive parenting are mutually dependent, co-designed features of evolution. At birth, mothers and infants do share mutually adapted instinctive behaviors orchestrating their transactions in feeding and caring. This primeval, biological kind of sharing is reflected at multiple levels, from the physiological (lactation and energy "fueling" via actual food transfer and digestion), to the psychological (intuitive parenting, infant early learning and preference), and the cultural (artifacts like bottles, milk pumps, pacifiers, diet, sleeping arrangements).

(2) Inter-subjective sharing (2 months and up) Beyond the biological sharing orchestrating mother–infant exchanges and transactions at birth, some major changes occur by approximately 6 weeks post partum, indexed by first signs of emotional co-regulation (i.e., first socially oriented smiles). A new kind of mutual sharing emerges, distinct from the primeval complex biological co-regulation expressed at birth. Sharing becomes psychological and inter-subjective, the sharing of experience proper. The emergence of socially elicited smiling as well as mutual smiling forms indices of unambiguous *awareness* and the beginning of a possibility for *co-awareness*, in reference to the roadmap of mind states in development proposed above.

In face-to-face interactions, infants and caregivers begin to share by co-constructing feeling experiences. As already discussed in relation to ownership, at this developmental juncture, infants take a novel, contemplative stance toward physical and social objects, exploring and modulating systematically the active embodied consequences they produce on them. Infants from 2 months start to grasp and to own their embodied agency toward objects. They do so equally toward people and caregivers who tend irresistibly to resonate to them with high-pitched infant-directed speech ("motherese") and amplified, contingent affective mirroring.[15]

[15] Gergely and Watson, "Early socio-emotional development."

In the social realm, two-way, deliberate sharing of affects emerges at this developmental juncture. This sharing has been extensively documented by infancy researchers in terms of rhythmical *turn taking*[16] and *two-way shared mutual gazes*.[17] While infants at birth open their eyes and orient their gaze toward faces, preferring face to non-face objects, and even though they are documented to imitate facial gestures and emotional expression (like tongue protrusion or sad faces),[18] the gaze of newborns remains often sluggish and hard to capture, as if it is passing through you. If we had to use adult criteria of visual impairment, infants at birth would be considered legally blind. Obviously they see something and are capable of detecting motion and strong contrasts. But starring straight at a newborn with open eyes often gives the impression that the child is looking through you rather than at you. By 6 weeks, this gaze becomes unmistakably *shared and mutual*, inaugurating a proto-conversational space of genuinely open-ended social exchanges made of turn taking and a novel sensitivity. It gives rise to prototypical narrative envelops co-constructed in interaction with others, made for example of tension build-ups and sudden releases of tension, as in the peek-a-boo games that are universally compelling to infants from the second month.[19] As can be seen in many baby diaries kept by mothers, it is also from this developmental juncture that parents often report meeting a person in their infant.

Classic research[20] on face exploration by young infants, looking at their precise eye movements while scanning the photograph or drawing of a person starring at them (presented very close to the child, about 30 cm away, beyond which the image would be too blurry), indicates that newborns tend to focus primarily on the outer edge of the face with only rare scanning of the internal features (eyes, nose, and mouth). Between 1 and 2 months, parallel to the emergence of socially elicited smiling, they begin to pay significantly more visual attention to the mouth and eyes, this attention falling into the "fateful" social attractor triangle linking mouth and eyes. It is also between 1 and 2 months that infants start spending significantly more time not simply awake, but awake and alert,[21] scanning the world around, revealing their naturally insatiable curiosity toward events and things in the environment, particularly talking heads: people attending to them, providing comfort, entertainment, and most importantly food.

16 Jaffe, "Rhythms of dialogue in infancy."
17 Stern, *The Interpersonal World of the Infant*, and Stern et al., "Affect attunement."
18 Meltzoff and Moore, "Imitation of facial and manual gestures"; Field et al., "Discrimination and imitation of facial expressions by neonates."
19 Stern, *The Interpersonal World of the Infant*; see also Rochat, *The Infant's World*.
20 Haith, Bergman, and Moore, "Eye contact and face scanning in early infancy."
21 Wolff, *The Development of Behavioral States and the Expression of Emotions in Early Infancy*.

People are the richest resource, providing the most rewarding stimulation. There is nothing like a talking face, or fishing for a smile or any other positive feedback by systematically engaging in highly structured proto-conversation and routine game exchanges with the infant. In this process, the eyes and the sharing of eye contacts play a particularly important role. In other primate species, eye-to-eye contact from a young age is often a threatening sign and tends to be avoided. Inversely, eye-to-eye contact is a major attractor in humans. From 2 months of age it becomes an index of social engagement for the infant. For example, by 5 months infants show less visual attention and significantly less smiling toward someone who avoids direct eye-to-eye contact. Infants show signs of relative displeasure in mutual exchanges with an adult staring at one of their earlobes rather than straight into the eyes. Note that this represents a remarkably slim optical angle difference, yet infants pick up the difference between a socially engaged or not engaged gaze from others, an elusive yet precise difference. Pupil-to-pupil eye contact becomes early on, and at least by 4–5 months, a critical index of engagement in proto-conversational and early inter-subjective exchanges. It is a variable picked up by the child as a measure of the relative degree to which others are socially engaged and attentive, affectively attuned and effectively "with" them. In relation to affective sharing, eye-to-eye contact, particularly pupil-to-pupil exchanges, the vitality contours of people in their affective exchange is primordial and the cornerstone of human communication. Statements like "All is in the eyes" or "The eyes have it"[22] are not just eye-catching slogans.

As a matter of fact, the human eye, as an organ, has evolved specific features serving this interactive, inter-subjective function, in the same way that some butterfly species have evolved designs of eyes on their wings as camouflage and to scare off predators. Compared to all other primate species, the anatomy of the human eye has evolved a uniquely high contrast between iris and sclera (white part of the eye) making gaze direction particularly public and conspicuous to others.[23] In primate evolution, this feature appears to be highly correlated with social complexity, and the relative size of the cortical frontal lobe, as well as the relative mobility of eyes in their sockets, independently of head movements. This evolution accompanies an apparent change in the function and meaning of gaze as a social signal.[24]

For humans, it correlates with a unique propensity toward "gaze grooming," a search for eye contacts and looking into each other's eyes

[22] For further discussion, see Rochat, "The gaze of others."
[23] Kobayashi and Kohshima, "Unique morphology of the human eye."
[24] Emery, "The eyes have it."

as expression of mutual affiliation and *belongingness*.[25] In development, and in particular with the emergence of independent locomotion, as infants increasingly gauge their social place and situation at farther distance, the monitoring of others' gaze is certainly facilitated by what amounts to a unique feature of the human eye, in the context of primate evolution. It all starts particularly by 2 months, with what we can consider as the inter-subjective birth of the young infant, in other words our true psychological birth as opposed to the biological birth or birthday that in Western cultures, but not all cultures, we celebrate every year. With the confluence of marked changes in visual attention, overall wakefulness to the world, and affective responses to others (i.e., socially elicited smile), the second month of life marks the first major, global qualitative change in human behavioral development. This is true in light of the well-documented, strong behavioral continuity between prenatal and postnatal development: between fetal behavior in the last trimester of gestation and how newborns behave immediately after birth and in the first 6 weeks of life.[26] The second month marks a major change and what we construe, once again, as human actual psychological birth: when infants open up to the world, particularly the social world. It is from this point on that children engage in first reciprocal sharing of experience, affective experiences that revolve primarily around gaze monitoring and exchanges in the healthy child.[27]

(3) Referential sharing (7–9 months and up) If by 2 months infants begin to co-construct inter-subjectivity, hence to share experience in face-to-face, open-ended proto-conversation with others, things change again radically by 7–9 months when the sharing becomes *about* objects that exist outside of the dyadic exchange. Infants become increasingly deictic (about something) in their social exchanges, starting to refer to things that can be jointly given attention. This is the sign of a "secondary" inter-subjectivity[28] adding to the first exchanges of 2–6-month-olds. This would represent the first "objectification" of sharing. By triangulation of attention, objects become jointly captured and shared. They start feeding into the exchange.

25 Kobayashi and Hashiya, "The gaze that grooms."
26 Prechtl, *Continuity of Neural Functions.*
27 There are currently many research attempts trying to detect in young infants early signs of autism, a devastating social handicap now diagnosed in over one percent of Western children; see for example Volkmar, Chawarska, and Klin, "Autism in infancy and early childhood."
28 Trevarthen, "The foundations of intersubjectivity."

This new triangulation emerging by 7–9 months is also, and maybe more importantly, about social affiliation and togetherness. Like the optical parallax that gives depth cues to viewers, first signs of joint attention give children a new measure of their social affiliation, a novel social depth. By starting to point to objects in the presence of others, by presenting or offering grasped objects to social partners, infants invite others' mental focus and this is done by their creating and advertising for a shared attention. This is a new objectified and referential creation. Psychologically, it also corresponds to the first *appropriation* of an object as topic of social exchange, in the same way that in the course of a conversation someone might spontaneously appropriate an object (pen, stick of wood, any small object) as a prop to help in the telling of a story. The object, used as a conversational prop in early bouts of joint attention, becomes the infant's new "fishing hook" to capture, gauge, and eventually possess others' attention against which they can gauge further their relative agentive role, control, and impact in relation to others: their situation and place in the social environment.

It is reasonable to state that in joint attention we find the roots of the child's first socially shared mental projection of control over an object (i.e., possession in the literal sense). In other words, we find the first explicit seeds of the "That's mine!" claim and the inseparable "Not yours!" affirmation that emerge by the end of the second year. In starting to bring other people's attention to things in the environment, the infant opens up the possibility of claiming ownership of both the initiation of a conversation about something and the thing itself. Pointing, offering, or presenting objects to others are all new social gestures becoming prominent in the healthy child from the age of 7–9 months. They express a marked qualitative shift in social-cognitive development[29] but also a crucial step in the development of possession: the origins of owning and sharing. It opens up, in particular, a new horizon of *centrifugal and centripetal sharing games*.

An object that is presented or offered can now be retrieved or taken away by others, given back, or ignored by them. This gives rise to all sorts of new, complex, and objectified social transactions. It is in these new objectified social transactions that the child consolidates the concept and idea of what eventually will become in a few months' developmental time and with the emergence of language the explicit claim of ownership: the assertion of "That's mine!" and "Not yours!"

[29] Tomasello, "Joint attention as social cognition."

From this point on and at this pre-linguistic stage of development, objectified and socially shared centrifugal and centripetal forces are the new playing field created by children.[30] It is a crucial step in the development of possession in general and the development of sharing in particular. In emerging joint attention, infants implement for the first time the control of others via objects. It is at this developmental juncture that children can begin to grasp the social power gained through objects of possession. Feeding their basic affiliation need, children learn from then on that, with objects, others' attention and recognition can be earned, thus shared.

Aside from new engagements in joint attention per se, 7-month-olds begin to manifest novel initiatives in social exchanges and emotional sharing using joint attention. They reveal a new sense of social agency and a novel autonomous role in promoting inter-subjectivity and social engagement with others, sometimes using objects of possession to instrument such initiatives. By 7 months, for example, an infant jointly focusing on a toy with an adult who suddenly adopts a frozen face will attempt at re-engaging the adult, for example shaking the object in front of her eyes or pushing it toward her.[31] In contrast, facing such social disruption or "entrapment" created by the adult, infants younger than 7 months tend simply to disengage, looking away, smiling less, and displaying self-comfort and negative affects.[32] Prior to this age, infants do not show re-engaging initiatives, nor any instrumentation of an object as tool for social re-engagement. Clearly, by 7 months, infants show a new rapport with objects as objects of possession that can be used as tools or

[30] These are triadic play activities that Tomasello et al., "Understanding and sharing intentions," describe as emerging by 9–12 months, such as giving, taking, rolling a ball back and forth, or building block towers with another person, showing that the infant is newly perceiving and understanding others as being goal directed, with whom goals can be shared (Tomasello et al., "Understanding and sharing intentions," p. 682). Our own research suggests precursor signs already by 7 months, as in the case of re-engagement initiatives in response to the sudden still face of a social partner (see below, Rochat and Striano, "Social cognitive development in the first year"). In general, Tomasello and colleagues describe what they view as the developmental origins of cultural cognition based on three successive types of *social sharing*, beginning from the outset with an understanding of animated actions, then from 9–12 months an understanding of goal directed actions, and finally by the second year an understanding of intentional (planned) actions. At this latter stage, children would start sharing psychological states (intentions and plans), negotiating "we" intention in collaboration, something they propose is unique to human cultural cognition.

[31] See Striano and Rochat, "Developmental link between dyadic and triadic social competence in infancy"; also Striano and Rochat, "Emergence of selective social referencing."

[32] Tronick et al., "The infant's response to entrapment between contradictory messages in face-to-face interaction."

instruments to control the social environment.[33] Objects do become endowed with social power.

(4) Intentional sharing (12 months and up) The instrumentation of sharing by initiating mutual engagement toward the same object or goal emerging by 7–9 months is probably not much different from a dog fetching a ball, retrieving it, and releasing it at the feet of the thrower for another run. If the person ignores it, is distracted, or looks away, the dog may grab the ball, drop it again at the person's feet, looking up while wagging its tail. Clearly the dog, like the 9-month-old, perceives goal orientation in others that is objectified in things like balls or toys which allow centrifugal and centripetal games (referential sharing described above). By 11–12 months, however, the child adds a novel layer of meaning to referential sharing. This layer corresponds to a novel understanding of the *manners* in which sharing and exchange games are played (whether the ball is thrown with irritation or not in the case of the dog).[34] The child becomes sensitive to the form of others' sharing actions. For example, by 11 months but not yet at 9 months, infants will tend to spend significantly more time attending to someone who is imitating them, compared to someone who is behaving contingently but not reproducing exactly what they do.[35] They begin to project themselves and identify with others,[36] becoming sensitive to the manner in which people behave in interactive games, therefore the way they share and the intentions they may have. They themselves begin also to modulate their ways of sharing and reciprocating, becoming more selective of the person they share with, and trying to imitate or to coordinate actions in attempts of cooperation.

From 12 months of age infants also begin to show significantly greater modulation and flexibility by engaging spontaneously in role reversal

[33] Longitudinal study of developing joint attention shows that passive joint engagement becomes increasingly active and initiated by infants from 12 months of age: Bakeman and Adamson, "Coordinating attention to people and objects in mother–infant and peer–infant interactions."

[34] The importance of this achievement is evident in research showing that autistic individuals tend to be significantly less sensitive to the vitality contours of actions they perceive in others, their detection of action goals remaining intact compared to healthy individuals; see Rochat et al., "Impaired vitality form recognition in autism."

[35] Agnetta and Rochat, "Imitative games by 9-, 14-, and 18-month-old infants."

[36] For an account of the importance of identification in developing imitation, see the work of Hobson and colleagues comparing healthy and autistic children. They point to the importance of identification in healthy developing imitation. Such identification appears to be lacking in autistic children along with depleted empathic feelings and emotions (i.e., depleted aptitude to get into the shoes of others). See Hobson, *The Cradle of Thought*; "On sharing experiences"; "Apprehending attitudes and actions."

imitation.[37] For example, imagine a situation where an adult engages the infant to play a collaborative game where the adult holds a basket and the infant throws toys into it. If the adult suddenly stops holding the basket and now wants to throw, 12-month-olds seeing this are able to switch role to continue the joint game: the infant will spontaneously stop throwing, and grab and hold the basket to let the adult throw the toys.[38]

From12 months, infants can follow through and maintain the sharing, collaborative game by taking the role of the other. What is new here is that the child begins to show signs of an implicit sense of reciprocity in sharing, with some rudiments of perspective taking and the budding ability to get into the shoes of others.

In relation to this developmental transition, Tomasello and collaborators write: "One possible explanation for the qualitative shift in infants' social engagements soon after the first birthday, then, is that they are in the process of developing a deeper understanding of intentional action in terms of underlying plans and intentions, and their motivation to share then leads them to create with others not only shared goals but also joint intentions with coordinated roles."[39] It is indeed, cognitively, a new layer of meaning added to referential and goal sharing. This layer is the layer of *intentionality* understanding that prefigures later developing theories of mind (e.g., false belief understanding).

From 11 to 12 months and beyond, adding to referential sharing, infants begin to consider and factor in their decision to share what others intend to do or want to do. This takes them deeper, beneath the surface monitoring of joint attention. They become sensitive to the forms and ways of sharing that they begin to perceive and understand as signs of intentions. Multiple studies of imitative games show that by 14 months infants differentiate intentional from unintentional or accidental actions. If the game is to imitate an action performed on an object, such as the pulling of a sleeve covering a dowel,[40] turning on a lamp by pressing on it,[41] or deciding what object an adult wants,[42] the child tends to detect intentions and reproduce selectively only those actions that they perceive as intentional, overlooking actions that are either failed attempts, accidental, or irrational. From this point on, sharing in imitation and children's budding collaborative

[37] Ratner and Bruner, "Games, social exchange and the acquisition of language"; Tomasello et al., "Understanding and sharing intentions."

[38] Carpenter, Tomasello, and Striano, "Role reversal imitation and language in typically developing infants and children with autism."

[39] Tomasello et al., "Understanding and sharing intentions," p. 683.

[40] Meltzoff, "Understanding the intentions of others."

[41] Gergely, Bekkering, and Kiraly, "Rational imitation in preverbal infants."

[42] Tomasello and Haberl, "Understanding attention."

engagement with others becomes intentional. Children now start to read and factor what others have on their mind in terms of plans and wants, adding to all the other forms of sharing expressed prior to the second year. By the second year, the child adds this fourth layer of meaning in sharing: the intentional layer. The intentional layer prepares and opens up the child toward a new range of social cognitive development that parallels the emergence of self-concept and the explicit sense of inalienable ownership that she starts to manifest by the end of the second year, with assertions like "That's mine!" and de facto saying, "Not yours!"

(5) Co-conscious sharing (21 months and up) What changes beyond the second birthday is unique to our species: it is the care for reputation and the manipulation of self-presentation with others in mind. Children become co-conscious of themselves, in other words they become explicitly aware of themselves as perceived and evaluated by others.

The expletive "Mine!" that children start to utter by the end of the second year (approximately 21 months)[43] is symptomatic of this major transition and needs to be understood in the context emerging co-consciousness. The explicit assertion of ownership parallels the emergence of self-recognition and self-objectification in the mirror, but also the emergence of self-conscious emotions[44] like blushing, shame, jealousy, envy, embarrassment, or pride that start shaping much of toddlers' social and affective lives as they roam more freely about their world, encountering new people, new social partners, particularly new peers at daycare centres and playgroups outside of the intimate family circle.

From this point on, children develop a renewed ability to conceal their mental states, manipulate what they expose of themselves to others, and, more to the point, become increasingly agile strategic manipulators in sharing. Based on their ability to infer intentions in others (intentional sharing), they now begin to add a layer of what we can label as co-conscious manipulation in sharing. A new negotiation channel in sharing develops that is flexible and adapted to what the child infers of what others might feel and want. The child probes and sees what works and what doesn't in sharing with others, starting a new era of bartering and endless negotiation of permissions that parents of 2- and 3-year-olds know too well. This era continues throughout the lifespan, a mark of our humanity, often exacerbated during adolescence.

[43] See Bates, "Language about me and you"; as well as Tomasello, "One child's early talk about possession."

[44] See in particular Kagan, *The Second Year*; Lewis et al., "Self development and self-conscious emotions"; Lewis, *Shame*.

With co-conscious sharing, children express new levels of deception and duplicity toward others. It is the time that children typically begin to cultivate the pleasures of dressing up and pretend games, adjusting their look and public appearance in the mirror and working on their self-presentation. They also begin to display growing pleasure in hide and seek games. They enjoy the concealment of themselves and the control of others in search of them. Children, at this developmental juncture, become self-conscious proper and co-conscious of their situation in the world. Sharing with others reaches a new level of meaning.

Nonverbal signs of deception appear early in development, in fact much earlier than all the explicit theories of mind and other false belief understandings children are universally reported to develop between 3 and 5 years.[45] Longitudinal studies and individual case reports suggest that already by 8–12 months infants can conceal actions, distract others to gain some privacy, and trick others to gain their attention.[46] By 18 months, some children are observed starting to make false claims of pain and injury in an apparent drive to obtain attention or sympathy, or even deflect criticism if they have done something wrong. By 20 months a majority of children tend to recognize themselves in the mirror, passing the mirror mark test. Active self-presentation and self-conscious emotions start to be at work and in the meantime, as a spinoff of emerging co-consciousness, by the second birthday children start being caught making false statements about themselves as well as reality. They also begin to understand pretense in others, able to generate as well as discriminate "as if" from "real" actions.[47] Children begin to delight in *sharing pretense with others*.[48] As a distinctive mark of childhood, they spontaneously invent pretend games, with or without the support of toys specifically designed by adults to replicate real things in miniature and to promote pretense in children. They may grab a banana pretending that it is a phone or get into the game of pretending by sticking a foot in a box as if it were a shoe. They also can communicate with others about such "as if" actions.[49] All is now pretext for pretending and suspending reality, sharing works of the imagination with others. A new level of participation is expressed in which the sharing is real but what is shared, its content, can be imagined with others.

45 See for example Callaghan et al., "Synchrony in the onset of mental-state reasoning."
46 Reddy, "Getting back to the rough ground."
47 Rakoczy, Tomasello, and Striano, "Young children know that trying is not pretending."
48 Piaget, *Play, Dreams, and Imitation in Childhood*; Leslie, "Pretense and representation"; Harris and Kavanaugh, "Young children's understanding of pretense"; Friedman and Leslie, "The conceptual underpinnings of pretense."
49 Striano, Tomasello, and Rochat, "Social and object support for early symbolic play."

In general, from this point on, children start a career of duplicity, manipulation, and lies that is also an intrinsic part of what it means to be human and to express *co-conscious* sharing. It represents, by necessity, the inseparable other side of the ability to be good, to show empathy, to take the perspective of others while trying to reach impartiality and some "veil of ignorance." No good without the bad too, and vice versa.

Duplicity and the manipulation of others represent the contrasting, other side of moral principles, the other side of the coin by which one should treat others in the same way one expects to be treated ("the golden rule"). This is also the other side of the explicit inequity aversion expressed when children from 3 years begin to manifest, sometimes with rage and much determination, that it is "Unfair!," increasingly providing explicit rationale as to why this is so.

Such an ethical stance is the mark of the last (sixth) layer of sharing that emerges in development, from approximately the third birthday, and that continues to develop throughout the lifespan. It is the last coarse veneer of our onion metaphor.

(6) Ethical sharing (36 months and up) There comes a point when children begin to act according to some ethical principles they have internalized and seemingly hold for themselves. They may start to question authority and refuse to abide by it when they feel and think it is ethically wrong or less right. Children slowly become autonomous moral agents as opposed to strict conformists who may obey and abide by the greater, more powerful majority in order to feed a basic social affiliation needs.

From this point on, children start to show signs that they care about their moral identity and to construct what sociologist Pierre Bourdieu calls *capital symbolique* (symbolic capital). Children begin to show clear signs that they are trying to maintain self-unity and coherence, avoiding moral dissonance for self in relation to others. They project moral rectitude in their self-presentation toward others. In the period between 3 and 5 years of age, children start opening up an area of lifespan development: the moral and ethical dimension of sharing possession with others, which will become, universally, the core issue of all politics in adulthood. They become sensitive to inequities in the distribution of scarce resources, trying to reach some "just" decisions in relation to others, but also to themselves. They open the perennial issue of what is fair: the conundrum of *fairness*.

Research on distributive justice by young children reveals this universal transition toward ethical sharing. For example, we asked children from all over the world to split between themselves and an adult experimenter small collections of treats (e.g., candies, stickers, or valuable coins) that were either even (e.g., N = 6) or odd (N = 7). In addition, in some conditions, the odd number included one item that was "special," all children agreeing beforehand that this item was much better than all the others in the collection (e.g., bigger and/or brighter).

We tested hundreds of children of 3 and 5 years of age from various socio-economic and cultural backgrounds (see Chapter 8 for more details of this particular cross-cultural study).[50] What we found was a robust, universal developmental trend toward an increase spontaneous equity in sharing. All over the world, 3-year-olds tend to be significantly more inclined to self-maximize, giving much more to the self than to the adult experimenter.[51] In the odd collection with a special item, not only do they give more to themselves, the vast majority of children also self-attribute the special item. Interestingly, this early "selfishness" is not innocent, nor is it nonchalant. Rather, it is deeply rooted and strategic. In one case, when the child is told that she will split the objects and then the adult will choose which one of the two created piles she wants (biblical or "perfect" sharing condition), 3-year-olds become suddenly much more equitable in their splitting.

By 5 years, children overall become significantly more equitable, often with remarkable instances in which the child actually *refuses* to go on splitting if the collection of treats cannot be distributed equally. Some children try to break in two the seventh item of the collection or insist on getting another one to reach equity. Five-year-olds do so even if they are not recipients of the distribution, when asked to split between two puppets (third party sharing).[52]

Further clear evidence of ethical sharing emerging by 5 years is the fact that, by this age, the child becomes increasingly willing to sacrifice some of his possessions to punish and make a statement of principle in the context of an unjust situation. Children become increasingly willing to engage in "costly punishment." In one piece of research,[53] we studied 3- to 5-year-olds splitting three ways a collection of nine valuable coins between themselves and two puppets animated by an adult experimenter. In four successive rounds, each protagonist (child and the two puppets) split the coins in turn. In each round, the same puppet (generous) started splitting

50 Rochat et al., "Fairness in distributive justice by 3- and 5-year-olds across 7 cultures."

51 See a similar developmental trend toward more other-concerned decision with older children using a different experimental paradigm (ultimatum game) in Murnighan and Saxon, "Ultimatum bargaining by children and adults"; see also Harbaugh, Krause, and Liday, "Bargaining by children."

52 Rochat et al., "Fairness in distributive justice by 3- and 5-year-olds across 7 cultures."

53 Robbins and Rochat, "Emerging signs of strong reciprocity in human ontogeny."

generously, giving one coin for itself, four for the other puppet, and four for the child. Then it was the turn of the other puppet (stingy) splitting stingily, giving seven for itself, one for the other puppet and one for the child. Then it was the child's turn to split three ways between himself and the puppets.

After each of the four successive splitting rounds, and with all the accumulated coins visible in front of the protagonists, the child was asked if the result was "fair," which obviously it wasn't, the stingy puppet typically ending up with markedly more coins for itself. After discussing the child's response and reaction to the inequitable situation, the adult experimenter offered the child the opportunity to give one of his own accumulated coins so he could take 5 coins out of the pile of one of the puppets (generous or stingy). In other words, we probed the child to see whether he would be willing to sacrifice one of his coins to penalize one of the other two protagonists (stingy or generous puppet). We tested children's inclination to engage in costly punishment.

The results are clear. First of all, as a function of the four rounds, 5-year-olds become increasingly inequitable in their distribution between the two puppets. As children come to grasp the stingy and generous characters of the two, they tend to increasingly favor the generous puppet compared to the stingy one when it is their turn to distribute. In comparison, younger 3-year-olds do not, invariably self-maximizing and giving equally less to either puppet. Hence 5-year-olds, but not 3-year-olds, clearly show sensitivity and discrimination of the distinctive stingy and generous characters of the puppets. They behave ethically in their distribution, favoring one over the other in an attempt to rectify what they perceive as inequitable. In other words, they show signs of inequity aversion, the tendency toward *egalitarianism* that appears to grow markedly beyond 5 years.[54]

The costly punishment test performed after the four-round distribution is even more specifically telling of the growing ethical stance children take in sharing between 3 and 5 years of age. When 3-year-olds are content to sacrifice one of their coins to punish one of two puppets, they do so essentially because they enjoy the game and want to continue playing. It is a surface expression of "ludic" inertia because they choose randomly which of the two to punish, either the stingy or the generous one. In contrast, by 5 years, children end up orienting their costly punishment 90 percent of the time toward the stingy puppet. Therefore, by 5 years costly punishment is selective of the puppet's stingy character. It reaches

[54] Fehr, Bernhard, and Rockenbach, "Egalitarianism in young children."

another layer of meaning, a sixth *ethical layer* following our onion metaphor. By 5 years, children begin to behave according to principles, ready to sacrifice their own resources to implement these principles and be recognized by others as possessing and being guided by such principles. The child is now forging a moral identity, adopting a perspective in what philosopher Charles Taylor calls "moral space."

Charles Taylor notes in his book *Sources of the Self*: "What we are constantly losing from sight is that being a self is inseparable from existing in a space of moral issues, to do with identity and how one ought to be. It is being able to find one's standpoint in this space, *being able to occupy a perspective in it*."[55] By 5 years, in relation to sharing, children begin to find and define their ethical standpoint. The quest for such moral bearing will accompany the child throughout life.

This increased sense of equity between 3 and 5 years also translates into new ways and more flexibility in bartering negotiation. In an ongoing study offering children stickers for later exchanges and bartering with an adult experimenter, we observe that by 5 years children tend to become significantly more apt and flexible at value negotiation. In a bartering of stickers situation, 5-year-olds spontaneously change their bid and "up the ante" if the experimenter turns an offer down. In contrast, a 3-year-old tends to insist on proposing the same offer that was turned down by the adult. They demonstrate a lack of flexibility in the exchange and a lack of strategic, *mutualistic* mind reading.

With the layer of ethical sharing added between 3 and 5 years, children change their rapport with others and open up the door to the possibility of a deliberately mutualistic and reciprocal kind of ownership transfer (sharing), therefore to morality: the ethical perspective and principles guiding decisions on what's right or wrong.[56]

Reciprocity and solidarity in development

In the history of ideas in philosophy but also in the social sciences in general, there are recurrent theories pointing to developmental progress, the fact that humanity is engaged in a long-term collective effort toward more social justice and greater, more sophisticated ethical considerations of how we should deal with one another, how social life should become better and more ethical. German idealist philosopher G. W. F. Hegel

[55] Taylor, *Sources of the Self*, p. 112.

[56] On the relation between emerging mutualism as roots of morality in human evolution, a perspective that can be applied by analogy to child development, see Baumard, André, and Sperber, "A mutualistic approach to morality."

(1770–1831) suggested that with the end of monarchy and the ancien régime, there should be an end of history and all its bloody wars. Karl Marx (1818–83) and Friedrich Engels (1820–95) endorsed this idealist view by projecting the end of social tensions and the bright future of humanity that would follow proletarians' victory with the collective appropriation of all the means of production.[57] In an analogous way, Emile Durkheim (1858–1917), founder of modern sociology, proposes an idealistic socio-evolutionary approach leading to more complex collective consciousness regarding "solidarity." Durkheim suggested that population growth in human evolution and history, in particular a marked increase in population density with the emergence of cities, pressured toward the division of labor, itself changing collective consciousness regarding "solidarity." According to Durkheim,[58] this evolution pressured a transition from the *mechanical* (tit-for-tat) solidarity of archaic small hunter-gatherer societies or rural living, to the more *organic* solidarity of large modern societies constrained to be governed by written laws and constitutions.[59]

Jean Piaget's (1896–1980) theory on social reasoning and moral development has the same teleological and idealistic overtones we find in Hegel, Marx, Engels, or Durkheim. Piaget insists on the moral "bettering" and increased conscientiousness that transcend the primordial egocentric propensities of the young child. This bettering would correspond to the progressive construction in child development of more mutualistic, balanced, hence altruistic tendencies. In the same vein, Lawrence Kohlberg (1927–87) further elaborated Piaget's six constructive stages in moral development, stretching moral development by describing them as emerging throughout the lifespan, with the ultimate culmination (only for the few) of an ability to adopt, compose, and empathize by embracing and weighing multiple perspectives while resolving complex moral dilemmas. This would lead children and adults alike toward more fair and balanced judgments, hence constructing an all-round sounder system of moral values.

Piaget's work on the development of moral reasoning in children,[60] particularly his seminal observations on how children develop an

[57] Marx and Engels, *The Communist Manifesto.*

[58] Durkheim, *The Division of Labor in Society.*

[59] For a different, more recent, anthropological, and less idealistic comparative view on human societies, see Fiske, "The four elementary forms of sociality." Fiske distinguishes societies that are primarily based on either communal sharing, authority ranking, equality matching, or finally market pricing. On related matters, see also the interesting book by David Graeber, *Debt.*

[60] Piaget, *The Moral Judgment of the Child.*

understanding of *rules* in games of marbles (chapter 1 of his book on moral development), is telling of the kinds of reciprocity he sees as naturally unfolding in the development of the individual child. For Piaget, the rules of the game are shared, but understood differently as children develop. This development ultimately translates into the growth of a more complex sense of social reciprocity and solidarity as Durkheim describes it. It would lead children toward a greater sense of mutualism and of being a citizen among other citizens, all governed by democratically decided and recognized rules. We recognize in Piaget the clear lineage with Jean-Jacques Rousseau, whose ideas on the social contract helped forge the French Revolution and who was arguably the most formative of the eighteenth-century French Enlightenment philosophers (i.e., explicit charter of basic and universal human rights).

Piaget observes four main developmental stages in the practice and application of rules children would construct between 2 and 12 years of age. The first stage (2 years of less) is purely active and motoric, the child only construing the rules of the game in terms of ritualized sensory-motor schemas, for example how to throw the marble and aim, but absolutely clueless about any collective norms. The second stage (3–5 years) is characterized by the child playing with others, but continuing to be oblivious of the social dimension of the game in terms of rules for winning and competing against others. Children do not show any regard for any shared rules, playing together but egocentrically, everybody potentially winning at the same time. Piaget observes that at this second stage children combine imitation of others "with a purely individual use of the examples received," which for Piaget is the prototypical mark of what egocentrism is in the social domain: an expression of non-democratic blind obedience and copying or conformity.

In a third developmental stage (7–8 years) of what Piaget calls "incipient cooperation" children try to win. In their reasoning about the shared rules of the game, they begin to show an awareness of the mutual control and unifying factor afforded by rules in the game of marbles. Yet, Piaget shows that rule understanding remains local, not generalized to various contexts, and, more importantly, not applied outside the groups of familiar friends. It is only by 11–12 years that Piaget observes the final and fourth stage of social cooperation and reciprocity, with the child now verbalizing ideas about rules that are universally codified following strict, intrinsic rules, the product of a logic that the child not only verbalizes and articulates, but also generalizes to the whole of society in making moral judgments.

This fourth stage would represent an ultimate point in development (and by extension in society) where the child is now cognitively equipped and has developed the potential to understand, and therefore espouses progressive democratic principles. In the idealist tradition of the Enlightenment, with such cognitive potential the child can now enter a civil society based on mutualistic, "properly moral" principles.[61] Those would be the ultimate form of a moral-based reciprocity that would define the politically correct, democratic, and conscientious modern individual. It would also correspond to what Kohlberg describes in his sixth stage of moral development, apparently only reached by a few, including emblematic historical and moral figures like Mahatma Gandhi, Nelson Mandela, or Mother Teresa.

Considering that we are certainly not all saints and in view of the enormous differences that still exist among adult individuals regarding moral issues, this progress-prone, idealistic view of moral development is rather restricted, if not flawed, not unlike the simplistic linear view of species evolution with Man supreme at its top. Nonetheless, it is true that in development, as in evolution, changes over time lead to more diversity, hence more complex physical and mental forms (psychologies). This would include more abstract forms of reasoning, integrating multiple perspectives that in the realm of moral reasoning would end up more "just," "reciprocal," and "mutualistic" in kind. In concrete terms, these progressive mental forms would correspond to various kinds of reciprocity in sharing. These forms are documented as emerging chronologically in child development. In development, reciprocity expressed in children does indeed become less tainted with marks of coercion and nepotism, more imbued with collective and institutional norm awareness.

In the field of comparative and evolutionary psychology, various kinds of sharing and cooperation are distinguished, corresponding to different ways of transacting or sharing resources with group members. These ways of sharing have various psychological values depending on how beneficial they are for each of the protagonists, and ultimately for the survival of the group. Within game theory's formulation,[62] sharing ways are basically classified either as *selfish* (beneficial for self and costly for the recipient or the group), *altruistic* (costly for self and beneficial for the recipient or the group), *spiteful* (costly for both self and recipient or group), or *mutualistic* (beneficial for all concerned). In development it appears that the

[61] See also Baumard et al., "A mutualistic approach to morality," for a theoretical rationale linking mutualism to morality, actually proposing a causal link in evolution from the former to the latter.

[62] See the original proposal in Hamilton, "The evolution of altruistic behaviour"; but also the discussion by Baumard et al., "A mutualistic approach to morality."

mutualistic kind of transacting or sharing ("win–win" solution) is a final-layer culmination, overlaying the three other kinds.

In general, and following the onion metaphor, children start off by expressing selfish sharing, adding new layers that culminate with ethical sharing. This latter kind is in essence mutualistic, the motivation behind it being the achievement of social harmony (as opposed to conflict and social tension) via the approximation of a "win–win" situation.

What characterizes the mutualistic kind of social transaction and sharing is the deliberate attempt at suppressing biases and controlling favoritism (i.e., nepotism and the construction of some "veil of ignorance"). In development, it would correspond to explicit signs that children are trying to reach equity by abiding by normative principles in the determination of what is right and what is wrong, appropriate or not appropriate: when children show first signs of morality or ethics (i.e., principled ways of transacting with others). Framed this way, ethical sharing would represent the first expression of morality emerging in the context of social tensions and conflicts, particularly conflicts over possession, the cradle of morality.[63]

From an evolutionary perspective, most social species demonstrate some degrees of sharing and cooperation. From vertebrates to invertebrates, most animals display complex joint efforts in creating reciprocal group benefits, building nests or habitat together, fighting predators or engaging in more or less organized group hunting, well documented for example among lions and male chimpanzees. In the perspective of evolution, an ant colony that cooperates in building a colony or chimpanzees hunting a monkey together and then sharing its meat employ different kinds of reciprocity. For example, research shows that chimpanzees hunting collectively and sharing the resulting meat do so mainly to create alliances and social bonds among males.[64] Bees cooperating in a hive do so, in all probability, for ontologically different reciprocal reasons. The question is how to differentiate and characterize different degrees and depth of cooperation, each corresponding to a different kind of social reciprocity.

Comparative and evolutionary psychologists continue to debate the relative complexity and psychological depth of cooperation found in different species where effort toward the same goal is clearly visible. In the meantime, no one would deny that insect and mammalian cooperation are qualitatively different, the latter entailing more than the former. The same applies to the six basic kinds of sharing we have described, building up and unfolding between birth and 5 years.

[63] See Rochat, "Possession and morality in early development.".
[64] Mitani and Watts, "Why do chimpanzees hunt and share meat?"

Observing young children aged 4 to 12 years exchanging candy, cards, or other treats among themselves in schoolyards,[65] as Piaget did with games of marbles many years ago, reveals a marked developmental change in the motives behind such "schoolyard economics." These motives correspond to at least two clearly distinct kinds of reciprocity accompanying the development of sharing (i.e., the transfer of ownership).

Children younger than 6 tend to exchange gifts essentially to create bonds with peers, what is described as *associative reciprocity*. At this young age, children articulate personal reasons for trading or not trading, often evoking threats or special bonds such as: "I will not trade my cards because yesterday you did not lend my your tricycle; if you don't lend me your bicycle I will not trade cards" or "You are nice, you gave me your teddy bear, I give you my marble."

Beyond 6 years, children articulate less and less associative reciprocity but rather trade explicitly to make a material gain in the exchange, or achieve the best deal possible. Their trades become more objective, involving negotiations that objectify the value exchange of items, going back and forth, and following certain implicit market rules. They begin to accept, for example, without tantrum or personal threat that an offer can be turned down. They argue, try to convince, and provide sale pitches. More importantly, children spontaneously, and after verbal bartering, agree on a reciprocal deal, either shaking hands or not stepping out of the negotiation.

In this development, beyond 6 years and increasingly with age, children refer to and abide by trade rules and the pragmatics of what become ritualized exchanges sanctioned by *institutions* (group norms, collective ways of being, school or playground culture). In their sharing, children become progressively more sensitive and aware of the cultural context: the institutional or consensual collective order that transcends and ultimately governs personal wants and inclinations.

It is with reference to this order that children beyond 6 years start building their reputation and status within the group, a lifetime enterprise. It is also against this order that children gauge the trust they can put in others. It is in sharing that children eventually develop and reveal their own moral identity. The way we share and are willing to relinquish power over things is indeed the great revealer of who we are as persons.

In adults and from a very early age, from the time children start expressing self-consciousness and self-conscious emotion, hence a new awareness of how one is perceived and evaluated by others, *indirect*

[65] Faigenbaum, *Children's Economic Experience*; and "The underground economy of schoolyards."

reciprocity comes into play in sharing. Indirect reciprocity adds to the simple tit-for-tat direct kind of reciprocity in sharing, by factoring reputation as a crucial determinant of how individuals relate to and deal with one another, in the present, but also in the future, based on memories of how they shared in the past. It opens up the notion of *accountability* and ethics that are both defining features of human sharing, in evolution as well as in child development.

What triggers such development and the driving mechanisms behind it remain for the most part a mystery, aside from a few theoretical speculations. Existing theories put more or less emphasis on unique human enculturation processes that would allow institutional transmission from one generation to the next. Alternatively, other theories emphasize more possible genetic mutations that allowed humans to develop particular social sophistications such as teaching and adopting a pedagogical stance toward others, an ability to elaborate theories of mind, or to detect "we" intentions allowing us, unlike other species, to collaborate creatively in resolving problems or achieving common goals. No matter what mechanisms are behind such evolution, what is certain is that all children, in the development of their ways of sharing, become more sensitive to what people think of them. Sharing is the primary context in which children build their own reputation and image, their own moral perspective and moral identity in the evaluative eyes of others. Ultimately, it determines their place in society.

Part III

Culture

Human possession in context

8 Culture and possession

The last part of the book focuses on possession *in situ*, trying to bring context, particularly cultural context, to the fore. As an opening chapter, we want first to circumscribe what we mean by culture and the various ways it is tentatively construed as a factor, not an easy task as we shall see.

In general, when we talk about culture, we talk about difference: what distinguishes this culture or that culture in the same way that we talk about this person or that person, her characteristics and presumed idiosyncrasies. But what are those distinct characteristics? On what conceptual or phenomenal grounds and in what perspective do we operate to make such distinctions? What constitutes a culture or a person? What qualifies people in their differences or distinctiveness? These are crucial questions, particularly in relation to possession.

Possession is first and foremost an instinct: a *basic instinct*. As a feeling experience, its origins are rooted in biology and not in culture. Culture may play a role in formatting the expression of such experience, but its origins are not cultural. These are rather deeply rooted in biological evolution. From a biological and evolutionary perspective, the inclination to possess does not have to be learned. It is instinctual and universal. No animals, including humans, need to learn the feeling experience of possession, in the same way that we do not need to learn how to fear attacks, be scared of being dispossessed. We do not need to learn envy or feel jealous. There are some necessary prerequisites in order to feel possession (to have a mature brain, to see, to smell, to move about and act, in the environment), but no learning is required. For example, the drive to latch on and control the nipple is innate in all mammals. As such, it is a prerequisite for the survival of the individual. At a basic level, possession is an instinct, analogous to fear, hunger, or sex in other social animals. Possession is another conspicuous kind of innate feeling experience. In this respect, from a basic biological and evolutionary point of view, possession as a feeling experience is not "cultural" per se, at least in its origins. It does not wait for culture to be part of our subjective experience.

Hard wired by evolution, there is thus an instinctive inclination to control and protect from potential predators, or more generally to protect against losing control once control is acquired (e.g., control over food, progeny, shelter, sexual partner, or prey). This said, it does not elude the question of whether the inclination to possess is equally expressed across individuals and groups of individuals, in particular whether cross-cultural differences exist in the *expression* of the basic, universal instinct to possess. Questions remain regarding how much culture actually shapes the expression of possession feelings via variable ways and manners of owning and sharing.

Defining culture

Etymologically, the word "culture" has horticultural and judgmental roots. It derives from an agricultural metaphor. First signs of this metaphor are found in Cicero (106–43 BC), the Latin philosopher and statesman, in his writings regarding the improvement and *cultivation* of the soul (*cultura animi*). Culture stands for learning and the bettering of the mind, in the same way gardeners attend to their plants. The gardening metaphor persists in the French language where "tutor" (*tuteur* in French) stands not only for guardian or teacher, but also for a garden support such as a trellis for climbing plants.

Originally, and persisting to this day, the vernacular sense of culture is often intuited as some forms of *bettering* of the person or of the group. Someone having "no culture" is someone who is a barbarian, an uncivilized "stranger," taken in the etymological sense of *barbaria* which in Latin is a foreign land.[1]

In general, there are two basic meanings attached to the concept of culture, one that tends to be judgmental and the other that tries, on the contrary, to be non-judgmental or "value-free." The judgmental meaning of *culture* refers to the degrees of civility of a person or a group. It does have a strong educational and "value" connotation. This connotation persists to this day. It is in the vernacular when, for example, self-proclaimed high-class or educated people stigmatize the lower classes for their ignorance and lack of culture, a common way to assert class distinction.

In the field of cultural anthropology, culture has a very different meaning. Modern and post-modern anthropologists try desperately to move away from any judgmental connotation, weary of the politics and power attached to the concept of culture. This defines a post-war, post-colonial, and post-modern approach to culture that shaped the field of anthropology and

[1] Note that the Latin word "barbaria" itself derives from the Greek *barbaros*, i.e., "ignorant and strange," what would need to be weeded out.

cultural psychology, for better or for worse. In this "value-free" perspective, the typical textbook definition of culture encompasses the specific ways groups of people in different regions of the world share values, beliefs, how they tend to classify and represent their experience as a group.

From a more evolutionary and comparative as well as psychological and developmental perspective, culture refers more narrowly to the human capacity of representing symbolically, classifying, and sharing experience with others, typically raising questions around the evolutionary origins of such capacity, the process of by which culture is transmitted from one generation to the next, assuming that it is not inscribed in our genes.[2]

The construal of culture, in its most generic and least judgmental (politically safe and "correct") acceptance, refers to an ensemble of characteristics and values that are shared and learned (i.e., not a given) by members of a society. These characteristics and values are by definition transmitted from generation to generation via learning. They are cultural because they do not strictly originate from biological inheritance.

Cultural characteristics and values include ways of behaving socially and carrying the body (so-called technique of the body[3]), the society's particular group norms and beliefs that children are exposed to from birth and even prior to birth in the ways parents live, what they believe in (e.g., parental views on child rearing), how they make a living, or what they eat. Food preparation, pre- and postnatal care, table manners or ways of greeting and sharing are indeed part of what defines culture, among many other things, including material artifacts, tools, and utensils, but also immaterial things like beliefs that take shape and materialize in group rituals and institutions like tribunals, churches, or schools. All of these are culturally transmitted from generation to generation and reach relative stability over time, becoming a group trademark, sometimes short lived and at other times long lasting.[4] All these cultural particularities have to be learned by each child who, in the process of socialization, picks up and assimilates their group "habitus."[5] Progressively, the child comes to embody the group ways or habitus, via an enculturation process that continues to be the source of

[2] See for example Tomasello, Kruger, and Ratner, "Cultural learning."

[3] See for example Mauss, "Le notion de technique du corps," the original essay by Marcel Mauss on ways of swimming and training the body across cultural groups. It is indeed striking how, for example, people in Central Park tend to run quite differently compared to those jogging in the Luxembourg Garden in Paris (personal observation). There are various running gaits in jogging, depending on culture and cultural ways in the practice of physical education.

[4] See Morin, *Comment les traditions naissent et meurent.*

[5] Marcel Mauss first introduced the concept of habitus in the realm of cultural anthropology, borrowing from the Greeks, in particular Aristotle, who originally coined it. Sociologist Pierre Bourdieu developed and popularized the concept further (see for example *The Logic*

much research and hot theoretical debates in both developmental, cross-cultural, evolutionary, and comparative psychology.[6]

Culture as sedimentation

Overall, culture arises from the more or less stable *sedimentation of group habits* becoming embodied by its members. Sedimentation is literally the process of depositing solid entities (rocks) from liquids, like the sediments accumulating on the banks of a river. Culture is at a group level, what happens to all of us at the individual level as we quickly build solid habits in our daily existence: networks of people, routine activities, and repetitive ways of being. We are indeed creatures of habit at both the individual and the group level, with the caveat that at the group level habits become *institutionalized* as they get transmitted from generation to generation and enter what we might call collective memory, just as jurisprudence is to the law.

This collective memory is not just a mental, immaterial phenomenon, but is embodied in group rituals and objects like environmental decor, churches, particular architecture, food, music, ways of moving and dancing, taste, table manners, and ways of cooking, celebrating, joking, working, and dealing with one another. Culture is the *sedimentation of all collective ways and norms of existing and sharing.* It is also what children learn and assimilate to integrate with their group and region, and in general adapt to the circumstances they inherit by birth. These circumstances are sociocultural and economic. They are also geographical, hence climatic (i.e., atmospheric) and physical circumstances, often thought to be the source of reliable differences in cultural institutions (laws and political regimes) as well as of the psychological profile of people within a culture. This idea has been floating around since antiquity.

Breathing culture

Pier Paolo Pasolini, the Italian movie director, essayist, and poet, compiled memories of a first short trip to India in a small and insightful book

of Practice), using it to capture ways of being and thinking as a member of a social class. In more specific terms, habitus corresponds to "an acquired system of schemes that allow for everyday instances of perception, categorization and the production of action and most importantly for the production of mundane judgments (e.g. judgments of moral propriety or impropriety, of likelihood or unlikelihood, of certainty or uncertainty, or judgments of taste such as likes and dislikes": Lizardo, "Habitus." See also Lizardo, "The cognitive origins of Bourdieu's habitus."

[6] See the target article by Tomasello et al., "Understanding and sharing intentions"; also Tomasello, *Cultural Origins of Human Cognition*; Bruner, *Child's Talk.*

entitled *The Scent of India*.[7] The title captures the fact that, at a primordial phenomenological (sensual) level, what emanates from group living is distinct *atmospheres* that we feel and smell. This is all-important when considering what distinguishes places and people around the world. We smell culture before we reason about it. This atmosphere or cultural air is breathed and felt, carrying unmistakable experiential specificities: smells, but also noises, voices, rhythms and movements, temperature, air quality. After landing, especially in tropical places, when the door of the plane opens and one steps out, one can experience a whiff of new air, in addition to novel colors, brightness, movements, all of which capture a specific atmosphere. This impression is *atmospheric* and sensory, combining an aggregate of novel sensations emanating from the climate, but also associated ways of collective living: particular demeanors and uniforms, but also particular cooking smells, different architecture and urbanization, different signs of relative wealth and opulence in cleanness and neatness, and on the contrary different signs of poverty and scarcity of resources with smells of mildew inside and outside of decrepit buildings. This is the first degree of culture as a primordial experience: it is first and foremost *breathed*, leaping to our nostrils and other senses as an immediate, global experience, before we put rational thoughts into it.

This "atmospheric" dimension of culture struck philosophers and early political thinkers, when pondering on how to explain the various patterns of mentalities found across races and cultures. For this, they tried to correlate and even sometimes attempted to demonstrate with empirical, pseudo-scientific observations what would amount to the direct relation between climate and specific collective temperaments or cultures. This tendency persists when people of southern regions are often stereotyped as lazier because of the heat. The stereotype is reinforced when, as in the United States, people tend to speak slower, with a drawling accent. On the other hand, they also tend to be more positively stereotyped as being more friendly because the climate would allow for more leisure time together. These are quick generalities or "cultural heuristics" heard all over the world since antiquity, often part of a rationalization in support of social views and racial attitudes toward certain minority groups, always with the intent of ultimately boasting about the values of one's own social group.

Extolling the virtues of his own Hellenistic culture, Aristotle writes in 350 BC:

> Having spoken of the number of the citizens, we will proceed to speak of what should be their character. This is a subject which can be easily understood by any

[7] Pasolini, *The Scent of India*.

one who casts his eye on the more celebrated states of Hellas, and generally on the distribution of races in the habitable world. Those who live in a cold climate and in Europe are full of spirit, but wanting in intelligence and skill; and therefore they retain comparative freedom, but have no political organization, and are incapable of ruling over others. Whereas the natives of Asia are intelligent and inventive, but they are wanting in spirit, and therefore they are always in a state of subjection and slavery. But the Hellenic race, which is situated between them, is likewise intermediate in character, being high-spirited and also intelligent. Hence it continues free, and is the best-governed of any nation, and, if it could be formed into one state, would be able to rule the world.[8]

Climate theories on cultural differences persisted through the centuries, first in the Arab world with the writings of Ibn Khaldun (1332–1406) reflecting on the causes of historical evolution that he attributed in part to climate variations, aside from sociocultural factors. In the Western history of ideas, it regained particular prevalence during the Enlightenment with the legal writings of Montesquieu (1689–1755). Montesquieu writes in *The Spirit of Laws* (1748): "It is the variety of wants in different climates that first occasioned a difference in the manner of living, and this gave rise to a variety of laws" (Book XIV, chapter 10). These ideas were later revived by romantics of the early nineteenth century, particularly in the writings of Madame de Staël (1766–1817) on the geographical variety of sensibilities and aesthetics in literature.[9]

Montesquieu's *Spirit of the Laws* influenced many political thinkers and in particular the writing of the US constitution. At its center, there is the idea that laws and political institutions should reflect the social and geographical character of the people that are conditioned by *ambient temperature*, hence latitude. In the scientism of the eighteenth-century Enlightenment, Montesquieu supports this idea, informed by some of his own empirical physiological observations exposed in chapter 2, Book XIV, of *The Spirit of the Laws*. Below is a relevant excerpt:

I have observed the outermost part of a sheep's tongue, where, to the naked eye, it seems covered with papillæ. On these papillæ I have discerned through a microscope small hairs, or a kind of down; between the papillæ were pyramids shaped towards the ends like pincers. Very likely these pyramids are the principal organ of taste. I caused the half of this tongue to be frozen, and, observing it with the naked eye, I found the papillæ considerably diminished: even some rows of them were sunk into their sheath. The outermost part I examined with the microscope, and perceived no pyramids. In proportion as the frost went off, the papillæ seemed to the naked eye to rise, and with the microscope the miliary glands began to appear. This observation confirms what I have been saying, that in cold countries the

[8] Aristotle, *Politics*, Book 7, Part 7, trans. Benjamin Jowett.
[9] De Staël, *De la littérature considérée dans ses rapports avec les institutions sociales.*

nervous glands are less expanded: they sink deeper into their sheaths, or they are sheltered from the action of external objects; consequently they have not such lively sensations. In cold countries they have very little sensibility for pleasure; in temperate countries, they have more; in warm countries, their sensibility is exquisite. As climates are distinguished by degrees of latitude, we might distinguish them also in some measure by those of sensibility. I have been at the opera in England and in Italy, where I have seen the same pieces and the same performers: and yet the same music produces such different effects on the two nations: one is so cold and phlegmatic, and the other so lively and enraptured, that it seems almost inconceivable.

And, corroborating the Latin lover myth embodied by the life of Giacommo Casanova (1725–98),[10] Montesquieu infers further on the basis of his physiological observation:

From this delicacy of organs peculiar to warm climates it follows that the soul is most sensibly moved by whatever relates to the union of the two sexes: here everything leads to this object. In northern climates scarcely has the animal part of love a power of making itself felt. In temperate climates, love, attended by a thousand appendages, endeavours to please by things that have at first the appearance, though not the reality, of this passion. In warmer climates it is liked for its own sake, it is the only cause of happiness, it is life itself.[11]

Ludicrous as these theories may sound today, they nonetheless capture and emphasize some ecological truth about cultures. For one, it is true that there are different characters and mentalities attached to various populations and that climate, hence food and diet, production of goods, and relative abundance of resources determine particular adaptive fitness of individuals as well as group characters. Reliably differentiable collective profiles (e.g., more or less competitive or equitable; different collective ways, rituals, cooking, games, pleasures, temperament, etc.) evolved through time as *local adaptations* that also might transform the genetic makeup of a population.[12]

Beyond climate and temperature, if we want to define cultural profiles and their origins, it is necessary to consider historical factors (i.e., the

[10] Casanova, *History of My Life*.

[11] Montesquieu, *Of the Difference of Men in Different Climates*, 1748, Book XIV, chapter 2.

[12] The theory of *gene-culture co-evolution* finds support in the fact, for example, that certain cultural practices evolving over time in certain groups of individuals change aspects of their biological constitution, these changes becoming genetically transmitted. The classic example is the impact of certain cultural practices in agriculture, i.e., herding and the introduction of dairy products that caused a genetic selection and transformation in the ability to digest lactose for these populations only. African and Asian populations for whom dairying is not part of their cultural practices tend not to digest milk, a large number of individuals being lactose intolerant. Their bodies react to milk as a poison (see Simoons, "Primary adult lactose intolerance and the milking habit"; Jersky and Kinsley, "Lactose deficiency in the South African Bantu").

mixing and interaction between populations and civilizations over time through wars, conquests, colonization, and migration). It is also necessary to consider the ways social norms, group traditions, cultural practices, and behavioral manners are learned and internalized by each individual child, transmitted from one generation to the next at the level of the group.

Love padlocks

Each social group, large or small, has its own normative ways of owning and sharing. Families within a particular society may vary sharply in their practices of ownership and sharing depending on multiple factors such as size of the household, religious beliefs, family traditions, income level, and overall resources. Between societies and groups at large, differences in ways of owning and sharing are most evident in light of the different collective principles ruling how individuals ought to behave relative to others regarding possession: how one can claim and transfer ownership in ways that are socially approved and recognized, what is "legitimate" in cases of conflict (e.g., property laws).

These collective principles are objectified in social institutions like legal codes, and explicit written or oral group rituals and traditions, but also implicit collective habitus governing ways to behave and of being socially appropriate, within specific norms of acceptable social sensitivity. As *sedimentation of group habits and practices*, social institutions survive beyond the passing of individuals, transmitted from one generation to the next with only slow changes and slight variability, except in instances of sudden, radical societal bouleversements and other major historical events like sudden expansionism and invasions (e.g., Roman imperialism and colonialism), or revolutions abolishing the privilege of the ancien régime (e.g., the French and Bolshevik revolutions).

The sedimentation of group habits and practices regarding possession can also be relatively sudden. A good example is the love padlocks or "locks of love" fad, a recent global tradition that became suddenly viral around the world, revived by a novel and a movie. Apparently an ancient Chinese tradition which has now spread around major cities all over the world, lovers attach at a particular location, usually the railings of a bridge, a padlock with their names or initials written on it, throwing the key away in the stream below as a wish for eternal love and enduring relationship. In only a few years, this symbolic ritual of sealing their love relationship by locking it to a railing is now a recognized practice by hundreds of thousand of couples. In most major cities in America, Europe, Asia, and Oceania, historical bridges and other landmarks are visually and physically altered by this sudden ritualistic tradition, spreading like an epidemic, viral since the publication of a popular Italian novel and film relating the practice.[13]

What is striking about the love padlocks phenomenon is its global appeal. What resonates with people across cultures is the symbolic way of expressing the basic need for possession and control in the realm of affective relationships. The padlock, straightforward hardware analog of control over possession, attached to a historical landmark and the throwing away of the key, combined with the anonymity engendered by the sea of other locks, contributes to the global appeal of a ritual that essentially conjures the perennial human angst of inescapable dissipation and entropy of all things, including love. In the meantime, it is also a romantic celebration of love, experienced so strongly that it should last forever, albeit a powerful demonstration of global conformism. Love bridges in Paris and Rome and other historical landmarks elsewhere (e.g., a fountain in central Montevideo, Mount Huang in China), with all their thousands of shiny padlocks, are the contemporary equivalent of ancient cathedrals where people, as individuals, can celebrate their love, their own particular relationship, their trust and affective commitment toward another elected individual. The padlock stands literally for the *mutual experience of possession* by lovers who are making a wish of perpetuity, writing their names on it with permanent ink, locking it, and in a charged ceremonial moment (long embraces and self-portraits via cellphones for posting on the social network), throwing away the key, presumably never to be found again. This love padlock ritual, currently a tradition going viral and that will probably die out in a few years, is repeated thousands of times by couples all over the world and from all walks of life. In many ways, it parallels traditional weddings but in a more casual and individualistic fashion as it does not involve the whole family. It is cheaper and has the historical recognition and authority of the culturally loaded site chosen for performing the ritual, anonymously but in resonance with all the thousands of other couples doing exactly the same thing. Lovers recognize themselves in the protagonists of the Italian love story, even if they have never read the book.

Less of a quick spreading of collective ways, groups of individuals over generations develop specific, implicit and explicit principles regarding possession. Often, these principles are highly contrasted and demonstrate radically different collective beliefs and intuitions in regard to the basic need to possess.

13 A 2006 novel by Italian novelist Federico Moccia and the 2008 film adaptation: *Ho vogila de te* (*I Want You*). See also an article in the *New York Times* of August 6, 2007, by I. Fischer, "In Rome, a new ritual on an old bridge."

Cultures of possession

Sri Lanka's indigenous inhabitants, the Wanniya-laeto (literally "forest-dwellers"), also called the Veddas, are descendants of an aboriginal Neolithic island population dating back to 14,000 BC. With successive invasions, in particular since independence from the British, the Veddas have been struggling to maintain their ancestral social organization (matrilineal exogamous clan organization based on female line of descent[14]). They have tried to maintain their hunter-gatherer way of life in the midst of radically different views on property.

As a good example of cultural variation, here is how the possession conundrum of the aboriginal forest-dwellers of Sri Lanka is described by an anthropologist documenting their ways of owning:

> The Waniyalaeto of Sri Lanka do not see themselves as owning the forest; rather, *the forest owns both them and their ancestors-spirits*. This understanding is in such radical opposition to how most other cultures understand the land and the forest within their territories that is difficult to see how any property concept might be introduced among the Wanniyalaeto which would not do a profound violence to the very foundations of their world view. The violence might be such that the culture collapses and those from whom it has been their only known way of life are made futureless and without hope.

Being owned by the forest rather than owning the forest is rather counter-intuitive to most cultures, particularly Western industrial cultures that tend to be less group-minded or "collectivistic," less governed by traditional beliefs and more grounded in plain, matter of fact legal property issues in defense of private "individualistic" principles.

Along the same lines, a few years ago, wandering on a small and remote Melanesian island of northern Vanuatu,[15] I asked a native who owned the garden we were visiting deep in the luscious island rainforest. "It is mine," said the man. "Really? How do you know and how do other people know that it is yours?" "Well, the land was maintained by my ancestors for me to maintain it for my descendants. It is mine and everybody knows it's mine because I am maintaining the land for those coming after me who will do the same. They will maintain the land like I do now and my ancestors did in the past." Clearly, for this Ni-Vanuatu islander, his sense of property rests primarily on a temporal continuity linking past (ancestors), present

[14] Seligmann, "Notes on recent work Among the Veddas"; see also http://vedda.org/wanniyalaeto.htm.

[15] Field notes, July 2007, Motalava in the Banks Islands of the Torba Province of Vanuatu, population approximately 1,500 people surviving mainly from fishing and small garden horticulture, with very little cash revenue, no harbour, and only a small airfield with one very rudimentary dirt road.

(self as temporary keeper), and future (offspring). This traditional sense of property transcends what would tend to be an individual sense of control and agency over possession, the sense that prevails in the industrial capitalistic world.

Less anecdotal is the unique ethnography done in the 1980s by French anthropologist Bernard Vienne on the people living on the same island of Motalava in the Torba Province of Vanuatu (Banks Islands).[16] Regarding the tradition of land ownership by Motalava people, Vienne reports in particular: "From a juridical point of view, arboriculture is clearly distinguished from horticulture. If it is common to grow and cultivate a garden on land for which we have no legal deeds or property rights; a more precise agreement is required for planting trees on a property that is not legally owned, because in that case the tree belongs, no matter what, to the one who planted it. In the case of a prejudice or a conflict with the owner of the land, the planter has the right to destroy the trees he planted."[17] Magic stones as marks of ownership are placed on trees and other objects of possession. These ownership marks constitute a "taboo" (a prohibition) that is backed up and overseen by the group members (chiefs) forming the ritual society of the island (p. 164).

Such collective habitus regarding possession does inevitably translate into particular ways of daily life and behaving in relation to others, particularly in the case of ownership conflicts. Westerners can often be shocked by how people relate to possession in small island villages of the South Pacific, as in many other non-Western cultural environments. For example, in most traditional villages of the South Pacific, you cannot leave a pair of flip flops at the entrance of your hut during the night, as they would probably be innocently taken away by any barefoot villager, seeing unused footwear, appropriating them for a while, not thinking twice. That is normal in the communal life of South Pacific villages. Not construed as the product of a theft, the pair can circulate from temporary owner to temporary owner within the close-knit community until you would find it again for your own use a few days later. This shows how much the sense of exclusivity, property, and justice can be determined by the cultural circumstances of the individual.

Anthropologist Brad Shore,[18] an expert in Samoan culture, recounts a story where one day he complained to his adoptive Samoan father that one of his brothers had stolen money from his wallet. In response, the father

[16] Vienne, *Gens de Motlap*, pp. 162–163; translated by the author.

[17] Barclay, *Manatuturu*, p. 88.

[18] Personal communication. For more thorough insights into Samoan values regarding ownership and property, see also Shore, *Sala'ilua*.

scolded the anthropologist, accusing him of having tempted his brother, creating inescapable envy by leaving his wallet unattended. Because of a profoundly different way of relating to one another, in a much more group-oriented, communal existence, the thief turns out to be the victim of temptation, a perspective that violates your typical Western individualistic perspective on possession.

In Samoa, as it is in most non-Western group-oriented ("collectivistic") cultures, it is the community's responsibility to guide and prevent individuals from falling prey to their own selfish desires and other envies. Likewise, when a child misbehaves, disrupting the classroom, Japanese preschool teachers tend to perceive that the class as a group is faulty and doing something wrong not to be able to integrate the problematic child. In the West we tend to attribute the cause of disruptive symptoms to the individual child, in some cases prescribing drugs and other one-on-one remedial treatment. In Japan, these symptoms tend to be perceived as collective rather than individual.[19]

In relation to possession and ownership, some cultures appear better than others at fostering the protection of what people own as well as ways of sharing what is owned. This is most evident in the often various and highly conspicuous socially acceptable ways of sharing and transferring ownership. These ways vary greatly across cultures. As already discussed in a preceding chapter, the seminal work of early French sociologist and anthropologist Marcel Mauss[20] on gift and donation systems describes different forms of the same general effort to give and transfer ownership in cultures. Extreme cultural variations are the famous potlatch of Northwestern American tribes studied by Franz Boas and the Kula of the Melanesian islanders studied by Malinowski.

In potlatch, a sometimes extremely agonistic form of gift giving, donors go as far as destroying goods, instead of giving them, in an apparent act of displaying disinterest in receiving back from others. Mauss writes, regarding potlatch: "In some instances, the point is not even to give and give back, but to destroy so to give the impression to the recipient that you are not even interested in getting something back. Houses and thousands of blankets are burned, the most expensive copper pieces are destroyed, all that in order to crush, to flatten his rival."[21]

Rules of equity and justice vary greatly in their interpretation among individuals, but also across cultures, even among Western, predominantly

[19] Tobin, Wu, and Davidson, *Preschools in Three Cultures*.

[20] Mauss, *The Gift*, pp. 201–202 of the French edition, translated by the author.

[21] Triandis and Gelfand, "Converging measurement of horizontal and vertical individualism and collectivism."

individualistic cultures like France and the United States. For example, in France and other European countries, the law stipulates that the organs of an individual do not belong to him or her once the person is dead.[22] This means that by default, once dead, French citizens lose the ownership of their own body. It now belongs to the state that, via its public and health services, has the exclusive prerogative to dispose of and harvest organs as needed by others. Historically, this default law exists in the mind of French lawmakers to foster public solidarity among citizens.

An inverted rationale prevails in the culture and justice system of the United States, where individuals are considered legal owners of their own organs beyond their own death. They, and only they, can relinquish their body for donation after death. Many Americans or US residents carry at all times an official document that authorizes such relinquishing. Sadly, some individuals of poor countries go as far as selling their own organs while alive for export to rich countries, for example one of their kidneys.

Culture and personality variations

Among people sharing the same collective habitus, inter-individual differences exist in the intensity and forms of possession experience. Possessiveness and the psychology surrounding possession can indeed greatly vary among individuals sharing the same ways of being together and relating to one another as a group. In all cultures, some individuals are more or less envious and jealous, more or less defensive and clingy about what they own, more or less willing to share and give. There are good tippers and bad tippers, people who donate to charities and others who don't. We know little about what might predict and explain such variation in personality traits. Aside from age, gender, or the individual's particular life history on which Freud and psychoanalysts would focus to explain inter-individual differences, culture plays a role as a buffering or "limiting" factor of such variability. This is what we want to consider here.

When comparing the numerous cultural ways of being together, it appears that there may be only a small number of basic forms of sociality among human groups. Anthropologist Alan Page Fiske[23] proposes that there are four basic forms, evidenced in the way resources are shared and distributed among people of various ethnicities and wealth levels from around the world. Fiske describes these basic forms as communal sharing, authority ranking, equality matching, and market pricing. Each represents

[22] Godbout, *The World of the Gift*, p. 103; Rochat, *Others in Mind*, p. 251.
[23] Fiske, "The four elementary forms of sociality."

a particular cultural way of sharing resources and transferring ownership. Each would also correspond to deeply different ways of relating to one another, setting different kinds of social obligations and exchange norms for the individual, hence possibly also different degrees of inter-individual variation in possessiveness within a culture.

In a similar approach, personality and social psychologists[24] have extensively compared cultures (primarily Euro-American and Asian cultures) that promote forms of collectivism or individualism within their group. Collectivistic cultures in general emphasize and promote group values. Individualistic cultures, on the other hand, tend to emphasize much more individual values, as is the case in most of the Western world where self-promotion, competition, and individual initiatives are strongly encouraged. Individualistic as well as collectivistic cultures may have one of two forms of possession: either it is inscribed into a strong hierarchical power ranking (vertical form), or it is inscribed into a more egalitarian framework (horizontal form).[25] What research shows is that these four basic cultural values and societal organizations correlate with the predominance of particular personality profiles among group members having a more or less strong sense of self or moral responsibility toward others.[26]

Cultural and societal organizations at large could determine an adaptive fitness favoring particular personality traits. It would set limits and calibrate inter-individual variations in the tendency to be more or less self-centered, possessive, envious, or competitive. Strong evidence exists that cultures value specific emotions. For example, embarrassment and self-erasing emotions are highly valued in most Asian cultures, particularly Japan. In contrast, most Western cultures put a premium on self-initiative and self-promotion.

As a case in point, Japanese culture is sometimes coined as a "shame" or "honor-shame culture" in contradistinction to Western cultures that tend to foster control of individuals by promoting and reinforcing feeling of guilt, i.e., the experience of regret mixed with a wish that one could undo mischiefs (so-called predominant Western "guilt culture"). Conceptually, in contrast to shame, guilt captures a painful experience that might befall the individual, either directly or indirectly (via other people), but that is not necessarily objective in the sense that its cause or

24 Triandis, "The self and social behavior in differing cultural contexts."

25 Triandis and Gelfand, "Converging measurement of horizontal and vertical individualism and collectivism."

26 Triandis and Gelfand, "Converging measurement of horizontal and vertical individualism and collectivism."

audience can be very elusive or in the imagination. In her classic 1946 book on Japanese culture (*The Chrysanthemum and the Sword*), anthropologist Ruth Benedict (1887–1948) captures something fundamental that specifies shame in contrast to guilt. She makes the following psychological observation in an attempt to seize the essence of Japanese cultural distinction: "A man is shamed either by being openly ridiculed and rejected or fantasizing to himself that he has been made ridiculous. In either case it is a potent sanction. But it requires an audience or at least a man's fantasy of an audience. Guilt does not . . . a man may suffer from guilt though no man knows of his misdeed and a man's feeling of guilt may actually be relieved by confessing his sin."[27]

Benedict's contrast between shame and guilt is conceptually as well as ontologically important. It helps specify the basic psychology behind it, hence why there is a distinct name for such human experience. A key hint of the psychology (and culture) behind shame revealed in contrast to guilt is the fact that we can "feel guilty of a crime that goes unnoticed." Not so with shame, as shame depends on the "objective" observations of others (quoted from Ian Buruma's foreword to Benedict's book). This is a subtle, yet significant and highly revealing difference, both psychologically and culturally, when comparing Eastern and Western cultures like Japan and the United States.[28] It is also revealing when comparing northern and southern regions of the same culture like the United States or Italy. People of the south, collectively, tend to put significantly more weight on honor, shame, and revenge values compared to people of the north.[29] It also demonstrates the close link that may exist between culture and the adaptive fitness of particular personality profiles, more or less valued within a particular context. This applies to the various ways individuals tend to possess. Culture would set limits to the range of inter-individual variability.

[27] Benedict, *The Chrysanthemum and the Sword*, p. 223.

[28] In passing, it is interesting that shame entails primarily the testimony of an objectified audience with an evaluative (negative) gaze on the self. This potential dread becomes part of what children know about others as potential judges. Interestingly, shame is a dreadful experience that cannot be alleviated with a confession. Once shamed, always shamed. Contrary to guilt, there tends to be no redemption for shame, as suggested by Benedict (see quote above). It is part of our human nature that we can forget shame, tame it, live with it, and eventually let the painful experience fade, but we cannot be redeemed from it via public disclosure. Aside from the fact that guilt can arise outside of the witnessing and testimony of an audience, in contrast to shame, innocence (the opposite of guilt) can be reclaimed through confession or payback toward the offended, whether via fines, prison time, or time outs for children: see Rochat, "The gaze of others."

[29] Nisbett and Cohen, *Culture of Honor*; Cohen and Nisbett, "Self-protection and the culture of honor"; Cohen and Nisbett, "Field experiments examining the culture of honor."

Material scarcity and possessiveness: the case of hunter-gatherers

Across cultures and among classes of the same culture (e.g., affluent neighborhood, city slum, rural area), wealth discrepancies and group differences in terms of possession opportunities loom large. Worldwide, wealth discrepancies are even getting larger:[30] the rich get richer and the poor get relatively poorer. The discrepancy grows, even if the physical situation of some of the poorest may get better in absolute terms of life expectancy and general public health. In relation to possession, some populations are in situations of great material abundance fostering consumerism and the accumulation of personal goods, as in most industrial regions of the world. In comparison, the majority of rural populations worldwide experience great material scarcity, putting many constrains on the kind of durable possession experience they might have. The question is what such blatant discrepancies may have on the way people relate to material, consumable, or non-consumable goods, what impact this has on the psychology of possession. Are rich people more greedy and possessive, as commonly thought? On the contrary, are poor people forced to become less pressed to possess, less defensive of the little they own, forced to be more nonchalant, less concerned about possession and the control over things?

There is a common myth that poor people, because of the material scarcity they are forced to live in, tend to be more generous and willing to share the little they have. This is a common reflection by rough travelers visiting poorer regions of the world and spending time with impoverished native populations. It is common to hear them dwelling on the kindness of such populations, their apparent pride and honor in receiving rich visitors into their poor compound, with no apparent signs of either envy or resentment toward them. If there is embarrassment, it is generally well concealed. For the rich traveler, there is unmistakable simple joy in the child pushing a stick with an empty can attached to its end, a seemingly universal poor-kid makeshift toy vehicle. Warm welcoming smiles tend to abound among villagers and for rich travelers these are manifestations of uncanny generosity in the midst of food insecurity, bad smells, poor hygiene, and toilet-less compounds, and overcrowded and decrepit, mildewed schools and family quarters. What if, in that poor reality that is still the reality of approximately 80 percent of the world's population, the

[30] Recent surveys indicate that 80 percent of the world's population live on a family income of less than $6,000 a year, with half of the world's population living on an average of 2 dollars a day. United Nations Development Programme, *Human Development Report, 2006.*

experience of possession has been essentially "depressed" because of the lack of opportunity to own, allowing people to be more disinterested and generous and more prone to be egalitarian? For example, would the lack of environmental maintenance and the trash spewing of poor living quarters that can be observed around the world indicate reduced possessiveness, some sort of *adaptive nonchalance* toward ownership of property (i.e., "who cares about owning" attitude)? What if the experience of possession and degrees of possessiveness varied depending on circumstances of material abundance? Would its magnitude be proportional to wealth, upholding the common comment by wealthy globetrotters about the uncanny generosity among people living in extreme poverty?

Despite these questions and the potential variability of possessiveness as a function of relative wealth, possession as an experience of power within the group seems to be universal. The power of giving, receiving, and reciprocating to foster social bonds cuts across rich and poor cultures. It is a constitutive aspect of human psychology above and beyond the great diversity of living circumstances. What might be highly variable across cultures and relative wealth contexts is the expression of such experience. Regarding inter-individual differences, as proposed earlier, culture and wealth contexts would play the role of setting limits in the range, form, and normative expression of such experience. In this respect, hunter-gatherer cultures are particularly interesting to consider because of their nomadic lifestyle that limits the accumulation of possession and wealth to a bare minimum. Hunter-gatherers, by definition, never settle for long. They do not cultivate and have no long-term food storage. Constantly moving, they chase and harvest food for immediate consumption.

Pre-agricultural populations of hunter-gatherers have traditionally been considered as "living fossils" of early, pre-historical human existence, possibly the model of our ancestors' (noble savage?) ways of living and sharing. They existed and to some extent their lifestyle still exists all over the world, on both hemispheres, from the North Pole (e.g., the Inuit) to South Africa (e.g., the Hazda or the !Kung San).

Because these populations are non-sedentary, always on the move tracking food resources, and because they also tend to consist of small assemblies of close kin, they have sometimes been described as *lacking possessiveness*, showing very depleted motives in acquiring possessions, and also as inclined to be highly egalitarian compared to other storing and accumulating agricultural, more sedentary, and larger-group cultures. Numerous careful ethnographies of hunter-gatherers have been compiled since the nineteenth century, some being "purer" than others depending on a population's level of contact or relationship with neighboring agricultural and pastoralist populations.[31] Furthermore, depending on context, surviving groups of hunter and gatherers (e.g., the Hadza of Tanzania and the !Kung San Bushmen of Botswana and Namibia) appear to be organized around two basic types of subsistence economy.[32] Some function around an *immediate return* system (immediate return from labor with food neither processed nor stored, on the harvest, hunt, and eat-as-you-go principle). Others are organized around *delayed return* (delayed return of processed and stored food, with material accumulation in fixed dwellings). These two kinds of subsistence economies depend in great part on the historical context of the group and in particular the history of their contacts with other pastoral and agricultural groups.[33] Presumably, pre-contact groups would be the most representative of our prehistoric ancestors and their economic ways, including the primeval possession psychology of modern humans.

Ethnographies of groups organized around immediate return subsistence economy (e.g., Hazda and !Kung San) tend to be strictly egalitarian with no institutions enforcing social norms. Harvest territories are named but are de facto open resources, free for all. There are no grounds for either defense or conflict over land and hunting territories.[34] The Hazda of Tanzania in particular, with an immediate return economy, live typically in bands or "camps" of twenty to thirty individuals. They may live, hunt, and gather in areas that are not asserted for rights, anyone being allowed to live wherever they choose in the vast Hazda country.

Hazda people have very few personal possessions which they hold and carry with them (leather pouch, pipes, clothing, beads). However, the accumulation of personal possessions is not sanctioned among the Hazda. In his thorough ethnography of these people, James Woodburn notes:

> Everywhere we find that there are sanctions against accumulation. This cannot be explained, as so many writers have mistakenly suggested, simply in practical terms: nomadic peoples who have to carry everything they possess are concerned that their possessions should be readily portable so that they can be carried with ease when the time comes to move camp, but sanctions against accumulation go far beyond meeting this requirement and apply even to the lightest objects such as beads, arrowheads or supplies of arrow poison.[35]

The mere fact that sanctions against accumulation are evident in Hazda culture indicates that possession experience exists. It may be minimal and

[31] See the two rich edited volumes by Ingold, Riches, and Woodburn, *Hunters and Gatherers*.
[32] Woodburn, "Egalitarian societies." [33] Stiles, "Hunter-gatherer studies."
[34] Marlowe, *The Hadza*. [35] Woodburn, "Egalitarian societies," p. 442.

contained, but it is indeed a psychological reality as in any other culture regardless of its economic organization. In the Hazda immediate return and highly egalitarian socio-economic system that would most resemble our prehistoric ancestors, we can conclude that possession experience is a fact that cannot be obliterated, defining a lesser-level, tamer expression of possessiveness compared to what is found in other delayed return cultures where competition is more pronounced.

James Woodburn summarizes the main aspect of the egalitarianism found in !Kung San and Hazda hunter-gatherers cultures by stating:

> *What it above all does is to disengage people from property, from the potentiality in property rights for creating dependency.* I think it is probable that this specialized development can only be realized without impoverishment in societies with a simple hunting and gathering economy because elsewhere this degree of disengagement from property would damage the operation of the economy. Indeed the indications are that this development is intrinsic, a necessary component of immediate-return economies which occurs only in such economies.[36]

A high degree of disengagement from property in hunters and gatherers does not mean that the experience of possession, possessiveness, and ultimately the sense of who owns what are merely obliterated in this culture. Another detailed ethnography over a seventeen-month period of two !Kung bands during the 1950s (Lorna Marshall, as part of the Marshall expedition, 1951–59)[37] indicates that gift giving and particularly meat distribution following a big game hunt is instrumental in the prevention and repairing of conflicts within and between bands. To work, gift giving necessarily entails a shared experience of possession and its transfer from individual to individual or group to group. Gift and reciprocal exchanges can be effective only if the giver and the receiver both recognize the value of relinquishing and receiving possession. Evidently, !Kung Bushmen demonstrate such recognition as they frequently engage in gift giving as a way of relieving social tensions they appear to be particularly weary of. This weariness might also account for the absence of stealing in !Kung societies reported by the same ethnographer, not because !Kung inclination to possess and a sense of ownership is absent.

!Kung share the meat they hunt. Interestingly, as a rule, the meat belongs to the owner of the arrow that killed the animal. As possessor of the meat, he takes the larger piece and is responsible for the distribution of the rest. However, arrows are often gifts or borrowed from others, and as a

[36] Woodburn, "Egalitarian societies," p. 445.
[37] Marshall, "Sharing, talking, and giving."

consequence the hunter who actually killed the animal often ends up not being the possessor of the meat and not endowed with the power to get the larger piece and distribute the rest.

In all, we see that even in highly egalitarian cultures where degrees of possessiveness are at a bare-bones minimum, the experience of possession remains central when the context is charged, such as collective hunting and situations of social conflict where gifts (hence a mutually perceived personal possession of the giver) are used to relieve social tensions and promote social harmony.

9 Possession in children across cultures

The context of child development is highly variable and the question is how to construe context, in particular cultural context, as a factor in the development of owning and sharing. Quantitatively, context may vary in terms of relative wealth and material resources, and qualitatively, in terms of general living atmosphere, beliefs, and larger group cultures and values. All of these combined factors contribute to forming each child's *developmental niche.* These niches may vary tremendously within and across cultures. But what kind of impact might they have on the developing psychology of possession? This is the question driving this chapter. But first, the challenge is to create meaningful supra-ordinal "cultural" groupings of children's developmental niches, not an easy feat as we shall see.

Wealth and material resources have concrete consequences at all levels: health, hygiene, life expectancy, education, as well as the relative "social toxicity" of the child's familial and extra-familial environment (crime, addiction, corporal punishment, and abuse). This is not trivial considering that half of the world's population lives on an average of 2 dollars a day, 80 percent of all people on this planet living on a family income of less than $6,000 a year.[1] Aside from great material and resource disparities, children may also, by birth, be immersed in radically different communal and cultural ways of being, learning and internalizing very different normative values regarding tastes and manners of being together, ultimately what is right or wrong, what is appropriate, tolerable, or not tolerable within the group culture. Culture is indeed selective of children's temperament, attitudes, and decisions, from the self-erased tendencies of the Japanese to the more boisterous ways of the Samoans; from the competitive and individualistic propensities that are at a premium in Western cultures, to the more group-oriented and group-attitude values in Eastern cultures.[2]

Depending on tradition, population density, and natural resources, some societies tend to emphasize more communal sharing as a cardinal

[1] Kent and Haub, "Global demographic divide." [2] Nisbett, *The Geography of Thought.*

aspect of sociality. In contrast, other societies tend to be organized primarily in relation to authority ranking or egalitarianism, or around principles of market pricing.[3] Some cultural systems put more emphasis on the general value of collectivism (group orientation), others more on individual achievements (individualistic orientation). Both also vary depending on whether they put more or less emphasis on either hierarchical ranking (vertical system) or egalitarianism (horizontal system).[4] These various ways of being together and sharing values as a group are reflected for example in the way children are cared for (e.g., maternal versus distributed child care),[5] family living arrangements (e.g., joint versus individual space and activities),[6] or the forms of early education (e.g., rote learning versus instruction).[7]

In relation to this multilevel variability, the obvious question is to what extent possession in children as well as adults depends on context and surrounding culture. What can be said on the relative impact culture has on the development of owning and sharing? Here, we want to gauge the influence culture has on possession and its development. The goal in this final chapter is to bring context and difference to the fore.

Factoring culture in child development

In trying to circumscribe culture as a factor in child development, theories offer different kinds of conceptualization of cultural influences and social contexts. Typically, these kinds are distinguished in relation to either proximal (caregivers and teachers) or more distal contexts (ritualistic group practices and ready-made institutions like school).

Ecological, systemic theories on child development, for example, break down children's social context into different zones of influence. Children are constrained to learn and adapt locally to the norms and rules characterizing each zone (family, peers, school, etc.). In development, children would eventually integrate what they have learned in each specific zone. Urie Bronfenbrenner (1917–2005), a prominent child psychologist interested in the context of development, defines developmental zones as *various scale environments* ranging from the microsystem of family and

3 See Fiske, "The four elementary forms of sociality."

4 See Triandis and Gelfand, "Converging measurement of horizontal and vertical individualism and collectivism."

5 Lamb et al., *Child Care in Context.*

6 Lancy, *Playing on the Mother Ground*; see also Harkness and Super, *Parents' Cultural Belief Systems.*

7 Odden and Rochat, "Observational learning and enculturation"; Rogoff, *The Cultural Nature of Human Development.*

peers, through the macrosystem of societal values and institutions like laws, and moral codes, to the more global economics and politics surrounding individuals.[8]

In his ecological theory of development, Bronfenbrenner distinguishes three other levels influencing micro- and macrosystems: the mesosystem capturing important interactions between microsystems (e.g., family and school environment), the exosystem capturing indirect environmental influences on the child (e.g., mother's profession and situation at work), and finally the chronosystem intended to capture the evolution of all the systems over developmental time, in particular historical changes in the sociocultural circumstances of the developing individual (e.g., global politics and economics).[9]

Returning to the onion metaphor used in preceding chapters, it is reasonable to think that the layers of ecosystems proposed by Bronfenbrenner have varying status and shaping power over developmental time. During the first 3 years of life and before crucial adaptations to extra-familial institutions like school, neighbourhood, and peer associations, the child develops strong habitus and predispositions in the context of basic care and intimate interactions with parents and close relatives. At the origins, influences from macrosystems exist but are farther removed, gaining in importance over developmental time when the child adds other experiences and zones of novel local adaptations like entry into school and other peer activities outside of the family environment.

It is one thing is try to parse what constitutes the *amalgam of factors* that culture represents in relation to development, quite another to figure what might be the mechanisms or process by which children learn and eventually become "encultured" within their own context, embodying the collective habitus of their group that we recognize as their culture. Some researchers propose that first-order effects of culture are related to specific ways the developmental niche or developmental environment of children is organized via specific practices.[10] These practices are initiated, reinforced, and established by caregivers and educators, reproducing particular group ways or traditions of being together and caring for children. At the level of teaching and the transmission of skills and knowledge, learning practices and beliefs regarding education vary across cultures. For example, learning in most rural,

8 Bronfenbrenner, *The Ecology of Human Development.*

9 For a different historic, cultural, and systemic approach to child development, see also Cole and Hatano, "Cultural-historical activity theory."

10 Super and Harkness, "The developmental niche"; Super and Harkness, "Culture structures the environment for development."

non-Western cultures, such as small traditional societies in the South Pacific[11] or rural Africa,[12] tend to be mainly fostered via observational learning and imitation as opposed to the more Socratic teaching and instructional learning fostered in children of urban and Westernized regions of the world.[13]

Culture in relation to child development can be operationalized in terms of the organizational aspects surrounding the child, embodied and created by caregivers in their reinforcement of certain practices, the elaboration of certain verbal and nonverbal (proto-conversational) themes, the implementation of particular values and beliefs guiding the particular chain of practices, the establishment of particular loci or settings for certain practices (e.g., school, schoolyards, playgrounds, etc.). Numerous anthropological works on childhood across cultures point to the influence of collective practices structuring in different ways the developmental niche of children, from the relative distribution of child care, corporal punishment, or ways of instructing or teaching children within the group. This second-order cultural factor[14] (i.e., group practices, educational beliefs, or child care norms) has an influence, for example, in the differential promotion of gender roles and temperament profiles across Western and Eastern cultures.[15]

Cultural dressage and dispositional habitus

The role of early intimate experiences of infants with their parents, siblings, and other caregivers in the immediate family environment is at the core of most theories of personality development. Since antiquity, long before Freud and psychoanalysis, philosophers and other social scientists pondered the influence of early intimate relationships (e.g., the mother–child relationship) in shaping individuals from the crib on, arguably what would be the main cradle of cultural influence and learning (enculturation).

For sociologist Pierre Bourdieu, it is in this primordial relational system, in particular in what he calls "body's *dressage*," that the first dispositions of the habitus are established. Bourdieu goes as far as suggesting that

11 Odden and Rochat, "Observational learning and enculturation."
12 Lancy, *The Anthropology of Childhood*; see also Lancy, *Playing on the Mother Ground*; Rogoff et al., "Development through participation in sociocultural activity"; Konner, *The Evolution of Childhood*.
13 Rogoff, *The Cultural Nature of Human Development*.
14 See the seminal cross-cultural comparison of preschools in Japan, China, and the United States showing significant differences in child-rearing practices and theories guiding early education in these societies: Tobin, Wu, and Davidson, *Preschools in Three Cultures*.
15 See Chen, Rubin, and Sun, "Social reputation and peer relationships in Chinese and Canadian children."

adults' biases toward submission or domination in relation to categories like gender, ethnicities, language, and other cultural ways leading to discrimination and hard-to-shake stereotypical attitudes toward others, find their roots in the early dressage and inscription into the child's body of deeply rooted preferential propensities. Those propensities correspond to perceptual and action schemes that are the foundation of practical and implicit (unconscious) cognitive biases. Bourdieu refers to them as the individual's long-lasting and obscure *dispositional habitus* that he defines as "the extraordinary inertia resulting from the engraving of social structures into the bodies."[16]

In *The Family Idiot*, his biography of Gustave Flaubert, Jean-Paul Sartre speculates at length and in remarkable depth on the formative impact and primordial influence found in the intimate social exchanges between infants and their proximal family environment. In the first part of this long study ("The constitution"), Sartre goes to great lengths in describing the initial experiential state of total abandon to the cares of others. He speculates that it is in this early submission to specific maternal gestures, attitudes, and attention that one can find the roots of Flaubert's apparent passivity as a child and subjective disconnection as an adult, possibly also the source of his genius as inventor of the modern novel. He writes: "Gustave as a child, is not *made* to act; what he feels is dizzying submission to this constitutive nature experienced within him as the product of *others*."[17] Sartre goes on a few pages later: "The newborn, molded every day by dispensed cares, internalizes the maternal activity of his own passive 'being there,' in other words the infant internalizes the maternal care activity as the passivity that conditions all the pulsions, and all the internal rhythms of desires, speeds, accumulated storms, schemas that reveal at the same time organic constancies and unspeakable wishes – in brief that his own mother, buried deep into that body, becomes the *pathetic* structure of affectivity" (p. 58).

Sartre insists on the inescapable determinant of the mother as a whole person who determines the affective core experience of cared newborns. Maternal constitution, relative sensitivity, and life story are inescapably reflected in the kind of care, attention, and gestures mothers are able to dispense to their infants. Indeed, in the experiential life of newborns that revolves primarily in the passive reception of cares molded by others, there is more than the serving of basic survival needs such as food, warmth, and hygiene. There is also, as Sartre points out, the transmission of unique trans-generational idiosyncrasies or family truth, what could be equated

16 Bourdieu, *Méditations pascaliennes*, p. 248.
17 Sartre, *The Family Idiot*, p. 48; author's translation.

to Bourdieu's dispositional habitus: "when the mother breastfeeds or cleans her infant, she expresses herself, like anybody else, in her personal truth, which, naturally, sums up in it all her life, from her own birth; in the meantime, she realizes a rapport that changes depending on circumstances and people – for which she is the *subject* and that we can call maternal love . . . But, at the same time, by this love and through it, by that person, skillful or unskillful, rough or tender, the way her history made her, the child is manifested to himself" (p. 57).

From Sartre the philosopher, at the end of his life, wearing the hat of psychoanalysis that for years he tended to dismiss, these reflections try to capture the larger cultural impact others can have while dispensing basic, indispensable cares to the needy infant. In particular, not unlike the dialectic of master and slave, newborns would start off extracting a sense of imposed passivity and submission. In return, the mother would extract a sense of duty and fulfillment in the instinctive call for maternal love and protection. This sort of basic inter-subjective rapport of force is paradigmatic of the context in which Bourdieu's obscure dispositional habitus would find its developmental roots.

Beyond dispositional habitus emerging from first interactions with intimate others, children eventually develop individual ways of fitting the larger group, beyond the mother and intimate family circle. They learn and adapt to the normative ways of the larger community: ways of being, acting, and experiencing as a group. These ways are particularly varied when it comes down to possession.

Cultural practices of parenting

Except for nuclear Western middle-class families that are overly represented in child development research, the vast majority of other children across cultures are exposed to multiple parenting practices involving older siblings as well as older generations within an extended family context. For these understudied majority children, the mother's role as a primary figure tends to be much less prevalent. It recedes to the background compared to the Western industrial family context.

Multiple parenting practices allow for much more flexibility and greater diffusion of parental responsibility, spread over the larger community. This is the case for example in the collective context of the Israeli kibbutz, but also in Oceania and many other urban and rural regions of the world. In Oceania, for example, adoption can become prevalent and a routine practice, children being used as gifts and marks of trust to reinforce inter-family alliances. This kind of voluntary adoption is a common practice in traditional Polynesian cultures like Samoa, shocking and uncanny, unthinkable for most Western middle-class parents.[18] But would that affect the child's budding sense of attachment and exclusivity that is so central in psychoanalytical theorizing?

As already discussed in a previous chapter, in a Western middle-class context, first signs of social exclusivity are manifested from 6 months of age with bouts of what researchers interpret as "jealousy," but particularly by 8 months when infants start to show exclusive interpersonal clinginess accompanied by a novel, unmistakable wariness of strangers (i.e., stranger anxiety).[19] These observations, however, are based primarily on samples of children exposed to Western middle-class parenting practices, an exception rather than the rule at a more global scale.

Marked differences in parenting practices exist across cultures, as documented in works by both anthropologists of childhood[20] and developmental psychologists.[21] Babies are cared for and handled very differently with various normative expressions of parental sensitivity. Physical proximity is more or less prevalent. In some contexts, proximity is quasi permanent, babies being carried around in adults' day-to-day domestic chores (e.g., on the back of the mother during field labor and food preparation). Sleeping arrangements vary as well as feeding schedules, all corresponding to different parental beliefs regarding the form and role of early parenting. Across cultures, adults project and implicitly endorse various collective views of infant psychology, the development and potential capacities of newborns. Conceptions of hygiene and ways of training or educating young children can vary considerably from one culture to the next. For example, in most cultures, observational learning and imitation are at the core of early education, in sharp contrast to the directive instruction promoted in the industrial Western world, particularly by the middle and upper socio-economic classes.[22] Marked differences also exist within a culture, depending on social and economic status (poor, working class versus rich, more affluent), each having evolved a particular

[18] In Samoa, and Polynesian culture in general, it is difficult to meet a family that did not raise a few adopted children, a common practice in the multi-parenting context of this culture. At birth, a child might be given as a gift to other group members within the large and close-knit extended family network that included villages within a chiefdom region, but also across chiefdom regions. As in the Japanese game of Go, parents place offspring to occupy space, and to create social links, alliances, and in the end social debts. See O'Meara, *Samoan Planters*; Shore, *Sala'ilua*.

[19] Hart and Carrington, "Jealousy in 6-month-old infants"; Spitz, *The First Year of Life*.

[20] For example, Lancy, *The Anthropology of Childhood*; see also Lancy, *Playing on the Mother Ground*; Konner, *The Evolution of Chilhood*.

[21] In relation to the significant impact of parental beliefs and practices across cultures on child development, see Keller, *Cultures of Infancy*; see also for example LeVine, *Child Care and Culture*.

[22] Rogoff, *The Cultural Nature of Human Development*; Lancy, *The Anthropology of Childhood*.

collective (class) habitus through generations of economic and educational segregation within the society.[23]

At a macro level, cultures of early education may vary among groups of people who are neighbors, sharing the same physical ecology and comparable wealth or living standards. Each can have evolved different collective norms of infant care practices. An example is the contrasted infant care practices found in the Aka hunter-gatherers of Central Africa and their neighbors, the Ngandu, a more sedentary and agricultural population.[24] Both form pre-industrial, traditional, small-scale, and egalitarian societies with no apparent socio-economic class structures aside from age and gender. However, each has evolved contrasted collective ways of handling, relating to, and caring for their young.

The systematic observation of typical (normative) infant care by the Aka and the Ngandu shows marked differences. Instances of adult–infant interaction at a distance (with no physical contact) increase markedly as a function of the infant's age by the Ngandu but not by the Aka. Aka babies tend to be held, often fed, and maintained in a state of sleepiness and drowsiness. In contrast, Ngandu infants are often left alone fussing or crying. Ngandu infants also show significantly more smiling, playing, and vocalizing compared to Aka babies. These observations show that different child care practices within a group can be associated with different emotional expressions and dominant temperament profiles in children.

Collective norms of caring for the young constrain affective self-regulation and infants' ways of gaining attention from others. These norms are sedimentation of group habits, an intrinsic part of each child's developmental niche. As in the case of the comparison between Aka and Ngandu infants, it appears that, early on, these norms determine the adaptive fitness of particular temperaments. They shape ways of relating to others that are most adapted to the practices and beliefs of the larger group culture.

Culture and early attachment

In the footsteps of Freud, modern theories of personality development consider the first relationship between mother and infant the crucial determinant of socio-emotional development throughout the lifespan. The theoretical assumption, upheld by numerous longitudinal and cross-sectional studies, is that the form of early attachment to the mother

[23] See in particular Bourdieu, *Distinction.*
[24] Hewlett et al., "Culture and early infancy among Central African foragers and farmers."

has enduring consequences on individuals' capacity to relate and share with others, their capacity to build social trust and intimacy.[25]

However, as we have seen, there are great cultural variations in parenting practices and in the role played by the biological mother in early development. Already by the beginning of the twentieth century, anthropologists questioned the Freudian assumption of a universal Oedipus complex, showing that in societies organized along matrilineal lines, no apparent signs of triangle tensions between children and their biological parents exist.[26] In fact, in many cultures, the biological tie is not the centerpiece of early parenting.

Since John Bowlby's original attachment theory,[27] the vast majority of developmental work tends to be informed by the narrow Western middle-class ideological perspective. As Heidi Keller notes:

> As concomitants of attachment theory, ideas about intergenerational transmission, organizing relationships in general, deviations and pathological behaviors, as well as experiences that mold the neurophysiology of attachment, rest in the assumption of monotropic relationships, exclusive attention between baby and caregiver, mainly the mother, sensitive responsiveness towards infants' signals, and elaborated mentalistic dialogues and trait-like organization of the psyche. These assumptions characterize the psychology of parent–child relationships in Western middle-class families, which compose less than 5% of the world's population. There are, however, accounts of substantial differences of socialization goals, caretaking strategies, and parent–child behavioral relationships across cultural communities that must have implications for the development of attachment relationships.[28]

As a matter of fact, cultural variations exist when measuring attachment (secure versus insecure or disorganized), as measured by the standardized *strange situation* introduced over forty years ago by Mary Ainsworth (1913–99).

In post-war England, Mary Ainsworth became a student and collaborator of psychiatrist and psychoanalyst John Bowlby, researching with him and others at the Tavistock Clinic in London the effect of maternal separation in children.[29] In the mid 1950s, having the opportunity to sojourn in Africa, Ainsworth launched a longitudinal field study of mother–infant interaction in Uganda.[30] She documented developmental patterns and infant care in Uganda analogous to those found in

[25] See in particular the seminal post-Freudian works of Bowlby, *Attachment and Loss*, and Erikson, *Childhood and Society*.

[26] See in particular Malinowski and Ellis, *The Sexual Life of Savages in North-Western Melanesia*.

[27] Bowlby, *Attachment and Loss*. [28] Keller, "Attachment and culture," at p. 179.

[29] Ainsworth and Bowlby, *Child Care and the Growth of Love*.

[30] Ainsworth, *Infancy in Uganda*.

British children. From this observational study published in the 1960s, Ainsworth upheld the idea of the universal character of early attachment.

In the 1970s, back in the United States, Ainsworth devised the standardized and highly influential *strange situation*, for the experimental measurement of early infant attachment toward the mother.[31] In this laboratory-controlled situation of approximately 20 minutes, the child is observed while mother and stranger come in and out of a room to sit quietly while the child plays with toys. Children's reactions to the mother's departure and her return, and the reaction to the stranger while alone with her, as well as the child's relative propensity to play and explore novel toys, are systematically analyzed. Based on this analysis, infants 9 months and older are categorized as falling into categories of either *secure attachment* (the child securely attached to the mother) or other forms of *insecure attachment* profiles (i.e., anxious-resistant, avoidant, or disorganized attachment to the mother).

The numerous studies using the strange situation tend to concur that the majority of 12–18-month-old infants fall into the category of secure attachment (approximately 60 percent), while a minority falls into one of the insecure attachment categories of either disorganized (approximately 8 percent), avoidant (approximately 21 percent), or anxious-resistant (approximately 12 percent). In the mid 1970s the large longitudinal "Minnesota study" was launched, testing infants at 12 and 18 months, but also through childhood, adolescence, and even now in adulthood. This study included 200 participants from low-income families, whose mothers were exposed to challenges and stresses typically linked to poverty. Interestingly, this inclusion almost doubled the proportion of anxious-resistant attachment cases (22 percent) compared to what is generally reported in the literature (approximately 12 percent) based on infants from primarily middle-class urban families visiting infant laboratories to be tested in the strange situation.[32] This suggests that the attachment profile developed in infancy is not immune to contextual variations and overall environmental stress.

In general, the longitudinal results from the Minnesota study provide complex yet clear evidence that, based on the strange situation, the form of attachment at 12 and 18 months is predictive of later emotional self-regulation, the propensity toward curiosity, and integration into the peer group during the preschool years, but also by middle childhood the propensity to make friends and to function as part of a group. By adolescence, it is also predictive of the ability to self-reflect, construct an

[31] Ainsworth et al., *Patterns of Attachment.* [32] Sroufe, "Attachment and development."

identity, and generate intimacy with others.[33] Early attachment to the mother is thus clearly a formative factor of social competence, corroborating what Bowlby and Ainsworth proposed in their original theory. It is also a relatively stable feature of personality development and individuals' relative capacity to affiliate and engage in intimate relationship with others as they enter adolescence and even adulthood. Patterns of early attachment are indeed found to be predictive of how individuals engage in and deal with intimate relationships when they reach adulthood.[34]

Early attachment patterns, however, do not seem to be immune from cultural influence. Based on the strange situation, research shows that, compared to North American and other Western samples, a significantly larger proportion of 12-month-old infants from either Germany, Japan, or a kibbutz in Israel fall into insecure attachment categories. In particular, significantly more cases of avoidant pattern are found in Germany,[35] more cases of resistant insecure pattern are found in Japan,[36] and more cases of ambivalent pattern are found in Israel.[37] These findings demonstrate that attachment is not immune from cultural variations in terms of prevalent normative child care practices and adult beliefs: German parents tend to put a premium on early independence, Japanese on the importance of closeness in mother–infant bonds (an emphasis increasing opportunities for greater stress around separation), and kibbutz children tend to be overall significantly less exposed to strangers.[38]

Early possession and transitional objects across cultures

Social selectivity and preference are first expressed when infants cling to their mother or primary caregiver(s) for soothing (self-regulation) and protection. Signs of social selection are evident immediately after birth as newborns tend to orient preferentially toward the scent of the maternal amniotic fluid or maternal milk compared to any stranger's.[39]

33 Sroufe et al., *The Development of the Person.*

34 Waters, Weinfield, and Hamilton, "The stability of attachment styles from infancy to adolescence and early adulthood."

35 See Grossmann et al., "German children's behavior toward their mothers at 12 months and their fathers at 18 months in Ainsworth's strange situation."

36 Takahashi, "Examining the strange-situation procedure with Japanese mothers and 12-month old infants."

37 Sagi et al., "Security of infant–mother, –father, and –metapelet attachments among kibbutz-reared Israeli children."

38 Grossmann et al., "Maternal sensitivity and newborns orientation responses as related to quality of attachment in Northern Germany"; see also Keller, "Attachment and culture."

39 Marlier, Schaal, and Soussignan, "Neonatal responsiveness to the odor of amniotic and lacteal fluids"; Marlier, Schaal, and Soussignan, "Bottle-fed neonates prefer an odor experienced in utero to an odor experienced postnatally in the feeding context."

By 6 months, Western middle-class infants manifest ownership (public expression of possession) in relation to their mother with first bouts of "jealousy," being jealous of their mother's exclusive attention.[40] Signs of jealousy are also evident by 8 months with the emergence of "stranger anxiety," children tensing with fearful emotional expressions and renewed clinging toward known people as they encounter novel people who try to contact them.[41] It is in the context of such selectivity that attachment develops, becoming more or less secure (see preceding section).

Aside from attachment to people and first social bonding, children also tend to develop exclusive attachment to one particular physical object in their environment (e.g., blanket, pacifier, stuffed animal, etc.), what psychoanalyst and child psychiatrist Donald Winnicott termed a *transitional object.*[42] It is an object of possession that is between "me" and "not-me," endowed with exceptional affective investment and bonding power, a primitive form of fetishism. In Winnicott's psychoanalytical perspective, transitional objects would help children to cope with social separation (e.g., going to sleep) and to self-regulate (i.e., self-soothing) in instances of stressful events.

At a more cognitive level, such object investment would also allow infants to create a zone of exploration that is at the intersection between self- and non-self world, an area of play and interplay between subjectivity and objectivity. In a playful way, transitional objects would allow children to explore and create links between these realms, providing some sort of in-between playful and creative "resting place." Interestingly, and beyond a mechanism allowing infants to cope with their separation from what he calls their "good-enough mother," Winnicott views the transitional object phenomenon as instrumental in a child's developing symbolic capacity, namely the ability to experience something (e.g., a blanket, a stuffed animal, a pacifier) as a *substitute*, hence standing for something else (e.g., the mother, the breast). It would allow children's active exploration and resulting awareness of the difference and similarity between the two (i.e., the real and the substitutive transitional object):[43]

[40] Hart and Carrington, "Jealousy in 6-month-old infants."

[41] Spitz, *The First Year of Life*. As I visit villages of different cultures in the South Pacific and elsewhere, it appears anecdotally that the phenomenon is rather universal in infants between 6 and 18 months.

[42] Winnicott, "Transitional objects and transitional phenomena."

[43] See also the following from Winnicott: "But the term transitional object, according to my suggestion, gives room for the process of becoming able to accept difference and similarity. I think there is use for a term for the root of symbolism in time, a term that describes the infant's journey from the purely subjective to objectivity; and it seems to me that the transitional object (piece of blanket, etc.) is what we see of this journey of progress towards experiencing." In Winnicott, "Transitional objects and transitional phenomena," p. 94.

> I have introduced the terms "transitional object" and "transitional phenomena" for designation of the intermediate area of experience, between the thumb and the teddy bear, between the oral eroticism and true object-relationship, between primary creative activity and projection of what has already been introjected, between primary unawareness of indebtedness and the acknowledgement of indebtedness ("Say: ta!"). By this definition an infant's babbling or the way an older child goes over a repertory of songs and tunes while preparing for sleep come within the intermediate area as transitional phenomena, along with the use made of objects that are not part of the infant's body yet are not fully recognized as belonging to external reality. (p. 90)

Transitional objects are common for Western, middle-class infants and toddlers, emerging in the first year of life and often persisting through early childhood. Children show a predilection for certain object kinds depending on age, the early prevalence of pacifiers being replaced by blankets and hard objects from 18 months.[44] Based on existing parental surveys but also direct laboratory observations, 50 to 75 percent of Western middle-class children show strong attachment to a particular physical object between 3 and 60 months. The transitional phenomenon disappears or becomes rare beyond 5 years of age.[45] However, there are marked cross-cultural differences, as we shall see, depending on living arrangements, child care practices, and socio-economic status of the child's family.

Regarding the quality of the transitional object, it is useful to distinguish two basic kinds. One is *absolute* in the sense of exclusive and rigid, like a doll or stuffed animal, an individuated pacifier or blanket. These are singular and not interchangeable objects, even if the object falls to pieces and is anything but appealing and hygienic for anybody but the child. The other kind is *relative* in the sense of interchangeable and more flexible. These are any objects that reproduce a particular experiential (sensory) experience that is a source of comfort for the child, presumably associated with the mother or anything/anybody the child is missing or separated from, the child coping by actively re-creating sensory comfort with object mediated self-stimulation. This second kind of transitional object can be something as simple as the small silk label found on most commercial clothing. The child can be very picky as to what label is of the right texture and feel when fingered and rubbed, for example.[46] It can also be any piece of material, regardless of

44 Passman and Halonen, "A developmental survey of young children's attachment to inanimate objects."

45 Ekecrantz and Rudhe, "Transitional phenomena"; Gaddini and Gaddini, "Transitional objects and the process of individuation."

46 Anecdotally, a French father and good friend (François Bertrand) recalls his daughter Aude being very picky and exclusive regarding the kind of silk label that would do the job for her to go to sleep or travel. By around 2 years, she would finger and do "label tasting" of any material, before deciding that it would do the soothing job.

color, but with a very specific scent (e.g., lavender) that the child might, in a ritualistic fashion, pass under and gently rub against his nose, typically engaging also in thumb sucking. This is a common sight when the light is turned off and the child is left alone in his room to sleep, but also when facing any stressful event and seeking comfort. At a generic level, all transitional objects (absolute or relative) are soothing instruments that the child uses to actively re-create sensory comfort and sensations that are associated with social contacts, particularly interactions with the mother. They are the first *self-regulating tools* of children, and in this sense are two primordial forms of possession and ownership. What is interesting is the fact that a relatively large proportion of children (approximately 40 percent) do not manifest such object attachment, and those who do, do so in idiosyncratic ways, favoring absolute over relative kinds. These early inter-individual differences remain for the most part mysterious, although some researchers have found correlations between transitional object expressions and secure attachment to the mother.[47] There are also some reports that young children who are institutionalized, placed early on in an orphanage and deprived of their mother, show less to no inclination in attaching to an inanimate object.[48]

In relation to culture and context, the question is whether the transitional object phenomenon as primordial expression of object possession and ownership would be as prevalent, for example, in the context of a small, close-knit village community with allo-parenting (distributed child care practices), the child from birth constantly being held by older siblings and growing up in an environment providing very few child-oriented objects like toys, blankets, or pacifiers. This is a legitimate question considering, once again, that those are the circumstances of most children on this planet.

In the Western world and within the particular national and cultural context of Italy, Italian children of peasant families living in rural villages demonstrate markedly less transitional object attachment (5 percent) compared to either Italian children (31 percent) or Anglo-Saxon children (60 percent) living with their family in the city of Rome.[49] Likewise, in the United States, infants and children from white affluent families tend to show significantly more transitional object attachment compared to children from black, less affluent families (77 versus 46 percent).[50]

47 Lehman et al., "Soft object and pacifier attachment in young children"; Litt, "Children's attachment to transitional objects"; Litt, "Theories of transitional object attachment."

48 Provence and Lipton, *Infants in Institutions*, cited in Hobara, "Prevalence of transitional objects in young children of Tokyo and New York."

49 Gaddini and Gaddini, "Transitional objects and the process of individuation," cited in Hobara, "Prevalence of transitional objects in young children of Tokyo and New York."

50 Litt, "Children's attachment to transitional objects," cited in Hobara, "Prevalence of transitional objects in young children of Tokyo and New York."

In general, research shows that there are substantial differences across cultures in children's getting attached to a particular object. For example, a lesser proportion of 2–3-year-old Korean children living in Korea show transitional object attachment (18 percent) when compared to same-age Korean children living either in Korea or in the United States (34 and 53 percent respectively).[51] These cultural and socio-economic variations in relative prevalence of transitional object attachment may depend on various child care practices and in particular sleeping arrangements that more or less alleviate stress from separation. When going to sleep with others in the same place, and when seldom alone during the day while cared for by multiple people, the child is not constrained, following Winnicott, to re-create symbolically, via the object, the lost union with the "good-enough" mother.

In Japan, where the dominant child care practice is for parents, and especially mothers, to sleep with their child through toddlerhood and beyond (typically around 6 years), transitional object attachment is less prevalent, cut almost by half, when compared to same-age children of North American urban populations of comparable middle to high socio-economic status (62 versus 38 percent).[52]

While traveling and staying in villages doing research in the South Pacific (Samoa, on the island of Savai'i in Polynesia, and Vanuatu, on the island of Motalava in Melanesia), we surveyed parents (N = 34 at each location) regarding their young child's attachment to inanimate objects.[53] We compared their responses using the same questionnaire with a sample of parents in the United States (N = 30) visiting our Lab with their infant or toddler as part of another study. At the time of the questionnaire, the child was between 1 and 96 months, with an average age of 48 months across locations, and comparable standard deviation of about 30. The questionnaire was administered by us to English-speaking parents in the South Pacific, and filled in by the parent in a written format in the United States during their visit at the Lab. US parents were in large majority from white middle-class background.

Question (1) was whether their child was given a particular object at birth and, if so, what kind of object it was (e.g., if it was for decoration or play). We also asked whether the child was still playing with it. In five subsequent short questions, we then asked: (2) what kinds of toys or objects the child likes to play with; (3) whether the child has a particular preferred toy to play with; (4) whether the child tends to carry a particular toy around the

[51] Hong and Townes, "Infants' attachment to inanimate objects," cited in Hobara, "Prevalence of transitional objects in young children of Tokyo and New York."

[52] Hobara, "Prevalence of transitional objects in young children of Tokyo and New York."

[53] Robbins and Rochat, "Transitional objects in the South Pacific and the United States."

community; (5) whether the child has a particular toy that she likes to sleep with; and if sleeping with a toy, (6) whether the child becomes upset when this is misplaced or lost. Based on the parental responses to this questionnaire, and in particular based on the last three "attachment" questions, we calculated an attachment index: minimum 0 if all questions are answered negatively, maximum of 3 (100 percent) if all are positive.

This quick survey relied on the parent's recollection and needs to be taken with a pinch of salt. However, in a nutshell, we do find that US parents report their child sleeping with an object, presumably their transitional object, significantly more compared to either Samoan or Ni-Vanuatu parents (respectively 68, 36, and 28 percent of the children). In Samoa and Vanuatu, the sleeping arrangement is typically communal, children sleeping with their mother as well as other siblings. Regarding the object attachment index, we found that it is significantly higher in the United States (0.6), compared to Samoa (0.37), but not Vanuatu (0.55).

In conclusion, based on our own as well as other cross-cultural observations, we conclude that while the transitional object appears to be a prevalent phenomenon for a large proportion of Western middle-class children, it tends to be significantly less prevalent in majority, non-Western cultures, as well as families of lower socio-economic status across societies. The material environment (e.g., relative abundance of toys and other child-oriented objects), parental practices within a culture (e.g., normative sleeping arrangement), and inter-individual differences within a particular group or cohort (e.g., attachment profile), all constitute contextual factors shaping the transitional object phenomenon. This could, in turn, influence each child's budding psychology of possession, a psychology that has to fit group practices and norms, as well as material living circumstances that can vary tremendously.

Sharing in children across cultures

Cross-cultural studies on sharing and pro-social behavior among peers in 3–5-year-old children from North America,[54] preschoolers from China and India,[55] North American and Chinese 7-year-olds,[56] and 6-year-olds from the United States and Columbia[57] indicate that the early propensity to share varies depending on culture and social context, but also gender,

[54] Birch and Billman, "Preschool children's food sharing with friends and acquaintances."

[55] Rao and Stewart, "Cultural influences on sharer and recipient behavior sharing in Chinese and Indian preschool children."

[56] Stewart and McBride-Chang, "Influences on children's sharing in multicultural setting."

[57] Pilgrim and Rueda-Riedle, "The importance of social context in cross-cultural comparisons."

degrees of friendship, and the relative desirability of the traded item (preferred or non-preferred food item).

For example, pairs of same-sex North American preschoolers were observed spontaneously sharing (or not sharing) snack food.[58] Instances of spontaneous or passive sharing (stealing) were rare, most instances typically elicited by the potential recipient. Girls tended to share significantly more than boys, particularly when they were friends rather than just acquaintances. Sharing was also influenced by the previous experience of the child as recipient and whether the food was preferred or non-preferred.

In a replication of the study with Indian and Chinese preschoolers, researchers found no influence of relative friendship on the propensity to share and, in general, more spontaneous sharing in these Asian children, particularly the Chinese children, compared to what has been reported with children from the United States.[59] In another cross-cultural study, the spontaneous, either anonymous or public donations to peers by Western and Asian second graders was further investigated.[60] Again, results show that donations varied depending on culture, gender, and condition of anonymity. To interpret these findings, researchers evoke differences in parenting practices and adult moral reasoning in the US and Asian context.[61]

Considering the great variability of children's developmental niches, at both micro and macro levels, it is legitimate to ask whether this variability might be at the origins of particular ways of feeling possession, together with particular ways of owning and sharing. The question is whether collective norms and habitus might early on dictate particular ways and propensities to possess, the larger culture and societal organization dictating specific adaptive fitness as the norm. For example, would children growing up in a more egalitarian and group-oriented culture show early on greater and earlier signs of egalitarianism in their spontaneous ways of sharing with others, compared to children growing up in a Western, economically rich, more individualistic culture? To what extent might culture impact on children's developing ethical and moral sense toward others? Depending on culture and relative wealth, would children develop a different sense of what is fair and just in terms of resource ownership and

58 Birch and Billman, "Preschool children's food sharing with friends and acquaintances."
59 Rao and Stewart, "Cultural influences on sharer and recipient behavior sharing in Chinese and Indian preschool children."
60 Stewart and McBride-Chang, "Influences on children's sharing in multicultural setting."
61 See Stewart and McBride-Chang, "Influences on children's sharing in multicultural setting"; for a convergent account, see also Pilgrim and Rueda-Riedle, "The importance of social context in cross-cultural comparisons."

distribution? These are the kinds of questions that a handful of developmental studies have considered, from the time children become explicit about ownership and can be observed from approximately 3 years as they are instructed to split and share food or toys.

The few existing cross-cultural studies comparing children's sharing present a mixed picture of universal and culture-specific developments. For example, a rare cross-cultural research[62] compares adults and children aged 5–16 years from Israel, either living in a kibbutz in Tel Aviv or middle-class individuals living in the United States on the basis of an open-ended interview regarding possession. In this study, the Israeli and US groups were construed as differentially exposed "in the degree to which personal possession is practiced and encouraged" (p. 64). The interview revolved around questions about what makes somebody own something. Results show common and putatively universal motives for possession across the three cultures: the *control of effects* one has on objects (sense of efficacy or "effectance motives" in relation to objects) and the *self-assertiveness* dimension attached to possession (self-defining motives in relation to others). However, further analyses indicate complex interactions between culture, age, and gender, as well as kind of object, all contributing to what individuals from the youngest age construe as possessed and what might be rightly owned. In general, the study shows that if the right of use and/or control of an object is a central aspect of what determines possession and ownership for all interviewed children, only the youngest children (5-year-olds) raised in a kibbutz viewed the acquisition process of an object as the main determinant of rightful ownership of possession. Overall, the results of this study show that although (not surprisingly) the range of meanings and reasons for possessing an object increases significantly with age across cultures, this development occurs at a significantly *different rate* in the three cultures. As we shall see, this is a common finding in existing cross-cultural studies on possession and ownership in development.

Another rare piece of cross-cultural research compared 1- to 3-year-old toddlers growing up in different Israeli kibbutz communities that differed in child care and rearing practices. Some promoted total collective child care. Others promoted partially collective care where children live with their biological parents but spend working hours in daycare centers.[63] Comparative behavioral analysis of these children indicates that there are significantly fewer conflicts over object possession amongst kibbutz children raised in total collective care compared to those in daycare. These observations suggest that, from at least the second year, there is a link

62 Furby, "Possession in humans."
63 Lakin, Lakin, and Costanzo, "Group processes in early childhood."

between various kinds of cultural practices (i.e., all communal versus mixed communal and nuclear) surrounding children and developing feelings, motives, and attitudes toward possession and sharing. The cultural value of self-assertiveness, and in particular the assertion of ownership in relation to others, may vary and play a role in early childhood development elsewhere than in an Israeli kibbutz. Research shows that cultural variations exist in terms of relative self-assertiveness when comparing infants and children growing up in rural Africa (Cameroon) to same-age urban children from Germany.[64]

Cultural psychology research points to the universality of some forms of concern with harm and unfairness toward others across known cultural groups, concern that overlaps over issues of injustice.[65] However, there is also evidence for marked cultural variations in the definition of personhood,[66] the kinds of acts considered as fair or unfair, as well as the relative emphasis on justice to resolve moral dilemmas.[67]

We have also seen that the adult literature on bargaining behaviors in ultimatum and dictator games can vary across cultures, sometimes drastically, and that the expression of punishment, fairness, and strategy in these games depends on culture.[68] If culture appears to play a significant role in determining adults' economic decisions and sense of fairness in distributive justice, questions remain as to how and when they might be acquired while factoring in the great variety of children's cultural contexts.

In adults, cultural variations exist in how individuals experience equity and respond to inequity in the sharing and distribution of possession. This is true also for children, from at least 3 years of age. Based on classic economics games[69] (one-shot dictator, first or third party ultimatum games; see brief description below), played by individuals of fifteen societies from five continents, ranging from small, rural, traditional, sedentary, or nomadic populations, to the urban middle-class and educated college ("WEIRD")[70] population that is overwhelmingly representative in behavioral and social science research in general. In the dictator game, a player is given a substantial sum of money (equivalent to one day's wage within the population, plus 20 percent for showing up to participate) to split with another individual, as a measure of their relative willingness to share more or less equitably. In the ultimatum game, a player makes an

64 Keller, *Cultures of Infancy.*
65 Snarey, "Cross-cultural universality of social-moral development."
66 Schweder, "Beyond self-constructed knowledge."
67 Miller, "Insight into moral development from cultural psychology."
68 Henrich et al., "Costly punishment across human societies."
69 Henrich et al., "Costly punishment across human societies."
70 Henrich, Heine, and Norenzayan, "The weirdest people in the world?"

offer to split the sum of money that can be either accepted or refused by the other recipient. If the recipient refuses the offer, no one gets anything. The ultimatum game is a simple way to probe the extent to which a person (the recipient) is willing to accept a lesser share. Rationally, he or she has nothing to lose by accepting any offer, however low it might be. However, people are shown often to refuse a small offer, and be willing to punish the one proposing too low an offer despite the cost (zero income in the end). Such costly punishment from the recipient who turns down low offers is irrational from a purely economic standpoint, but makes sense from an ethical point of view, as expression of fairness principles. Such principles could be at the origins of the human unique propensity to cooperate and the evolution of preventive mechanisms against cheating and freeloading.

Dictator and ultimatum games can be played either as potential first party distributor and recipient, or as second party recipient only, but also as a third party player who can be either indirectly or not at all a beneficiary of the economic transaction, simply providing a third person judgment or refereeing on the outcome of the game and the way stakes are split. This is an important variation as it allows some measurement of how principled and unselfish (disinterested) a person might be in her ethical stance. Using these games, research shows that across cultures all adults rarely self-maximize their gains as much as they could if they were only self-serving, even in anonymous, one-shot deals, where their reputation theoretically is not at stake. This means that across cultures individuals show signs of altruism and hence are not totally self-interested. When looking at people's relative propensity to engage in costly punishment, then culture appears to be a significant factor. Individuals of some cultures tend to punish not only those participants who go astray for being egalitarian, but also those who are being too generous, overwhelmingly favoring others. Analyses show that factoring age, sex, education level, household size, or relative wealth does not explain these cultural differences.[71]

However, follow-up studies using the same economic games with adults in fifteen different cultural contexts, ten of which were new,[72] show that the degree of market integration (i.e., average number of calories purchased per capita) and the extent to which the culture is part of a large world religion do predict individuals' propensity to be generous as well as to engage in costly punishment. It appears that larger institutions (integrated global market and religion) create supra-ordinal norms by which individuals abide and which shape their ways of sharing with

[71] Henrich et al., "Costly punishment across human societies."
[72] Henrich et al., "Markets, religion, community size, and the evolution of fairness and punishment."

others, above and beyond what might be more proximal innate determinants (e.g., instinct to favor biological kin).

Specific local adaptations translating into particular cultural practices and local adaptations entrenched in the culture, transmitted from generation to generation, would explain these differences: "consistent with recent evolutionary models of altruistic punishment, in particular, culture–gene co-evolutionary models in which strategies of cooperation and punishment predict that local learning dynamics generate between-group variation as different groups arrive at different 'cultural' equilibria. These local learning dynamics would create social environments that favor the genetic evolution of psychologies that predispose people to administer, anticipate, and avoid punishment by learning local norms" (p. 1770). In short, if the propensity to engage in costly punishment, hence abiding by ethical principles that override purely economic self-interest, is evident in all cultures, these principles can have very different forms and intensities. They reveal various underlying social values, often described by ethnographers and cultural anthropologists courageously immersing themselves in field studies. These studies try to capture collective feelings and norms in language and other group practices that each individual learns and eventually transmits to new generations within the confine of their own collectivity.

Regarding children, we conducted a cross-cultural study on sharing in 3- and 5-year-olds across seven cultures from three continents (USA, and three sites in Brazil, Peru, China, and Fiji).[73] These cultures varied in environment (rural versus urban) and socio-economic status (very low to middle–high), including children from a small traditional island village (Fiji), pupils at a communist party run preschool (China), and children with little to no adult supervision living on the street (Recife in Brazil). We compared a total population of 200 children, assessing their relative equality in distributing small collections of even or odd numbers of more of less desirable candies. In each successive trial, there were six or seven candies in the collection, sometimes including a bigger one that was more desirable and could not be split. In seven successive trials, children were asked to split the collection either between themselves and an adult experimenter, or between two puppets, forcing them to take a third party perspective by not being a recipient of the sharing. In a final condition, we also tested children in a "biblical or Solomon" sharing condition in which the child splits and then the experimenter chooses. Based on this simple dictator game, we assessed children's relative fairness in justice distribution (i.e., spontaneous propensity toward more or

[73] Rochat et al., "Fairness in distributive justice by 3- and 5-year-olds across 7 cultures."

less equitable sharing). We were interested in children's psychological approach to the distribution of possession, their relative "greediness" as a function of age and culture. Overall we found that, across cultures, there is a universal developmental trend toward more equity between 3 and 5 years of age, children becoming more "conscientious" about others and taking increasingly what amounts to an ethical stance in splitting possessions. In general, children across culture and age tend to be less equitable when they are a recipient of the sharing. From 3 years of age also, they show signs of being strategic, becoming suddenly more even in their split in the biblical sharing condition where the experimenter makes the final decision of which pile to choose. However, we also found that compared to all the other cultures, children from small-scale urban (Peru) and traditional rural (Fiji) populations tend on average to be significantly more fair in their distribution, splitting more evenly and being less tempted to self-appropriate the more desirable candy of the collection. This culture effect supports the idea that local adaptations to particular societal norms take place early in development and probably from the time children become explicit and strategic about ownership (3 years and up). Although we did not test this interpretation directly, explaining our cultural findings, we propose that the societal norms of equitable resource distribution are particularly prevalent, more visible, and implicitly enforced in the close-knit communal living circumstances of the Fijian and Peruvian children we tested.

We repeated the same experiment, using exactly the same design, with another cohort of 138 same-age children (3 and 5 years) in a poor region of Brazil and in the United States.[74] The Brazilian children (N = 60 boys, 30 girls) were very poor, unschooled, unsupervised kids living on the streets of Recife, a large city in northeastern Brazil.[75] The United States children were from middle-class families in Greater Atlanta, tested at our Laboratory. We were particularly interested in whether children would behave differently and possibly be tempted toward more self-maximizing if the items to be split were more fungible, rather than immediately consumable like candies or cookies. In Brazil we used real coins (centavos) while in the United States, plastic poker chips were to be exchanged after the game against small toys in a makeshift toy store at the Lab. At the end of the game, the maximum accumulation for the child was set to be no more than 1 dollar. In Brazil, we tested children in the living room of the manager of a small neighborhood general store. Home and store were part

[74] Rochat et al., "Coin versus food sharing in children growing up in highly contrasted socio-economical circumstances in north-eastern Brazil and the United States of America."
[75] Aneci Rosa et al., "The street children of Recife."

of the same house. After the game, children were asked to spend their earned coins at the store, as a reward to our host, but also to have control over the child's spending since drug use (i.e., glue sniffing) is prevalent among the gangs of street children they belonged to. In general, we replicated the original findings whereby, overall, 5-year-olds tend to be more equitable in their sharing compared to 3-year-olds, with no significant culture effect comparing these two populations. Compared to candies, using coins and more fungible poker chips did not change our basic findings. However, worth reporting is what street children of Recife chose to buy at the neighborhood store with what they earned in the dictator game. Most of them, instead of candy and other age-appropriate knick-knacks and snacks, purchased items of collective consumption such as a large sausage or a long bar of soap sold by weight. Survival necessities and the idea of sharing with the larger community dictate these children's choice, an interesting fact on how, early in development, possession choices are shaped by overall sociocultural circumstances.

In a series of new exploratory studies, we compared 3- and 5-year-old children of varying socio-economic status in the United States (high versus low SES in Atlanta, Georgia), and same-age children from Japan (middle-class Kyoto), street children in Recife (Brazil, very low SES), and village children from independent Samoa (Polynesia) and Vanuatu (Melanesia, Banks Islands).[76] We recorded systematically how these children split food between two puppets (third party dictator game) depicted as having different needs. We also compared their ways of distributing food between the puppets and between themselves and the adult experimenter, trained and fluent in the local language. We replicate the overall tendency to self-maximize in sharing when the child is a recipient, this tendency generally decreasing between 3 and 5 years of age. From a cross-cultural comparison, one cardinal and seemingly reliable observation is the fact that, when recipient of the sharing (first party dictator game), Japanese and Ni-Vanuatu children are distinctive in their tendency to accumulate significantly less for themselves compared to all the other cultures.

When distributing food between two puppets (third party dictator game), one of which is ostentatiously described as poor and very hungry (crying and with tears wiped from its face), while the other is described as happy and living in abundance (satiated), only United States children

[76] Work underway and to be published in collaboration with Jamie Lawler (University of Minnesota), Shoji Ikatura (Kyoto University), Erin Robbins (Emory University), Maria Grazia Dias (Federal University of Pernambuco), and Claudia Passos (Federal University of Rio de Janeiro).

from middle-class families tend to be significantly more biased toward the poor one, distributing much more food to it compared to the rich one. Again, these simple observations demonstrate the complex overlay of a universal early developmental tendency toward more egalitarianism, this tendency being moderated by local (socio-economical and cultural) adaptations to dominant norms within the societal group such as the overtone of *political correctness* in rectifying inequity that tends to be prevalent in middle-class families of the United States, for example. Of interest is the fact that low SES children from the United States do not show the same inclination, supporting the idea that local adaptation to adult norms can vary across social classes within the same overall culture (e.g., North American culture). This shows, once again, how difficult and in the end how arbitrary it is to circumscribe and define culture as a factor in child development. Such arbitrariness cannot be overstated.

Costly punishment in children across cultures

The developmental tendency toward increased egalitarianism is now demonstrated using various economics games with children, sometimes but rarely in a cross-cultural perspective. To the best of our knowledge, we performed the first study comparing children of two cultures in their relative propensity to engage in costly punishment: their willingness to sacrifice possession to make a stance and correct a situation that the child perceives as unfair. We now know that there is a development toward *egalitarianism* (i.e., the propensity to share possessions equitably) in children above 5 years of age. With only a few exceptions presented above,[77] this is mainly shown on the basis of research with children from Western middle-class families, like Swiss children.[78] Only a few studies have considered such development systematically across various social classes and cultures, as has been painstakingly done with adults from fifteen different cultures using dictator and various forms of ultimatum games (see above[79]). These adult studies demonstrate that the tendency toward costly punishment or propensity to sacrifice possession to make an ethical stance can vary tremendously across cultures, depending on whether they are part of a global market system or a world religion, for example.[80]

77 For example, Furby, "Possession in humans."
78 Fehr, Bernhard, and Rockenbach, "Egalitarianism in young children."
79 Henrich et al., "Costly punishment across human societies."
80 Henrich et al., "Markets, religion, community size, and the evolution of fairness and punishment."

A few years ago, we conducted a cross-cultural study with young children on their relative propensity to engage in costly punishment, a first attempt of its kind as far as we know.[81] Samoan children were from a coastal village with a population of approximately 500 on the eastern side of the island of Savai'i (population approximately 50,000), the largest of three inhabited islands in Samoa (population approximately 180,000, with a nominal per capita GDP of 2,608 US dollars, as opposed to $46,900 in the United States).

Samoa is at the heart of Polynesia and still maintains strict ancestral Polynesian traditions despite successive colonial dominations by the British, Germans, and New Zealanders, and notwithstanding a widespread conversion to Christianity of almost all denominations from the middle of the nineteenth century. Gaining its political independence in 1962, and despite years of Western influence and governance, Samoa has managed to uphold strong traditions of collective living organized around a highly hierarchical chief ("Mataï") system that is typical of Polynesian culture. In Samoa, this system is maintained in arguably its purest form within the Polynesian context of the South Pacific.[82] Samoan culture and societal organization is a good example of what is sometimes characterized as "vertical" as opposed to "horizontal" or "egalitarian" collectivism.[83]

Samoan children were tested in the village of Faga, which engages in horticulture, fishing, and marine foraging for survival and as a means to a small cash revenue, aside from remittance money sent from family members living and working abroad, primarily in New Zealand. Before children attend school (at around age 3 to 5), they typically spend the day with their immediate and extended family, playing outdoors with other young children, or observing alongside adults as they perform their daily duties. There is minimal adult supervision after the child begins to walk; however, children tend to be supervised collectively by the adults and older children in the village (distributed child care). Aside from collective games with balls and a very few other shared objects, these children develop in a culture that does not emphasize individual possession. Children's toys are rare in the Samoan context that emphasizes communal properties and living space, rather than individual possession and private quarters.

We compared Samoan children (5-year-olds) with age and gender matched children from middle-class families in the United States (Atlanta, Georgia) in a three-way sharing game between the child and

[81] Robbins and Rochat, "Emerging signs of strong reciprocity in human ontogeny."
[82] O'Meara, *Samoan Planters*; Shore, *Sala'ilua*.
[83] Triandis and Gelfand, "Converging measurement of horizontal and vertical individualism and collectivism."

two puppets, a "stingy" and a "generous" puppet animated by a trained experimenter fluent in the native language of the child. Nine valuable coins were successively shared three ways between the protagonists, starting with the generous puppet keeping one coin for itself and giving four to the other puppet and four to the child. Then it was the turn of the stingy puppet to share, keeping seven coins for itself and giving one to the child and one to the other puppet. Then it was the child's turn to split three ways. There were four successive rounds in this sharing game, each time ending with the child's turn to split, which was systematically recorded.

At the end of the fourth round, the experimenter questioned the child on the total amount of coins accumulated by each protagonist, asking her what she thought about it. In a crucial costly punishment test, the experimenter then offered the child the chance to give up one of her coins to punish one of the puppets, by taking away four coins from their accumulated win. If the child accepted, then the experimenter asked which puppet (stingy or generous) should she "punish" by taking away four coins. The proposal was then repeated until the child declined to proceed any further with the punishment.

In general, we found that North American children, across the four rounds, tended to accumulate significantly more coins for themselves, hence self-maximizing more compared to Samoan children. They also tended to share significantly more with the generous compared to the stingy doll. Regarding costly punishment, 5-year-old American children (not 3-year-olds), when opting to use some of their accumulated win to punish, do so by choosing systematically to penalize the stingy puppet, and only very rarely the generous puppet. They are thus ethically oriented in their costly punishment. In sharp contrast, the 5-year-old Samoan children do not show any signs either of favoritism toward the generous puppet in the course of the four sharing rounds, or of any systematic orientation of their costly punishment toward the stingy puppet.[84] Note that a comparable proportion of American and Samoan children accepted the proposal to sacrifice in order to punish, only the former showing systematic orientation toward the stingy puppet.

Overall, compared to the US children, Samoan 5-year-olds displayed a heightened tendency toward egalitarianism and a lesser propensity to self-maximize or orient their costly punishment. These cross-cultural observations illustrate the role culture plays in how children develop a sense of fairness in the distribution of possession as measured by our sharing game and costly punishment test. Culture and context do play a role in the early

[84] See Robbins and Rochat, "Emerging signs of strong reciprocity in human ontogeny," for more details.

expression of an ethical stance in child development. The sharp contrast between the middle-class, overall more individualistic, materially abundant culture of US children versus the small-village, and overall more collective and traditional chief culture of Samoan children appears to be reflected in their developing sense of fairness in terms of the propensity to self-maximize and engage in retributive justice. Once again, we interpret these cross-cultural differences as early expression of children's local adaptations to the adult norms enforced and emphasized in their culture: strongly hierarchical and authoritarian group practices and default egalitarianism in Samoa; individual initiative and self-assertiveness in middle-class America.

Reasoning about ownership in children across cultures

Considering that important variations exist across cultures in how claims and conflicts of possession (i.e., ownership) are adjudicated within a group, from the proximal sphere of the family (e.g., nuclear, extended, religious, not religious, high status, low status) to the macro sphere of institutions governing the society at large (e.g., schools, churches, clubs, tribunals, political ideologies, economic policy), an important developmental question is the extent to which these collective traits may shape children's ways of reasoning about ownership, and whether early on these traits trickle down to influence individual children's intuitions and practices regarding ownership, when for example they have to decide *who should own what and why*. The question is how early and to what extent children's implicit practices and explicit reasoning about ownership are a reflection of their inherited cultural circumstances, the collective ways surrounding them and defining their developmental niche.

In relation to the transfer and distribution of ownership (sharing) by young children (5 years and younger), we have already presented some evidence that there are variations across cultures and contexts in the way young children relate to possession in terms of their willingness to relinquish what they own, as well as their relative propensity to self-maximize.[85] As we have seen, it varies between rural and urban industrial circumstances that emphasize more or less communal ways of living,[86] but it also varies across gender, degrees of friendship, and the relative desirability of the traded item (preferred or non-preferred food item).

Recently, we conducted a study testing how young children from seven highly contrasted cultural backgrounds tended to reason about

[85] See Chapter 6, in particular Rochat et al., "Fairness in distributive justice by 3- and 5-year-olds across 7 cultures."

[86] Rochat et al., "Fairness in distributive justice by 3- and 5-year-olds across 7 cultures."

ownership.[87] We probed their intuitions in a justice distribution task involving two puppets fighting over an object, both claiming: "This is mine!" – "No this is mine," etc. We asked them to tell us which of the two puppets should own the object and why.

In *Brazil*, we tested three cohorts of children: a group growing up in great poverty (street children of Recife), a group of less poor children but living in a crime-infested slum or favela of Rio de Janeiro, and finally a group from the middle to upper class attending an expensive private preschool in Rio de Janeiro. In the *United States*, we tested a group of low socio-economic status African American children and a group from middle-class predominantly Caucasian families in Atlanta. In *China*, we tested children attending a highly communal, communist party run preschool in Shanghai. Finally, in a remote corner of the *South Pacific*, we tested children from a traditional and rural, also highly communal Melanesian village in Vanuatu, on the small and isolated island of Motalava in the Banks Islands (Torba Province). Across all cultures, we tested approximately 200 children aged 3 and 5 years in five conditions of a guessing game involving a pair of identical puppets. In each condition, the experimenter (trained and fluent in the local language) told the child a story involving a fight between the two puppets about an object of possession.

The experimenter animating both puppets first described them as friends who decide to go for a walk. During the walk, they discover together a toy they both want, ending up fighting over it. Once the story had been told, the child was asked three questions about ownership: "Whose toy is it? Who should have it? Could you give it to the puppet?"

In each of the five different experimental conditions, each time with different pairs of physically identical puppet protagonists, children were given various kinds of information about the puppets. This information potentially provided different grounds or rationale for distributive justice. Our aim was to probe children's relative sensitivity and understanding (choice) for various reasons in attributing ownership to either one of the puppets. In other words, the aim was to place the child in the role of a judge, giving her the authority to referee, take sides, and resolve the fight between the two puppets. We recorded their judgments as a function of the conditions and information given regarding the two fighting protagonists.

These conditions and information given to the child were inspired by classical rationales evoked for property determination in the history of

[87] Rochat et al., "Development of ownership reasoning in children of 7 cultures."

political philosophy. It probed whether children's intuition about ownership matched more or less the labor theory of John Locke, the egalitarian views of Jean-Jacques Rousseau, the first possession and discovery principle of imperialist (conquistador) ideologies, or the historical-traditional precedence arguments (temporal roots or "we were here first") that are typical of nationalist and other ethnic cleansing ideologies all over the world.[88]

In one condition, one of the puppets was depicted as the creator who built with its own hands the contentious toy object (labor or *creation condition*). In another, one of the puppets was designated as very familiar with the object, it always having been part of its household (precedence or *familiarity condition*). In another condition, one of the puppets, during the walk, saw the object first while the other rushed to physically grab it first (visual versus forceful physical *first contact condition*). In a fourth condition, one of the puppets was described as wealthy, owning lots of similar toys, and the other as poor and materially deprived (rich versus poor or *wealth condition*). Finally, in a control condition, there was no preliminary information about the puppets (*neutral condition*). Each child was tested in all conditions in a randomized order. An important point is that each condition was repeated, once with the toy object of contention being *solid and unsplittable*. The script was then repeated with the same object, but this time *splittable* in two halves, connected with velcro along its axis of symmetry. This variation was meant to provide children with the opportunity to resolve the conflict by splitting the object into two equal halves.

We thus tested close to 200 preschoolers spread across three continents, varying along multiple dimensions, including demographic (large urban areas versus semi-urban or small rural regions), socio-economic (middle-class versus poor), and cultural dimensions (individualistic versus more collectivist and traditional value systems as in the case of Vanuatu). The choice of the research sites was in part opportunistic, based on possible research collaboration offered to us that gave access to a large variety of cultural circumstances surrounding children in their development. Opportunism aside, the choice was also guided by the working assumption of a contrast between cultures that promote different values attached to collective living, activities, and the sharing of more abundant or less abundant resources or possessions.

Conceptually, we thought of these cultures as potentially nurturing a variable sense of interdependence in children beyond the nuclear family, educated around different communal concerns and values, as well as

[88] Seniority is the recurrent rationale of nationalist ideologies around the world, from the Middle East (Palestine) to Kosovo and Myanmar.

obviously facing drastically different challenges within their developmental niche. How would all these cultural contrasts reflect on young children's intuitions about third party distributive justice regarding who should own what and why. That was the question. Although we did not have any readymade answer, we expected to find some differences, and particularly a contrast for cultural environments putting a major emphasis on communal values like the Chinese preschool and the Vanuatu village, as compared to all the others. But this was only a general working hypothesis.

In a nutshell, results yielded complex interactions between age, culture, and condition. For some conditions, development varies significantly across cultures, typically with a clustering of various sites within one nation's culture (the three Brazilian and the two North American cohorts). A propensity to split the object in equal halves in the "splittable" object condition was generally high among the Chinese children and almost nonexistent in the Ni-Vanuatu children. Across cultures, children are significantly more consistent and decisive in attributing ownership when one of the protagonists created the object. The reason appears to be more primordial and stable across cultures than is relative wealth or first contact.

In other words, we observe a combination of remarkable stability and variability across cultures in young children's reasoning about ownership. We found that, in general and not surprisingly, children tend to become more consistent and decisive in their ownership attribution between 3 and 5 years. This is a global, transcultural trend that is actually consistent with the universal development of theories of mind based on the classic false belief task, as we demonstrated some time ago testing children in India, Peru, Thailand, Japan, and North America.[89] What we also found is that, globally, across cultures, the *creation* (labor) rationale for ownership attribution is consistently prevalent in children from 5 years of age.

Interestingly, however, the relative wealth of the puppet is a significantly more prevalent rationale for the wealthier North American cohort as well as, to some extent, the Chinese communist preschool cohorts only. Compared to all the children across cultures, the Chinese show a significantly greater inclination spontaneously to split the object of contention in halves, when splittable. We found another interesting cross-cultural difference in the relative wealth (rich–poor) condition whereby North American children and Chinese children tended to attribute ownership to the poor puppet significantly more compared to all the other cultures.

[89] Callaghan et al., "Synchrony in the onset of mental-state reasoning."

Children were globally random in their ownership attribution in the first contact or neutral/control conditions (see description above).

With this study, we detect both stability and variability across cultures in children's reasoning about ownership. What is globally stable is the fact that, in the perspective of development, John Locke's principle of labor (creation) appears to be more primordial across cultures. In contrast, the equity principle of relative wealth is more dependent on children's cultural circumstances. This cultural difference in relative sensitivity to inequity is difficult to interpret. It appears that US and Chinese contexts somehow promote significantly more inequity aversion in children. No simple explanation can account for this phenomenon. However, it shows that cultural context does play a role in children's early reasoning about ownership: the question of who should own what and why. Children's budding reasoning about possession is not immune from macro cultural and collective habitus influences.

We can assume that not one single sociocultural mechanism but a bundle of different ones may underlie the reliable cross-cultural differences we observed. These mechanisms might include various degrees of in-group preference (parochialism) across cultures, a tendency constrained by various circumstances, such as extreme situations of war, exile, and political stress surrounding the young child. This is what we found comparing 3–5-year-old *North American* middle-class children with a same-age cohort of *Palestinian* children living in a dilapidated refugee camp in Beirut, Lebanon. Again, we tested these children in a third party distributive justice game situation, but this time we asked them to determine the ownership of a piece of land.

Judgment of land ownership by Palestinian and US children

There are early signs of *parochialism* ("nepotism" or in-group favoritism) in children when asked to distribute justice and to determine who should own what and why.[90] In-group favoritism thus can be added to the principles of creation, precedence, familiarity, or equity in ownership attribution discussed earlier from a cross-cultural perspective. Early parochialism tends to be particularly exacerbated in politically charged

[90] Much research documents the remarkably early propensity of children, even infants, to prefer and explicitly favor in-group members, based for example on the way they speak their maternal language (with or without accent) (e.g., Kinzler et al., "Accent trumps race in guiding children's social preferences"; Kinzler, Dupoux, and Spelke, "The native language of social cognition"; Shutts et al., "Race preferences in children."

situations that can surround young children, like war or exile. A large number of children, all over the world, grow up in war-torn places, experiencing from birth tense atmospheres that are part of their developmental niche. War and exile are typically compounded with material scarcity and high societal toxicity, as in the case of Palestinian refugee camps. All over the world, many children live in crime-infested circumstances, in great insecurity, and with disintegrated families, not to mention poor hygiene and only transient legal status, as in the case of the street children in Recife or refugee Palestinian children we tested in Lebanon. The question we asked is to what extent extreme poverty and political stress accompanying the life of people in exile would impact on their children's reasoning about who should own what and why. In other words, what might be the impact of such a context on the child's reasoning about possession?

To address this question, we performed a study[91] on *judgment of land ownership*, testing a group of refugee Palestinian children (3- and 5-year-olds again), living in a very dilapidated camp in Beirut (Bourj el-Barajneh). We compared these children to a cohort of same-age children from middle-class families of Atlanta in the United States, using basically the same experimental paradigm as before. However, rather than telling children about puppets fighting over possession of a toy object, this time the puppet protagonists in the script were fighting over a *piece of land*.

We were particularly interested in whether the high political and social pressures surrounding young Palestinian refugee children living in a densely populated and impoverished Lebanese camp, immersed in prolonged tensions (three generations), and political discourses that pertain to the lost ownership of their land, would develop different ways of reasoning about who should own land and why. In our study, we therefore examined whether 3–5-year-old preschoolers living in a context of political unrest and poverty display a different sense of distributive justice compared to middle-class Western children growing up in significantly safer, more materially stable, and much less contentious circumstances.

As before, children were required to make distributive justice decisions about four scripted scenarios that involved a pretend conflict between different types of neighbors of the same or different material wealth (rich versus poor), or of the same or different nationality and cultural affiliation as the child (in-group versus out-group). For the Palestinian children, in-group was signified with one of the puppets wearing the traditional

[91] Zebian and Rochat, "Judgment of land ownership by young refugee Palestinian and US children."

Palestinian scarf, and for the American children, one of the puppets wearing an American flag wrapped around it.

In brief, there were five scenario scripts corresponding to five conditions of the experiment. All scripts were told by an adult experimenter, fluent in the child's native language. Following the same basic paradigm, in all conditions the scripts ended with a dispute over the empty plot of land desired for exclusive appropriation by both puppet neighbors. Following each script, the child was asked "Whose land is it?," "Who should have the land?," and "Can you put the puppet that owns the land on the land?"

The five experimental conditions varied as follows: In a *neutral/control* condition, the puppets were identical, sitting and living on identical lands. In a color *stigma* condition, the puppets were identical but one of them was totally covered with solid white paint. Both were depicted as sitting and living on identical plots of land (large green rectangles lying on the testing table). In a *rich–poor* condition, there were identical puppets but one depicted as rich, sitting on a larger plot of land. Children were explicitly asked to compare the plots of lands owned by each puppet to ensure they understood that the rich one had more land than the poor one. Finally, and more crucially, in a last *rich/in-group* condition, the puppets were identical but sitting on unequal lands, but one covered either by a Palestinian scarf (in-group totemic symbol for the Palestinian children) or by an American flag (in-group totemic symbol for the US children). The script scenario of this last condition was determined by the child's response on the always immediately preceding rich–poor condition. If the child chose in the preceding rich–poor condition the poor puppet as the legitimate owner of the disputed land, then the rich one was draped with the in-group totemic symbol. Each child passed all conditions in a partially randomized order (see the published paper for more details). For all children, the five conditions were each repeated in succession with the additional prop of a river running through the empty plot disputed by the two neighbors. In other words, half of the scenarios included the river prop that served as a visual cue splitting the contentious land in two equal parts. The rationale for this "river" variation was to capture the impact of surface (obvious) perceptual cues (as opposed to deeper, non-obvious moral reasoning and sensitivity) influencing children to resolve the land dispute. As in the splittable or unsplittable object conditions of the preceding research on object ownership, we recorded the extent to which children were enticed to split the disputed plot along such a perceived natural feature.

In summary, what we observed once again was a mixed indication of stability and difference across US and refugee camp contexts. On one hand, 5-year-old Palestinian and American children both showed inequality aversion. All tended to favor the poor neighbor over the rich in their distributive justice decisions. Three-year-olds, across cultures, do not show such an ethical stance, the latter developing in relative independence of context, as part of a more universal ontogenetic trend. From 5 years of age, being born into political stress and poverty (i.e., Palestinian cohort) does not make young children more sensitive to material inequity, even if the object of dispute is of particular cultural relevance (land that is at more of a premium in the Palestinian context compared to the United States).

This said, in the condition where parochialism (in-group versus out-group) is pitted against wealth (rich versus poor), we do find that 5-year-old Palestinians side significantly more with their in-group, even though it is wealthier than the out-group. In contrast, North American middle-class children stick to favoring the poor puppet, even if the rich one is identified as American by the flag wrapped around it.

This latter finding does point to the fact that the extreme developmental circumstances of the Palestinian refugee children do translate into enhanced in-group partialities, above and beyond what seems to be a more global normative trend toward inequity aversion. In subtle, yet powerful ways, once again, the larger sociocultural context does impact on children's early determination of who should own what and why: how they feel and shape their decision to distribute justice as they forge what will become eventually their own perspective in moral space. Although this perspective is individual, it always reflects the larger sociocultural context that, in the end, children learn to embody and perpetuate.

Conclusion
Great Transformation

What led creatures from having a possession "instinct" to eventually come up with a shared notion of property? That is the main issue running through the book. This issue can be equated to the Great Transformation[1] of the first industrial revolution that led human societies toward a market economy, but also to the emergence of the modern nations dividing the world today, for better or for worse. The question is how we can account for such profound changes.

From a comparative perspective, the question is how protective instincts regarding progeny, food, or territories came about in evolution and compare across species. From a developmental point of view, the question is what might account for the ontogenetic changes leading children from rudimentary feelings of possession and control over things, something that we share with all other animals, to holding and eventually *abiding by* the notion of who should own what and why. In other words, what leads children from possessing to recognizing property?

If the transition from possession to property is a major transformation at the level of child development, it is equally a major step in the evolution of group living and cooperation. As we know, animal co-existence comes in many different forms and structures, with highly predictable, yet distinct social dynamics. This is true from invertebrate to vertebrate, fish, insects, birds, and all mammals. Compared to all other social species, what is clearly distinctive in human co-existence is the *codification* of rules, as shared representational systems regarding the dos and don'ts of being together, the right and wrong ways of co-existing and sharing resources. This codification of rules is most explicit in written books of law like the ancient Roman code regulating property rights. But it is also made explicit in oral tales and group traditions, modeling normative (appropriate versus inappropriate ways) of being together, exchanging, relating to one another. This is what we typically refer to as culture, the generic word

[1] Polanyi, *The Great Transformation*.

for the bundle of norms collectively expressed and memorized, what individuals "breath in" from birth and rapidly internalize, what impinges on and structures the behavior of individuals forming the dispositional habitus and other dressage of the body that are transmitted to offspring.

In its most generic sense, culture is indeed the sedimentation of group habits and ways of co-existing that are explicitly codified in shared (collective) representational systems like the tablets of the Ten Commandments or any other books of law, but also in group rituals and traditions like marriage, funeral rites, rites of passage from puberty to adulthood, collective artifacts such as totems and flags, table manners, collective intuitions about parenting and education, the architecture and landscaping of public places, and dress codes. What glues this vast bundle of cultural phenomena and distinguishes human ways from any other group living ways found in nature is the *explicit codification of collective norms* ruling appropriate versus inappropriate ways of being together. These collective norms range from aesthetic principles to simple etiquette enhancing class distinction within and across groups (e.g., taste, style, table manners, appropriate attire, politeness), to the codified judicial ruling regarding abuses of power or conflicts over property (e.g., homicide, embezzlement, copyrights). All of this explicit, often highly abstract codification is unique to humans, and the question is how it all came about in evolution. What is the evolutionary link between the instinctive defense of a territory against predators and other competitors that all animals across species are capable of carving for themselves in the environment, to planting a flag on a piece of unknown land and, from then on, claiming that this piece of land is national property protected by international laws?

Obviously, dealing with this question is the duty of biologists, anthropologists, and prehistorians. They perform it via archaeological research, computer simulation, comparative brain research and genetics, trying to pinpoint evolutionary links that might account for major evolutionary emergence like symbolism, art, and language,[2] memory systems,[3] or the causes and consequences of erect posture and bipedal locomotion in proto-humans.[4] Intriguing post-hoc (just-so) stories are offered regarding what might have triggered the great symbolic transformation in the *Homo* lineage. These stories try to put together the pieces of the gigantic puzzle of human evolution. They may evoke events associated with particular mutations or group selection associated with sudden climate changes, cataclysms, or major migratory events. They also speculate on particular

[2] See for example Deacon, *The Symbolic Species*.
[3] See for example Donald, *Origins of the Modern Mind*.
[4] Leroi-Gourhan, *Gesture and Speech*.

selective pressures that emerged on the way individuals within a group dealt with one another. One recent just-so story[5] is for example that, in human evolution, groups that survived, hence the groups of proto-humans selected to form the modern *Homo* lineage, were those who under selective pressure evolved the capacity to discriminate the relative value of their peers within the group. Cooperation among individuals started to operate on the novel basis of "partner choice." This process is viewed as one potential trigger mechanism leading to the uniquely human sense of reputation and fairness (morality). But those are post-hoc speculations even if they are based on sophisticated computer simulation, hence hard data, from which one can assess their relative plausibility.

The developmental approach to the Great Transformation question has a major advantage over all the others. Child psychologists can witness in the development of each and every child – in vivo and in all its vast complexity – the rapid emergence of what makes us the symbolic and self-conscious creatures we are. Here I want to conclude this book by offering, from a developmental perspective, what I see as an important factor to the Great Transformation leading children from possession to property: from experiencing possession as any other animals, to having the collective sense of property that is unique to our species.

Aside from genetic factors and other innate predispositions inscribed in the cognitive and affective architecture of each and every child, my view is that these factors and innate predispositions come to life only in the context of particular, predictable existential events or fundamental crises that are in essence relational and inter-subjective. My argument is that this relational context is the necessary backdrop, the existential force field by which all the dormant genetic predispositions of the child can come to fruition and de facto become psychologically *actualized*.[6]

In other words, what is proposed here is that innate cognitive architecture or all the core knowledge and mental states that infants appear to own from birth are enacted, and hence become psychologically real, in the context of particular, predictable existential and affective events that each and every child has to deal with and resolve early in life. These events revolve around the basic need to affiliate with caregivers, in particular the fear of separation and social rejection that are the necessary counterpart of the basic affiliation

[5] Baumard, André, and Sperber, "A mutualistic approach to morality."

[6] This view is broadly analogous to the idea behind the diathesis-stress model of psychopathology in which genetic predispositions (diathesis = predisposition in Greek) interact and become actualized with particular stress events. Here I propose that there are universal and predictable stress events linked to separation in the life of children that are instrumental in the actualization of their innate potentials. By analogy, see for example Gazelle and Ladd, "Anxious solitude and peer exclusion."

need. By strict analogy, these events revolve around the basic need to possess and control, and its necessary counterpart: the fundamental fear of being *dispossessed and losing control over things*. But how does all of this come about in child development? What is the configuration of these triggering existential "stress" events each child has to resolve?

As discussed in Chapter 5, there is a peculiar evolutionary context to human childhood arising from the basic fact that it is first and foremost incomparably *protracted* in duration. Compared to any other primate species, humans are born too soon, greatly immature and markedly dependent on others to survive. As a species we are both "precocious" (born early) and "altricial" (in need of extended intensive care from others to survive).[7] Human precocious birth leads to intensely assisted "external gestation."[8] This human peculiarity evolved under the combined pressure of a proportionally larger brain and the narrowing of the female's birth canal that is associated with the emergence of bipedal locomotion.[9] Accordingly, the narrowing of the birth canal in human evolution led to a precocious birth, and, in turn, shaped the unique ways we are brought up and cared for in order to survive over a uniquely protracted period of dependency. The *human prolonged immaturity* is what developmental psychologists see as a crucial opportunity for learning and exploration, with basic needs covered by parental and other group care. In a seminal paper, Jerome Bruner elaborates on the nature and "use" of immaturity that is the protracted character of human childhood.[10]

It is in the necessary adult parenting care and supervision that we need to look for the cradle of human cultural transmission and sophistication. For the human young to survive requires years of total support and protection, total parenting care. The necessity of such protracted care put much evolutionary pressure on human social practices, probably having much to do with the human evolution of culture as sedimentation and transmission of shared values and group ways. There is no equivalent in nature to the ways humans teach and nurture (as well as scold) their younglings.

Aside from imitation and observational learning, teaching and pedagogy are at the roots of human cultural learning,[11] what underlies human cultural evolution: the ratcheting (exponential) invention of cultural artifacts, from tools to institutions over a period of only 200,000 years. This slice of time represents only a tiny portion, a minuscule sliver at the scale of evolution

[7] See Gould, *Ontogeny and Phylogeny*.
[8] See Montagu, "Neonatal and infant immaturity in man."
[9] See in particular Trevarthan, "Human birth."
[10] See Bruner, "Nature and uses of immaturity."
[11] Tomasello, Kruger, and Ratner, "Cultural learning."

(approximately 3.5 billions years).[12] Obviously there are an unfathomable number of interacting factors at the origins of human cultural evolution, from the micro (molecular) to the macro (societal) level. We can only parse a few and approximate their plausible contribution at each level of analysis (cellular, neurophysiological, cognitive, and behavioral).

At the level of cognition, there are unmistakable traits children develop as they enter the culture of their parents. In parallel to symbolic (referential) and linguistic (syntactic) abilities, these traits include the capacity for "recursive inferences." This corresponds to the cognitive ability of repeating an inference in embedded clauses as for example in the reflective abstraction "I think that he thinks that they think that I think, etc." This recursive ability is equivalent to a bootstrapping of infinite mirror reflections inside the head of the individual for contemplation and objectification. This emerging trait is particularly relevant because it is directly linked to self-consciousness, the human trademark propensity to infer how other people feel about the self. Presumably, it is on the basis of such recursive capacity that children might begin to elaborate "theories" about the mental states of others (i.e., theories of mind), for example whether others hold true or false beliefs. In relation to human self-conscious psychology, this recursive or reflective capacity happens to be quickly and irresistibly turned toward the self in order to figure how others perceive us.

The self-conscious human trait did not elude early theorists of evolution. Charles Darwin (1809–82) was struck and puzzled by the unique and selective human flushing of the face, a region of the body that is most conspicuous to others. In his book *The Expression of the Emotions in Man and Animals*,[13] he writes: "Blushing is the most peculiar and the most human of all expressions" (p. 309). Observing blushing in his son from approximately 3 years of age, and not before, Darwin highlights the mental states that seem to induce human blushing: "It is not the simple act of reflecting on our own appearance, but the thinking what others think of us, which excites a blush. In absolute solitude the most sensitive person would be quite indifferent about his appearance. We feel blame or disapprobation more acutely than approbation; and consequently depreciatory remarks or ridicule, whether of our appearance or conduct, causes us to blush much more readily than does praise" (p. 325).

These observations capture something fundamental and distinctive about humans, a unique motivation behind their social cognition: the exacerbated quest for approbation and affiliation with others, as well as its necessary counterpart that is an unmatched fear of being rejected by others,

[12] Klein, *The Human Career*.
[13] Darwin, *The Expression of the Emotions in Man and Animals*.

an insatiable quest for social recognition and unique care for reputation.[14] In human development, the self becomes eventually a cognized entity that is objectified and valued in reference to others, through their evaluative eyes and in anticipation of praise and criticism. The enormous energy we spend deliberately working on our self-presentation attests to this: from reputation boosting moves, distinctive class manners (e.g., snobbishness), body building, accessories, plastic surgery and other systematic staging of the self for the public eye, the self-packaging, self-advertising (e.g., résumé), and self-staging that sociologist Erving Goffman (1922–1982) described in his book *The Presentation of Self in Everyday Life.*[15]

The uniquely self-conscious psychology we evolved, and that each and every child develops, is by definition recursive and referential, symbolic as opposed to literal. It refers to an objectified (represented and recognized) as well as evaluative sense of self, *not just for itself*, but primarily in reference to others.

What is specific to human self-conscious psychology is that it elevates the here and now of social perception and action to a "re-presented" realm of referential (symbolic), recursive, and reflective thoughts and abstractions. It leads toward systematic imagination and mental re-presentation, the opening of the human mind's pretend and great "simulacrum" theater.

The capacity for recursive thoughts and reflective abstraction applies to all domains of cognition, yet it has particularly heavy experiential consequences in the realm of social cognition because it primarily refers to the self, and to self-reputation in particular. Recursive thoughts do open the door to shame and guilt as well as issues of moral identity and conscientiousness, not just the knowledge of what others have on their mind, what they are going to do next that is typically considered in theories of mind research. They open doors to morality, shared agreements, and mutually binding norms regarding who should own what and why. They transform the minimal experience of possession and possessiveness that all animals experience into the sense of property as a shared, mutually binding concept.

It is important to note that mutually binding concepts like property are embodied in institutions and cultural artifacts such as schools, and written or oral codes of law and tribunals. These societal institutions are products of an accumulated sedimentation of group habits that transcend the life of individuals. They survive it. These institutions define "game rules" and set ready-made goals and values for individuals, as in schools for children or banks for businessmen. It is against money, honorary medals, diplomas, accumulated personal properties, or any other institutions that social

[14] See Rochat, *Others in Mind.* [15] Goffman, *The Presentation of Self in Everyday Life.*

affiliation and recognition can be gauged. It is against institutional systems like family, school, and workplace that ultimately we measure the degree to which we possess control over things, but more importantly over people: how socially recognized we are. Institutions are indeed the major backdrop of possession psychology.

"*The first man who, having fenced in a piece of land, proclaimed 'That is mine,' and found people naïve enough to believe him, was the true founder of civil society.*" With this seminal statement on the origins of property, Rousseau captures the Great Transformation accompanying the emergence of the human self-conscious, self-reflective, and socially referred psychology. He points to the necessary self-conscious twist required for possession and ownership to become the mutually shared concept of property. Unlike possession or public claims of possession (ownership), property entails mutual trust: the trust that my claim of ownership is not simply heard, but *recognized* as such by others and that I recognize that others recognize me as possessor of what I claim to own.

Self-reflection and recognition in reference to others is thus at the core of property as a normative, socially shared, and mutually binding concept that transcends individual possession and ownership claims. Property as a normative, mutually binding "moral" concept is another offshoot of human self-conscious psychology, the only psychology that makes creatures prone to blush or feel guilty, that makes them care about reputation and their moral identity in the evaluative eyes of others.

These remarks beg the question as to what mechanism or cause could account for the emergence of self-conscious psychology, and would, as a direct consequence, transform the basic experience of possession that all animals share, into the normative, institutional notion of property, something that we humans legally adjudicate via tribunals and other cultural institutions in the case of conflicts regarding who should own what and why.

As for mechanism or causal explanation, I can only offer a developmental account that would be paradigmatic to all children. It is an existential conundrum that would put decisive pressure on each and every child to actualize and *prime* their cognitive potential as recursive and referential, as opposed to being literal perceivers, actors, and thinkers. It would also decisively prime their potential for self-conscious psychology. Note that this account eludes the question of what might explain the prerequisite of a cognitive potential. In my account, this potential would be just actualized, as opposed to created or constructed. It would be actualized in the context of the proposed existential conundrum that each and every human child has to deal with. The idea is that children are equipped and well prepared to resolve this existential conundrum. However, this potential is revealed in the context of a particularly charged affective and existential situation. This paradigmatic situation is as follows.

From 7 to 9 months of age, with the rapid development of postural mobility and the enjoyment of new degrees of behavioral freedom, infants begin to have an insatiable need to explore away from the secure base of their mother, while trying to maintain joint attention and intimate proximity with her or any other primary caregiver(s). As already mentioned, this existential conundrum is particularly exacerbated because of the prolonged immaturity and the hyper-dependence of the human young on the care of others.

The human infant's proximity maintenance versus independent roaming conundrum would be resolved via the actualization of the potential for referential communication, the deliberate effort at incorporating the gaze of others (e.g., the mother), into the compulsive roaming activity of the child. Resolving the proximity maintenance versus independent roaming dilemma would put pressure on children to quest for social attention and adopt a third person perspective, keeping in mind and controlling their mother's attention *on themselves* as they answer their irresistible call to roam the environment away from the secure base of the mother.

I propose that it is in the paradigmatic context of separation (i.e., the fear of losing control over others' attention), the felt dilemma of being either alone or together, that children would become self-conscious, constrained emotionally to behave for the first time in reference to something else. It would be in this highly charged affective context of *separation* that children would first experience having others in mind, that they would be at the threshold of human self-conscious psychology, what will eventually lead them to say to whoever wants to hear, "That's mine!" and for us to be naïve enough to believe them. It is also what will lead them to the rich moral soil of ownership conflicts, the unmatched exposure to the normative ruling as to who owns what and why, who is entitled to what and why.

From both an evolutionary and a developmental perspective, I have tried to show in this book that possession is at the heart of morality, that possession as property is a direct spinoff of human self-conscious psychology which is arguably the product of the greatest, most mysterious transformation in nature. It is also the product of the most devastating advances in being aware of our own situation in this world while experiencing our own embodied self. Coming back to the opening line of the book, only one issue is above all the others: the knowledge of our more or less imminent death.

References

Addessi, E., Crescimbene, L., and Visalberghi, E. (2007). Do capuchin monkeys (*Cebus apella*) use tokens as symbols? *Proceedings of the Royal Society B: Biological Sciences*, 274(1625), 2579–2585.

Agnetta, B. and Rochat, P. (2004). Imitative games by 9-, 14-, and 18-month-old infants. *Infancy*, 6(1), 1–36.

Ainsworth, M. D. (1967). *Infancy in Uganda*. Baltimore, MD: Johns Hopkins University Press.

Ainsworth, M. and Bowlby, J. (1965). *Child Care and the Growth of Love*. London: Penguin Books.

Ainsworth, M. D., Blehar, M. C., Waters, E., and Wall, S. (1978). *Patterns of Attachment*. Hillsdale, NJ: Erlbaum.

Ainsworth, M., Blehar, M., Waters, E., and Wall, S. (1978). *Patterns of Attachment*. Hillsdale, NJ: Erlbaum.

Alsaker, F. D. and Valkanover, S. (2001). Early diagnosis and prevention of victimization in kindergarten. In J. Juvonen and S. Graham (eds.), *Peer Harassment in School: The Plight of the Vulnerable and Victimized* (pp. 175–195). New York: Guilford Press.

Anand, K. J. S. and Hickey, P. R. (1987). Pain and its effects in the human neonate and fetus. *New England Journal of Medicine*, 317, 1321–1329.

Andonotopo, W. and Kurjak, A. (2006). The assessment of fetal behavior of growth restricted fetuses by 4D sonography. *Journal of Perinatal Medicine*, 34, 471–478.

Andonotopo, W., Stanojevic, M., Kurjak, A., Azumendi, G., and Carrera, J. M. (2004). Assessment of fetal behavior and general movements by four-dimensional sonography. *Ultrasound Review of Obstetrics and Gynecology*, 4, 103–114.

Aneci Rosa, C., Rute, S., de Sousa, E., Borba, R., and Ebrahim, G. J. (1992). The street children of Recife: a study of their background. *Journal of Tropical Pediatrics*, 38, 34–40.

Arnott, G. and Elwood, R. W. (2007). Fighting for shells: how private information about resource value changes hermit crab pre-fight displays and escalated fight behavior. *Proceedings of the Royal Society B: Biological Sciences*, 274(1628), 3011–3017.

Asma, S. T. (2012). *Against Fairness*. University of Chicago Press.

Atran, S. (2003). Genesis of suicide terrorism. *Science*, 299, 1534–1539.

Augé, M. (1994). *Le sens des autres*. Paris: Fayard.

Bakeman, R. and Adamson, L. (1984). Coordinating attention to people and objects in mother–infant and peer–infant interactions. *Child Development*, 55, 1278–1289.

Banks, M. S. and Shannon, E. S. (1993). Spatial and chromatic visual efficiency in human neonates. In C. E. Granrud (ed.), *Carnegie-Mellon Symposium on Cognitive Psychology* (pp. 1–46). Hillsdale, NJ: Erlbaum.

Barclay, B. (2005). *Manatuturu: Maori Treasures and Intellectual Property Rights.* Auckland University Press.

Barsalou, L. (1999). Perceptual symbol systems. *Behavioral and Brain Sciences*, 22, 577–660.

Bates, E. (1990). Language about me and you: pronominal reference and the emerging concept of self. In D. Cicchetti and M. Beeghly (eds.), *The Self in Transition: Infancy to Childhood* (pp. 165–182). University of Chicago Press.

Bauer, P. (2006). *Remembering Times of our Lives: Memory in Infancy and Beyond.* Hillsdale, NJ: Erlbaum.

Baumard, N., André, J-B., and Sperber, D. (2013). A mutualistic approach to morality: the evolution of fairness by partner choice. *Behavioral and Brain Sciences*, 36, 59–122.

Belk, R. W. (1978). Assessing the effects of visible consumption on impression formation. *Advances in Consumer Research*, 5, 39–47.

(1991). The ineluctable mysteries of possessions. *Journal of Social Behavior and Personality*, 6(6), 17–55.

(1995). *Collecting in a Consumer Society*. New York: Routledge.

(1999). Shoes and self. *Advances in Consumer Research*, 30, 27–33.

(2000). Are we what we own? In A. L. Benson (ed.), *I Shop, Therefore I Am: Compulsive Buying and the Search for Self* (pp. 76–104). Oxford: Rowman and Littlefield.

Benedict, R. (1946). *The Chrysanthemum and the Sword.* Boston: Houghton Mifflin.

Benson, A. L. (ed.) (2000). *I Shop, Therefore I Am: Compulsive Buying and the Search for Self.* Oxford: Rowman and Littlefield.

Benson, J. B. (1993). Season of birth and onset of locomotion: theoretical and methodological implications. *Infant Behavior and Development*, 16(1), 69–81.

Berger, K. (2007). Update on bullying at school: science forgotten? *Developmental Review*, 27, 90–126.

Bertenthal, B. and Campos, J. J. (1990). A systems approach to the organizing effects of self-produced locomotion during infancy. In C. Rovee-Collier and L. P. Lipsitt (eds.), *Advances in Infancy Research* (vol. 6, pp. 1–60). Norwood, NJ: Ablex Publishing Corp.

Binet, A. (1887). Du fétichisme dans l'amour (Fetishism in love). *Revue Philosophique*, 24, 143–167.

Birch, L. L. and Billman, J. (1986). Preschool children's food sharing with friends and acquaintances. *Child Development*, 57, 387–395.

Blake, P. and Harris, P. L. (2009). Children's understanding of ownership transfers. *Cognitive Development*, 24, 133–145.

(2011). Early representations of ownership. In H. Ross and O. Friedman (eds.), *Origins of Ownership of Property. New Directions for Child and Adolescent Development*, 132, 39–51.

Block, N. (2007). Consciousness, accessibility, and the mesh between psychology and neuroscience. *Brain and Behavioral Sciences*, 30, 481–548.

Bourdieu, P. (1984). *Distinction: A Social Critique of the Judgement of Taste*. New York: Routledge.

(1985). The social space and the genesis of groups. *Theory and Society*, 14(6), 723–744.

(1986). The forms of capital. In J. Richardson (ed.), *Handbook of Theory and Research for the Sociology of Education* (pp. 241–258). New York: Greenwood.

(1989). Social space and symbolic power. *Sociological Theory*, 7(1), 14–25.

(1990). *The Logic of Practice*. Cambridge: Polity Press.

(1994). *Raisons pratiques* (Practical Reasons). Paris: Editions du Seuil.

(1997/2003). *Méditations pascaliennes* (Pascalian Meditations, French edition, author's translation). Paris: Editions du Seuil.

Bowlby, J. (1969/1982). *Attachment and Loss*. New York: Basic Books.

(1988). *A Secure Base: Parent–Child Attachment and Healthy Human Development*. New York: Basic Books.

Breuer, J. and Freud, S. (2000). *Studies on Hysteria*. New York: Basic Books, first published in German in 1895.

Bronfenbrenner, U. (1979). *The Ecology of Human Development: Experiments by Nature and Design*. Cambridge, MA: Harvard University Press.

Brosnan, S. and DeWaal, F. (2001). A proximate perspective on reciprocal altruism. *Human Nature*, 13(1), 129–152.

Bruner, J. S. (1969). Eye, hand and mind. In D. Elkind and J. H. Flavell (eds.), *Studies in Cognitive Development: Essays in Honor of Jean Piaget* (pp. 223–236). Oxford University Press.

(1972). Nature and uses of immaturity. *American Psychologist*, 27(8), 687–708.

(1983). *Child's Talk*. New York: Norton.

Brusseau, R. R. and Mashour, G. A. (2007). Subcortical consciousness: implications for fetal anesthesia and analgesia. *Behavioral and Brain Sciences*, 30(1), 86–87.

Caillois, R. (1958/2001). *Man, Play, and Games*. Urbana-Champaign: University of Illinois Press.

Callaghan, T., Rochat, P., Lillard, A., Claux, M. L., Odden, H., Itakura, S., Tapanya, S., and Singh, S. (2005). Synchrony in the onset of mental-state reasoning: evidence from five cultures. *Psychological Science*, 16(5), 378–384.

Carey, S. (2011). The origin of concepts: a précis. *Behavioral and Brain Sciences*, 34, 113–167.

Carlson, B. M. (1994). *Human Embryology and Developmental Biology*. St. Louis: Mosby.

Carnevalli, B. (2011). *Romantisme et reconnaissance: figures de la conscience chez Rousseau* (Romantism and Recognition: Rousseau and the Figures of Consciousness). Geneva: Droz Publishers, Collection Bibliothèque des Lumières.

(2013). "Glory": la lutte pour la réputation dans le modèle hobbesien ("Glory": the struggle for reputation in the Hobbesian model). *Communications*, Special issue on reputation, ed. G. Origgi.

Carpenter, M., Tomasello, M., and Striano, T. (2005). Role reversal imitation and language in typically developing infants and children with autism. *Infancy*, 8, 253–278.

Casanova, G. (1797/2006). *History of My Life*. New York: Everyman's Library.

Charles, S. and Lipovetsky, G. (2006). *Hypermodern Times*. Cambridge: Polity Press.

Chen, X., Rubin, K. H., and Sun, Y. (1992). Social reputation and peer relationships in Chinese and Canadian children: a cross-cultural study. *Child Development*, 63, 1336–1343.

Clark, G. (2007). Specialisation, standardisation and Lapita ceramics. In S. Bedford, C. Sand, and S. P. Connaughton (eds.), *Oceanic Explorations: Lapita and Western Pacific Settlement* (pp. 289–296). Terra Australis 26. Australian National University.

Cohen, D. and Nisbett, R. E. (1994). Self-protection and the culture of honor: explaining southern violence. *Personality and Social Psychology Bulletin*, 20, 551–567.

(1997). Field experiments examining the culture of honor: the role of institutions in perpetuating norms about violence. *Personality and Social Psychology Bulletin*, 23, 1188–1199.

Cole, D. T. (1955). *An Introduction of Tswana Grammar*. Parktown: Longman Penguin South Africa.

Cole, M. and Hatano, G. (2007). Cultural-historical activity theory: integrating phylogeny, cultural history, and ontogenesis in cultural psychology. In S. Kitayama and D. Cohen (eds.), *Handbook of Cultural Psychology* (pp. 109–135). New York: Guilford Press.

Cyencek, D., Greenwald, A., and Meltzoff, A. (2011). Measuring implicit attitudes of 4-year old children: the preschool implicit association test. *Journal of Experimental Child Psychology*, 109, 187–200.

Darwin, C. (1872/1965). *The Expression of the Emotions in Man and Animals*. University of Chicago Press.

Deacon, T. W. (1997). *The Symbolic Species: The Co-evolution of Language and the Brain*. New York: Norton.

Debord, G. (1977/1967). *The Society of the Spectacle*. St. Petersburg, FL: Black and Red Publishers.

DeCasper, A. J. and Fifer, W. P. (1980). Of human bonding: newborns prefer their mother's voices. *Science*, 208, 1174–1176.

Dennett, D. C. (1981). *Brainstorms: Philosophical Essays on Mind and Psychology*. Cambridge, MA: MIT Press.

(1987). *The Intentional Stance*. Cambridge, MA: MIT Press.

De Staël, Madame (1799). *De la littérature considérée dans ses rapports avec les institutions sociales* (On literature considered in relation to social institutions). Paris: Nabu.

deVries, J. I. P., Visser, G. H. A., and Prechtl, H. F. R. (1985). The emergence of fetal behavior. II. Quantitative aspects. *Early Human Development*, 12, 99–120.

De Waal, F. B. M. (1989). Food sharing and reciprocal obligations among chimpanzees. *Journal of Human Evolution*, 18, 433–459.

(1997). The chimpanzee's service economy: food for grooming. *Evolution and Human Behavior*, 18, 375–386.

(2006). *Primates and Philosophers: How Morality Evolved*. Princeton University Press.

Dewey, J. (1922). *Human Nature and Conduct: An Introduction to Social Psychology*. New York: Carlton House.

Dittmar, H. (1992). *The Social Psychology of Material Possessions: To Have Is to Be*. New York: St. Martin's Press.

(2000). The role of self-image in excessive buying. In A. L. Benson (ed.), *I Shop, Therefore I Am: Compulsive Buying and the Search for Self* (pp. 105–132). New York: Rowman and Littlefield.

Donald, M. (1991). *Origins of the Modern Mind: Three Stages in the Evolution of Culture and Cognition*. Cambridge, MA: Harvard University Press.

Dubreuil, D., Gentile, M. S., Visalberghi, E. (2008). Are capuchin monkeys (*Cebus apella*) inequity averse? *Animal Cognition*, 11(2), 275–282.

Dunham, Y., Baron, A., and Banaji, M. (2008). The development of implicit intergroup cognition. *Trends in Cognitive Sciences*, 12(7), 248–253.

Dunn, J. (1988). *The Beginnings of Social Understanding*. Cambridge, MA: Harvard University Press.

Durkheim, E. (1893/1997). *The Division of Labor in Society*. New York: Free Press.

Ehrlich, P. R., Dobkin, D. S., Wheye, D., Pimm, S. L. (1994). *The Birdwatcher's Handbook* (pp. 228–232). Oxford University Press.

Ekecrantz, L. and Rudhe, L. (1972). Transitional phenomena: frequency, forms and functions of specially loved objects. *Acta Psychiatrica Scandinavia*, 48, 261–273.

Emery, N. J. (2000). The eyes have it: the neuroethology, function and evolution of social gaze. *Neuroscience and Biobehavioral Reviews*, 24, 581–604.

Erikson, E. H. (1993). *Childhood and Society*. New York: W. W. Norton.

Faigenbaum, G. (2005). *Children's Economic Experience: Exchange*. Buenos Aires: Libros En Red.

(2013). The underground economy of schoolyards (manuscript submitted).

Fair, D. A., Bathula, D., Mills, K. L., Costa Dias, T. G., Blythe, M. S., Zhang, D., Snyder, A. Z., Raichle, M. E., Stevens, A. A., Nigg, J. T., and Nagell, B. J. (2010). Maturing thalamocortical functional connectivity across development. *Frontiers in Systems Neuroscience*, 4(10), 1–10.

Fehr, E., Bernhard, H., and Rockenbach, B. (2008). Egalitarianism in young children. *Nature*, 454, 1079–1084.

Field, T. M. et al. (1982). Discrimination and imitation of facial expressions by neonates. *Science*, 218(4568), 179–181.

Fiske, A. P. (1992). The four elementary forms of sociality: framework for a unified theory of social relations. *Psychological Review*, 99(4), 689–723.

Fonagy, P., Target, M., and Gergely, G. (2006). Psychoanalytic perspectives on developmental psychopathology. In D. Cicchetti and D. J. Cohen (ed.), *Developmental Psychopathology* (2nd edn., pp. 701–749). New York: Wiley.

Freud, S. (1905/2000). *Three Essays on the Theory of Sexuality*. New York: Basic Books.

Friedman, O. (2008). First possession: an assumption guiding inferences about who owns what. *Psychonomic Bulletin and Review*, 15, 290–295.

Friedman, O. and Leslie, A. M. (2007). The conceptual underpinnings of pretense: pretending is not "behaving-as-if." *Cognition*, 105, 103–124.

Friedman, O. and Neary, K. R. (2008). Determining who owns what: do children infer ownership from first possession? *Cognition*, 107, 829–849.

Friedman, O., Neary, K. R., Defeyter, M. A., and Malcolm, S. L. (2011). Ownership and object history. In H. Ross and O. Friedman (eds.), *Origins of Ownership of Property. New Directions for Child and Adolescent Development*, 132, 79–89.

Furby, L. (1978). Possession in humans: an exploratory study of its meaning and motivation. *Social Behavior and Personality* 6(1), 49–65.

Gabalda, B. (2012). Development of the sense of ownership: social and moral evaluations. Doctoral dissertation, Université René Descartes Paris.

Gaddini, R. and Gaddini, E. (1970). Transitional objects and the process of individuation: study in three different social groups. *Journal of American Academic Child Psychiatry*, 9, 347–365.

Gallagher, S. and Zahavi, D. (2008). *The Phenomenological Mind: An Introduction to Philosophy of Mind and Cognitive Science*. New York: Routledge.

Gazelle, H. and Ladd, G. W. (2003). Anxious solitude and peer exclusion: a diathesis stress model of internalizing trajectories in childhood. *Child Development*, 74, 257–278.

Gergely, G., Bekkering, H., and Kiraly, I. (2002). Rational imitation in preverbal infants. *Nature*, 415, 755.

Gergely, G. and Watson, J. S. (1999). Early socio-emotional development: contingency perception and the social-biofeedback model. In P. Rochat (ed.), *Early Social Cognition: Understanding Others in the First Months of Life* (pp. 101–136). Mahwah, NJ: Erlbaum.

Gibbon, E. (1776/2001). *The History of the Decline and Fall of the Roman Empire*. London: Penguin.

Gibson, J. J. (1979). *The Ecological Approach to Visual Perception*. Boston: Houghton-Mifflin.

Godbout, J. (1998). *The World of the Gift*. Montreal: McGill-Queen's University Press.

Goffman, E. (1959). *The Presentation of Self in Everyday Life*. New York: Doubleday.

Gomes, C. M. and Boesch, C. (2009). Wild chimpanzees exchange meat for sex on a long-term basis. *PLoSONE*, 4, e5116.

Gomes, C. M., Mundry, R., and Boesch, C. (2009). Long-term reciprocation of grooming in wild West African chimpanzees. *Proceedings of the Royal Society B: Biological Sciences*, 276 (1657), 699–706.

Gottlieb, G. (1971). Ontogenesis of sensory functions in birds and mammals. In A. Tobach, L. R. Aronson, and E. Shaw (eds.), *The Biopsychology of Development* (pp. 67–128). New York: Academic Press.

Gould, S. J. (1977). *Ontogeny and Phylogeny*. Cambridge, MA: Harvard University Press.

Graeber, D. (2011). *Debt: The First 5000 Years*. New York: Melville House.

Granrud, C. E. (1987). Size constancy in newborn human infants. *Investigative Ophthamology and Visual Science*, 28 (Supplement), 5.

Groos, K. (1898). *The Play of Animals*. New York: Appleton.

Grossmann, K., Grossmann, K. E., Spangler, G., Suess, G., and Unzner, L. (1985). Maternal sensitivity and newborns orientation responses as related to quality of attachment in northern Germany: growing points in attachment theory and research. *Child Development*, 50, 233–256.

Grossmann, K. E., Grossmann, K., Huber, F., Wartner, U. *et al.* (1981). German children's behavior toward their mothers at 12 months and their fathers at 18 months in Ainsworth's strange situation. *International Journal of Behavioral Development*, 4, 157–184.

Haith, M. M., Bergman, T., and Moore, M. J. (1977). Eye contact and face scanning in early infancy. *Science*, 198, 853–855.

Hamilton, W. (1963) The evolution of altruistic behavior. *American Naturalist*, 97, 354–356.

Hansell, M. (2000). *Bird Nests and Construction Behaviour*. Cambridge University Press.

Harbaugh, W. T., Krause, K. S., and Liday, S. J. (2003). Bargaining by children. *Social Science Research Network*, 1–40.

Hardin, G. (1968). The tragedy of the commons. *Science*, 162(3859), 1243–1248.

Harkness, S. and Super, C. M. (eds.) (1996). *Parents' Cultural Belief Systems: Their Origins, Expressions, and Consequences*. New York: Guilford Press.

Harlow, H. F. (1958). The nature of love. *American Psychologist*, 13, 673–685.

Harris, P. L. and Kavanaugh, R. D. (1993). *Young Children's Understanding of Pretense*. Monographs of the Society for Research in Child Development, 58, 1.

Hart, S. and Carrington, H. (2002). Jealousy in 6-month-old infants. *Infancy*, 3(3), 395–402.

Hata, T., Dai, S. Y., and Marumo, G. (2010). Ultrasound for evaluation of fetal neurobehavioural development: from 2-D to 4-D ultrasound. *Infant and Child Development*, 19(1), 99–118. Special issue: Towards a fetal psychology.

Haun, D. and Tomasello, M. (2011). Conformity to peer pressure in preschool children. *Child Development*, 82(6), 1759–1767.

Haye, D. F. (2006). Yours and mine: toddlers talk about possessions with familiar peers. *British Journal of Developmental Psychology*, 24, 39–52.

Hebdige, D. (1994). *Hiding in the Light*. London: Routledge.

Heider, F. and Simmel, M. (1944). An experimental study of apparent behavior. *American Journal of Psychology*, 57(2), 243–254.

Heine, B. (1997). *Possession: Cognitive Sources, Forces, and Grammaticalization* (pp. 1–44). Cambridge University Press.

Heller, M. C. (2012). *Body Psychotherapy: History, Concepts and Methods*. New York: Norton.

Henrich, J., Ensimger, J., McElreath, R., Barr, A., Barrett, C., Bolyanatz, A., Cardenas, J. C., Gurven, M., Gwako, E., Henrich, N., Lesorogol, C., Marlowe, F., Tracer, D., and J. Ziker (2010). Markets, religion, community size, and the evolution of fairness and punishment. *Science*, 327, 1480–1484.

Henrich, J., Heine, S. J., and Norenzayan, A. (2010). The weirdest people in the world? *Behavioral and Brain Science*, 33, 1–75.

Henrich, J., McElreath, R., Barr, A., Ensminger, J., Barrett, C., Bolyanatz, A., Cardenas, J. C., Gurven, M., Gwako, E., Henrich, N., Lesorogol, C., Marlowe, F., Tracer, D., and Ziker, J. (2006). Costly punishment across human societies. *Science*, 312(5781), 1767–1770.

Hepper, P. G. (2002). Prenatal development. In A. Slater and M. Lewis (eds.), *Introduction to Infant Development* (pp. 39–60). Oxford University Press.

Hepper, P. G. and Shahidullah, S. (1994). Development of fetal hearing. *Fetal and Maternal Medicine Review*, 6, 167–179.

Hewlett, B., Lamb, M., Shannon, D., Leyendecker, P., and Schölmerich, A. (1998). Culture and early infancy among Central African foragers and farmers. *Developmental Psychology*, 34(4), 653–661.

Hinde, R. (1966). *Animal Behavior*. New York: McGraw-Hill.

Hobara, M. (2003). Prevalence of transitional objects in young children of Tokyo and New York. *Infant Mental Health Journal*, 24(2), 174–191.

Hobson, R. P. (1989). On sharing experiences. *Development and Psychopathology*, 1, 97–203.

(1995). Apprehending attitudes and actions: separable abilities in early development? *Development and Psychopathology*, 7, 171–82.

(2002). *The Cradle of Thought*. London: Macmillan.

Hofeld, W. H. (1913). Some fundamental legal conceptions as applied to judicial reasoning. *Yale Law Journal*, 23, 16–59.

Hooker, D. (1952). *The Prenatal Origin of Behavior*. University of Kansas Press.

Huizinga, J. (1938/1955). *Homo Ludens: A Study of the Play Element in Culture*. Boston: Beacon Press.

Hume, D. (1739/1928). *A Treatise of Human Nature*. Oxford: Clarendon Press.

Hustvedt, S. (2005). *Mysteries of the Rectangle: Essays on Painting*. Princeton Architectural Press.

Huttenlocher, P. R. and Dabholkar, A. S. (1997). Regional differences in synaptogenesis in human cerebral cortex. *Journal of Comparative Neurology*, 387(2), 167–178.

Ingold, T., Riches, D., and Woodburn, J. (eds.) (1988). *Hunters and Gatherers*, vol. 1: *History, Evolution and Social Changes*; vol. 2: *Property, Power and Ideology*. Oxford: Berg.

Jaffe, J., Beebe, B., Feldstein, S., Crown, C., and Jasnow, M. D. (2001). Rhythms of dialogue in infancy. *Monographs of the Society for Research in Child Development*, 66(2), Serial No. 265.

James, W. (1884). What is an emotion? *Mind*, 9, 188–205.

(1890/1950). *The Principles of Psychology*. New York: Dover.

Jersky, J. and Kinsley, R. H. (1967). Lactose deficiency in the South African Bantu. *South African Medical Journal*, 41(Dec.), 1194–1196.

Kagan, J. (1981). *The Second Year: The Emergence of Self-awareness*. Cambridge, MA: Harvard University Press.

Kanngiesser, P., Gjersoe, N., and Hood, B. (2010). The effect of creative labor on property-ownership transfer by preschool children and adults. *Psychological Science*, 21, 1236–1241.

Karmiloff-Smith, A. (1996). *Beyond Modularity: A Developmental Perspective on Cognitive Science*. Cambridge, MA: MIT Press.

Keller, H. (2007). *Cultures of Infancy*. Mahwah, NJ: Erlbaum.

(2013). Attachment and culture. *Journal of Cross-Cultural Psychology*, 44(2), 175–194.

Kellman, P. J. and Arterberry, M. E. (2006). Infant visual perception. In D. Kuhn, R. S. Siegler, W. Damon, and R. M. Lerner (eds.), *Handbook of Child Psychology*, vol. 2: *Cognition, Perception, and Language* (6th edn., pp. 109–160). Hoboken, NJ: Wiley.

Kent, M. M. and Haub, C. (2005). Global demographic divide. *Population Bulletin*, 60(4), 1–24.

Kinzler, K. D., Dupoux, E., and Spelke, E. S. (2007). The native language of social cognition. *Proceedings of the National Academy of Sciences of the United States of America*, 104(30), 12577–12580.

Kinzler, K. D., Shutts, K., DeJesus, J., and Spelke, E. S. (2009). Accent trumps race in guiding children's social preferences. *Social Cognition*, 27, 623–634.

Kisilevsky, B. S. and Hains, S. M. J. (2010). Exploring the relationship between fetal heart rate and cognition. *Infant and Child Development*, 19(1), 60–75. Special issue: Towards a Fetal Psychology.

Klein, Melanie (1932). *The Psycho-analysis of Children*. London: Hogarth Press.

Klein, R. G. (1999). *The Human Career: Human Biological and Cultural Origins* (2nd edn.). University of Chicago Press.

Klimach, V. J. and Cooke, R. W. (1988). Maturation of the neonatal somatosensory evoked response in preterm infants. *Developmental Medicine and Child* Neurology, 30(2), 208–214.

Klopfer, P. H. (1969). *Habitats and Territories: A Study of the Use of Space by Animals*. New York: Basic Books.

Kobayashi, H. and Hashiya, K. (2011). The gaze that grooms: contribution of social factors to the evolution of primate eye morphology. *Evolution and Human Behavior*, 32, 157–165.

Kobayashi, H. and Kohshima, S. (1997). Unique morphology of the human eye. *Nature*, 387, 767–768.

Konner, M. (2010). *The Evolution of Childhood*. Cambridge, MA: Harvard University Press.

Kretschmann, H. J., Kammradt, G., Krauthausen, I., Sauer, B., and Wingert, F. (1986). Brain growth in man. *Bibliotheca Anatomica*, 28, 1–26.

Kummer, H. (1971). *Primate Societies: Group Techniques of Ecological Adaptation*. Chicago: Aldine-Atherton.

Lakin, M., Lakin, M. G., and Costanzo, P. R. (1979). Group processes in early childhood: a dimension of human development. *International Journal of Behavioral Development*, 2(2), 171–183.

Lamb, M. E., Sternberg, K. J., Broberg, A. G., and Hwang, P. (1992). *Child Care in Context: Cross-Cultural Perspectives*. Erlbaum.

Lancy, D. F. (1996). *Playing on the Mother Ground: Cultural Routines for Children's Development*. New York: Guilford.

(2008). *The Anthropology of Childhood: Cherubs, Chattel, Changelings*. Cambridge University Press.

Lecanuet, J.-P., Granier-Deferre, C., and Busnel, M.-C. (1988). Fetal cardiac and motor responses to octave-band noises as a function of central frequency, intensity and heartrate variability. *Early Human Development*, 18, 81–93.

Lecanuet, J.-P., Granier-Deferre, C., DeCasper, A. J., Maugeais, R., Andrieu, A.-J., and Busnel, M.-C. (1987). Perception et discrimination foetales de stimuli langagiers, mise en évidence à partir de la réactivité cardiaque, résultants préliminaires. *Compte-Rendus de l'Académie des Sciences, Paris (III)*, 305, 161–164.

Lecanuet, J. P. and Schaal, B. (1996). Fetal sensory compentencies. *European Journal of Obstetrics and Gynecology and Reproductive Biology*, 68, 1–23.

Lehman, E. B., Denham, S. A., Moser, M. H., and Reeves, S. L. (1992). Soft object and pacifier attachment in young children: the role of security attachment to the mother. *Journal of Child Psychology and Psychiatry and Allied Disciplines*, 33, 1205–1215.

Leroi-Gourhan, A. (1993). *Gesture and Speech*. Cambridge, MA: MIT Press.

Leslie, A. M. (1987). Pretense and representation: the origins of "theory of mind." *Psychological Review*, 94, 412–426.

LeVine, R. A. (1994). *Child Care and Culture: Lessons from Africa*. Cambridge University Press.

Lewis, M. (1992). *Shame: The Exposed Self*. New York: Free Press.

Lewis, M. and Brooks-Gunn, J. (1979). *Social Cognition and the Acquisition of Self*. New York: Plenum Press.

Lewis, M., Sullivan, M., Stanger, C., and Weiss, M. (1989). Self development and self-conscious emotions. *Child Development*, 60, 146–156.

Lipovetsky, G. (2005). *Hypermodern Times*. Cambridge: Polity Press.

Litt, C. J. (1981). Children's attachment to transitional objects: a study of two pediatric populations. *American Journal of Orthopsychiatry*, 51, 131–139.

(1986). Theories of transitional object attachment: an overview. *International Journal of Behavioral Development*, 9(3), 383–399.

Lizardo, O. (2004). The cognitive origins of Bourdieu's habitus. *Journal for the Theory of Social Behaviour*, 34, 375, 401.

(2013). Habitus. In Byron Kaldis (ed.), *Encyclopedia of Philosophy and the Social Sciences*. London: Sage Publications.

Locke, J. (1689/1997). *An Essay Concerning Human Understanding*. Ed. Roger Woolhouse. New York: Penguin Books.

(1690/1980). *The Second Treatise of Civil Government*. Cambridge: Hackett.

Malinowski, B. (1932). *Argonauts of the Western Pacific: An Account of Native Enterprise and Adventure in the Archipelagoes of Melanesian New Guinea*. London: Routledge.

Malinowski, B. and Ellis, H. (1929). *The Sexual Life of Savages in North-Western Melanesia: An Ethnographic Account of Courtship, Marriage, and Family Life among the Natives of the Trobriand Islands, British New Guinea*. London: Routledge.

Marcuse, H. (1955/1987). *Eros and Civilization* (2nd edn.). London: Routledge.

Marlier, L., Schaal, B., and Soussignan, R. (1998a). Neonatal responsiveness to the odor of amniotic and lacteal fluids: a test of perinatal chemosensory continuity. *Child Development*, 69(3), 611–623.

(1998b). Bottle-fed neonates prefer an odor experienced in utero to an odor experienced postnatally in the feeding context. *Developmental Psychobiology*, 33, 133–145.

Marlowe, F. W. (2010). *The Hadza: Hunter-Gatherers of Tanzania*. Berkeley: University of California Press.

Marr, D. (1982/2010). *Vision: A Computational Investigation into the Human Representation and Processing of Visual Information*. Cambridge, MA: MIT Press.

Marshall, L. (1961). Sharing, talking, and giving: relief of social tensions among !Kung Bushmen. *Africa: Journal of the International African Institute*, 31(3), 231–249.

Marx, K. and Engels, F. (1888/1998). *The Communist Manifesto*. New York: Penguin.

Mauss, M. (1934). Le notion de technique du corps. *Journal de Psychologie*, 32, 3–4, reprinted in *Sociologie et Anthropologie*. Paris: Presses Universitaires de France.

(1952/1967). *The Gift: Forms and Functions of Exchange in Archaic Societies*. New York: Norton.

Meltzoff, A. N. (1995). Understanding the intentions of others: re-enactment of intended acts by 18-month-old children. *Developmental Psychology*, 31, 838–850.

Meltzoff, A. N. and Moore, M. K. (1977). Imitation of facial and manual gestures. *Science*, 198(4312), 75–78.

(1992). Early imitation within a functional framework: the importance of person identity, movement, and development. *Infant Behavior and Development*, 15, 479–505.

Merker, B. (2007). Consciousness without a cerebral cortex: a challenge for neuroscience and medicine. *Behavioral and Brain Sciences*, 30, 63–134.

Merskey, H. and Bogduk, N. (eds.) (1994). *Classification of Chronic Pain: Descriptions of Chronic Pain Syndromes and Definitions of Pain Terms* (pp. 209–214). New York: IASP Press.

Metzinger, T. (2003). *Being No One: The Self-Model Theory of Subjectivity*. Cambridge, MA: MIT Press.

Michotte, A. (1946/1962). *The Perception of Causality*. Andover, MA: Methuen.

Miller, J. G. (2006). Insight into moral development from cultural psychology. In M. Killen and J. Smetana (eds.), *Handbook of Moral Development* (pp. 375–398). Mahwah, NJ: Lawrence Erlbaum.

Mitani, J. C. and Watts, D. P. (2001). Why do chimpanzees hunt and share meat? *Animal Behaviour*, 61(5), 915–924.

Moessinger, P. (2000a). *Le jeu de l'identité*. Paris: Presses Universitaires de France.

(2000b). *The Paradox of Social Order: Linking Psychology and Sociology*. New York: Aldine de Gruyter.

Montagu, A. (1961). Neonatal and infant immaturity in man. *Journal of the American Medical Association*, 178(23), 56–57.

Morin, O. (2011). *Comment les traditions naissent et meurent: la transmission culturelle* (How traditions arise and die out: cultural transmission). Paris: Odile Jacob.

Morton, J. and Johnson, M. H. (1991). CONSPEC and CONLERN: a two-process theory of infant face recognition. *Psychological Review*, 98(2), 164–181.

Murnighan, J. K. and Saxon, M. S. (1998). Ultimatum bargaining by children and adults. *Journal of Economic Psychology*, 19(4), 415–445.

Nijhuis, J. G., Prechtl, H. F. R., Martin, C. B., and Bots, R. (1982). Are there behavioral states in the human fetus? *Early Human Development*, 6, 177–195.

Nisbett, R. E. (2003). *The Geography of Thought: How Asians and Westerners Think Differently . . . and Why*. New York: The Free Press.

Nisbett, R. E. and Cohen, D. (1996). *Culture of Honor: The Psychology of Violence in the South*. Denver, CO: Westview Press.

Noles, N. S., Keil, F. C., Bloom, P., and Gelman, S. A. (2012). Children's and adults' intuitions about who can own things. *Journal of Cognition and Culture*, 12, 265–286.

Nordgreen, J., Joseph, P., Garner, J. P., Janczak, A. M., Ranheim, B., Muir, W. M., and Horsberg, T. E. (2009). Thermonociception in fish: effects of two different doses of morphine on thermal threshold and post-test behaviour in goldfish (*Carassius auratus*). *Applied Animal Behaviour Science*, 119(1–2), 101–107.

Nozick, R. (1974). *Anarchy, State, and Utopia*. New York: Basic Books.

Odden, H. and Rochat, P. (2004). Observational learning and enculturation. *Educational and Child Development*, 21(2), 39–50.

O'Meara, T. (1990). *Samoan Planters: Tradition and Economic Development in Polynesia*. Fort Worth: Holt, Rinehart, and Winston.

Oppenheim, R. W. (1991). Cell death during development of the nervous system. *Annual Review of Neuroscience*, 14, 453–501.

Over, H. and Carpenter, M. (2009). Eighteen-month-old infants show increased helping following priming with affiliation. *Psychological Science*, 20, 1189–1193.

Papoušek, H. and Papoušek, M. (1995). Intuitive parenting. In Marc H. Bornstein (ed.) (1995). *Handbook of Parenting*, vol. 2: *Biology and Ecology of Parenting* (pp. 117–136). Hillsdale, NJ: Lawrence Erlbaum.

Parnas, J. et al. (2005). EASE: Examination of Anomalous Self-Experience. *Psychopathology*, 38, 236–258.

Pasolini, P. P. (1962/1984). *The Scent of India*. London: Olive.

Passman, R. H. and Halonen, J. S. (1979). A developmental survey of young children's attachment to inanimate objects. *Journal of Genetic Psychology*, 134, 165–178.

Piaget, J. (1932/1977). *The Moral Judgment of the Child*. Harmondsworth: Penguin.

(1936/1952). *The Origins of Intelligence in Children*. New York: International Universities Press.

(1938/1955). *The Construction of Reality in the Child*. New York: Routledge and Kegan Paul.

(1962). *Play, Dreams, and Imitation in Childhood*. New York: Norton.

Pierce, J. L. and Jussila, I. (2011). *Psychological Ownership and the Organizational Context: Theory, Research Evidence and Application*. New Horizons in Management Series. Cheltenham: Edward Elgar.

Pilgrim, C. and Rueda-Riedle, A. (2002). The importance of social context in cross-cultural comparisons: first graders in Columbia and the United States. *Journal of Genetic Psychology*, 163(3), 283–295.

Polanyi, K. (1944/2001). *The Great Transformation: The Political and Economic Origins of our Time*. Boston: Beacon Press.

Porges, S. W. (2001). The polyvagal theory: phylogenetic substrates of a social nervous system. *International Journal of Psychophysiology*, 42, 123–146.

(2004). Neuroception: a subconscious system for detecting threats and safety. *Zero to Three*, May, 19–24.

Poss, S. and Rochat, P. (2003). Referential understanding of videos in chimpanzees (*Pan troglodytes*), orangutans (*Pongo pygmaeus*), and children (*Homo sapiens*). *Journal of Comparative Psychology*, 117(4), 420–428.

Prechtl, H. F. R. (1977). Assessment and significance of behavioural states. In S. R. Berenberg (ed.), *Brain, Fetal and Infant: Current Research on Normal and Abnormal Development* (pp. 79–90). The Hague: Martinus Nijhoff.

(ed.) (1984). *Continuity of Neural Functions: From Prenatal to Postnatal Life*. Oxford: Blackwell.

Proctor, D., Williamson, R. A., de Waal, F. B. M., and Brosnan, S. F. (2013). Chimpanzees play the ultimatum game. *Proceedings of the National Academy of Science*, 110, 2070–2075.

Provence, S. and Lipton, R. C. (1962). *Infants in Institutions*. New York: International Universities Press.

Rakic, P. (1972). Model of cell migration to the superficial layers of the fetal monkey neocortex. *Journal of Comparative Neurology*, 145, 61–84.

Rakoczy, H., Tomasello, M., and Striano, T. (2004). Young children know that trying is not pretending: a test of the "behaving-as-if" construal of children's understanding of pretense. *Developmental Psychology*, 40, 388–399.

Rakoczy, H., Warneken, F., and Tomasello, M. (2008). The sources of normativity: young children's awareness of the normative structure of games. *Developmental Psychology*, 44(3), 875–881.

Rao, N. and Stewart, S. M. (1999). Cultural influences on sharer and recipient behavior sharing in Chinese and Indian preschool children. *Journal of Cross-Cultural Psychology*, 30(2), 219–241.

Ratner, N. and Bruner, J. (1978). Games, social exchange and the acquisition of language. *Journal of Child Language*, 5, 391–401.

Rawls, J. (1999). *A Theory of Justice*. Cambridge, MA: Harvard University Press.

Reddy, V. (2007). Getting back to the rough ground: deception and "social living." *Philosophical Transactions of the Royal Society B: Biological Sciences*, 362(1480), 621–637.

Reed, E. S. (1984). An outline of a theory of action systems. *Journal of Motor Behavior*, 14, 98–134.

Rigo, B. (2005). *Conscience occidentale et fables océaniques: la dynamique de la contradiction*. Paris: Editions L'Harmattan.

Robbins, E. and Rochat, P. (2011). Emerging signs of strong reciprocity in human ontogeny. *Frontiers in Psychology*, 2(353), 1–14.

(2014, in preparation). Transitional objects in the South Pacific and the United States.

Rochat, M. J., Veroni, V., Brushweiler-Stern, N. et al. (2014, in press). Impaired vitality form recognition in autism. *Neuropsychologica*.

Rochat, P. (1983). Oral touch in young infants: response to variations of nipple characteristics in the first months of life. *International Journal of Behavioral Development*, 6, 123–133.

(1987). Mouthing and grasping in neonates: evidence for the early detection of what hard or soft substances afford for action. *Infant Behavior and Development*, 10, 435–449.

(ed.) (1999). *Early Social Cognition*. Mahwah, NJ: Lawrence Erlbaum.

(2001). *The Infant's World*. Cambridge, MA: Harvard University Press.

(2009). *Others in Mind: Social Origins of Self-consciousness*. Cambridge University Press.

(2011a). Possession and morality in early development. *New Directions in Child and Adolescent Development*, 11(132), 23–38.

(2011b). The self as phenotype. *Cognition and Consciousness*, 20(1), 109–119.

(2013). The gaze of others. In M. Banaji and S. Gelman (eds.), *Navigating the Social World*. Oxford University Press.

Rochat, P., Dias, M. D. G., Guo, L., Broesch, T., Passos-Ferreira, C., Winning, A., and Berg, B. (2009). Fairness in distributive justice by 3- and 5-year-olds across 7 cultures. *Journal of Cross-Cultural Psychology*, 40(3), 416–442.

Rochat, P., Goubet, N., and Shah, B. (1997). Enhanced sucking engagement by preterm infants during intermittent gavage feedings. *Journal of Developmental and Behavioral Pediatrics*, 18(1), 22–26.

Rochat, P. and Hespos, S. J. (1997). Differential rooting response by neonates: evidence of an early sense of self. *Early Development and Parenting*, 6(3–4), 105–112.

Rochat, P. and Passos-Ferreira, C. (2008). Becoming *Homo negotiatus*: ontogeny of the unique ways humans own and share. In S. Itakura and K. Fujita (eds.), *Origins of the Social Mind: Evolutionary and Developmental Views* (pp. 141–156). New York: Springer.

Rochat, P. and Senders, S. J. (1991). Active touch in infancy: action systems in development. In M. J. Weiss and P. R. Zelazo (eds.), *Infant Attention: Biological Constraints and the Influence of Experience* (pp. 412–442). Norwood, NJ: Ablex.

Rochat, P. and Striano, T. (1999a). Emerging self-exploration by 2 month-old infants. *Developmental Science*, 2(2), 206–218.

(1999b). Social cognitive development in the first year. In P. Rochat (ed.), *Early Social Cognition* (pp. 3–34). Mahwah, NJ: Lawrence Erlbaum.

Rochat, P., Querido, J., and Striano, T. (1999). Emerging sensitivity to the timing and structure of protoconversation in early infancy. *Developmental Psychology*, 35(4), 950–957.

Rochat, P., Robbins, E., Dias, M., and Passos-Ferreira, C. (2014). Coin versus food sharing in children growing up in highly contrasted socio-economical circumstances in North-eastern Brazil and the United States of America (in preparation).

Rogoff, B. (2003). *The Cultural Nature of Human Development*. Oxford University Press.

Rogoff, B., Baker-Sennett, J., Lacasa, P., and Goldsmith, D. (1995). Development through participation in sociocultural activity. In J. J. Goodnow, P. J. Miller, and F. Kessel (eds.), *Cultural Practices as Contexts for Development* (pp. 45–65). San Francisco: Jossey-Bass.

Rose, C. M. (1985). Possession as the origin of property. *University of Chicago Law Review*, 52(1), 73–88.

Ross, H., Conant, C. M., and Vickar, M. (2011). Property rights and the resolution of social conflict. In H. Ross and O. Friedman (eds.), *Origins of Ownership of Property. New Directions for Child and Adolescent Development*, 132, 53–64.

Ross, H. and Friedman, O. (eds.) (2011). Origins of Ownership of Property. *New Directions for Child and Adolescent Development*, 132 (special issue).

Rossano, F., Rakoczy, H., and Tomasello, M. (2011). Young children's understanding of violation of property rights. *Cognition*, 121, 219–227.

Rousseau, J.-J. (1755). *Discours sur l'origine et les fondements de l'inégalité parmi les hommes*. (Discourse on the origin and the foundations of inequality among men). Paris.

Rudmin, F. W. (1991). "To own is to be perceived to own": a social cognitive look at the ownership of property. In *To Have Possessions: A Handbook on Ownership and Property*, special issue of *Journal of Social Behavior and Personality*, 6(6–7), 85–104.

Sagi, A., Lamb, M. E., Lewkowicz, K. S., Shoham, R., Dvir, R., and Estes, D. (1985). Security of infant–mother, –father, and –metapelet attachments among kibbutz-reared Israeli children. *Monographs of the Society for Research in Child Development*, 50(1–2, 209), 257–275.

Sahlins, M. (1963). Poor man, rich man, big man, chief: political types in Melanesia and Polynesia. *Comparative Studies in Society and History*, 5(3), 285–303.

Saks, E. (2007). *The Center Cannot Hold: My Journey through Madness*. New York: Hyperion.

Salas, C., Broglio, C., Durán, E., Gómez, A., Ocana, F. M., Jiménez-Moya, F., and Rodriguez, F. (2006). Neuropsychology of learning and memory in teleost fish. *Zebrafish*, 3(2), 157–171.

Sartre, J.-P. (1971/1981). *The Family Idiot: Gustave Flaubert 1821–1857*, vol. I. Trans. Carol Cosman. University of Chicago Press.

Saussure, F. de (2002). *Ecrits de linguistique générale*. Paris: Gallimard.

(2006). *Writings in General Linguistics*. Oxford University Press.

Scaife, M. and Bruner, J. S. (1975). The capacity for joint visual attention in the infant. *Nature*, 253, 265–266.

Schaal, B., Orgeur, P., and Rognon, C. (1995). Odor sensing in the human fetus: anatomical, functional, and chemio-ecological bases. In J.-P. Lecanuet, W. P. Fifer, N. A. Krasnegor, and W. P. Smotherman (eds.), *Fetal Development: A Psychobiological Perspective* (pp. 205–237). Hillsdale, NJ: Lawrence Erlbaum.

Schachter, S. and Singer, J. (1962). Cognitive, social, and physiological determinants of emotional state. *Psychological Review*, 69, 379–399.

Schweder, R. A. (1982). Beyond self-constructed knowledge: the study of culture and morality. *Merrill-Palmer Quarterly*, 28(1), 41–69.

Seligmann, C. G. (1908). Notes on recent work among the Veddas. *Journal of the Royal Asiatic Society (Ceylon)*, 21(61), 74.

Seyfarth, R. M., Cheney, D. L., and Marler, P. (1980). Vervet monkey alarm calls: semantic communication in a free-ranging primate. *Animal Behavior*, 28(4), 1070–1094.

Sherrington, C. S. (1906). *The Integrative Action of the Nervous System*. New Haven, CT: Yale University Press.

Shore, B. (1982). *Sala'ilua: A Samoan Mystery*. New York: Columbia University Press.

Shutts, K., Kinzer, K., Katz, R., Tredoux, C., and Spelke, E. (2011). Race preferences in children: insights from South Africa. *Developmental Science*, 14, 1–9.

Simoons, F. J. (1969). Primary adult lactose intolerance and the milking habit: a problem in biological and cultural interrelations. I. Review of the medical research. *Digestive Diseases and Sciences*, 14(12), 819–836.

Slater, A., Mattock, A., and Brown, E. (1990). Size constancy at birth: newborn infants' responses to retinal and real size. *Journal of Experimental Child Psychology*, 49, 314–322.

Slomp, G. (2000). *Thomas Hobbes and the Political Philosophy of Glory*. New York: St. Martin's Press.

(2007). Hobbes on glory and civil strife. In P. Springborg (ed.), *The Cambridge Companion to Hobbes's Leviathan* (pp. 181–198). Cambridge University Press.

Smith, Adam (1759/2002). *The Theory of Moral Sentiments*, ed. Knud Haakonssen. Cambridge University Press.

Smith, S. (1996). *Commission of Inquiry into Fetal Sentience*. London: CARE.

Snarey, J. (1985). Cross-cultural universality of social-moral development: a critical review of Kohlbergian research. *Psychological Bulletin*, 97, 202–232.

Sneddon, L. U., Braithwaite, V. A., and Gentle, M. J. (2003). Do fish have nociceptors? Evidence for the evolution of a vertebrate sensory system. *Proceedings of the Royal Society of London Series B*, 270, 1115–1121.

Spaepen, E., Coppola, M., Spelke. E., Carey, S., and Goldin-Meadow, S. (2011). Number without a language model. *Proceedings of the National Academy of Sciences*, 108(8), 3163–3168.

Sperber, D. (1974). *Le symbolisme en général* (Symbolism in general). Paris: Hermann.

Spitz, R. A. (1965). *The First Year of Life: A Psychoanalytic Study of Normal and Deviant Development of Object Relations*. New York: Basic Books.

Sroufe, A. (2005). Attachment and development: a prospective, longitudinal study from birth to adulthood. *Attachment and Human Development*, 7(4), 349–367.

Sroufe, L. A., Egeland, B., Carlson, E., and Collins, W. A. (2005). *The Development of the Person: The Minnesota Study of Risk and Adaptation from Birth to Adulthood*. New York: Guilford.

Stern, D. N. (1985). *The Interpersonal World of the Infant: A View from Psychoanalysis and Developmental Psychology*. New York: Basic Books.

(1991). *The Diary of a Baby: What Your Child Sees, Feels, and Experiences*. London: Fontana Press.

Stern, D. N., Hofer, L., Haft. W., and Dore, J. (1985). Affect attunement: the sharing by means of intermodal fluency. In T. M. Field and N. A. Fox (eds.), *Social Perception in Infants* (pp. 249–286). Norwood, NJ: Ablex.

Stewart, S. M. and McBride-Chang, C. (2000). Influences on children's sharing in multicultural setting. *Journal of Cross-Cultural Psychology*, 31, 333–348.

Stiles, D. (2001). Hunter-gatherer studies: the importance of context. *African Study Monographs*, Suppl. 26, 41–65.

Strathern, A. (1971). *The Rope of Moka: Big-men and Ceremonial Exchange in Mount Hagen, New Guinea.* Cambridge University Press.

Striano, T. and Rochat, P. (1999). Developmental link between dyadic and triadic social competence in infancy. *British Journal of Developmental Psychology*, 17(4), 551–562.

(2000). Emergence of selective social referencing. *Infancy*, 1(2), 253–264.

Striano, T., Tomasello, M., and Rochat, P. (2001). Social and object support for early symbolic play. *Developmental Science*, 4(4), 442–455.

Super, C. M. and Harkness, S. (1986). The developmental niche: a conceptualization at the interface of child and culture. *International Journal of Behavioral Development*, 9, 545–569.

Super, C. M. and Harkness, S. (2002). Culture structures the environment for development. *Human Development*, 45(4), 270–274.

Takahashi, K. (1986). Examining the strange-situation procedure with Japanese mothers and 12-month old infants. *Developmental Psychology*, 22(2), 265–270.

Taylor, C. (1989). *Sources of the Self: The Making of the Modern Identity.* Cambridge, MA: Harvard University Press.

Thomsen, L., Frankenhuis, W. E., Ingold-Smith, M., and Carey, S. (2011). Big and mighty: preverbal infants mentally represent social dominance. *Science*, 331, 477–480.

Tobin, J. J., Wu, D. Y. H., and Davidson, D. H. (1989). *Preschools in Three Cultures: Japan, China, and the United States.* New Haven: Yale University Press.

Tomasello, M. (1995). Joint attention as social cognition. In C. J. Moore and P. Dunham (eds.), *Joint Attention: Its Origins and Role in Development* (pp. 103–130). Hillsdale, NJ: Lawrence Erlbaum.

(1998). One child's early talk about possession. In J. Newman (ed.), *The Linguistic of Giving* (pp. 349–373). Amsterdam: John Benjamins.

(1999). *Cultural Origins of Human Cognition.* Cambridge, MA: Harvard University Press.

(2009). *Why We Cooperate.* Cambridge, MA: MIT Press.

Tomasello, M., Carpenter, M., Call, J., Behne, T., and Moll, H. (2005). Understanding and sharing intentions: the origins of cultural cognition. *Behavioral and Brain Science*, 28, 675–735.

Tomasello, M. and Haberl, K. (2003). Understanding attention: 12- and 18-month-olds know what is new for other persons. *Developmental Psychology*, 39, 906–912.

Tomasello, M., Kruger, A. C., and Ratner, H. H. (1993). Cultural learning. *Brain and Behavioral Sciences*, 16, 495–552.

Trevarthan, W. R. (1987). *Human Birth: An Evolutionary Perspective.* Hawthorne, NY: Aldine de Gruyter.

Trevarthen, C. (1980). The foundations of intersubjectivity: developments of interpersonal and cooperative understanding in infants. In D. R. Olson (ed.), *The Social Foundations of Language and Thought: Essays in Honor of Jerome S. Bruner.* New York: Norton.

Triandis, H. C. (1989). The self and social behavior in differing cultural contexts. *Psychological Review*, 96(3), 506–520.

Triandis, H. C. and Gelfand, M. J. (1998). Converging measurement of horizontal and vertical individualism and collectivism. *Journal of Personality and Social Psychology*, 74(1), 118–128.

Tronick, E., Als, H., Adamson, L. B., Wise, S., and Brazelton, T. B. (1978). The infant's response to entrapment between contradictory messages in face to face interaction. *Journal of the American Academy of Child Psychiatry*, 17, 1–13.

United Nations Development Programme (UNDP) (2006). *Human Development Report, 2006*. New York: United Nations.

Veblen, T. (1899/1994). *Theory of the Leisure Class: An Economic Study in the Evolution of Institutions*. New York: Dover.

Veyne, P. (1976). *Le pain et le cirque* (Bread and Circuses). Paris: Le Seuil.

(2006). *The Roman Empire*. Cambridge, MA: Harvard University Press.

Vienne, B. (1984). *Gens de Motlap (People of Motlap)*. Paris: Musée de L'Homme.

Volkmar, F., Chawarska, K., and Klin, A. (2005). Autism in infancy and early childhood. *Annual Reviews of Psychology*, 56, 315–336.

Von Hofsten, C. (1982). Eye–hand coordination in newborns. *Developmental Psychology*, 18, 450–461.

Walker, L. J. and Frimer, J. A. (2007). Moral personality of brave and caring exemplars. *Journal of Personality and Social Psychology*, 93, 845–860.

Walker, L. J., Frimer, J. A., and Dunlop, W. L. (2010). Varieties of moral personality: beyond the banality of heroism. *Journal of Personality*, 78, 907–942.

Waters, E., Weinfield, N. S., and Hamilton, C. E. (2000). The stability of attachment styles from infancy to adolescence and early adulthood: general discussion. *Child Development*, 71, 703–706.

Weber, M. (1904/2009). *The Protestant Ethic and the Spirit of Capitalism*. New York: Norton.

Weiner, A. (1992). *Inalienable Possessions: The Paradox of Keeping-while-Giving*. Berkeley: University of California Press.

Wellman, H. M., Cross, D., Watson, J. (2001). Meta-analysis of theory-of-mind development: the truth about false belief. *Child Development*, 72(3), 655–684.

Winnicott, D. (1953). Transitional objects and transitional phenomena. *International Journal of Psycho-Analysis*, 34, 229–242.

Wolff, P. H. (1987). *The Development of Behavioral States and the Expression of Emotions in Early Infancy*. University of Chicago Press.

Woodburn, J. (1982). Egalitarian societies. *Man*, 17(3), 431–451.

Yang, M. M. (2007). Ritual economy and rural capitalism with Chinese characteristics. In D. Held and H. Moore (eds.), *Cultural Politics in a Global Age: Uncertainty, Solidarity and Innovation* (pp. 226–233). Oxford: Oneworld Publications.

Zahavi, A. and Zahavi, A. (1997). *The Handicap Principle: A Missing Piece of Darwin's Puzzle*. Oxford University Press.

Zebian, S. and Rochat, P. (2012). Judgment of land ownership by young refugee Palestinian and US children. *International Journal of Behavioral Development November*, 36(6), 449–456.

Index

For EU product safety concerns, contact us at Calle de José Abascal, 56–1°, 28003 Madrid, Spain or eugpsr@cambridge.org.

www.ingramcontent.com/pod-product-compliance
Lightning Source LLC
LaVergne TN
LVHW011527200926
848484LV00001B/180

* 9 7 8 1 1 0 7 0 3 2 1 2 5 *